BROKERAGE AND CLOSU

Brokerage and Closure

An Introduction to Social Capital

Ronald S. Burt

OXFORD

UNIVERSITY PRESS

OXFORD
UNIVERSITY PRESS

Great Clarendon Street, Oxford OX2 6DP

Oxford University Press is a department of the University of Oxford.
If furthers the University's objective of excellence in research, scholarship,
and education by publishing worldwide in

Oxford New York

Auckland Cape Town Dar es Salaam Hong Kong Karachi
Kuala Lumpur Madrid Melbourne Mexico City Nairobi
New Delhi Shanghai Taipei Toronto

With offices in

Argentina Austria Brazil Chile Czech Republic France Greece
Guatemala Hungary Italy Japan Poland Portugal Singapore
South Korea Switzerland Thailand Turkey Ukraine Vietnam

Oxford is a registered trade mark of Oxford University Press
in the UK and in certain other countries

Published in the United States
by Oxford University Press Inc., New York

British Library Cataloguing in Publication Data
Data available

Library of Congress Cataloging in Publication Data
Data available

Typeset by SPI Publisher Services, Pondicherry, India
Printed in Great Britain
on acid-free paper by
Ashford Colour Press Ltd, Gosport, Hampshire

ISBN 978–0–19–924914–5 (Hbk.)   978–0–19–924915–2 (Pbk.)
1 3 5 7 9 10 8 6 4 2

This one's for my Raytheon colleagues,
as emotionally and intellectually provocative a set
as one can realistically hope to have.

Thirty spokes meet in the hub.
Where wheel isn't is where it's useful.

Hollowed out, clay makes a pot.
Where the pot's not is where it's useful.

Cut doors and windows to make a room.
Where the room isn't, there's room for you.

So the profit in what is
is in the use of what isn't.

Lao Tzu, *Tao Te Ching*, 500 BC
(from Le Guin, 1997: 14)

TABLE OF CONTENTS

FIGURES

TABLES

Introduction

SATURDAY probably began like most days for George Temple. He woke up hungry, perhaps hesitant to get out of his warm bed. This Saturday would turn out to be unique: George will be dead at the end of it. But that would be later. Now was about breakfast and waking up.

The trouble started just before noon when the regiment rounded the edge of town and started up the two linked hills known locally as Marye's Heights, because of the Marye family farm at the top. Confederates were dug in behind a stone wall with cannon and musket trained on the approach. It was December 13th, 1862 in Fredericksburg, Virginia. Fourteen times Union soldiers attacked the Confederate line. Fourteen times they failed. When they quit, around dinner, George was one of twelve thousand Union casualties.

Civil War Competence–Capability Gap: Fire Power

Consider two views of the carnage. One highlights the admirable resolution and élan of the Union troops repeatedly attacking the difficult Confederate line. This view is expressed with feeling in a popular documentary film in which the battle is discussed (Burns, 1990).

From a second angle, also mentioned in the documentary, the Union deaths were a foolish waste, reflecting the generic problem of social competence lagging technological capability. Union troops were massed and marched against the Confederate line because that was the strategic thinking of the day. Generals were trained to mass their men to achieve the firepower needed to break a fortification. The thinking was correct with respect to smoothbore muskets, but that was yesterday's technology. The French "Minie" ball, adopted in the decade before the Civil War, made practical the deadly potential of rifled gun barrels. Guns previously accurate to 150 yards were now accurate to 450 yards. Troops could blow apart one another's formations from a distance. Massive casualties were the cost of using smoothbore strategy in a fight with rifled weapons. The tragedy would recur on other Civil War battlefields, and on a larger scale fifty years later when massed troops in Europe were thrown against machine-gun fortifications.[1]

---

[1] As one military historian describes the setting (O'Reilly, 2003: 7): "Prior to the Civil War, military leaders had been inculcated with Napoleonic tactics, which were based on smoothbore musket fire. Smoothbore muskets had proven notoriously inaccurate and

Contemporary Capability–Competence Gap: Social Networks

The image of old thinking wasting young lives is repugnant, but hold that emotion as you look at contemporary organizations. We today fight in our own Fredericksburg, with its own staggering potential for casualties. Technology has expanded our ability to communicate across geographic and social distance. Our ability to coordinate across markets has expanded accordingly. "Global" is the word of the day. The limited scale of yesterday's organizations is today inefficient. We removed layers of bureaucracy and laid in fast, flexible communication systems.

Ask the leader of any large organization about the most difficult barriers he or she has to manage to harvest the coordination potential of our communication capabilities. They inevitably talk about people issues, culture issues. People continue to work the way they learned in legacy organizations, in yesterday's organization silos. We are capable of coordinating across scattered

---

rarely damaged a target beyond a hundred yards. Rifling, however, made shoulder weapons accurate at ranges exceeding four hundred yards. Massed fire practice—or close-order tactics—planted men shoulder to shoulder firing in unison, to compensate for the inaccuracy of smoothbore muskets by creating a dense concentration of fire. But close-order tactics for attacking forces had become a liability in the face of superior firearms. Military practice had failed to evolve past massed formations, so weaponry decidedly favored the defender over the attacker. Fredericksburg would prove that better than anywhere else." Here is an excerpt from the diary of Union officer Josiah Favill on the evening after the attack:

" . . . the head of the column appeared in the open and the rebel batteries opened fire. Pandemonium at once broke loose. The whizzing, bursting shells made one's hair stand on end. We marched rapidly forward—passing a huge pile of bricks which the round shot was scattering in every direction, then came a mill race, and on the other side of it a high board fence—clearing these obstacles in the face of a terrible fire, then in full line of battle.

We marched directly forward in front of Marye's house, the strongest point of the enemys' works. It seemed a terrible long distance. We hurried forward with bated breath and heads bowed down, the rebel guns plowing great furrows in our ranks at every step; all we could do was to close up the gaps and press forward. When within some three hundred yards of the rebel works, the men burst into a cheer and charged for the heights.

Immediately the hill in front was hid from view by a continuous sheet of flame from base to summit. The rebel infantry poured in a murderous fire while their guns from every available point fired shot and shell and canister. The losses were so tremendous that before we knew it our momentum was gone, and the charge a failure. Within one hundred yards of the base of the hill we dropped down, and then flat on our bellies, opened fire while line after line of fresh troops, like ocean waves, followed each other in rapid succession, but none of them succeeded in reaching the enemy's works. A few passed over our line, but the bulk of them dropped down before they reached us. Looking over the field in rear, from where I lay, the plain seemed swarming with men, but it was easy to see that the attack was a failure, and that nothing that could be done would amount to anything.

Our losses were heavy, while those of the enemy sheltered behind superb works were almost nothing. Just then there was no romance, no glorious pomp, nothing but disgust for the genius who planned so frightful a slaughter."

markets of human endeavor. We are not yet competent in how to take advantage of the capability.

In this period of competence trying to catch up with capability, authority in the formal chain of command no longer provides the answers it once did. Matrix structures have people reporting to multiple superiors, which weakens the authority of each reporting relationship. Efficiencies gained by removing layers of bureaucracy shift control from vertical chains of authority to horizontal peer pressure. Work once defined by superiors in the formal organization is now negotiated between colleagues who have no authority over one another. People are more than ever the authors of their jobs, not told what to do, so much as expected to figure it out. Feeling that someone must be at fault, people blame one another for problems created by the capability–competence gap. I do not wish to make too much of the Fredericksburg analogy because it is only one of many such, but it is interesting to hear Fredericksburg soldiers voice complaints I so often hear in contemporary organizations: Officers in the field recognize the folly of attacking the Confederate line and so hope there is no truth to the rumor of headquarters ordering an attack.[2] Staff officers blame failure on a "want of cooperation" in the organization.[3] Then as now, technological capability exceeds social competence and we blame one another for failure: "... if only we put in more effort and pulled together as a team."

In our zeal to cut costs and coordinate more broadly with our communication capabilities, we weakened vertical chains of authority relations and deepened our dependence on informal, discretionary relations. When people are confused, they turn to friends and colleagues for advice. When authority is unclear, people turn to friends and colleagues for support. Accountability flows through the formal organization of authority relations. All else flows through the informal—advice, coordination, cooperation, friendship, gossip, knowledge, trust. Formal relations are about who is to blame. Informal

---

[2] My information on the Fredericksburg battle comes primarily from O'Reilly (2003) but internet access to soldier letters and diaries was useful. Here is an excerpt from Union field-officer Josiah Favill's diary five days before the attack: "We hear to-day that Burnside has made up his mind to cross the river, and attack the rebel works. It hardly seems possible, as they are now fortified in the most approved manner, and garrisoned by the best army the Confederacy has in the field. Whoever undertakes it is sure to be beaten; therefore we hope the rumor may prove untrue."

[3] Here is an excerpt from Union surgeon Alfred Castleman's diary after the attack: "Night has come, and the firing has ceased. It has been a terrible day. The wounded have been sent in to us in great numbers. I have been amputating and otherwise operating all day. The result of the battle I do not know. The enemy is very strongly posted, and I exceedingly doubt our ability to dislodge him. In my letter of the 10th, I prophesied that we would cross without much fighting; that when we crossed, the enemy would contest every inch of ground, but that if Burnside was heartily sustained by his officers he would drive the enemy. The two first have been fulfilled to the letter. Burnside has not yet driven the enemy, but the fight is not over. Has he had hearty co-operation? I hear hints of the want of co-operation from our subordinate Generals. I have feared this from the start."

relations are about who gets it done. Informal relations have always been with us. They have always mattered. What is new is the range of activities in which they matter, and the emerging clarity we have about how they create advantage for certain people at the expense of others.

Social Capital

The advantage created by a person's location in a structure of relationships is known as social capital. Reflecting the coordination capability–competence gap bedeviling our time, social capital has become a core concept in business, political science, and sociology. There are an increasing number of research articles and chapters on social capital, with the attendant reviews and books that accompany an exciting idea.[4] The term "social capital" appears across the internet as a business competence, a goal for non-profit organizations, a legal category, and subject of university conferences.

The concept begins as a metaphor about advantage. The advantage is visible when certain people, or certain groups of people, do better than equally able peers. The advantage can be visible in higher incomes. Some people become prominent more quickly. Some lead more important projects. More generally, the interests of some are better served than the interests of others. The human capital explanation of the inequality is that the people who do better are more able individuals; they are more intelligent, more attractive, more articulate, more skilled.

Social capital is the contextual complement to human capital in explaining advantage. Social capital explains how people do better because they are somehow better connected with other people. Certain people are connected to certain others, trusting certain others, obligated to support certain others, dependent on exchange with certain others. One's position in the structure of these exchanges can be an asset in its own right. That asset is social capital, in essence, a concept of location effects in differentiated markets. For example, Bourdieu is often quoted defining social capital as the resources that result from social structure (Bourdieu and Wacquant, 1992: 119, expanded from Bourdieu, 1980): "social capital is the sum of the resources, actual or virtual, that accrue to an individual or group by virtue of possessing a durable network of more or less institutionalized relationships of mutual acquaintance and recognition." James Coleman, another often-cited source, defined social capital as a function of social structure producing advantage (Coleman, 1988: S98, 1990: 302):

---

[4] For example, Adler and Kwon (2002), Baker (2000), Baron, Field and Schuller (2001), Cohen and Prusak (2001), Flap and Volker (2004), Foley and Edwards (1999), Leenders and Gabbay (1999), Lesser (2000), Lin (1999, 2002), Lin, Cook and Burt (2001), Nahapiet and Ghoshal (1998), Portes (1998), Sandefur and Laumann (1998), Woolcock (1998). Also, Monge and Contractor (2003) and Cross and Parker (2004) draw heavily on social-capital mechanisms to describe instrumental behavior in communication networks.

"Social capital is defined by its function. It is not a single entity but a variety of different entities having two characteristics in common: They all consist of some aspect of social structure, and they facilitate certain actions of individuals who are within the structure. Like other forms of capital, social capital is productive, making possible the achievement of certain ends that would not be attainable in its absence." Putnam (1993: 167) grounded his influential work in Coleman's metaphor, preserving the focus on action facilitated by social structure: "Social capital here refers to features of social organization, such as trust, norms, and networks, that can improve the efficiency of society by facilitating coordinated action." I echoed the above to begin my argument about the competitive advantage of structural holes (Burt, 1992: 8, 45).

So there is a point of general agreement to begin talking about social capital. The perspectives cited above are diverse in origin, and diverse in their style of accompanying evidence, but they agree on a social capital metaphor in which social structure defines a kind of capital that can create for individuals or groups an advantage in pursuing their ends. People and groups who do well are somehow better connected.

This Book

Clear-thinking observers can be frustrated with the vagaries of social capital left as a metaphor. Social capital is the Wild West of academic work. There are no skill or intellectual barriers to entry. Contributions vary from rigorous research to devotional opinion, from carefully considered to bromide blather. Research and theory in economics, political science, and sociology are distributed across loosely related perspectives and specialties, each a group of connected experts purporting to have a productive view across groups. The variety is as interesting and exciting as it is corrosive to cumulative work.

What struck me while reviewing social-capital research a few years ago (Burt, 2000b) was the variety of theoretical and practical questions on which useful results were being obtained—and the degree to which more compelling results could be obtained and integrated across projects if attention would cut beneath the metaphor to reason from concrete network mechanisms responsible for social capital. Social capital has the potential to be a powerful technology applied to a critical issue. The technology is network analysis. The issue is performance. Social capital promises to yield new insights, and more rigorous and stable models, describing why certain people and organizations perform better than others. In the process, new light is shed on related concerns such as coordination, creativity, discrimination, entrepreneurship, leadership, learning, teamwork, and the like—all topics that will come up in the following pages.

My goal for this book is to state the concept of social capital in four reliable and general facts that span the space of issues described by social capital. These facts are stylized to apply across study populations, but precise enough to provide a frame of reference for integrating research projects and posing new questions.[5] I cover diverse sources of evidence, however, I focus on organizations and managers because that is where I have found the highest quality data on the informal networks that provide social capital.[6]

---

[5] The manner in which I construct the stylized facts, and the uses to which I put them, explains their substance and function in this book. Nevertheless, the term "stylized fact" warrants a footnote because it is more familiar in economics than in sociology. For example, a November, 2004 search of JSTOR (Journal STORage service at www.jstor.com) shows more than 200 articles in economics mentioning stylized facts versus 22 articles in sociology, and the bulk of the 22 in sociology were authored by people in business schools or appeared in journals at the intersection of economics and sociology such as the *Industrial and Labor Relations Review* and *Journal of Human Resources*. The first JSTOR article in an economics journal mentioning stylized facts is Corry's (1966) article in the *American Economic Review*: "In an effort to limit the possible theoretical permutations that can be dreamed up, resort has been made to what I shall call (following Kaldor) the constraint of the stylized fact." British economist Kaldor (1985: 8–9) explains in a later lecture entitled, "Stylized facts as a basis for theory building": "I called them 'stylized facts,' a term used also by Okun, because in the social sciences, unlike the natural sciences, it is impossible to establish facts that are precise and at the same time suggestive and intriguing in their implications, and that admit no exception. ... we do not imply that any of these 'facts' are invariably true in every conceivable instance but that they are true in the broad majority of observed cases—in a sufficient number of cases to call for an explanation that would account for them." This is an image of empirical data summarized to be descriptive of the "broad majority of observed cases" on a point that is theoretically intriguing. I am using stylized facts in this book to represent empirical data at a level of abstraction targeted by Merton's (1948a, 1968: ch. 2) argument for middle-range theories, and Hedstrom and Swedberg's (1998) renovation of Merton's argument to propose that contemporary work would do well to focus on social mechanisms. I offer a stylized fact on the mechanism by which brokerage constitutes social capital (Figure 2.3) and evidence of its association with performance (Figure 1.8). I offer the same for closure (Figures 4.8 and 3.5 respectively). Some colleagues have expressed discomfort with the variation ignored by my deliberate oversimplification, but data representation is not my primary goal. The four stylized facts are empirical reference points for integrating alternative explanations, reference points meant to facilitate comparison between alternative explanations by cutting beneath the social-capital metaphor to reason from the network mechanisms responsible for social capital.

[6] The focus on managers probably means that I will find more evidence of social capital than would be found in a representative cross-section of occupations. For example, Carroll and Teo (1996) use survey network data on a probability sample of Americans to show that manager networks (relative to non-managers) involve more participation in voluntary associations, more core discussion contacts, a larger proportion of contacts who are colleagues or co-workers, and more contacts who are total strangers to one another. Also, managers have more job autonomy than non-managers and social capital is more of an advantage for people who have more autonomy (see Section 3.3). More evidence of social capital makes professionals and managers a productive research site for studying social capital, but warrants a caution against generalizing to other populations. The caution should not be taken too far. Business students sometimes ask whether social capital is irrelevant to their small organization because every one knows one another within the organization and key contacts are outside—so

In terms that will become clear across the chapters, here are the four stylized facts around which the book is organized:

The first two facts describe the mechanism and returns to network brokerage, which is about the value of increasing variation in a group. Informal relations form a small world of dense clusters separated by structural holes (Figure 1.1). People whose networks bridge the holes are brokers rewarded for their integrative work, rewarded in the sense of more positive individual and team evaluations, compensation higher than peers, and faster promotion (Figure 1.8). Simply put, the first fact is that brokers do better. Second, improved vision is the mechanism responsible for returns to brokerage. Information is more homogeneous within groups such that people who bridge the holes between groups are at greater risk of having creative ideas and more likely to see a way to implement ideas (Figure 2.3).

The third and fourth facts describe the mechanism and returns to network closure, which is about the value of decreasing variation in a group. Closure increases the odds of a person being caught and punished for displaying belief or behavior inconsistent with preferences in the closed network. In so doing, closure reinforces the status quo. It protects against decay in new relations between friends of friends, and amplifies strong relations to extremes of trust and distrust (Figure 4.8). Facilitating the trust and collaborative alignment needed to deliver the value of brokerage, closure is a complement to brokerage such that the two together define social capital in a general way in terms of closure within a group and brokerage beyond the group (Figure 3.5).

I close, in Chapter 5, with implications of the four stylized facts for images of stability and change. The two main points are, first, that network models of brokerage and closure measure forces that bear a striking similarity to the market metaphor in the Austrian school of economics, most notably in the work of Schumpeter and Hayek. Second, the productive potential of brokerage as an engine of endogenous change is more clear in theory than in fact. Closure's inertial forces typically prevail, deepening the structural holes that segregate groups. Legacy organizations can survive in spirit long past the formal organizations in which they developed. In the pages to follow, you will find a world in which reputation replaces authority, pursued opportunity

---

closure is complete allowing no brokerage. I do not wish to make too much of this because the response is obvious, but it deserves mention in a footnote. It is true that social capital evidence comes disproportionately from large organizations (research sites often number employees in the thousands while the median organization in which Americans work contains fifty full-time employees and two part-time people operating on an annual budget of three million dollars; Kalleberg, Knoke, Marsden, and Spaeth, 1996: 49). However, managers in all settings have contacts in their immediate workgroup along with contacts in the rest of the world. In a large organization, the rest of the world is typically elsewhere in the same firm. In a small organization, the rest of the world is the external environment of suppliers, competitors, and customers. In either situation (anticipating the structural autonomy model in Figure 3.5), closure is productive within the workgroup combined with brokerage beyond the group.

replaces assignment, and reward is associated with competitive advantage in a social order of continuous disequilibrium.

Personal Note

This book is based on the 2001 Clarendon Lectures in Management Studies at the Said Business School, University of Oxford. I appreciate the engaging audience and the opportunity to assemble my thoughts that the Lectures provided. The bulk of my research reported in the book was funded by work for private clients. In addition, I appreciate support from CEDEP, the University of Chicago Graduate School of Business, INSEAD, and the Kauffman Foundation. I have acknowledged in papers published over the last few years colleagues whose comments helped shape the work reported here. I owe a special debt to three people who read through this book manuscript, Valdis Kreps, Holly Raider, and Don Ronchi. Valdis, with his network entrepreneur breadth of involvements, brought to my attention productive analogies I had missed. Holly caught inconsistencies in the internal logic of the argument. Don I watched as a barometer of my target audience. Don is an entrepreneur between the academic and corporate. He has a Ph.D. in Psychology from the University of Chicago, a successful career in management consulting, and the responsibilities of serving as the Chief Learning Officer at Raytheon Company. That is a rare cluster of attributes; not my target demographic. Don represents my target audience in the sense that he is not wedded to any particular cluster of jargon and he brings a literate, analytical mind to practical problems of how to create value. My target audience is people like Don whose analytical efforts do not fit easily in the traditional categories of basic or applied research. The fit is better to what Stokes (1997) described as "Pasteur's Quadrant," a category of research in which general models emerge from solutions to practical problems.

More broadly, the book is a product of the social capital it describes. I am a sociologist in a business school, and there is an element of brokerage in any such appointment. Brokerage is facilitated by the workshop culture of the Chicago GSB, but it is fair to say that there remains an element of brokerage in negotiating group boundaries (see Chapter 4). In part to better understand business in Europe, I began in 1999 teaching part-time as the Shell Professor of Human Resources at INSEAD. Beginning in 2000, I had an opportunity to put my ideas about social capital into practice by becoming a full-time manager in Raytheon Company, eventually Vice President of Strategic Learning. I mention the mix of roles in part to indicate that I draw on different sensibilities in writing about brokerage, from American mixed with European, from academic as well as corporate. I also mention the mix of roles because it forced me to better appreciate how it feels to work coordination problems. In juggling contradictory demands within and between my roles at Chicago, INSEAD, and Raytheon, I experienced the richness and difficulty of what is described in this book. Weeks spent more often away than at home, emotions ground between divergent groups, and long periods of weekly commuting between Chicago and Paris are exemplary sour memories from the period. I know mine were minor coordination problems on the scale of what is possible, and what many manage. Regardless, it was more than I want to do again. As Jim Baron described my abundant mileage points with his usual biting verve, I was "getting two surgeries for the price of one." Better you read the book.

ONE

The Social Capital of Structural Holes

O NE of the opening acts for the twenty-first century was venture capital discovering social networks. Tens of millions of dollars were invested in software companies purporting to make people better off through network services providing lucrative or emotionally rewarding relationships.

Companies sprang up one after another like spring flowers, drawing comment from establishment media such as *Fortune* (Kirkpatrick, 2003) and the *Wall Street Journal* (Bulkeley and Wong, 2003), which in turn sent technology gossip all a-blog. From Boston's Route 128, Monster facilitated connections between employers and job seekers; Manhattan's SelectMinds targeted corrections among a company's former employees; Manhattan's theSquare targeted graduates of "quality" schools; while Classmates Online, in Reston, took care of people from elsewhere. It was in Silicon Valley that the market tornado touched down: Friendster facilitated connections among registered users looking for companionship and Google's invitation-only network service, Orkut, made social life more active and stimulating by facilitating existing relations and introducing friends of friends. Data-rich Craigslist provided love and business contacts all in one screen. Targeting business, companies like Linke dIn, Tacit Knowledge Systems, and Spoke Software focused on facilitating new connections between professionals.

There is a common-sense business case to be made for these companies. More lucrative and emotionally rewarding relationships must be a good thing. Certainly, "bowling alone" is not good (Putnam, 2000). Motivational anecdotes posted on company websites describe people who used the company's service and are better off today. But what contribution did the network service make to those people being better off? Would the better-off people have been better off whether or not they had used the service? How does an average user benefit from the service?

The concrete promise is volume. Network services increase the number of people connected to you. Access to thousands, even millions, of people will provide, as one service put it, "a secure, private method for getting personal introductions," that will, as another service claimed, "expand the circumference of your social circle."

The focus on volume can create ambivalence in people new to network services. If such services are the breakthrough technology they purport to be, you don't want to miss the boat. On the other hand, no honorable person wants to become that sebaceous careerist at the party, promiscuously flitting from person to person in self-serving pursuit of opportunity. On a less emotional note, there are logistic costs to maintaining an architectonic network. Dealing with inquiries from service-generated contacts can become a full-time job.

It is a cross-eyed strategy that focuses on contact volume. The focus on contact volume is reminiscent of the internet pre-bubble view of value in terms of "eyeballs" viewing a website—and it is just as wrong.[1] Counts of relationships will never measure network value, and in the worst case are associated with social pathologies. At best, a business model based on network size will be inefficient, typically dramatically so.

Here is why: The value of a relationship is not defined inside the relationship; it is defined by the social context around the relationship. Explaining that point, and the consequent inefficiency of optimizing for contact volume, is the substance of this chapter. Section 1.1 is about the association, in theory, between network and value. Section 1.2 describes the association as it occurs in an example organization; Sections 1.3, 1.4, and 1.5 follow with corroborating evidence in other populations. I conclude in Section 1.6 with a first stylized fact for the book: Brokers do better.

1.1 Brokerage

Begin with a population of people, a set of people selected for study. The population could be a category of people in an organization, the people in a project, the people in an invisible college or community of practice, the people in a neighborhood, or any other interrelated group to be studied.[2]

At any moment, there is a social history to the people in the population. Certain people have sought out certain others. Some have met frequently. Certain people have completed exchanges with one another.

---

[1] Czernich and Heath (2002) describe the evolution of the idea that website value could be measured by the number of people who looked at it.

[2] In theory, a population is bounded by the same network criteria that define a social cluster: cohesion (a set of connected people such as a project team or larger organization) or structural equivalence (a set of people having similar relations to external groups, such as a functional category in a company or an industry in the economy). Cohesion and equivalence criteria are discussed below with reference to Figure 1.2. See Marsden (2004) for summary discussion and references.

1.1.1   Social Structure

In short, there is a network residue to social history, a network in which individuals are variably connected as a function of prior contact, exchange, and attendant emotions. Figure 1.1 depicts a generic structure. Lines indicate where information flows more routinely, or more clearly, between people or groups represented by dots. Solid (dashed) lines indicate strong (weak) flow. The lines and dots are a sociogram of the social structure.

The defining feature of the structure is clusters of dense connection linked by occasional bridge relations between clusters. As a point of reference for later discussion, a network segment is enlarged in the overlay box to highlight four clusters. Clusters A, B, and C are variably closed-network groups in the sense that relations are more dense within than beyond the group (density table shows average relations within and between groups). Cluster D (white dots in the figure) is defined by structural equivalence (density table shows that people in cluster D have stronger relations with group C than with one another).

The clusters in Figure 1.1 are associated with events that bring people together such as involvement in the same project, employment in the same firm or location, participation in the same church or school. The events create a "homophily" bias in networks, which means that relations are more likely between people who share socially significant attributes such as income, education, age, gender, and so on (also familiar in the old saying "birds of a feather flock together"). Feld (1981, 1982) analyzes the cluster-inducing events as social foci.[3] A social focus is anything that brings people together in an activity with the result (intended or unintended) of facilitating relations among the people. For example, high-school friendships often develop between same-age students. One could argue that high-school students are going through rapid change, so students of the same age have more in common, and are therefore more attracted to one another for friendship. That would be a reasonable inference if the students lived in an open friendship market in which friendship is equally possible between any two students. But the market is segmented into classrooms. Students who attend the same classes have opportunities to strike up a casual conversation with one another that could

---

[3] There are numerous papers documenting homophily, with socio-economic status and age among the most often documented in the United States (e.g., Laumann (1966) is a classic description of homophily associated with occupational prestige, and Burt (1991) describes the network structure of age homophily). McPherson and Smith-Lovin (1987) is one of the most thorough assessments of homophily, distinguishing between homophily induced by social foci and homophily chosen. Feld's social foci, and McPherson and Smith-Lovin's homophily are grounded in Blau's (1977) parameters of social structure. McPherson, Smith-Lovin, and Cook (2001) provide comprehensive research review.

develop into friendship. Same-age friendships develop because students in the same classroom are typically the same age. Classrooms are a social focus for students. A similar story can be told for other potential foci such as occupations, income levels, geographic regions, industries, organizations, divisions, products, or teams. For example, Festinger, Schachter, and Back (1950) studied the friendships that developed among MIT students assigned to two-story dormitories. Friendships were most likely with students assigned to rooms at the foot of the stairs to the second floor. Foot-of-the-stairs students were more likely to bump into second-floor residents coming and going. The chance encounters led to recognition, greetings, casual conversation, and friendship. A relationship can be discontinued at any stage in its development to friendship, but it certainly won't develop if it doesn't begin. Time can be a social focus (Melbin, 1987). People who work in the same shift are more likely to develop friendships than people who work different shifts. People working different shifts are segregated in time. They have fewer opportunities for the random encounters that develop into friendships.

The structure in Figure 1.1 is sometimes discussed as a "small world" structure because of a phenomenon that occurs in such structures. You meet a stranger at a social event and learn that you two have a mutual friend—"Isn't it a small world!" There are social reasons why you and the stranger are attending the same event. It is not too surprising that you have mutual friends (which is Feld's argument about social foci), but the point remains that we are often connected to people in other cities more strongly than we are to a colleague next door. Milgram (1967; Travers and Milgram, 1969) coined the term "small world" to describe the tendency for people at geographic remove to be connected through a few intermediaries. Granovetter (1973) drove the point home with respect to "weak ties" providing the key intermediaries and Watts (1998, 1999) rekindled interest in the small-world phenomenon (including illustrative descriptions of organization bridges and clusters, such as Kogut and Walker, 2001, on the small world of large German companies in the 1990s, treating two companies as connected when they are owned by one or more of the same institutional investors; Davis, Yoo, and Baker, 2003, on the small world of interlocking directorates among large U.S. companies in the 1990s; and Baum, Shipilov, and Rowley, 2003, on the small world of Canadian investment banking from the 1950s through the 1980s, treating two banks as connected if they participated in one or more underwriting syndicates together).

Whatever the reasons for networks having the small-world structure illustrated in Figure 1.1, it is sufficient for the purposes here to say that such structures occur in a variety of circumstances and levels of analysis (Watts and Strogatz, 1998). Whether communities in a geographic region, divisions in a corporation, groups in a profession, or people in a team, people specialize within clusters and integrate via bridges across clusters.

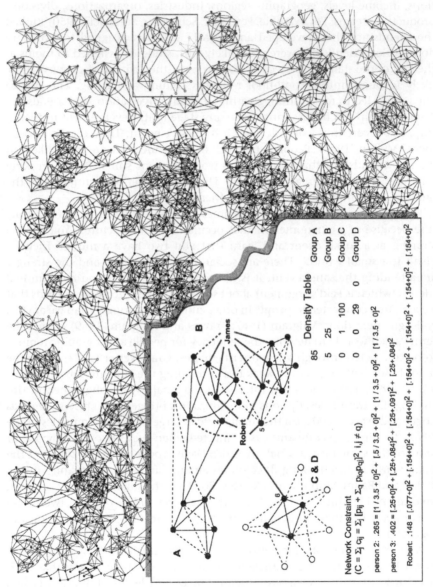

Fig. 1.1: The small world of organizations and markets

1.1.2 Structural Holes

Social history can be irrelevant to behavior. In a market, I buy from the seller with the most attractive offer. That seller may or may not be the seller I often see at the market, or the seller from whom I bought yesterday. So viewed, the network in Figure 1.1 would recur tomorrow only if buyers and sellers come together as they have in the past. Network stability would have nothing to do with the prior network as a causal factor. Exchange tomorrow between yesterday's exchange partners would be only a by-product of buyers and sellers seeking one another out for their personal best exchange.

Selecting the best exchange, however, requires that people have information on available goods, sellers, buyers, and prices. Even if information is of high quality, and eventually reaches everyone, diffusion requires channels and an interval of time. Information can spread across the people in a population, but the higher density of relations within groups mean that information circulates more within than between groups; within a work group more than between groups, within a division more than between divisions, within an industry more than between industries.[4] When people specialize on their immediate tasks to the exclusion of adjacent tasks, they lose track of other groups and the external environment. Variation in belief and practice develops between groups. People here do it differently than people over there. In fact, in-group communication can create barriers to information inconsistent with prevailing beliefs and practice. People talk with colleagues when faced with decisions that cannot be decided with concrete data (decisions such as selecting a production process, selecting between alternative growth strategies, selecting between alternative job opportunities, and so on). In discussing their opinions, people converge over time to share similar views of the future and proper ways to get there. In other words, Figure 1.1 is an information Polynesia in which the clusters are islands of opinion and behavior. Information is not always different between the island clusters, but when information varies, variation will be more pronounced between clusters.[5]

---

[4] Continuing the market metaphor, the structure in Figure 1.1 corresponds to a division of labor, familiar from the early sociology of Durkheim (1933 [1893]), but here focused on network structure within and across cluster specializations. Illustrative work on factors responsible for such structures ranges from Hayek (1937, 1945) on the division of labor dependent on coordination across individuals with specialized knowledge to Becker and Murphy (1992) on the incentives to integrate rather than specialize. See Birner (1999*a*) for the network imagery in Hayek's market model, Birner (1999*b*) on network imagery as a point of similarity between Durkheim and Hayek, and Ellis (2003) for application to Asia-Pacific trade companies. I return to Hayek's market metaphor in Chapter 5.

[5] This seems to be a point for which everyone has examples from their life or field of study, but an example relevant to a broad variety of people is the small-world clustering of medical procedures in the United States. The "unwarranted variations" are compellingly illustrated, and readily available, in state and local maps provided by The Center

Gaps between clusters in Figure 1.1 are holes in the structure of information flow, or more simply, structural holes. A structural hole between two groups need not mean that people in the groups are unaware of one another. It means only that the people are focused on their own activities such that they do not attend to the activities of people in the other group. Holes are buffers, like an insulator in an electric circuit. People on either side of a structural hole circulate in different flows of information. Structural holes are the empty spaces in social structure. The value-potential of structural holes is that they separate nonredundant sources of information, sources that are more additive than overlapping.

1.1.3   Social Capital

Variable exposure to structural holes is the foundation for network models of social capital and a fulcrum for comparing models. Recall that social capital refers to an advantage created by the way people are connected, then consider James and Robert in Figure 1.1. The two men have the same number of contacts, six strong ties and one weak tie, but different structures surround them. James is connected to people within group B, and through them to friends of friends all within group B. Like James, Robert is tied through friends of friends to everyone within group B. In addition, Robert's connection with contact 7 is a conduit for information from group A, and his connection with 6 is a conduit for information from group C. His relationship with 7 is for Robert a network bridge in that the relationship is his only direct connection with group A. Robert's relationship with contact 6 meets the graph-theoretic definition of a network bridge: break the relationship and there is no connection between groups B and C.

Relative to James, Robert is three ways advantaged by his position in the social structure: access to a wider diversity of information, early access to that information, and control over information diffusion.[6] The three advantages

---

for the Evaluation Clinical Sciences at Dartmouth College (downloadable from www.dartmouthatlas.org; see Murphy, 2003, for brief overview).

[6] Belief and behavioral implications of the analytical duality illustrated by Robert and James have been the subject of extensive work. There is, for example, Schumpeter (2002 [1911*a*], 1934 [1911*b*]) on entrepreneurial "leaders" bringing together elements from separate production spheres in which people live by routines (see Ch. 2 n. 6, and Section 5.1), or Merton (1949), and Katz and Lazarsfeld (1955) on the diffusion of tastes through cosmopolitan "opinion leaders" whose relationships bridge the gaps between social worlds (see Section 2.4), Rees (1966) on "extensive" search for information on job opportunities versus "intensive" search for information about a specific opportunity, Milgram (1967; Travers and Milgram 1969) on the "small world" phenomenon in which people at great geographic remove can communicate with one another through surprisingly few intermediaries because of bridges between social worlds (see Watts 1999), Granovetter (1973) on the critical role that "weak ties" would play in information access and flow if bridge relations were weak rather than strong, Klapp (1978) on people

together give Robert an opportunity for information arbitrage: the strategic deployment of information to create value. On the first point, Robert's bridge relations give him access to less redundant information. Contacts to the three separate groups means that his information contains fewer redundant bits of information. Second, Robert is positioned at a crossroads in the flow of information between groups, so he will be early to learn about activities in the three groups. Robert is what early diffusion research identified as an opinion leader; a person responsible for the spread of new ideas and behaviors (discussed in Section 2.4). Robert's more diverse contacts mean that he is more likely to be a candidate discussed for inclusion in new opportunities. More, there is a feedback loop to be expected: Robert's experience with bridge relations is an asset in detecting and maintaining such relationships, and his early access to diverse information makes him more attractive to other people as a contact in their own networks.

Third, Robert is more likely to know when it would be rewarding to bring together separate groups, which gives him disproportionate say in whose interests are served when the contacts come together. More, the structural holes between his contacts mean that he can broker communication while displaying different beliefs and identities to each contact. A certain amount of self interest can be expected, but there is much more: Opinions and behaviors within a group are often expressed in a local language, a dialect fraught with taken-for-granted assumptions shared within a group. The local language makes it possible for people in the group to exchange often-repeated data more quickly (see Sections 3.2 and 3.3.5 on network closure, tacit knowledge, and efficiency). The more specialized the language within groups, however, the greater the difficulty in moving ideas between groups. Robert's connections across groups gives him an advantage in translating opinion and behavior familiar in one group into the dialect of a target group. Simmel and Merton introduced the sociology of people who derive such benefits: The ideal type is the *tertius gaudens* ("the third who benefits").[7] The *tertius* is literally an

---

"opening" or "closing" to new information, Burt (1982, 1992) on the information access and control advantages created when relations span the "structural holes" between groups (see Burt, 1992: 25–30, on the connection between weak ties and structural holes), March (1991) on organizations "exploring" new opportunities versus "exploiting" known revenue streams, or Padgett and Ansell (1993) on the "robust action" made possible by structural holes between groups (see Brieger, 1995, on the connection between robust action and structural holes).

[7] The structural-hole argument draws on network concepts that emerged in sociology during the 1970s; most notably Granovetter (1973) on the strength of weak ties, Freeman (1977) on betweenness centrality, Cook and Emerson (1978) on the benefits of exclusive exchange partners, and Burt (1980, 1982, 1992) on the autonomy created by complex networks. More generally, sociological ideas elaborated by Simmel (1922) and Merton (1957) on the autonomy generated by conflicting affiliations are mixed in the hole argument with concepts of monopoly power and oligopoly to produce network models of competitive advantage.

entrepreneur, a person who adds value by brokering connections between others.[8] In this view, a structural hole is a potentially valuable context for action, brokerage is the action of coordinating across the hole with bridges between people on opposite sides of the hole, and network entrepreneurs, or brokers, are the people who build the bridges. These network entrepreneurs operate somewhere between the force of corporate authority and the dexterity of markets, building bridges between disconnected parts of markets and organizations where it is valuable to do so. The social capital of structural holes comes from the opportunities that holes provide to broker the flow of information between people, and shape the projects that bring together people from opposite sides of the hole.

There is tension here, but not the hostility of combatants so much as the uncertainty of change. Robert lives in a world of contradictory variation. In the swirling mix of preferences across groups, value is created by network entrepreneurs strategically moving accurate, ambiguous, or distorted information between people on opposite sides of structural holes in the routine flow of information. The information access and control benefits of bridging the holes reinforce one another at any moment in time, and cumulate together over time.

Where James is positioned to integrate the work of people who have much in common, Robert is positioned to benefit from differences between people who vary in their behavior and opinion. Where James is positioned to drive variation out of group B (discussed in Chapter 4), Robert is positioned to introduce into group B variation from the other groups A and C with which he is familiar. Given greater homogeneity within than between groups, people whose networks bridge the structural holes between groups have earlier access to a broader diversity of information and have experience in translating information across groups. People whose networks bridge the structural holes between groups have an advantage in detecting and developing rewarding opportunities. Information arbitrage is their advantage. They are able to see early, see more broadly, and translate information across groups (a point developed in Chapter 2).

Thus, people with networks rich in structural holes are the people who know about, have a hand in, and exercise control over, more rewarding opportunities. The behaviors by which they develop the opportunities are many and varied, but opportunity itself is defined by a hole in social structure. In

---

[8] See Burt (1992: 30–32) for review. As Stewart (1990: 149, deleting quotation marks and citations from original) reports from economic anthropology, entrepreneurs focus on: "those points in an economic system where the discrepancies of evaluation are the greatest, and ... attempt to construct bridging transactions. Bridging roles are based on the recognition of discrepancies of evaluation, which requires an edge in information about both sides of the bridge. Because this requires an information network, bridgers will commit time, energy, travel, and sociability to develop their personal networks. For many entrepreneurs, their most significant resource is a ramifying personal network."

comparisons between otherwise similar people like James and Robert in Figure 1.1, Robert has more social capital. His strong relations to otherwise disconnected groups give him a competitive advantage in detecting and developing rewarding opportunities.

1.1.4 Seeing Holes

There are shades of gray. Robert is better positioned than James for brokerage, but note in the Figure 1.1 insert box how James connects a northern and southern segment of cluster B. Within his immediate environment, James has strong ties into both segments and so is positioned to broker their integration. The caution here is that structural holes and brokerage can be found in almost any task, depending on point of view. What is Grand Canyon to one person is dirt dent to another.

In teaching social capital, the material in Figure 1.2 has been useful to help people overcome two common misperceptions of holes.

First, the shaded area in Figure 1.2 contains three networks. I hire you to do a job and make four personal introductions to people whose support I believe you will need to do your job effectively (network A). You immediately take off, doubling the network to eight contacts (network B), soon quadrupling it to sixteen contacts (network C). What has happened to your information as you moved from network A, to B, to C? Has it increased, remained the same, or decreased?

Most people say it has increased. When asked for their logic, they explain (after a frown crosses their face because the explanation is so obvious) that you are talking to more people in network C so you have more information. The assumption is that each person has a unique view so more people means more information. Note the analogy to the idea, with which I began the chapter, of measuring the value of network services in terms of the number of contacts provided.

There is always someone who says that information has remained the same. You are talking to the same four groups with which you began. Instead of seeing people as the source of information, clusters are the source and people are ports of access to the information that circulates around them. Network C does not provide more information, it requires you to manage email with sixteen people to get the views of the four clusters initially connected to the job.

This illustrates the point of information redundancy and the importance of context for determining value. The value of a contact in terms of the information he or she provides depends on the information you already have. If a new person provides information that you already have, the new person adds coordination cost but no value.[9]

---

[9] This sentence warrants a caution. To some degree, different individuals do have different views. If you are monitoring an environment for variation, however, variation

There are two network scalpels used to identify redundant sources. These are illustrated in the box that overlays the shaded area of Figure 1.2. The first network scalpel, cohesion, has been the focus up to this point: People strongly connected are likely to provide redundant information. Clusters A, B, C around James and Robert in Figure 1.1 are an example, as are the four clusters around YOU in the shaded area of Figure 1.2. The other network scalpel is structural equivalence.[10] The three contacts at the bottom of the box in Figure 1.2 do not talk to one another, but all three are strongly connected to the same source of information. Cluster D in the lower-left of Figure 1.1 is composed of people who have no direct contact with one another, but have in common ties to group C. Go to a McDonald's in Boston, then another in Los Angeles. The two store managers are probably not in close contact with one another, but their understanding of how to run the store comes from the same Hamburger University in Chicago. Talking to either the Boston or the Los Angeles store manager will give you a sense of the McDonald's model of how to run a store. Tight bureaucracy connecting people in separate clusters increases redundancy in the information available in the clusters. This will be an important point in Chapter 3 for regional economies and the contingent value of brokerage.

Armed with the cohesion-equivalence scalpels, consider the BEFORE and AFTER networks in Figure 1.2. Imagine this is you BEFORE reading this chapter and AFTER reading the chapter. You have a budget of five relationships. The five relations are deployed differently in the two networks. How many nonredundant contacts do you have in the BEFORE network? If the five contacts all provide redundant information, then you have one nonredundant contact. Or there could be two, three, four, up to a maximum of five nonredundant contacts (if every one of the five provides nonredundant information).

Most people say one. When asked for their logic, they explain (again with the it-seems-obvious frown, this time less confident than when they answered the first question) that the five contacts are all connected, so they constitute one nonredundant source of information. Tracing the connections usually converts a few more people to say one nonredundant contact—contact 1 is tied to 3, 3 to 2, 3 to 5, and 5 to 4.

There is usually someone who says that there are two nonredundant sources. They explain that contacts 1, 2, and 3 get you into a cluster of people at the top

---

between individuals in the same group is less than variation between individuals in separate groups. Information is the same across networks A, B, and C in Figure 1.2 in terms of the breadth of information covered. Once you decide to focus on building a bridge between two specific clusters, it is time to read intra-cluster variation more closely to know how to most effectively coordinate across the clusters. The second phase of work is discussed in Chapter 3 with respect to the value of closed networks.

[10] Readers not familiar with the network concepts of cohesion and structural equivalence, are probably new to network analysis. Scott (2000) and Kilduff and Tsai (2003) are good introductions. Wasserman and Faust (1994) offer a more formal introduction.

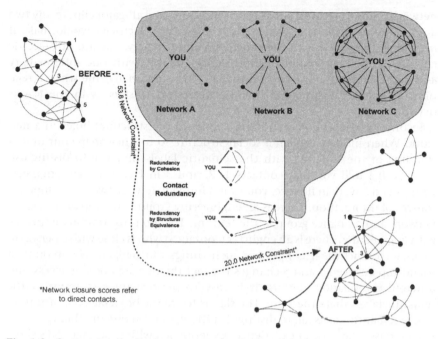

Fig. 1.2: Optimizing for brokerage opportunities

of the network while contacts 4 and 5 get you into a cluster of people largely disconnected from the top cluster. The two clusters are not connected except for the connection between 3 and 5, which is too little to make the clusters redundant. (I am putting aside clinically interesting world views in which there are three, four, even five nonredundant sources.)

Two points are illustrated in the discussion.[11] First, something happens when people begin to think analytically about social networks. They turn into electrical engineers, replacing social intuition with circuitry. If the BEFORE

---

[11] There is a third caution on seeing holes that is not illustrated in Figure 1.2 and is not, in my experience, as serious as the issues illustrated, but warrants a quick mention. On average, people in higher job ranks manage across more structural holes. For example, the table at the top of Figure 1.3 shows people in higher job ranks have larger networks, less constrained networks, and shorter path distances across the supply-chain organization. My third caution is against assuming that the social capital of brokerage is exclusive to senior people. There is wide variation within job ranks. Johnson and Miller (1983) illustrate with fieldwork on an isolated Alaskan camp of Italian fishermen. Two factions in the camp were integrated through the least successful fisherman among them. His joking banter and attachments in both groups prevent the two groups from spinning off into opposing factions, which could be destructive in an isolated camp. His reward was fishing assistance from his colleagues. As colleagues explained (Johnson and Miller, 1983: 67): "He is the bridge between the two groups," and "He belongs to everyone."

network were an electrical circuit, and you connected alligator clips to any two dots in the network, you would close the circuit—electricity would make it from one alligator clip to the other. But human networks are not electric circuits. Influential communication decays sharply with one intermediary and disappears into noise beyond that.[12] This is especially true when a relationship spans the structural hole between two clusters as in the BEFORE network.

Second, preconceptions can blind people to the structural holes in a network. When insiders explain a social structure to us, they shape our understanding of the structure with the semantic labels they use to distinguish clusters. If I told you that contacts 1, 2, and 3 in Figure 1.2 are engineers while 4 and 5 work in finance, you would immediately see two nonredundant sources of information. There is an engineering group at the top of the BEFORE network and a finance group at the bottom. The job is to coordinate finance with engineering. There is an engineer (contact 3) who is close with a person in finance (contact 5). It is rare, but such things can happen. No amount of friendship between 3 and 5 changes the fact the two are ports of access into different information clusters. It is easy to see structures in terms of the semantic labels that others use. The skill is to see the brokerage opportunities where semantic labels fail to distinguish them, or even obscure them.

That raises the issue of experience. Experiments with small networks show that people find it difficult to see a structural hole (Freeman, 1992), especially if their own network contains none (Janicik, 1998; Janicik and Larrick, 2005).[13] With experience, people learn to see the structural holes in a network; in fact, they can be trained to see the structural holes.[14] The implication is that people

---

[12] I have found Friedkin's (1983) evidence useful on this point (see Friedkin, 1998, for later developments). I return to this issue in Section 2.4 on contagious ideas.

[13] Susskind, Miller, and Johnson (1998) offer a related bit of evidence. They describe three panels of network and opinion data on 97 employees who survived their company being downsized from 130 employees. Some of the employees forced to leave created structural holes in the networks of continuing employees. Employees whose networks contained more structural holes after the downsizing were more likely to describe the organization as chaotic and less open to organization change. It is difficult to interpret the statistical results because several dimensions of network structure are mixed together, but the interesting intuition is that people not accustomed to structural holes find it stressful to have them introduced to their network.

[14] The comment on training is an inference from results reported in Burt and Ronchi (2004), though even minor training in a laboratory experiment can improve hole detection (Janicik and Larrick, 2005: 357–358). For several years, senior people in a large organization had been attending an executive education program on thinking strategically about brokerage, closure, and social capital (288 senior people through seven sessions of the program, leaving several thousand people in the same job ranks who had not been through the program). Using company data on position, performance, and background for everyone in job ranks eligible to attend the program, Burt and Ronchi estimate a logit model defining each person's risk of attendance each year. With risk defined, an annual control group was assembled of people who look just like the senior people who attended the program. Here are summary statistics illustrating the program effects:

from a closed network move into a new situation looking for ways that people are connected. They will find them because people are typically connected through a surprisingly short number of intermediaries. In looking for connections, however, these people will not see the brokerage opportunities to create value. People experienced with structural holes more quickly identify the holes in a new situation, so they can target brokerage opportunities to create value. In other words, looking for the structural holes in a network is a kind of perceptual test (which can be put to analytical advantage, e.g., Krackhardt, 1990). Two people in the same room can see different networks, one sees brokerage opportunities, the other sees a closed network of already-connected people. Truth is not an average. If several inexperienced consultants fail to see the structural hole in a situation, it does not mean that the hole is not there. It means the brokerage opportunity awaits a more experienced eye to see it.

The AFTER network in Figure 1.2 shows the budget of five relations allocated to reach five clusters. Instead of three contacts in engineering and two in finance, the person has one contact in the engineering group and new contacts in other engineering groups to see how they do the same work. Instead of two contacts in finance, the person has one contact in the finance group and a new contact in the finance group of another division to see how they do the same work. The three benefits of bridging structural holes can be expected: Access to alternative opinion and practice, early access to new opinion and practice, and an ability to move ideas between groups where there is advantage in doing so.

	Participant Active	Participant Passive	Control Group	All Others Eligible
"Outstanding" in Recent Performance Evaluations	43%	40%	31%	17%
Promoted Since Being at Risk of Attending Program	26%	16%	14%	6%
Left the Company for a Job Elsewhere	3%	10%	14%	11%

For example, 31% of the control group received an "outstanding" evaluation in the last arrival performance review. The first two rows distinguish program participants who were active in the program versus the people who said little or nothing (decided at end of program by lead instructor and a senior company observer in the program). Three points are illustrated: First, a point legitimating the control group is that program participants and people in the control group are similarly different from the "other" people in the eligible job ranks. Second, the program participants show the expected results of improved social capital. Relative to the control group, program participants (combining active and passive participants) are 31% more likely to be evaluated "outstanding," are 29% more likely to be promoted after graduating from the program, and are 51% more likely to stay with the company. The program effects are all statistically significant beyond a .001 level of confidence. Third, program benefits are higher for participants who were active in the program. In fact, passive participants are no more likely to receive a high evaluation or be promoted than people in the control group.

1.1.5   Network Terminology and Constraint Index C

Relationships are the fundamental elements in a network. They have form in the strength of a relationship, and content in the substance that passes through a relationship (confiding, advice, cash, etc.). Granovetter (1973: 1361) provides a widely cited definition of strength: "the strength of a tie is a (probably linear) combination of the amount of time, the emotional intensity, the intimacy (mutual confiding), and the reciprocal services which characterize the tie." We know a little more now about emotional closeness being a primary dimension of relations independent of how often people talk to one another (as in semantic distinctions more generally, Osgood, Suci, and Tannenbaum, 1957), but I postpone content distinctions between kinds of relations to Section 1.5.

A bridge is a (strong or weak) relationship for which there is no effective indirect connection through third parties. In other words, a bridge is a relationship that spans a structural hole. There is a bridge relation in Figure 1.1 between Robert and contact 6. Robert has no relationship with anyone who is also connected to contact 6. Robert lives in cluster B. Contact 6 lives in cluster C. Their relationship is a bridge across the structural hole between clusters B and C.[15]

---

[15] The text gives a working definition of structural hole: the relationship between two people is a hole-spanning bridge when there is no effective indirect connection between the people. In studying the social capital of investment bankers, for example, I counted as a bridge each colleague relationship for which banker and colleague had no positive indirect connection through mutual contacts (and a banker's bonus compensation relative to peers is strongly associated with the count of bridges in which the banker is involved, Burt, 2002).

However, I do not wish to imply with the working definition that the concept of a structural hole has an absolute meaning. Indirect connections not found in one network might have been found if another network had been measured, or a broader population had been included. The same definitional issue exists for the absolute meaning of a relationship, which is a fundamental element in network theory. When is the interaction between two people a relationship? When they first say hello? When they join a mutual colleague for coffee? When they work on the same project? All three kinds of interaction can be relationships. There is no absolute meaning—and there are often disagreements in which one person sees as casual interaction what the other person sees as a relationship. Network analysts work around the definition issue by asking people to define their own relationships (e.g., two people are connected by a relationship if either or both say they have a relationship) or by using concrete archival data (so whatever a relationship means, it can be replicated by other scholars, e.g., two people are connected if they are involved in the same project). Either methodology, self-report or archive, leaves open the question of what a relationship means. There is no reason to expect that a concept less central to network theory, such as structural hole, would be more clearly defined.

A definition of structural hole more general than the working definition in the text would define hole in terms of effect rather than structure. Rather than defining a structural hole and saying that brokerage is the act of creating value by bridging the

The network is closed around a relationship between two people to the extent that the people have no contacts through whom they are not indirectly connected. Where a set of people are connected to one another by strong direct or short indirect connections (e.g., through a few leaders), I will refer to the set as a cluster, a group, or, more generally, a closed network. A strong relationship in a closed network is a bond between the people connected.

Relations can be measured for strength and context such that they can be sorted into three categories: bridges, bonds, and something else (more than a bridge and less than a bond). The gist of my argument in this book is that bridges are valuable for creating information variation, while bonds are valuable for eliminating variation and protecting connected people from information inconsistent with what they already know.

The contrast between bridges and bonds distinguishes two research strategies for estimating returns to brokerage. One strategy is to study returns to the people connected by brokers. The other is to study returns to the broker.

Illustrating the first strategy, Garmaise and Moskowitz (2003) study the effects of brokers in the commercial real estate market: "Informal intermediaries fulfill a crucial function in markets in which borrowers seek financing relatively infrequently and have little opportunity to develop relationships with lenders themselves....Hiring a broker raises the probability that a transaction will be financed with bank debt from 40% to a striking 58%." The increase from 40% to 58% is a conservative estimate. Other estimates holding constant transaction differences associated with bank financing show an increase from 34% bank loans in nonbrokered transactions to 63% in brokered transactions (Garmaise and Moskowitz, 2003: 1024). Garmaise and Moskowitz have authoritative data on real estate transactions that did not involve a broker, so they can compare features of brokered versus nonbrokered transactions to estimate returns to brokerage. The same research strategy could be used to advantage in estimating returns to brokerage in other capital markets (e.g., with prestigious banks as intermediaries; De Long, 1991; Boot, Greenbaum, and Thakor, 1993) or labor markets (e.g., Murray, Rankin, and Magill,

---

hole, define a structural hole as a place in a network where brokerage could create value. A structural hole exists between two people or groups when either party is unaware of value available if they were to coordinate on some point. This leaves open the possibility that the people or groups are already coordinated in some fashion. The structural hole refers to a missing element of coordination that would be valuable. There is a self-correcting feedback loop to holes defined in terms of effect: (a) the greater the connection between two groups in prior projects, (b) the more likely they will coordinate on their own in subsequent projects and the less likely they will bring new information to the coordination, so (c) the lower the value available to brokerage between the groups, and therefore (d) the more shallow the structural hole between the groups. Holes defined in terms of effect might be a productive foundation for network diagnostic work in future. For testing hypotheses, however, such a definition is not useful because value, the predicted outcome, becomes part of the definition of the predictor. For the purposes of this book, I stay with the working definition in the text.

1981, on graduate students obtaining first jobs with a senior professor as intermediary; Burt, 1998, on senior managers as intermediaries on behalf of women and young men moving into senior ranks; also see Chapters 3 and 4 of returns to "structural embedding" within a closed network).

Problems arise if brokers are not clearly defined because the clear baseline of nonbrokered relations becomes ambiguous. Garmaise and Moskowitz have a code in their transaction data that distinguishes a broker present or absent. Such a code is rarely available. Coordination between two groups can come from various people connecting across the structural hole between the groups. There can be clear rules within groups of who is eligible to play the broker role, but there are no consistent rules across groups. More, a few strong relations between people in the two groups can be sufficient to coordinate the groups, so it is difficult to identify the baseline of nonbrokered relations in which coordination would have occurred if there had been brokerage. There is an element of this baseline issue in the commercial real estate market studied by Garmaise and Moskowitz. Given the large difference in financing available to brokered versus nonbrokered transactions, how many possible transactions did not occur, and therefore do not appear in the data on executed transactions, because no broker was available? If data on the failed transactions were available, returns to brokerage would be higher than the estimates reported by Garmaise and Moskowitz.

Studies of social capital typically describe situations in which there is no binary variable distinguishing brokers. The strategy used to estimate returns to brokerage (and the strategy used in this chapter) is to distinguish networks by the extent to which they limit brokerage opportunities, then estimate the extent to which rewards accumulate disproportionately in the hands of people who have more opportunities for brokerage. This is a strategy of estimating brokerage returns to the person or group providing the brokerage.

There are three ways that network can be closed to brokerage. It can contain too few contacts, contacts too interconnected, or contacts too connected indirectly through a central person. For the purposes of this book, I use a summary index that combines all three conditions: The network constraint index, C, is a concentration measure that varies from zero to 100 with the extent to which all of a person's network time and energy is concentrated in one contact (Burt, 1992: ch. 2; 2000*b*).[16] Network constraint on a person is

---

[16] The network constraint index and its composition in terms of network size, density, and hierarchy are discussed elsewhere (Burt, 1992: ch. 2; 2000*b*; cf. Borgatti, Jones, and Everett, 1998; and for a triad version implicitly capturing constraint, Täube, 2004). The index begins with the extent to which manager i's network is directly or indirectly invested in the manager's relationship with contact j: $c_{ij} = (p_{ij} + \Sigma_q p_{iq} p_{qj})^2$, for $q \neq i,j$, where p_{ij} is the proportion of i's network time and energy invested in contact j, $p_{ij} = z_{ij}/\Sigma_q z_{iq}$, and variable z_{ij} measures the zero to one strength of connection between contacts i and j. The total in parentheses is the proportion of i's relations that are directly or indirectly invested in connection with contact j. The sum of squared proportions,

high if he or she has few contacts (small network), the contacts are closely connected with one another (dense network, e.g., the cohesion examples in Figure 1.2), or they share information indirectly via a central contact (hierarchical network, e.g., the equivalence example in Figure 1.2).

For illustration, look along the dashed line in Figure 1.2 to see the 54 points of network constraint in the BEFORE network decrease to 20 points in the AFTER network. In Figure 1.1, James has a constraint score twice Robert's (31.3 versus 14.8) and Robert is the least constrained person in the inset box.[17] Figure 1.1 contains three illustrative computations. Person 2 illustrates the constraint of having few contacts (26.5 points of constraint). Person 3 illustrates the constraint of densely connected contacts (40.2 points of constraint). Robert illustrates the low constraint of having many contacts in separate groups (14.8 points of constraint, versus James' 31.3 points). To the extent that brokerage is social capital in a population, network constraint should have a negative association with measures of achievement and rewards. The people whose networks span structural holes in the population should be the people more recognized and rewarded.

1.1.6 Goal or By Product?

If experience serves, a word of caution is useful here before I document the returns to brokerage.

Assume, as will be shown, that the brokerage argument is correct in identifying a social-capital advantage for people like Robert in Figure 1.1. The normative implication is that everyone should optimize their access to structural holes so they look more like Robert.

My word of caution is that such a conclusion is a reasonable inference from the argument thus far, but the conclusion is premature and wrong-headed. The conclusion is premature because I have not yet introduced the formidable advantage created when closure is combined with brokerage. That is the subject of Chapter 3 and illustrated in Figure 3.5 as my third stylized fact. The optimum network combines Robert's brokerage reach with a closed, reputation-inducing, structure among select peers and subordinates.

Second, the conclusion to optimize for structural holes is wrong-headed in assuming that Robert set out to create his brokerage position in Figure 1.1. Given the accumulating evidence of returns to brokerage, it is a short step to

---

$\Sigma_i c_{ij}$, is the network constraint index C. I divided by the maximum score possible to bound scores in small, dense networks, and multiply by 100 to discuss integer points of constraint.

[17] Network betweenness, proposed by Freeman (1977), is an index that measures the extent to which a person brokers indirect connections between everyone else in a network. Robert's betweenness score of 47.0 shows that almost half of indirect connections run through him. His score is the highest in the Figure 1.1 inset box, well above the average 6.5, and much higher than James' below-average 5.2 score.

talk about people strategically building bridges to increase their social capital. I use language to that effect in discussing Figure 1.2 with respect to managers building a network optimized for nonredundant contacts. However, my instrumental language was only a heuristic to engage the reader in a puzzle that illustrates the value of brokerage by highlighting reasonable alternatives that would not create the value. It is not obvious that people set out to build bridges so much as bridges are a by-product of pursuing other ends. For one thing, brokerage is not all that obvious. People vary in their ability to detect holes in social structure (Freeman, 1992; Janicik, 1998; Janicik and Larrick, 2005), and inaccurately diagnose the value of their network (Burt, 1998: fig. 8). More, clusters in the small world emerge from people being proximate while they pursue other interests (Feld's, 1981, "social foci"). As Coleman (1990: 312, also pp. 313, 317–318) puts it, "A major use of the concept of social capital depends on its being a by-product of activities engaged in for other purposes." Moreover, there is no empirical research at this point that establishes the value of a network in terms of its etiology. We know brokerage creates an advantage, but we know little about how people come to be brokers. Consider the French and American managers discussed below. Bridge relations among the Americans are often between recent acquaintances. Bridge relations among the French are often between people who have known one another for a long time. Returns to brokerage are similar for the Americans and French (Figure 1.5), but their paths to brokerage are different.

In short, this chapter is about the instantaneous effect of brokerage: networks that span structural holes create an advantage in detecting and developing rewarding opportunities. With respect to etiology, I return in Chapter 5 to the issue of structures changed by people pursuing brokerage opportunities, after I have introduced in Chapters 3 and 4 the way that closure works with brokerage to stabilize a structure. The task remaining in this chapter is to document the returns to brokerage.

1.2   Example Organization

I begin with an illustrative case. In the summer of 2001, a new leadership team took command of the supply chain in one of America's largest electronics companies. The head of the new team decided that a network analysis of senior people in the organization would be a way to come up to speed quickly in thinking about, and communicating, strategy for integrating the supply chain.[18]

---

[18] This is an overview of the project. See the published report for details on research design, measurement, and results (Burt, 2004).

Data started to come in right after the head of the new leadership team sent his email message to each of the 673 supply-chain managers under him. The message explained the survey, assured confidentiality and respondent access to a final report, and directed the recipient to a webpage containing a brief questionnaire. The questionnaire asked for their name and email address, a description of their best idea for increasing the value of the supply chain, then presented two network name generators.[19] After managers typed in their idea, they were asked if they had discussed the idea with anyone. If yes, they were asked to provide the name of the person with whom they had the most detailed discussion. Next they were asked: "More generally, who are the people with whom you most often discuss supply-chain issues?" Five response boxes were provided for names. The questionnaire then listed two name interpreters. The first asked for years of acquaintance with each cited person. The second asked about connections among the cited contacts. The respondent was guided through a matrix in which the respondent's perceived connection between each pair of cited people was coded as "often," "sometimes," or "rarely" discussing supply-chain issues with one another.

Slightly more than a thousand people were cited as discussion partners. The cited contacts included 480 of the 673 supply-chain managers. The other 193 managers were social isolates. They surely had a local circle of contacts. They must have been talking to someone. All I know is that they did not respond to the survey and were not cited for discussion by other supply-chain managers. The cited discussion partners who were not supply-chain managers were supply-chain subordinates below manager rank and contacts beyond the supply chain.

1.2.1 Brokerage Opportunities

Figure 1.3 is a sociogram of the network data. Each dot represents one of the 480 managers active in the discussion network. Five levels of network connection can be distinguished from the survey, with information presumed more likely to move between people more strongly connected. Scores for the five levels range from 0 between two people who do not cite one another or are perceived to rarely talk, up to 1.0 between two people where one cited the other or a mutual colleague reported that the two people often discussed supply-chain issues with one another. A line between two dots in Figure 1.3 indicates that one or both connected managers cited the other as often discussing supply-chain issues. Managers are close in the sociogram to the extent that they cited one another and had the same other people as discussion

---

[19] Issues in obtaining network data, especially from surveys using name generators and interpreters, are reviewed by Marsden (1990, 2004). The use of web-based surveys follows the same general rules as other surveys. The primary difference is speed and reliability. Data collection is facilitated on the web by the computer server assembling lists of contacts across the interview.

partners. The 193 social isolates would be distributed around the periphery of the diagram, disconnected from anyone else in the network.

The sociogram in Figure 1.3 shows a center–periphery pattern associated with job rank and business division. The tightly interconnected individuals at the center of the sociogram work at company headquarters. Radiating out from the center are spokes corresponding to business divisions (one to the northwest, another to the southwest, one to the south, another to the southeast, and a large one to the northeast). Within each spoke, managers tend to be more-connected and higher-rank at the center of the sociogram; less-connected and lower-rank at the periphery of the sociogram. The connection with job rank is illustrated by the first two columns of the table in Figure 1.3. Social isolates are at the periphery of the sociogram and more often lower-rank managers. No Vice President or Director was a social isolate. Two Senior Managers were isolates. The largest concentration was among first-rank managers, where it is easy to imagine a local circle of people cut off from colleagues elsewhere. People at the center of the sociogram are connected to more colleagues. In the second column of the Figure 1.3 table, network size, the number of colleagues connected to a manager, shows that managers had a handful of discussion contacts on average and the average varied with rank: Directors and Vice Presidents had 12.6 contacts on average, versus 3.4 for managers in the first rank. In short, informal discussion between managers flowed along command lines in the corporate hierarchy. The informal organization was patterned by the formal organization.

Structural Holes around the Function

The organization is rich in brokerage opportunities. The first set of opportunities concerned contacts missing from the network. Every person cited by three or more supply-chain managers is included in Figure 1.3, but everyone in the sociogram is a supply-chain manager. Contacts beyond the supply-chain were named, but almost all were named by a single respondent (95%). The few named by multiple respondents were cited twice. No one was named by more than two respondents. In other words, no business leaders outside the supply chain were a shared point of reference for managers inside the supply chain. The supply-chain managers focused on one another, an island unto themselves—which was an opportunity for enterprising managers to build bridges to the business units and other functions to better integrate supply-chain processes into production.

Structural Holes between the Business Units

Second, there were structural holes between supply-chain organizations in separate business units. Checking company data on job rank and business

	Percent Social Isolates	Mean Network Size	Mean Network Constraint	Mean Number Cited as Discussion Partners	Mean Network Constraint Cited Discussn. Partners	Mean Path Distance (min–max) for the 476 connected managers in graph
VP or Director (25)	0%	12.6	29.8	4.9	70.2	3.3 (2.7–4.2)
Senior Manager (41)	5%	8.5	37.3	3.8	78.1	3.7 (2.9–6.4)
Manager III (121)	11%	6.4	50.2	3.7	77.9	4.0 (3.0–6.4)
Manager II (199)	27%	4.1	65.0	2.8	83.1	4.3 (2.8–6.4)
Manager I (287)	44%	3.4	73.6	2.4	83.4	4.6 (3.4–7.4)
Mean (673)	29%	5.0	60.5	2.9	81.0	4.2 (2.7–7.4)

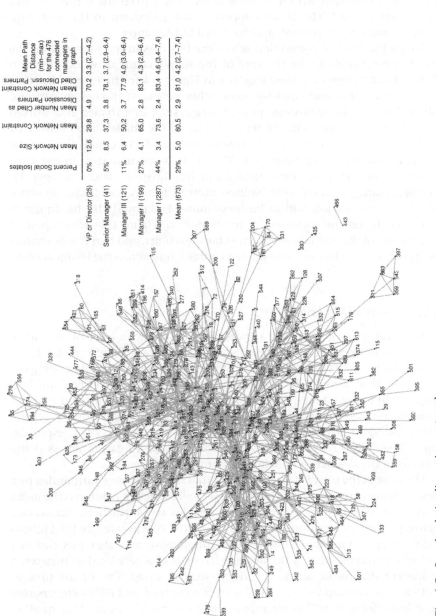

Fig. 1.3: Supply-chain discussion network

unit shows that the people in the center work at corporate headquarters. Clusters of managers within business units radiate from the center like five spokes on a wheel. The clusters appear in the sociogram to the southeast, south, southwest, northwest, and northeast of the center.

To see the level of connection across the business units, I focused on the most senior people to see the core of the supply-chain network, drawn in Figure 1.4. Managers are close together in Figure 1.4 to the extent that they cited one another and cited the same other people as discussion partners. Shaded areas indicate business units. Managers not in a shaded area worked at headquarters. The concentrations of lines in the shaded areas show that discussion is concentrated within business units: Of 514 connections in the sociogram at the top of Figure 1.4, 62% are between managers in the same business unit, 35% are with managers at headquarters, and a meager 3% connect managers in different business units (fifteen connections). To better see the concentration within business units, I removed the headquarters managers to get the sociogram at the bottom of Figure 1.4—which is stark illustration of the fragile contact across business units, and that fragile contact is opportunity for brokerage to tighten coordination across the business units.

The Small World of Leadership

A third category of brokerage opportunities was at the level of individual managers. Bridges and clusters can be seen in Figure 1.3 and Figure 1.4, but Watts and Strogatz (1998, and Watts, 1999) provide metrics for describing the small world at a micro level. There is a bridge and cluster structure in a population to the extent that two conditions occur: relations are dense within clusters, and short path distances connect people across the clusters. Bridges make the short path distances possible (see Granovetter, 1973, especially pp. 1373–1376 on a community's difficulty in coordinating across dense clusters in the absence of bridging relationships).

The table at the top of Figure 1.3 shows that managers were surrounded by a dense cluster of discussion partners. The second to the last column is the mean network constraint among a manager's cited discussion partners. The average across job ranks is a near-maximum 81.0, and the 70.2 average for the highest-rank managers is not much lower. To put this in more concrete terms, consider network density, which is the average strength of a relationship between a manager's discussion partners: partners were reported 52% of the time to "often" discuss supply-chain issues with one another, and 80% were reported to at least "sometimes" discuss supply-chain issues with one another. In other words, the average manager worked in a small clique within which he or she discussed work.

Despite the dense clustering within business units and around individual managers, managers who had any connection with one another were con-

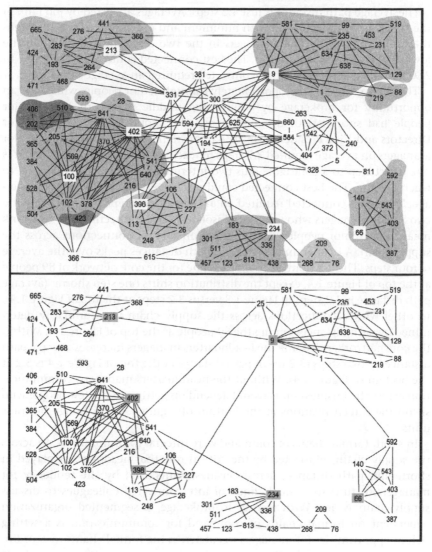

Fig. 1.4: Core of the network

nected by few intermediaries. Path distance is the minimum number of relations required to connect two people. Managers who cite one another were separated by a path distance of one. Path distance to friends of direct contacts is two, and so on. Try tracing a path of indirect connections across Figure 1.3. Intermediaries add up quickly. A computer search for the shortest paths between people shows that the longest path distance is eleven steps.

The average path distance is just 4.2 steps. Averages are listed by job rank in the last column of Figure 1.3 with minimum and maximum means in parentheses (excluding the four managers in the two disconnected dyads in the lower-right corner of Figure 1.3). The best-connected could reach everyone in 2.9 steps on average. The worst-connected required an average of 6.4 steps.

The short paths go disproportionately through senior people, which was an opportunity for brokerage by enterprising middle managers. More senior people had shorter path distances across the supply chain (3.3 mean for Directors and Vice Presidents versus 4.6 for Manager I). For example, Senior Managers on average required 3.7 steps to reach anyone in Figure 1.3— that is one direct step to a colleague, plus two intermediaries past the colleague, to reach anyone. The best connected could reach everyone in 2.9 steps on average. The worst-connected required an average of 6.4 steps (putting aside the two Senior Managers who were social isolates). The connection with job rank means that senior people were more responsible for connections across the supply chain. A histogram of Figure 1.3 path distances peaks over the average of four steps. The distribution looks the same for the core network of 89 people at the top of Figure 1.4, except the distribution shifts one step shorter (average path distance is 4.2 steps in Figure 1.3 versus 3.2 steps at the top of Figure 1.4). In other words, connections across the supply chain were primarily determined by path distances among the 89 people at the top of Figure 1.4. Within the core network, removing the headquarters managers increases average path distance by two steps (3.2 mean path distance at the top of Figure 1.4 is 5.2 at the bottom of Figure 1.4). Without the headquarters managers, communication across the business units would depend on getting to the few people who sit on the fifteen relations at the bottom of Figure 1.4 that bridge business units.

In short, formal chains of command were integral to communication across the supply chain; illustrated by the critical role that headquarters played in shortening path distances across business units, and by the tendency for managers to turn to a small clique of interconnected colleagues to discuss supply-chain issues. With respect to brokerage, a segmented organization dependent on formal chains of command for communication is a setting rich in opportunities for managers to cut across the formal chains to coordinate directly.

1.2.2   Returns to Brokerage

The many opportunities for brokerage raise a question about incentives. If managers had incentives to coordinate across structural holes in and around the supply chain, why do so many holes still exist?

It is easy to imagine the lack of incentive: The network structure just described would result from managers encouraged to a focus on their immediate assignments, relying on headquarters for strategic thinking about how to coordinate across the supply chain. In fact, such a view was crisply stated to me by a program manager describing how he ran his group: "I don't want my people even thinking about alternatives. They spend two weeks thinking about an alternative, only to learn that what we have is 90% as good. The result is that they wasted two weeks and I'm behind schedule. I get some complaints about stifling creativity, but all I want is to be good enough and on schedule." Combine this view with a premium on personal loyalty from subordinates, the relative ease with which complex knowledge moves over strong connections between people in a dense network (Reagans and McEvily, 2003), and one can quickly imagine an organization of managers rewarded for sticking to an interconnected circle of colleagues focused on their immediate tasks.

Despite views such as the one quoted, the company recognized and rewarded brokerage. Managers who often discussed supply-chain issues with managers in other groups were better paid, received more positive job evaluations, and were more likely to be promoted.

Brokerage Measured by Low Network Constraint

The table in Figure 1.3 shows the distribution of network constraint across the supply-chain managers. I measured the constraint on each manager with respect to the immediate network of discussion partners, comprised of anyone that the manager cited as a discussion partner and anyone who cited the manager.[20] As is usual, constraint is more severe on managers in lower ranks, increasing from a mean of 29.8 points for Directors and Vice Presidents, up to an average of 73.6 points for a Manager I. There are 60.5 points of constraint

---

[20] Building on previous research, I compute constraint for the immediate discussion network around each manager. Alternatively, I could have computed constraint to take into account the broader structure around a manager. Person 3 in Figure 1.1 illustrates the difference. Person 3 has four contacts: Robert, James, and two others. Equal proportions of 3's network time and energy are allocated to each contact ($p_{ij} = 1/4$). The indirect proportion for 3's tie with Robert is zero because Robert has no direct contact with the other people. The indirect proportion for 3's tie with the other three contacts is high because all three are connected ($\Sigma_q p_{iq} p_{qj} = 165$). However, the three contacts have relationships not considered in this computation. James, for example, has four contacts beyond 3's network. Ignoring them makes 3's network look more constrained than it is. James could bring new information into 3's network even though he is strongly connected within the network. If contact ties beyond 3's network were taken into account, the indirect proportions would be lower, so the network constraint on person 3 would drop to 40.2 from the 70.8 reported in Figure 1.1 ($.402 = [.25 + 0]^2 + [.25 + .084]^2 + [.25 + .091]^2 + [.25 + .084]^2$). I don't take this as a problem because I want to be consistent with previous survey network research and I am only making inferences from relative levels of constraint. The point to note is merely that the absolute level of constraint reported here for each manager's network is higher than it would be if constraint were computed from the entire network across managers.

on the average manager in the discussion network (27.3 standard deviation). As a frame of reference, Robert and James in Figure 1.1 would both look like network entrepreneurs in the supply chain. Robert would be almost two standard deviations less constrained than the average in Figure 1.3 ([14.8–60.5]/27.3). James would be about one standard deviation less constrained than the average ([31.3–60.5]/27.3). The 193 social isolates not in Figure 1.3 are assumed to have local discussion partners and so given the constraint score of someone who had one discussion partner or a completely interconnected circle of discussion partners (100 points). The statistically significant associations in Figure 1.5 between brokerage and performance are evident with or without the 193 social isolates included in the analysis.

Compensation

Graph A in Figure 1.5 (hereafter Figure 1.5A) shows higher compensation paid to senior managers who bridged holes in the supply-chain organization. Compensation in this study population was primarily salary, so compensation measured cumulative performance in that this year's salary is typically an incremental addition to last year's salary. Salaries were stable before and after the network survey. They increased slightly in the second year (5.5% on average, 2.8% standard deviation, 0% minimum, 30% maximum), but relative salary changed little (.99 correlation between the two years).

The vertical axis in the graph measures relative salary at the time of the network survey. The zero point is the salary typical of a manager's peers, where peers are people who share the manager's job rank, work role, age, education, business unit, and geographic location (Burt, 2004: 371). Scores are standardized residuals that measure the extent to which a manager's salary was higher than peers (positive score) or lower (negative score). A score of 1.0 indicates that a manager's salary was one standard deviation higher than the salary typical of his or her peers.

The strong negative association in the compensation graph is evidence of the social capital created by bridging structural holes. To the left, managers with discussion partners in diverse groups had low network constraint and tended to enjoy salaries higher than their peers. To the right, managers isolated in a group of discussion partners who all spoke to one another frequently were under high network constraint and tended to receive salaries lower than the average person their age at their rank and in other ways their peer.

Performance Evaluations

When the head of human resources saw the association between brokerage and salary, she was suspicious because so many factors affect salary. She said

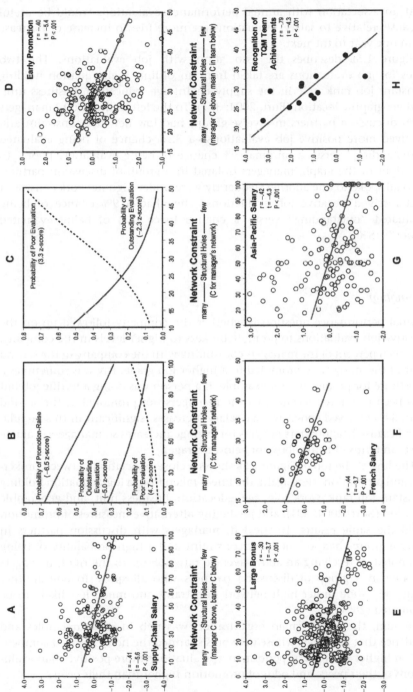

Fig. 1.5: Performance and network constraint

that an association with annual performance evaluations would be useful because, relative to salary, evaluations are more free to increase or decrease from one year to the next.

Figure 1.5B describes the association with job evaluations. The two lines for job evaluations are taken from an ordinal logit equation holding constant job rank, role in the supply chain, age, education, business unit, and geographic location (Burt, 2004: 371). To the left in the graph, managers with discussion partners in diverse groups had low network constraint and received more positive job evaluations—a 32% chance of being evaluated "outstanding" versus a minimal 3% chance of being evaluated "poor." To the right in the graph, managers isolated in a group of discussion partners who all spoke to one another frequently were under high network constraint and received negative job evaluations. They had a 9% chance of being evaluated "outstanding" versus a chance twice that of being evaluated "poor" (18%).

Promotion

A final performance question is whether the company followed up on the positive job evaluations to promote brokers to higher levels in the company. Fourteen percent of the managers continuing with the company in the second year of the study were promoted to a higher job grade. Pay was sometimes a substitute for promotion, for example, if a person was doing a terrific job but had been promoted recently. Of the managers not promoted in the second year, 34% received above-average salary increases (significant in this population because headquarters budgets for average increases so managers evaluate raises in terms of being above or below average).

The line at the top of Figure 1.5B shows a close association between brokerage and promotion. Here again, the line is taken from a logit equation holding constant job rank, work role, age, education, business unit, and geographic location (Burt, 2004: 371), and predicting alternative measures of promotion yield the same results. To the left, managers with discussion partners in diverse groups had low network constraint and a high probability of being promoted or receiving an above-average raise (68%). To the right, managers isolated in a group of discussion partners who all spoke to one another frequently were under high network constraint and much less likely to be promoted (28%).

In sum, the supply-chain organization was rich in structural holes and evidence that managers whose networks spanned the holes enjoyed compensation higher than peers, performance evaluations more positive than evaluations of their peers, and odds of promotion higher than their peers.

1.3 Corroboration

Evidence of association between performance and brokerage has been replicated in other populations. This section offers a selection of the evidence and
references to detailed reviews. Evidence began to accumulate in the 1970s with
research on the career advantages of contact networks. Related lines of work
developed at about the same time on experiments with small-group exchange
networks[21] and market structures,[22] but the work on networks and careers was
more readily absorbed into the prevailing research using survey methodology
to explore stratification theory. A widely cited early study is Granovetter's
(1995 [1974]) demonstration that white-collar workers find better jobs faster
through weak ties that bridge otherwise disconnected social groups. Lee (1969)
similarly found that women searching for an abortionist (when abortion was
illegal) were successful more quickly when they began their search with contacts outside their immediate social circle. Lin, Ensel, and Vaughn (1981)
combined probability surveys with Milgram's (1967) small-world and Granovetter's (1973) weak-tie arguments to present evidence of the importance of
ties to distant and diverse contacts as a social resource for status attainment
(see Lin, 1999, 2002, for review).

---

[21] Cook and Emerson (1978) showed that the most central, or powerful, people in a
network need not be the people who most benefit from exchanges with others. The
people who did best were brokers with exclusive exchange relations to otherwise disconnected partners. The idea that competitive advantage came from brokerage rather
than a dominant central position drew the attention of able researchers and spawned a
cottage industry on small-group exchange networks (e.g., Cook et al., 1983; Markovsky,
Willer and Patton, 1988; see Willer, 1999, for review).

[22] Input–output tables of national and regional economies can be used to compute
network measures of the extent to which producers in an industry, market, or sector
have a network of buying and selling that spans structural holes among suppliers and
customers. Producers that have such a network have the information and control
advantages of social capital and so can be expected to enjoy higher profit margins.
Lustgarten (1975) and Burt (1983) were early efforts describing the association in 1967
with profits in American manufacturing markets defined at broad and detailed levels of
aggregation. Burt (1988, 1992) extended the results to include nonmanufacturing
through the 1960s and 1970s, and Burt, Guilarte, Raider, and Yasuda (2002) refined
the nonlinear form of the model to more accurately describe the association between
performance and market network, and extended the results through the early 1990s.
Using profit and network data on markets in other countries, similar results have been
found in Germany during the 1970s and 1980s (Ziegler, 1982), Israel in the 1970s
(Talmud, 1994; Talmud and Mesch, 1997), Japan in the 1980s (Yasuda, 1996), and
Korea in the 1980s (Jang, 1997). This work seems most productive not in the study of
market behavior so much as in providing a market criterion for corporate behavior (e.g.,
Piskorski, 2001).

1.3.1 Evaluation and Promotion

Research expanded dramatically in the 1990s with interest in the career implications of social capital (see Burt, 2000b; Lin, 2002; Borgatti and Foster, 2003, for review; Lin, Cook, and Burt, 2001; Flap and Volker, 2004, for a sense of research diversity). Podolny and Baron (1997) present evidence on a probability samples of managers in an electronics firm showing that senior people with networks richer in structural holes are more likely to get promoted early. Mehra, Kilduff, and Brass (2001) find that supervisors in a small technology company give higher performance evaluations to employees whose networks bridge otherwise disconnected parts of their organization. Mizruchi and Sterns (2001), studying loan officers in a large commercial bank, show that the officers whose approval networks span structural holes in the firm (in the sense of being less dense and less hierarchical) are more likely to be successful in bringing a deal to closure.

Working with more limited data, Sparrowe and Popielarz (1995) innovatively reconstruct past networks around managers to estimate the effects of holes in yesterday's network on promotion today (cf. Hansen, 1999: 93), Gabbay (1997) shows that promotions occur more quickly for sales people with strong-tie access to structural holes, and Gabbay and Zuckerman (1998) show that expectations of promotion are higher for research and development scientists whose networks are richer in spanning structural holes. Seibert, Kraimer, and Liden (2001) find that alumni whose networks span structural holes report more contact with senior executives and colleagues in other functions, which is associated with self-reports of more access to information, resources and sponsorship, which is in turn associated with promotions and higher salary. Godechot and Mariot (2004: 259–262), comparing the Ph.D. juries of doctoral candidates in political science, show that (quote from p. 243): "having a heterogeneous jury, i.e., whose members have only slight connections to the thesis director, adds to the value of the doctoral degree within the discipline and helps successful candidates find jobs."

Replicating the Section 1.2.2 results on performance evaluations in an example organization, Figure 1.5c describes a representative sample of staff officers in a large financial organization in 1996 (Burt, Jannotta, and Mahoney, 1998). The network data come from a survey of all senior people in the staff function.

The criterion variable in Figure 1.5c is annual performance evaluations, taken from company personnel records. Employees were evaluated at the end of each fiscal year and sorted into three categories of outstanding to poor. Holding constant background differences between the officers, the regression lines in Figure 1.5c show that outstanding evaluations tended to go to officers with contacts in diverse groups (-2.3 z-score test statistic with network constraint) and poor evaluations tended to go to officers in a closed network (3.3 z-score with network constraint).

Replicating the Section 1.2.2 promotion association with brokerage in an example organization, Figure 1.5D describes a probability sample of senior managers in a large computer manufacturer in 1989. Performance and network data on these managers have been discussed in detail elsewhere (Burt, 1992; 1997*a*; 1997*b*). The network data come from a survey of the sample managers. Manager performance and background data were taken from company personnel records.

The criterion variable in Figure 1.5D is early promotion to senior rank. Whether promoted internally or hired from the outside, people promoted to senior rank in large organizations have several years of experience preceding their promotion. A period of time is expected to pass before people are ready for promotion to senior rank (see Merton, 1984, on socially expected durations). How much time is an empirical question, the answer to which differs between individual managers. Some managers are promoted early. Early promotion is the difference between when a manager was promoted to his current rank and a human-capital baseline model predicting the age at which similar managers are promoted to the same rank to do the same work: $E(age) - age$. Expected age at promotion $E(age)$, is the average age at which managers with specific personal backgrounds (education, race, gender, and seniority) have been promoted to a specific rank within a specific function (rank, function, and plant location). The vertical axis in Figure 1.5D is the early promotion variable standardized to zero mean and unit variance. The statistically significant negative association in the graph (-5.4 t-test) shows that early promotion to senior rank is associated with having contacts in diverse groups (low-constraint networks).

1.3.2 Compensation

Research on the brokerage association with compensation has been less compelling than the work on evaluation and promotion.

One complication is the permeable wall between research on job search and research on job execution. There is a large literature on job search. It seems from this research that personal contacts do not, on average, locate better-paid jobs than other sources of information. This point is a general conclusion in Lin's (1999) review, and Mouw (2003) argues that what evidence there is can be attributed to the tendency for people to build relations with contacts like themselves. There is a thorny methodological challenge to identifying the independent role of personal contacts in job search (Lin, 1999: 482).

The research question is less complex once the person is employed. All employees, certainly managers, use personal contacts in the execution of their work. The research question is not whether employees work through personal contacts, but how. Do they scan and mobilize via a closed network of close colleagues or a brokerage network of scattered contacts?

The shift to job execution does not eliminate data problems. Compensation is a sensitive issue on which most companies are reluctant to release data. Also there can be a close connection between job rank and salary which leaves little salary variation for social capital to explain between peers at the same rank. That variation has been increasing as firms moved to broad salary bands in response to layers of bureaucracy being removed.

Whatever the reasons, there is less replication on compensation than there is on evaluation and promotion. For example, Meyerson (1994) is helpful in showing an association between income and strong connections outside the firm for managers in a selection of large Swedish companies in the mid-1980s, but income is a self-report by the manager and the network data are incomplete (cf. Boxman, DeGraaf, and Flap, 1991).[23] Seibert, Kraimer, and Liden (2001) use an alumni survey to look at the career effects of social capital. They have network data with and among each survey respondent's contacts. They describe an interesting pattern of correlation from brokerage, to information and resources, and from there to promotions, satisfaction, and salary. However, salary is self-report on an alumni survey and there are no controls for differences between occupations and industries, so it is difficult to interpret the results.

Three graphs at the bottom of Figure 1.5 replicate the Section 1.2.2 brokerage association with compensation using compensation data obtained from employer archives. These graphs are useful for the quality of the compensation data and for showing the brokerage association with compensation in different settings. To produce these graphs, the compensation expected for a person is computed from data on compensation and background characteristics in the population. The vertical axis in the Figure 1.5 compensation graphs is a z-score measure of the extent to which a manager's compensation exceeds the level expected for his or her peers.

Figure 1.5E describes a brokerage association with bonus compensation in a large American financial organization in 1993 (Burt, 1997a). The population includes bankers responsible for client relations, along with backroom administrative and support people who participate in the bonus pool. For easy reference, I will refer to everyone in the bonus pool as a banker. The network data come from annual peer evaluations in which each banker names colleagues with whom he or she had substantial business over the preceding year,

---

[23] Meyerson's (1994) analysis is a nicely reasoned use of the data she had available. Her network data are incomplete in that she only knows people named by her survey respondents. There are no data on connections between a manager's external contacts, so she cannot distinguish a manager with N external contacts into separate groups from a manager who has N external contacts all in one group. Meyerson does know whether a manager's contacts were named by other managers in the same company. From that knowledge, she measures the extent to which a manager's contacts overlap with colleagues, which is a kind of redundancy measure, but she finds no associations with the overlap measure.

then reports on what it was like to work with the colleague. I identified colleagues cited by each banker, then found their evaluations of one another. Network constraint is computed from evaluations with and among a banker's colleagues. Network constraint is high if a banker's colleagues all had substantial business with one another. These data will be discussed in Chapter 4 for the evidence they provide on trust and reputation.

Performance and background data are taken from company personnel records. Annual bonuses were decided five months after the network data were gathered. Bonuses varied from zero to several million dollars. Seventy-three percent of the variance in bonuses can be predicted from job rank and seniority. With rank and seniority held constant, there are no statistically significant bonus differences across banker gender, race, or other background factors on which the firm has data. The residual 27% of bonus variance defines the performance variable in Figure 1.5E. Relative bonus in the graph is based on the difference between the bonus a banker was paid and the bonus typical for someone in his rank, at her age, with his years of seniority at the firm: bonus − E(bonus). The scores plotted of the vertical axis of Figure 1.5E are studentized residual bonuses standardized across all bankers in the population to zero mean and unit variance. A score of 1.5, for example, means that the banker's bonus is one and a half standard deviations higher than the bonus typically paid to people at his or her rank, age, and seniority. The statistically significant negative association in the graph (−3.7 t-test) shows that bankers who receive bonuses higher than their peers tend to have (low constraint) collaboration networks spanning structural holes in the firm.

It could be argued that the social capital of structural holes is a culture-bound argument, swept up in the rhetoric of American markets and limited to those markets (Burt, Hogarth, and Michaud, 2000). The results in graphs F and G are useful because they replicate in a European and an Asia-Pacific organization the brokerage associations seen in America. Unlike the banker data, there is no time ordering here. Network and compensation data refer to the same time period. The empirical question is whether there is an association between compensation and brokerage when background variables are held constant. Figure 1.5F contains a representative sample of senior managers across functions in a division of a large French chemical and pharmaceuticals company in 1997. The data come from a network survey of the managers. Salary and background data come from company personnel records (Burt, Hogarth, and Michaud, 2000). Seventy-two percent of the study-population variance in annual salaries can be predicted from a manager's job rank and age. The residual 28% of salary variance defines the performance variable in Figure 1.5F. Relative salary is the difference between a manager's salary and the salary expected of someone in his rank at her age: salary − E(salary). Studentized residual salary is standardized across all managers in the division to zero mean and unit variance. The statistically significant negative association in Figure 1.5F shows that managers with salaries higher than their peers tended to have (low constraint) discussion networks across structural holes in the firm.

The island segregation of Asia-Pacific cultures and resources has long made the region rich in structural holes and active in entrepreneurial activity. Informed network analysis of contemporary activity highlights the role of brokerage in the region (e.g., Ellis, 1998, 2000, 2002, and especially his 2003 article on international trade associations). At a more modest, micro level, Figure 1.5G describes the association between brokerage and salary in the Asia-Pacific operations of one of the region's largest electronics organizations. The network data come from an unpublished survey in 2004 of several hundred managers in the organization. Salary and background data come from company personnel records. Salary was adjusted by the company finance department for currency differences between countries in the region. With country differences removed from the salary data, 65% of salary variance can be predicted from manager differences in job rank, job function, and seniority (salary associations with other predictors were statistically negligible). Studentized residuals from the prediction are standardized across all managers in the population to zero mean and unit variance to define the vertical axis in Figure 1.5G. The statistically significant negative association (-4.3 t-test), shows that managers with salaries higher than their peers tended to have (low constraint) networks across structural holes in the company's regional operations.

1.3.3   Team Performance

The social capital of teams is the subject of Chapter 3, but there is evidence even at this point that the social capital of individuals aggregates to the teams on which they serve. Figure 1.5H is taken from Rosenthal's (1996) dissertation research on the social capital of teams. Troubled by the variable success of total quality management (TQM) and inspired by Ancona and Caldwell's (1992a, 1992b) demonstration that networks beyond the team are associated with team performance, Rosenthal wanted to see whether the structure of external relationships for TQM teams had the effect predicted by the hole argument. She gained access to a midwest manufacturing firm in 1994 that was in the process of using TQM teams to improve quality in all of its functions in its several plants (a total of 165 teams). She observed operations in two plants, then asked the senior manager responsible for quality in each plant to evaluate the performance of each TQM team in his or her plant. Evaluations were standardized within plants, then compared across plants to identify functions in which team performance most varied. The study population was teams assigned to a function with high success in some plants and low success in other plants. Selecting two functions for study, Rosenthal sent to each employee on the selected teams a network questionnaire and the survey data were used to compute constraint in each person's network within and beyond the team. The vertical axis in Figure 1.5H is senior-manager evaluation of each team standardized across teams working issues in the same function, and the horizontal axis is average constraint on people in the team. The association is as predicted by the hole argument, and quite striking (−.79 correlation). Teams composed of people whose networks extend beyond the team to span structural holes in the company are significantly more likely to be recognized as successful.

Without adumbrating the discussion of team social capital in Chapter 3, I can mention other work showing the social capital of teams with brokerage connections beyond the team. Hansen (1999) studied new-product teams in a leading American electronics firm segmented by geography and product lines into forty-one divisions. The network data are aggregate in that Hansen asked the R&D manager in each division to describe the extent to which people in his or her division had frequent and close working relationships with other divisions. Team performance is measured by the relative speed with which a team moves from initiation (first employee dedicated to the project) to completion (product released to shipment). Faster solutions are to be expected from teams with the social capital of bridge relationships that span the structural holes between divisions, and Hansen found that teams reached completion more quickly when they were in divisions with frequent and close relations to other divisions.[24] Hansen, Podolny and Pfeffer (2001) study the interpersonal networks around the teams. Each team member was asked to name intra-division contacts from whom he or she had regularly sought information and advice, then asked about relations between the contacts. Teams more quickly completing their assigned task contained people with more non-redundant contacts beyond the team (discussed in the analysis as "advice size" and "sparseness").

Related findings are reported by Krackhardt and Stern (1988) on higher performance in student groups with cross-group friendships, and in numerous studies of inter-organization networks (also see Leana and Van Buren, 1999, on corporate social capital): Fernandez and Gould (1994) on organizations in broker positions within the national health policy arena being perceived as more influential; Provan and Milward (1995) on higher performing mental health systems that have a hierarchical, rather than a dense, network structure; Geletkanycz and Hambrick (1997) and Park and Luo (2001) on higher performance for companies in which top managers have boundary-spanning

---

[24] More, the social-capital prediction is only true for teams coordinating poorly documented, personal knowledge across divisions. Where knowledge was unambiguous, teams reached completion more quickly if they didn't have to coordinate at all (in the sense that they were in a division that had infrequent and distant relations to other divisions, "tie weakness" main effect, Hansen, 1999: 102). The point illustrated is that brokers aren't worth their costs on tasks that involve unambiguous information. The more tacit the knowledge to be coordinated across groups, the more valuable network entrepreneurs can be in moving knowledge from one group to another. This issue comes up again in Chapter 2 on adaptive implementation.

relationships beyond their firm and beyond their industry; Pennings, Lee and Witteloostuijn (1998) on the survival of accounting firms as a function of strong partner ties to client sectors; Stuart and Podolny (1999) on the higher probability of innovation from semiconductor firms that establish alliances with firms outside their own technological area; McEvily and Zaheer (1999) on the greater access to competitive ideas enjoyed by small job manufacturers with more nonredundant sources of advice beyond the firm; Sørensen (1999) on the negative effect on firm growth of redundant networks beyond the firm; Llobrera, Meyer and Nammacher (2000) on the importance of nonredundant networks to the development of Philadelphia's biotechnology district; Baum, Calabrese and Silverman (2000) on the faster revenue growth and more patents granted to biotechnology companies that have multiple kinds of alliance partners at start-up; Rowley and Baum (2004) on the larger market share of Canadian investment banks who form underwriting syndicates with partners who have not done deals together in the past; and Koput and Powell (2003) on the higher earnings and survival chances of biotechnology firms with more kinds of activities in alliances with more kinds of partner firms.

At the same time that group performance is enhanced by the social capital of its members, group social capital can enhance employee performance. For example, Bielby and Bielby (1999) describe a decade of data on the careers of almost nine thousand film and television writers. Social capital in their study is held by the talent agency that represents a writer. About half of the writers had no representation (52% in 1987, down to 38% in 1992; Bielby and Bielby, 1999: 73). A quarter had the traditional representation of an agency that "finds work ... and in exchange it receives a 10-percent commission from the client's earnings" (Bielby and Bielby, 1999: 66). The remaining quarter of the writers were advantaged by having what Bielby and Bielby (1999: 66–67) describe as "core" representation; representation by an agency that brokers connections between functional areas to propose whole projects in which the writer is a component: "Instead of seeking out projects for their clients, they initiate projects on their own. They negotiate unique arrangements with the talent guilds and cultivate long-term relationships with those who finance, produce, and distribute new projects." Bielby and Bielby (1999: 70, 72) do not have network data, so they reduce social capital to binary distinctions between those who have it and those who do not; nevertheless, they obtain strong evidence of more likely employment and higher compensation for writers affiliated with the agencies that have it (cf. Yair and Maman, 1996, on the social capital of songwriters attributable to their country's network position among other countries; Jacob, Lys, and Neale, 1999, on the more accurate company earnings predictions from analysts employed in brokerage houses providing the information advantages of many other analysts and specialists in the company's industry).[25]

---

[25] The implication is that it would be productive to separate two levels of social capital. Distinguish the "first-order" social capital of a person's personal network (see

1.4　Kinds of People

Brokerage opportunities do not by themselves turn into success, and people are not equally comfortable in the role of broker. It is reasonable to ask whether the performance association with brokerage is contingent on having certain kinds of people as employees. My conclusion from available evidence is to separate network etiology from consequences. Kinds of people differ in the way they build networks, but the performance association with brokerage occurs across kinds of people.

There are three ways to deal with the question. One is to assume it away. For example, if individuals are rationally self-interested, personal preference about brokering connections is not a contingency factor. To know who succeeds, you only need to know who had the opportunity to succeed.

A second option is to assume that the structure around a person indicates the kind of person he or she is, so motivation does not have to be measured once one has a measure of network structure. I took this second option in *Structural Holes* (Burt, 1992: 34–36). For reasons of a clear path to success (a person is more likely to see brokerage opportunities in a large, sparse network), or the personality of the individual who constructed the network (people

---

Barnes, 1969, on the first-order zone of a person's network), from the "second-order" social capital of the organization, or contacts more generally, with which the person is affiliated (cf. Burt, 1992: 38–44, on primary versus secondary structural holes; Podolny, 1993; Stuart, Hoang, and Hybels, 1999, on status-enhancing affiliations). The two levels are combined in Bielby and Bielby's (1999: 74–79) analysis: A writer with a contact network that spans structural holes had a competitive advantage in securing and delivering on projects such that (*a*) his or her earnings would be correlated in adjacent years, and (*b*) he or she would be more attractive to the "core" agencies. Therefore, core agencies had more social capital for the reasons given by Bielby and Bielby, and because they could attract writers with more social capital. The task for future research would be to separate the performance effects of an individual's (first-order) social capital from the (second-order) social capital of the organization(s) with which he or she is affiliated.

The task is more difficult than estimating social capital effects within organizations because performance has to be compared across organizations, and organizations differ in performance criteria. Consider professors at major and minor universities. The distinction can be difficult, but universities differ in quality such that a major–minor distinction can be drawn where a major university has more organizational social capital because of its central location in a great many extramural networks of high quality faculty and students (a "core" university to use Bielby and Bielby's term). Given two professors of equal ability, one at a major, the other at a minor, university, the professor at the major university is more likely to be well compensated (major universities treat their faculty well to attract the most sought-after faculty) and be stimulated to produce important work (able people more often meet and exchange ideas at major universities). This is the performance effect of organizational social capital discussed in the text. However, minor universities can compete for able faculty by offering early promotion to tenure or other senior rank. This is the "promotion paradox" that Phillips (2001) observes in lawyer promotions to partner (and Phillips and Sørensen, 2003, observe in promotions to manage television stations): The probability of promotion to senior rank is higher in young, small, low-status organizations.

inclined toward brokering connections between others build large, sparse networks), or the nature of exogenous factors responsible for the structure of the network (persons forced to live in large, sparse networks are more likely to learn about brokering connections between others)—large, sparse networks are more likely to surround a person motivated to be entrepreneurial in the sense of building networks that span structural holes.

A third option is to address the question directly by adding personality or culture to the equation predicting performance. If the performance association with brokerage is stronger for certain kinds of people or people who live in certain kinds of cultures, then personality–culture distinctions between kinds of people is a contingency factor. For example, McClelland (1961) argues that the childhood formation of a need to achieve is a personality factor critical to later entrepreneurial behavior, and Weber (1930 [1905]) makes the culture argument that Protestant beliefs encouraged capitalism by making entrepreneurial behavior righteous.

The personality index in Figure 1.6 comes from a sociologist, businessman, and psychologist working to identify the kinds of people whose networks span structural holes (Burt, Jannotta, and Mahoney, 1998). The ten items in Figure 1.6 were culled from a 252-item personality questionnaire widely used in career advising. The items were selected because they best distinguished MBA students with closed networks from MBA students whose networks spanned structural holes. Student scores on the personality index in Figure 1.6 were closely associated with brokerage.[26] Students living with brokerage, like Robert in Figure 1.1, claimed the personality of an entrepreneurial outsider, in search of authority, thriving on advocacy and change. Students in closed networks claimed the personality of a reliable team player, in search of security, thriving on stability.

However, the MBA students were themselves a kind of person. They were younger than employees on average and worked in lower-level white collar jobs. This matters because network and personality data on a wider spectrum of people show a more complex pattern.

The personality association with brokerage is strong for people in technical and clerical jobs. But there is no evidence of performance associated with brokerage in technical and clerical jobs. People were free to build relations to suit their personal preferences.

At higher job ranks, where Burt, Jannotta, and Mahoney (1998) find brokerage associated with performance, the personality association with brokerage disappears. In other words, managers have networks that fit their work more

---

[26] To score responses to the index in Figure 1.6, sum across the ten items adding one for each of the following options selected: 1A, 2B, 3A, 4A, 5B, 6B, 7A, 8B, 9B, and 10A. The graph in Figure 1.6 is a logit regression line predicting, from student index scores, the probability that a student has a contact network rich in structural holes (Burt, Jannotta, and Mahoney, 1998: 80).

Select the phrase under each item that better describes you (circle A or B). Select one phrase per item. If you disagree with both phrases, select the one with which you disagree less. It is important to select phrases that describe how you actually operate, rather than how you feel you should or would like to operate. There are no right or wrong answers. When you are finished, you should have a total of ten phrases circled. To score your responses, see footnote 26 and compare your score to the graph below.

1. When evaluating opportunities, I am likely to look . . . .
  A. for a chance to be in a position of authority
  B. for the long-run implications

2. My strength lies in the fact that I have a knack for . . .
  A. being easygoing
  B. getting a point across clearly

3. In discussions among peers, I am probably seen as . . .
  A. an outspoken advocate
  B. motivating people to my views

4. In evaluating my aims in my career, I probably put more emphasis on . . .
  A. my ability to create an aura of excitement
  B. being in control of my own destiny

5. I believe that people get into more trouble by . . .
  A. being unwilling to compromise
  B. not letting others know what they really think

6. In a leadership role, I think my strength would lie in the fact that I . . .
  A. won people over to my views
  B. kept everyone informed

7. As a member of a project team, I . . .
  A. seek the advice of colleagues
  B. closely follow original mandate of the group

8. Others are likely to notice that I . . .
  A. let well enough alone
  B. let people know what I think of them

9. In an emergency, I . . . .
  A. take the safe approach
  B. am quite willing to help

10. I look to the future with . . .
  A. unshakable resolve
  B. a willingness to let others give me a hand

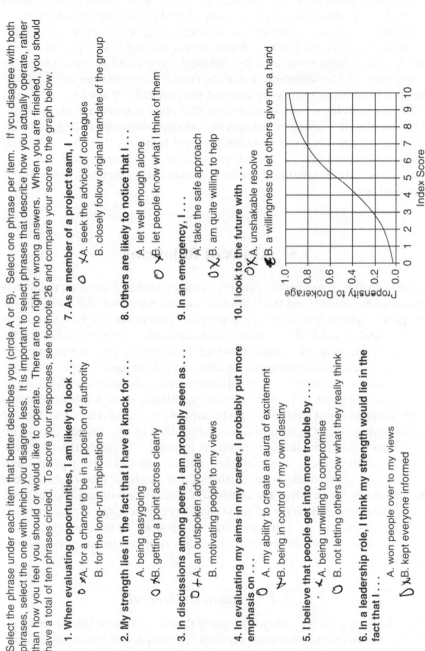

Fig. 1.6: Network entrepreneur personality index

than their personal tastes (see Mehra, Kilduff, and Brass, 2001, for an analysis in which the performance effects of network and personality are additive).

Culture is another criterion for distinguishing kinds of people. Burt, Hogarth, and Michaud (2000) compare senior managers in a pair of French and American firms because of the different French and American views of bureaucracy. The key difference is that the French networks were built on long-standing friendships that rarely spanned the boundary of the firm, while the Americans built from work relationships that often reached outside the firm. Differences in the etiology of network connections notwithstanding, performance in both firms is associated with personal networks that span structural holes (see Figure 1.5F). The French and American managers built their networks differently, but performance for both was enhanced when they bridged structural holes.

1.5   Kinds of Relations

Network analysis separates the pattern of connections in a network, the who is connected to whom, from the substance that flows through the connections. The pattern is form. The substance is content. Content is a factor to consider in social capital research if the performance association with brokerage is contingent on the network content in which brokerage occurs. For example, is brokerage in a friendship network a source of value or merely rude? Is brokerage in an authority network productive or merely a disruption to the chain of command? It can be difficult to separate questions about kinds of relations from questions about kinds of people because people can differ in their view of a relationship. What is friendship and obligation in one culture can be no more than business in another culture. It is useful to separate the two questions for analysis (content distinctions cutting across kinds of people and personality–culture distinctions cutting across kinds of relationships), but the two are closely related. My conclusion is that content can be, but need not be, a contingency factor for brokerage. Nevertheless, the most consistent performance effects are with brokerage in informal discussion relations. It would be wise to include informal discussion relations in any social capital analysis.

1.5.1   Content in General

When network data are gathered on more than one content there is always a risk that the analyst's distinctions between contents do not match distinctions in the study population. What is friendship distinct from business in one study population can be combined in the same relationships in another population.

Measuring population distinctions between contents is a generic issue in network analysis, for which there are various solutions (e.g., Romney and D'Andrade, 1964; Burt and Schøtt, 1985; Carley, 1986; Burt, 1990; Krackhardt, 1990; Faust and Skvoretz, 2002).

The solutions assume that behavioral distinctions precede cognitive distinctions. Two kinds of relations distinguished in a questionnaire are in fact the same kind of relationship to the extent that everyone with whom I have the first kind of relationship, I also have the second. For example, Figure 1.7 contains two spatial maps of content distinctions by senior people in an American technology firm in comparison to similar people in a French firm (see Burt, Hogarth, and Michaud, 2000, for the research design and discussion of the maps). Each map is a multidimensional scaling of joint probabilities. Kinds of relations are close together to the extent that they tend to reach the same people.[27] For example, the French managers cited a total of 275 colleagues as most valued, 227 as essential sources of buy-in, and 115 as both, defining a joint probability of .297 between valued and buy-in. "Valued" and "buy-in" are close together in the French map in Figure 1.7 because the .297 joint probability of a contact being cited for buy-in and valued is higher than most other joint probabilities.

The most obvious feature of the maps is their similarity (see Faust and Skvoretz, 2002, for statistical analysis of content-map similarity across poulations). Three kinds of relations distinct in each map are circled (personal, work, and negative). Personal relations (in the southeast of each map) are to people with whom the manager socializes and discusses personal matters such as leaving for a job with another firm. These are people to whom the manager feels especially close and with whom he speaks daily. Work relations (in the northeast of each map) are to people the manager cites as his most valued contacts at work and essential sources of buy-in for initiatives coming out of his office. These are people to whom the manager feels close, but not especially close, and with whom he speaks once a week or so. Negative relations (to the west of each map) are with people to whom the managers feels emotionally distant, or people cited for having most made it difficult for the manager to carry out his job responsibilities.

The two broad content distinctions illustrated in Figure 1.7 are evaluative between good and bad (east–west in each map), and work versus personal (north–south in each map). These broad distinctions also occur in survey network data on national probability samples, so they are probably reliable

---

[27] The two multidimensional scalings in Figure 1.7 are based on Kruskal's (1964) algorithm preserving monotonic distances between points, and the spatial displays are a good summary of the data (.21 and .23 stress coefficients for the French and American maps respectively; .91 correlation between logs of the observed and predicted distances between elements in the French map, .90 for the American map).

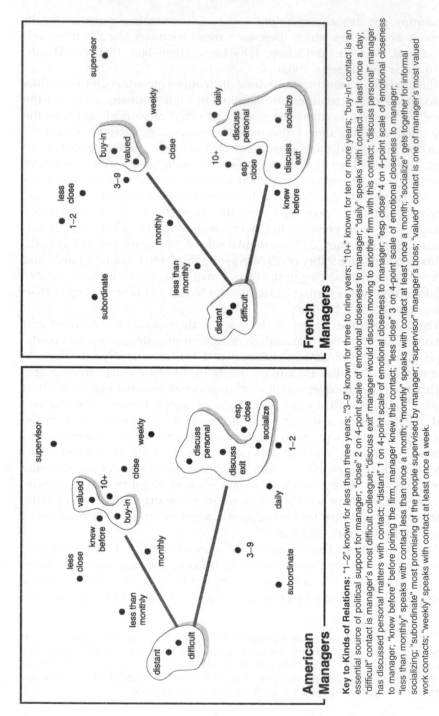

Key to Kinds of Relations: "1–2" known for less than three years; "3–9" known for three to nine years; "10+" known for ten or more years; "buy-in" contact is an essential source of political support for manager; "close" 2 on 4-point scale of emotional closeness to manager; "daily" speaks with contact at least once a day; "difficult" contact is manager's most difficult colleague; "discuss exit" manager would discuss moving to another firm with this contact; "discuss personal" manager has discussed personal matters with contact; "distant" 1 on 4-point scale of emotional closeness to manager; "esp close" 4 on 4-point scale of emotional closeness to manager; "knew before" before joining the firm, manager knew this contact; "less close" 3 on 4-point scale of emotional closeness to manager; "less than monthly" speaks with contact less than once a month; "monthly" speaks with contact at least once a month; "socialize" gets together for informal socializing; "subordinate" most promising of the people supervised by manager; "supervisor" manager's boss; "valued" contact is one of manager's most valued work contacts; "weekly" speaks with contact at least once a week.

Fig. 1.7: Manager distinctions between kinds of relations (relations close together reach the same contacts)

content distinctions for social capital research.[28] The evaluative distinction occurs in network data on probability samples of Americans (Marsden and Campbell, 1985, Burt, 1990), as does the distinction between work and personal relationships (Burt, 1990).[29] The distinction between positive and negative is an obvious distinction between network contents, but the positive–negative distinction has not been prominent in social capital research. Virtually all social capital research has been on networks of variably positive relationships (exceptions include Labianca, Brass, and Gray, 1998; Gulati and Westphal, 1999; Labianca and Brass, 2004; see Section 4.2 on the strategic importance of negative relationships for integrating the concepts of trust and brokerage).

---

[28] There are more fine-grain readings of content maps that can illuminate features of specific study populations. Lazega and Pattison (1999) offer an example in their analysis of mechanisms by which lawyers in a three-city law firm maintain status competition without the firm devolving into competing factions (also Lazega, 2001: ch. 5). Lazega and Pattison show that work and advice relations tend to occur together, which they interpret as evidence of status differences being used to resolve otherwise difficult work negotiations as Blau (1955) described people in a government agency giving respect to colleagues from whom they obtained advice as a way of paying for the advisor's effort. Lazega and Pattison also show that advice and friendship relations tend to occur together (are close in a content map), which they interpret as evidence of friendship being used to soften status competition. Another example is the time difference between the French and American managers in Figure 1.7. Personal relations in the southeast quadrant of the maps tend to be long-standing relations for the French managers ("10+" years known) but recent acquaintances for the Americans ("1–2" years known). Work relations in the northeast quadrant of the maps tend to be recent acquaintances for the French managers but long-standing relations for the Americans. The time difference led to seeing trust build more slowly for the French managers (see Figure 3.2c) and a lack of French contacts from the time before a manager joined the firm (Burt, Hogarth, and Michaud, 2000: 137).

[29] Montgomery (1998) explores the intuition that a relationship can be divided into its constituent roles, the business component in a relationship, for example, being played separately from the friendship component. The intuition depends on people being able to segregate roles (e.g., by one or another of the role segregation strategies that Merton, 1957, described for preventing conflict between roles in the same role-set). Content maps such as illustrated in Figure 1.7 could site fruitful research applications of Montgomery's model. The closer two kinds of relations are in the content map for a study population, the less likely that people can play the relations as separate roles. It would be difficult to separate business from friendship, to use Montgomery's example, in a population where friends are the people with whom you do business and business is only done with friends. Trying to behave in inconsistent ways in two kinds of relations that are always combined would be received as contrived, presumably for selfish interests. The more distant relations are in a content map, the more that people in the study population have ways of segregating the relations, and so the more likely that Montgomery's role model could yield substantive insights on strategic combination and manipulation of the relations.

1.5.2   *Authority in Particular*

Podolny and Baron (1997) argue that brokerage is more valuable in networks of personal relations, such as confiding and socializing in the southeast of the maps in Figure 1.7. Such relations are discretionary connections through which managers derive early access to information and shape its distribution. In contrast, Podolny and Baron argue, performance can suffer from structural holes in the authority network, as defined by relations such as buy-in and work advice in the northeast of the maps in Figure 1.7. Such relations are the channels through which a manager receives normative information about what is proper, and instrumental information on priorities to be pursued. Structural holes in the authority network increase the odds of a manager receiving contradictory information on proprieties and priorities, which could be confusing and so erode performance.

Using data on a representative sample of managers in a high-technology engineering and manufacturing company, Podolny and Baron show that large, sparse networks of contacts cited for task advice and strategic information increase the odds of manager promotion. They also show, as predicted by their content distinction, that large, sparse networks of buy-in relations lower the odds of manager promotion.

Following Podolny and Baron, I found similar results among the senior people in a large technology company (Burt, 1997b). Early promotion was associated with brokerage in networks of personal relations (socialize, discuss personal matters, discuss exit). There was no association in the authority network (supervision and essential sources of buy-in).

Nevertheless, evidence is mixed on the destructive nature of structural holes in the authority network. For one thing, I found many contacts cited for both work and personal reasons, which creates an extended network in which managers develop personal relationships with key sources of buy-in. Though replicating the Podolny and Baron content distinction, I found that early promotion was most closely associated with brokerage in the networks defined by pooling work relations with personal relations (Burt, 1997b: 369). Similarly, Flap, Völker, and Bulder (2000) report from a study of two government agencies that material job satisfaction increases with instrumental work ties while satisfaction with the social aspects of a job increased with other contents. However, "networks that branch out" enhance satisfaction with both the material and social aspects of a job.

Douthit's (2000) analysis of direct reports raises a second issue. If structural holes are a problem in the buy-in network around manager, they must be a particularly difficult problem when they separate manager and boss. With network data on samples of staff officers from two financial organizations, Douthit compared supervision in a segregated context of manager and boss sharing no key contacts, to supervision embedded in an integrated context of manager and boss sharing mutual key contacts. Supervision in the segregated context is a bridge that spans the structural hole between manager and boss. She discusses bridge supervision as the exercise of authority across a structural hole, and argues that bridge supervision should be less productive than embedded supervision. There are two empirical results. In an analogy to segregated networks in Bott's (1957) analysis of conjugal roles, Douthit describes the tendency for bridge supervision to accompany social disintegration between manager and boss (less joint decision-making, less informal discussion of office politics, less personal compatibility). But disintegration associated with bridge supervision does not affect the association between network constraint and performance evaluations. Interaction between network constraint and bridge supervision is negligible in predicting performance evaluations. Officers with networks that span structural holes are more likely to receive high performance evaluations, whether or not they work under bridge supervision.

1.6   Conclusions

This chapter is an introduction to structural holes and the social capital inherent in bridging them. The argument is as follows: informal organization consists of dense social clusters, or groups, between which there are occasional bridge relations when somone in one group has a friend, acquaintance, or former colleague in another group (Figure 1.1). Opinion and practice vary more between than within groups due to structural holes in the flow of information across groups. A person whose network spans structural holes has contacts in multiple groups, and that contact across holes can be an advantage in terms of breadth of knowledge, early knowledge, and opportunities for strategically coordinating across groups (Robert versus James in Figure 1.1; AFTER versus BEFORE in Figure 1.2). A hole-spanning network that provides these advantages is social capital. People who have the social capital of brokering connections across structural holes have an advantage in detecting and developing rewarding opportunities.

The social-capital advantage of brokerage is manifest in recognition and resources. I described the structural holes in an example organization (Figures 1.3 and 1.4) and offered illustrative evidence that company systems were successfully targeting and rewarding managers who bridged the holes (graphs A and B in Figure 1.5). I generalized the illustrative evidence with research on other populations (Figure 1.5). For individuals and groups, networks that span structural holes are associated with more positive evaluations, earlier promotion, and higher compensation.

Figure 1.8 is my summary interpretation of the evidence. Network constraint is on the horizontal axis. Performance relative to peers is on the vertical axis. The data are pooled from the eight graphs in Figure 1.5 and the

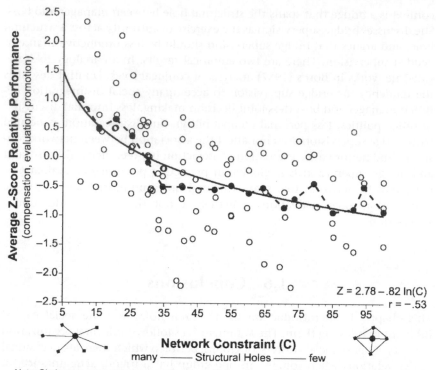

Note: Circles are average z-score performance (Z) for a five-point interval of network constraint (C) within each study population. Dashed line goes through mean values of Z for intervals of C. Bold line is performance predicted by the natural logarithm of C.

Fig. 1.8: Performance increases with brokerage, especially at high levels of brokerage (stylized fact #1)

association in the graph is a stylized fact in that many factors are held constant to highlight the association.[30] The graph is an informed guess about the distribution of social capital across levels of network constraint. Putting aside important contingencies discussed in Chapter 3, the graph shows two

---

[30] The data are a rough aggregation intended to push observers away from population specifics to a broader view of the evidence—but without losing a sense of data variation. Network constraint comes unchanged from Figure 1.5. This is an awkward step because it assumes points of network constraint have the same meaning across the populations. That seems unlikely since the networks were measured in different ways (e.g., see n. 20). The z-score performance scores in Figure 1.5 are ready to compare across populations because they are adjusted for population-specific peformance variation predicted by the many background variables on which I had data (job rank, kind of job, age, race, gender, education, geographic location, etc.). Each dot in Figure 1.8 is an average performance score in a study population within a five-point interval of network constraint, and on the horizontal axis, the average study-population constraint score within a five-point interval.

things: First, relative performance decreases as structural holes are eliminated from a network. This point was discussed at length with respect to Figure 1.5 and related research. Second, the decrease is steeper at low levels of network constraint: constraint on a high level of brokerage opportunity is more destructive to social capital benefits than incremental additions to already high levels of constraint. The nonlinearity is a subtlety not discussed in the chapter. The associations in Figure 1.5 are all linear, published research usually reports tests for a linear brokerage association with performance, and a linear association fits the pooled data in Figure 1.8 almost as well as the nonlinear curve displayed in Figure 1.8 (.53 correlation in Figure 1.8 for the log of constraint, versus .47 for a linear fit or .43 for an exponential fit to the z-scores converted to positive numbers). I use the nonlinear association in Figure 1.8 for four reasons: First, it fits the pooled data better, even if only slightly. Second, it looks more consistent with the data. There is an occasional bulge of performance underestimated at low levels of network constraint (most notably in Figure 1.8 and in graphs D, E, and G of Figure 1.5). More, the pooled data in Figure 1.8 show a kinked association. The dashed line through average performance scores in Figure 1.8 is steep at low levels of network constraint, then almost horizontal for constraint higher than 40 points. Third, there is an intuitive appeal to the displayed nonlinear association: initial increments of constraint are more destructive than incremental additions to already high levels of constraint. Fourth, the nonlinearity in Figure 1.8 is consistent with curves that are going to come up in later chapters. All together, the association in Figure 1.8 is the first stylized fact I infer from the evidence on social capital.

TWO

Creativity and Learning

B ERNIE Marcus caught it from Jack Welch, the legendary CEO of General
Electric. It was during a game of golf, in Florida, in 1995. Marcus, co-
founder and then CEO of Home Depot, was exchanging golf-game tidbits
with friend Welch about how things were going at Home Depot. Home
Depot had been dramatically successful; shares in the company had increased
in value by 28,000% since it went public in 1981, and the company continued
by a large margin to be the most admired retail company in America.[1] By 1995,
however, Home Depot's growth had slowed appreciably and age was catching
up with Marcus. The next generation of leadership was an issue. In their
discussion, Welch described how 360 evaluations had been an effective tool
for developing senior executives at General Electric (360s are multi-source
evaluations in which the usual job evaluation by the boss is extended to
include evaluations from a manager's peers, subordinates, and even customers). Marcus took the idea home and Home Depot soon developed its
own program.

The new program put Home Depot on the bandwagon of businesses using
multi-source evaluations. Rare in the 1970s, multi-source evaluation swept
through corporate America during the 1980s and 1990s to help managers
adapt to the ambiguity of flatter organizations in which bureaucratic chains
of command were replaced by networks of negotiated influence. Estimates at
the end of the century had as many as 90% of the *Fortune* 1000 using some
form of multi-source evaluations (Atwater and Waldman, 1998).

This chapter is about interpersonal moments, such as the exchange between
Marcus and Welch, that are the social origins of good ideas and the mechanism
by which brokerage creates value. The Marcus–Welsh connection was a bridge
across the structural hole between their respective companies. Marcus became
aware of an idea through his bridge to Welch, then productively adapted the
idea to his own organization.

The Marcus–Welsh exchange illustrates the essence of how brokerage is
social capital—it is about a vision advantage. Section 2.1 is a statement of

---

[1] For example, Home Depot led competitors in *Fortune*'s 1997 annual popularity poll
of "most admired companies" with a score of 8.0 (ahead of Circuit City Stores and Office
Depot both with scores of 6.6, Toys "R" US at 6.5, and Lowe's at 6.4). The exchange
between Marcus and Welch is taken from Sellers (1996).

the vision advantage. Section 2.2 contains illustrative evidence from the distribution of good ideas among the supply-chain managers introduced in Chapter 1, and Section 2.3 is an overview of corroborating anecdotal and aggregate evidence. Section 2.4 is about ideas being more contagious across bridge relations than they are through relations inside a group (peer pressure makes ideas contagious whether or not peers talk directly to one another), which further highlights the critical role that brokerage plays in the creative moment of informed meeting ignorant. Section 2.5 is about thinking creatively to implement an idea. The chapter conclusion is that where relationships bridge structural holes, people are more likely to encounter new ideas, create good ideas, as well as express, discuss, and see how to implement ideas.

2.1 Vision Advantage

The argument in Chapter 1 was that opinion and behavior are more homogeneous within than between groups, so people connected across groups are more familiar with alternative ways of thinking and behaving, which is an advantage in detecting and developing rewarding opportunities. Specifically, there is a vision advantage. Like an MRI in a medical procedure, or over-the-horizon radar in an airplane, brokerage across structural holes provides a vision of options otherwise unseen. New ideas emerge from selection and synthesis across structural holes. Unintentional learning is a feature of the process. Golf was the purpose of Marcus' meeting with Welch; the new evaluation system was a by-product (cf. Gladwell, 2000, for an engaging account of big change as a by-product of incidental events). Brokerage puts people in a position to learn about things they didn't know they didn't know. Some fraction of the brokerage-spawned new ideas are good. "Good" takes on specific meaning with empirical data, but for the moment let a good idea be broadly understood to be one that people praise and value. The hypothesis for this chapter is that people who stand near the holes in social structure are at higher risk of good ideas.

Novelty is not a feature of the hypothesis. It is familiar in the sociological theory of Simmel (1955 [1922]) on conflicting group affiliations, or Merton (1948b, 1957) on roles sets and serendipity in science, but the hypothesis is so much more broadly familiar that one can see it in the remarks of prominent creatives. For example, discussing commerce and manners, Adam Smith (1982 [1766]: 539) noted that: "When the mind is employed about a variety of objects it is some how expanded and enlarged." Swedberg (1990: 3) begins his book on academics working the boundary between economics and sociology with John Stuart Mills' (1987 [1848]: 581) opinion: "It is hardly possible to overrate the value … of placing human beings in contact with persons dissimilar to themselves, and with modes of thought and action unlike those with which they are familiar. .... Such communication has always been, and is peculiarly in the present age, one of the primary sources of progress." Jean-René Fourtou, former CEO of the chemical giant Rhône-Poulenc, observed that his scientists were stimulated to their best ideas by people outside their own discipline. Fourtou emphasized *le vide*—literally, the emptiness; conceptually, structural holes—as essential to coming up with new ideas (Stewart 1996: 165) "*Le vide* has a huge function in organizations. ... Shock comes when different things meet. It's the interface that's interesting. ... If you don't leave *le vide*, you have no unexpected things, no creation. There are two types of management. You can try to design for everything, or you can leave *le vide* and say, 'I don't know either; what do you think?'" Biochemist Alex Zaffaroni is an exemplar. A former subordinate is quoted in an INSEAD video case explaining Zaffaroni's value to his organization: "... he is reading and thinking very widely. He is totally unafraid of any new technology in any area of human creativity. He has wonderful contacts with people in many different areas, so he sees the bridges between otherwise disparate fields."[2]

2.1.1 Active Ingredient in Brokerage

The hypothesis makes up for its lack of novelty in the significance of its role in the theory of social capital, and its practical implications for people who work with ideas. On the first point, the hypothesized vision advantage is the mechanism by which structural holes provide social capital. There is abundant and accumulating empirical evidence of returns to brokerage (Chapter 1). Evidence on the mechanism is not abundant. Initial research established the social-capital potential of brokerage by focusing on returns to brokerage, but the association cannot be causal. Networks do not act, they are a context for action. The next phase of work is to understand the information-arbitrage mechanisms by which people harvest the value buried in structural holes.

---

[2] Productive analogy can be drawn to Merton's (1948b) view of serendipity in science. Expanding on research's familiar passive role in testing theory, Merton discusses active roles that research can play in shaping theory, one of which is the serendipity pattern in which an "unanticipated, anomalous, and strategic datum" exerts pressure for initiating theory (p. 158). Serendipity must involve an unanticipated result (datum) inconsistent with established facts or the theory being tested, but the third attribute, strategic, is the key that distinguishes Merton's view. The strategic value of a research result lies in its implications for generalized theory, by which Merton (1948b: 159) refers to: "what the observer brings to the datum rather than to the datum itself." Research has strategic value when an observer sees how a finding has implications for what other people see as unrelated theory. The creative spark on which serendipity depends is to see bridges where others see holes. Polanyi (1983 [1966]: 21–23) makes a similar point in describing a hole intuition involved in selecting a good problem for scientific study. Polanyi's little book on tacit knowledge is especially relevent here because he defines tacit knowledge in terms of seeing connections between items that are separate in the minds of people who do not have the tacit knowledge (Polanyi, 1966: 9–10).

The sociology of information will be central in the work, but it can take many forms.[3] For example, consider four levels of brokerage through which a person could create value: The simplest act of brokerage is to make people on both sides of a structural hole aware of interests and difficulties in the other group; so much conflict and confusion in organizations results from misunderstandings of the constraints on colleagues in other groups. Transferring best practice is a higher level of brokerage. People familiar with activities in two groups are more able than people confined within either group to see how a belief or practice in one group could create value in the other, and to know how to translate the belief or practice into language digestible in the target group (e.g., Marcus taking the idea of 360 evaluations from Welch to apply them in his own organization). A third level is to draw analogy between groups ostensibly irrelevant to one another. Something about the way in which those people think or behave has implications for the value of operations in my group. This step can be difficult for people who have spent a long time inside one group, living by Thoreau's (2004 [1854]: 22) advice to "beware of all enterprises that require new clothes."[4] Such people look for ways they differ

---

[3] I ignore idea content across the four levels of brokerage. I have two reasons: data and traction. It would be difficult to evaluate ideas accurately and reliably across content domains. Below, I defer to senior management in the study population. Second, I have no tools that provide novel insights into idea content (relative to the network analysis tools that can pry open the link between ideas and social structure). The presumption in this chapter is that the content of ideas reflects the social structure in which they emerge. Vary the groups to which a person is attached and you vary the content of the person's ideas. I do not believe that this is entirely true, but my intuition is that there is truth to it. The other extreme would be to ignore social structure to focus entirely on the organization of bits and bytes within an idea. Czernich and Heath (2002) provide an illustration. They describe the dot.com evolution of the idea that website value increases with its number of viewers. They describe analogies to other ideas, and recombinations of elements within the idea. Sociologists will recognize the sociolinguistics of ethnomethodology and the indexical nature of expressions in the analysis (e.g., Hudson, 1980), but the micro-level insights familiar in sociology are used by Czernich and Heath to describe macro-level change in market rhetoric. The subject could be analyzed from the perspective of this chapter. The brokerage argument would be that analogies and recombinations in the evolution of "eyeballs to websites" should have come disproportionately from people with attachments to the separate groups focused on the elements across which analogies and combinations were made. For example, Collins (1987: 67) refers to an imaginary social life of intellectuals (cf. White 1993, on the dialogue between artist and art world; Collins 1998: ch. 1, for elaboration): "The intellectual alone, reading or writing . . . is not mentally alone. His or her ideas are loaded with social significance, because they symbolize membership in existing and prospective coalitions in the intellectual network. New ideas are created as combinations of old ones; and the intellectual's creative intuitions are feelings of what groups these ideas are appealing to (and against which intellectual enemies). The market structure of the intellectual world is transposed into the creative individual's mind."

[4] Chapter 4 is about the mechanism responsible in closed networks for aversion to views not already familiar. The quote comes from Thoreau's introductory material explaining his search for an authentic life in the simplicity of living in isolation at

from others to justify their assertion that "our situation is different" so they can feel comfortable ignoring beliefs and behaviors different from their own. Differences can always be found if one wants to find them. The question is whether there are by analogy elements of belief or practice in one group that could have value in another. Synthesis is a fourth level of brokerage. People familiar with activities in two groups are more likely to see new beliefs or behaviors that combine elements from both groups.

A conclusion across the industry and organization stories one could tell about these four levels of information arbitrage is that brokers are critical to learning and creativity. People whose networks span structural holes have early access to diverse, often contradictory, information and interpretations which gives them a competitive advantage in seeing good ideas. To be sure, ideas come over a variety of paths from a variety of sources (e.g., Von Hippel, 1988; Geroski and Mazzucato, 2002), but idea generation at some point involves a person moving knowledge from this group to that, or combining bits of knowledge across groups. Where brokerage is social capital, there should be evidence of brokerage associated with good ideas, and vice versa.

2.1.2   *Creativity as a Transaction*

The hypothesized vision advantage is further interesting because of its implications for intellectual property and what it means to be creative. Stories about the creation of a good idea are often heroic, distinguishing exceptional people from the mundane. The creator is attributed with great intellectual ability, a fresh perspective, a productive way of thinking, a creative personality, or some other quality that enabled him or her to generate the good idea. Psychological research is today less focused on creative personalities than on a range of factors that can predispose a person to be creative (Runco, 2004), but there remains a belief, certainly among people I meet in my classes, that creativity is a quality of individuals. Creativity is a dimension on which people sort themselves. At one extreme are the people who think of themselves as having a gift for being creative. At the other extreme are the folks who keep quiet in situations that call for creativity. Every discipline has its heroes and heroines, stories about whom serve productive ends other than truth. There is even evidence to support such stories. For example, Simonton (1984) reports that creativity is less likely after age 40 (p. 111), is most likely in people with almost

---

Walden Pond from 1845 to 1847. I learned of the quote when I joined the Berkeley Sociology Department for my first full-time job as a professor. The quote was scrawled in large letters across my otherwise clean office blackboard. I was several months from finishing and defending my dissertation. I arrived a contested appointment to represent quantitative methodology in a department prominent at the time for its struggle against the spread of quantitative methods. Smelser and Content (1980) describe Berkeley's hiring that year. I was the quantitative hire. Thoreau's quote has remained with me.

a college education (pp. 65, 191), is more likely in first-born sons (pp. 26–28), increases with IQ score (p. 45), and so on.

Sociologists typically emphasize environmental factors in the prediction, factors such as the family and era variables in Simonton's analysis (e.g., Kavolis 1966, on the link between artistic creativity and social disequilibrium). In fact, the link between creativity and sociometric citations was a central theme in the early development of network analysis, though the link is obscured in mystical terminology (e.g., Moreno 1940, 1955; Northway and Rooks 1955). Individual and environment can be difficult to disentangle with available data. For example, age is a personal attribute negatively associated with creating good ideas in science (Stephan and Levin 1992, for review; Chandrasekhar, 1987 [1975], for engaging illustration).[5] Beyond the person-specific factors of youthful energy and skills is the environmental factor of a new generation less invested in, or blinded by, the prevailing paradigm (Kuhn 1970 [1962]). The view is bluntly phrased in physicist Planck's (1968 [1949]: 33) comment: "a new scientific truth does not triumph by convincing its opponents and making them see the light, but rather because its opponents eventually die." Of course, the environment exists in its own right. Collins' (1998) analysis, with its emphasis on philosopher greatness adjacent to structural holes, could be viewed as a Simonton kind of analysis run by a gifted structural sociologist.

The more consequential creativity-implication of analyzing good ideas in terms of brokerage is the shift in focus from the production of ideas to the value produced. What matters is the value produced by the idea, whatever its source. Debate over individual and environment factors predisposing a person to create is an aside. The source of an idea is no longer the focal question. The brokerage value of an idea resides in a situation, in the transaction through which an idea is delivered to an audience; not in the source of the idea, nor in the idea itself. People with connections across structural holes have early access to diverse, often contradictory, information and interpretations which gives them a competitive advantage in seeing and developing good ideas.[6] People

---

[5] Chandrasekhar (1987 [1975]) is after the point that the negative age-creativity correlation in science is reversed in the arts, where good ideas are more likely from more experienced minds (cf. Simonton 1984: ch. 6). He (pp. 47–48) presents a novel contrast between obituaries to illustrate what is lost by the early death of a creative in the arts versus the sciences. For example, playwright Christopher Marlowe's early death at age 29, and poet Shelley's early death at age 30, were bemoaned for the loss of what the artists could have given us in their mature years. In contrast, the early death of mathematician Ramanugan did not deny us his best work: "his death may be less of a catastrophe than it seems" because "a mathematician is comparatively old at thirty." Or, as mathematician Hardy (1940: 72) expresses it: "If a mature man loses interest in and abandons mathematics, the loss is not likely to be very serious either for mathematics or for himself."

[6] To further appreciate the network model on this point, consider how Schumpeter, despite his respect for, and emphasis on, what I have discussed as the social capital of brokerage, left the mechanism a mystery (1947: 150, the mechanism is "it" in the

connected to groups beyond their own can expect to find themselves delivering valuable ideas, seemingly gifted with creativity.[7]

This is not creativity born of deep intellectual ability. The creativity associated with brokerage surely involves synaptic event, but it is primarily an import–export business. Creativity by brokerage involves moving an idea mundane in one group to another group where the idea is new and valued. In our age of egocentrism and ready technology, people can easily make the mistake of thinking that they create value when they have an idea born of sophisticated analysis. In fact, what seems valuable to the source of an idea is often not what others value.

---

quote): "from the standpoint of the observer who is in full possession of all relevant facts, it can always be understood *ex post*; but it can practically never be understood *ex ante*; that is to say, it cannot be predicted by applying the ordinary rules of inference from the pre-existing facts." Schumpeter as a young man similarly discusses the phenomenon—with admiration (1934 [1911*b*]: 85, "Carrying out a new plan and acting according to a customary one are things as different as making a road and walking along it"), and mystery (1911*b*: 85, "the success of everything depends on intuition, the capacity of seeing things in a way which afterwards proves to be true, even though it cannot be established at the moment, and of grasping the essential fact, discarding the unessential, even though one can give no account of the principles by which this is done"). The creative act of the entrepreneur stands in contrast to the existence of other people who simply follow routines (Schumpeter, 1911*b*: 84): "All people get to know, and are able to do, their daily tasks in the customary way and ordinarily perform them by themselves; the 'director' has his routine as they have theirs; and his directive function serves merely to correct individual aberrations. This is so because all knowledge and habit once acquired becomes as firmly rooted in ourselves as a railway embankment in the earth. ... Everything we think, feel, or do often enough becomes automatic and our conscious life is unburdened of it." For elaboration, see the discussion below of network closure, efficiency, and groupthink (Sections 3.5 and 4.5). These quotes are from the 1934 translation of the 1926 revision of the 1911 chapter containing the quotes, but consistent across the three editions is an image of the entrepreneur that attributes creativity to individual superiority (see Becker and Knudsen, 2002: 392–395, on the 1911 text giving more emphasis to the superior-individual theme, and Schumpeter, 2002 [1911*a*], for their translation of sections from the 1911 text that were deleted from the later versions). As Dahms (1995: 6) summarizes: "Any given society has a minority of individuals who possess the 'sharpness of mind' and the 'flexiblity of imagination' that enables them to envision new combinations." Or, as Brouwer (2002: 89) more strongly puts it: "There are some overtones of the Nietzschean leader in Schumpeter's description of the entrepreneur." In contrast, the import–export nature of creativity in network brokerage leverages individual ability against situational advantage, making less heroic the task of detecting and developing a good idea.

[7] With respect to the creative arts, see Hatch (1999) on the importance of empty places to integrated improvisation among jazz musicians playing together, Giuffe (1999) on the greater attention given to photographers with careers in networks of sparsely connected photographers, Trolander and Tenger (2004) on the role that the holes between literary circles (coteries) played in the careers of agents and authors, or more broadly, White (1993) on art as a struggle to establish identity in a network of brokering arrangements among agents and other artists.

More specifically, an idea is as valuable as an audience is willing to credit it. An idea is no less valuable to its recipients because there are people elsewhere who do not value it.[8] The certain path to feeling creative is to find a constituency more ignorant than yourself and poised to benefit from your idea. This is a familiar phenomenon in academic work (e.g., see Stigler 1986 [1982], on the quick acceptance of his economic analysis of information, or Lamont 1987, on the popularity of Derrida's work in culture markets as different as France and the United States). If the small world in Figure 1.1 were a map of an academic area, the clusters would correspond to people specialized by method, theory, or topic. It is impossible to keep up with developments in other specialties. It would be inefficient even if it were possible. So there is a market for the information arbitrage of network entrepreneurs. The evidence of their work is that valuable new ideas in one specialty are often a familiar concept in some distant specialty.

Across the clusters in an organization or market, creativity is a diffusion process of repeated discovery. A good idea is carried across structural holes to be discovered in one cluster of people, rediscovered in another, then rediscovered in still others—and each discovery is no less an experience of creativity for people encountering the good idea.[9] Value accumulates as an idea moves through the social structure, each transmission having the potential to add value. In this light, there is an incentive to define work situations such that people are forced to engage diverse ideas. That incentive underlies the Rhône-Poulenc quote in Section 2.1 on managing *le vide*.

Here too I do no more than reassert a common understanding. The brokerage view of creativity can be seen in popular sayings such as the observation attributed to the French philosopher, Voltaire, that "Originality is nothing but judicious plagiarism," or the later adaptation attributed to English clergyman, Dean William R. Inge; "What is originality? Undetected plagiarism." More seriously, Gladwell (2004: 47–48) offers engaging rumination on the implications for copyright protection: "The ethics of plagiarism have turned into the narcissism of small difference: because journalism cannot own up to its heavily derivative nature, it must enforce originality on the level of the sentence.

---

[8] The word "elsewhere" refers to network parameters of diffusion. People elsewhere are neither part of a cohesive group containing the individuals now evaluating the idea, nor structurally equivalent to the current evaluators. Disbelievers cohesive with, or structurally equivalent to, current evaluators would certainly affect the perceived value of the idea (see Section 2.4). There is also status insecurity to consider (Phillips and Zuckerman 2001; Menon and Pfeffer 2003). Knowing that an idea has low value among elites, or is advocated by competitors, can affect the idea's value for people aspiring to look like elites.

[9] As Fleck (1979 [1935], pp. 109–110) so long ago described the social construction of facts with respect to ideas that move between scientific disciplines, "communication of ideas always results in a shift or a change in the currency of thought. ... This change in thought style, that is, change in readiness for directed perception, offers new possibilities for discovery and creates new facts."

... Creative property, Lessig reminds us, has many lives—the newspaper arrives at our door, it becomes part of the archive of human knowledge, then it wraps fish. And, by the time ideas pass into their third and fourth lives, we lose track of where they came from, and we lose control of where they are going. The final dishonesty of the plagiarism fundamentalists is to encourage us to pretend that these chains of influence and evolution do not exist, and that a writer's words have a virgin birth and an eternal life." In the words of urban pundit, Fran Lebowitz (1981: 14): "Original thought is like original sin: both happened before you were born to people you could not have possibly met."

2.2   Good Ideas

What I can add to the popular sayings is evidence of the brokerage–idea connection. I return to the supply-chain managers in Chapter 1. Given the performance association with brokerage documented in Chapter 1, there should be evidence of good ideas associated with brokerage—if brokerage provides the hypothesized vision advantage.

2.2.1   Idea Data

Managers were asked: "From your perspective, what is the one thing that you would change to improve [the company's] supply chain management?" The box into which responses were typed held a maximum of 2,000 characters. The survey elicited 455 ideas.

Evaluating the ideas requires a point of view. I deferred to top management. I do not recommend this point of view for all studies, nor propose it as the best point of view. At the same time, the view from the top is an eminently reasonable frame of reference: Top management was the expert panel familiar with business operations in the organization. They were the people who would reward ideas. They were the people whose careers would rise or fall with the value of the ideas they sponsored.

Two senior managers evaluated the ideas. Each led one of the company's largest business units, geographically distant from one another. Both judges were prominent for their experience in running the supply chain for their respective businesses. Each was given a list of the ideas, unattributed to source, and the question: "How much value could be generated if the idea were well executed?" The scale ranged from one ("low value or can't say") to five ("value could be high").[10]

---

[10] The judges were under pressure from the new leadership to provide quality evaluations, but rating 455 ideas is a daunting task. It seemed likely that the judges would fatigue. It also seemed likely that higher-quality ideas would come from more senior

Table 2.1 contains four ideas to give you a sense of the data. The first two ideas, judged high-value, propose extending supply-chain operations into exogenous sources of inefficiency. Supply-chain managers were widely viewed by company engineers as administrative assistants who executed equipment orders. Engineers were deemed better informed about alternative vendors, so the decision between vendors was theirs to make. Often, however, equivalent vendors existed for a product but the local engineer had dealt with only one vendor in the past, which was the vendor written into the proposal. The first idea in Table 2.1 is to move supply-chain operations into the proposal process so that the company could benefit from the scale economies of purchasing from preferred vendors before low-volume, high-price equipment purchases get written into a contract. A related inefficiency was created in large subcontracts to vendors familiar to local engineers. The second idea in Table 2.1 is to move supply-chain operations into subcontracts to control high prices that subcontractors paid for supplies, which were then charged back to the company.

The bottom two ideas in Table 2.1 were judged low in value. Both judges gave a score of one to the third idea, which is a call for more consistency across geographic locations. The bit of strategic thinking missing in the idea is to focus on consistency as it creates value as opposed to consistency for its own sake. As stated, the third idea is a classic lament from bureaucrats—we need people to adhere more consistently to agreed-upon processes. The fourth idea in Table 2.1 has a tone of the bureaucrat's lament, but it offers substantive detail, in fact so much detail that it is difficult to judge the value of the idea. The respondent is down in the weeds with details about his Six Sigma project and the computer systems utilized in the project. It is difficult to evaluate the value of this idea without knowing more about the specific project and computer systems (cf. Reagans and McEvily 2003). One of the two judges gave the idea a score of one, the minimum on the printed rating scale. The other judge dismissed the idea without rating it (scored as zero, resulting in the 0.5 average

---

people because they had a broader view across the bureaucratic silos in the supply chain (illustrated in Figures 1.3 and 1.4). To guard against unreliable evaluations of the better ideas, ideas were presented anonymously to the judges in two categories: The first 48 ideas were a random order of responses from respondents in the three highest ranks (Vice President, Director, and Senior Manager). The subsequent 407 were a random order of ideas offered by managers in lower ranks. As expected, ratings are lower for ideas later on the list (-3.5 t-test; 2.7 mean value for the first 50 ideas, 1.4 mean value for the last 50 ideas), and higher for the ideas from people in more senior ranks (6.9 t-test; 3.0 mean value of ideas from Directors and Vice Presidents, 2.5 for ideas from Senior Managers, and 1.8 for ideas from the less senior managers). Effects of respondent rank and judge fatigue are confounded in the ratings (since ideas from high-rank managers were listed before ideas from other managers), but the two factors do not need to be separated for the purposes of this chapter so much as it is important to hold constant both job rank and an idea's sequential order of evaluation when predicting the value of ideas. This, and other bias issues, are discussed below.

Table 2.1: Four illustrative ideas, two high-value and two low-value

---

(4.5 value, 38 network constraint)–Involve SCM in the proposal process. Most of the risk in supply chain is at the front end of the busines, where little involvement from the SCM community is found. Opportunities to improve our win rate through innovative SCM ideas and out-of-the-box procurement are often overlooked or missed altogether. For example, on a proposal with a plug number for material, SCM is oftentimes not considered. We could be utilizing our powerful processes to decrement that material cost substantially, thus creating a competitive advantage.

(4.5 value, 31 network constraint)–We need to develop and train our SCM people in the Subcontracts area to manage our critical subcontractors. We need to institute a standard process for subcontract mangement and a training program to deploy this process within SCM across our locations. We also need to have sufficient experienced subcontracts people available to support the program offices in order to adequately manage the subcontract process.

(1.0 value, 72 network constraint)–If you go through all the training to unify a process then the whole supply chain regardless of location should be required to continue to use the process. We tend to train alot, but are not required to continue to use the process once it has been incorporated. Supply Chain has a lot of great processes, but they get lost after the initial training, or not everyone is required to follow the process, based on location. We need to continue to work with our counterparts to ensure that the processes are being followed. Where there is a lack of training, we must take the time to train our fellow team members so that it benefits us in the long run.

(0.5 value, 80 network constraint)–My SixSigma Team was tasked with developing an easier method to get Budgets and Targets posted, by part number, so that the buyers would not waste time contacting individual SCMs. This process requires utilizing the Materials System and Buyer Web System. The team ran into several roadblocks, but we identified solutions to resolve those roadblocks. Some programming changes were required (none of which was extremely high cost). In addition, we tried to have all SCMs directed to get all of their contracts loaded into the system by a certain cut-off date. We went through three or four cut-off date delays for various reasons, and each time our team met the challenge. So much time went by, however, the programmers were all diverted to the new SAP system. Without the programming changes, meeting the initial goals of the team (making *all* budgets and targets available to the buyers) is no longer possible. Therefore, the one thing I would change is to implement the changes that my team came up with. This would make the buyer much more efficient, and less frustrated.

Note: SCM stands for supply-chain management or supply-chain manager.

across judges) and explained with a note at the end of his ratings: "for ideas that were either too local in nature, incomprehensible, vague, or too whiny, I didn't rate them."

As an indicator of construct validity, the ratings imply that good ideas came from people expected to provide good ideas (Burt, 2004: 380). For example, judges saw more value in the ideas of managers in more senior ranks. Average ratings of their ideas were higher (3.0 average for Directors and Vice Presidents versus 1.5 for the first rank of managers), and their ideas were less likely to be dismissed (0% of Director and Vice President ideas were dismissed by both judges versus 47% of ideas from first-rank managers were dismissed). Better ideas came from the purchasing managers, whose work brought them into contact with other companies. More educated managers had better ideas. Managers in the urban centers had better ideas. In keeping with the brokerage hypothesis, managers constrained in a closed discussion network were less likely to have valuable ideas (1.5 average) and more likely to have their ideas dismissed by both judges (43%).

2.2.2 Ideas Engaged

The results in Figure 2.1 support the hypothesized association between good ideas and brokerage.[11] The left-hand graph shows a nonlinear association with brokerage. The steepest drop in value happens with initial network constraint, in other words, when a manager first begins to rely on redundant discussion

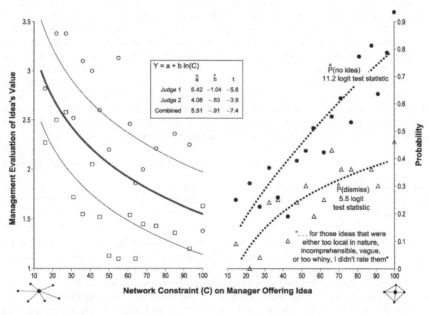

Fig. 2.1: Good ideas and brokerage

---

[11] Regression models and control variables for the predictions in Figure 2.1 are given in the published report (Burt, 2004: 381).

partners. Circles in the graph indicate ratings by one of the two judges (averaged across five-point intervals of network constraint), and squares indicate pooled ratings from the other judge. Thin lines through their respective ratings differ in level but have similar slopes: both show a strong negative association with network constraint.

In predicting idea value, I held constant the background variables associated with salary (job rank, role in the supply chain, age, education, business unit, and geography). None is associated with idea value when network constraint is held constant (Burt, 2004: 381). Higher-rank managers were more often the source of valuable ideas, but the zero-order association with rank disappears when network constraint is held constant. Even in the top ranks, people limited to a small circle of densely interconnected discussion partners were likely to have weak ideas for improving supply-chain operations.[12] Education does have a zero-order association: Higher value is seen in ideas from managers

---

[12] There is an intuitive difference, associated with a manager's rank, between bridge relations that connect groups in the same business unit and bridges across the business units themselves. Tushman and Scanlan (1981a, 1981b) emphasize such a distinction in comparing internal and external communication stars. Täube (2004) draws an analogy between such a distinction and Merton's (1949) distinction between locals and cosmopolitans (discussed below in Section 2.4). I looked into this by sorting the supply-chain managers into three categories: *non-brokers* (312 managers in a group of densely interconnected discussion partners as indicated by above-average network constraint), *local brokers* (196 managers with discussion partners in other groups, but all within the manager's own business unit, e.g., persons 283, 504, 528 in Figure 1.3), and *enterprise brokers* (165 managers with discussion partners in other groups, some outside the manager's own business unit, e.g., persons 9, 234, 402 in Figure 1.3). The hypothesis for this chapter is that good ideas are borne of engaging alternative ways of thinking and behaving. Since variation is more likely between than within business units, enterprise brokers have the most of whatever brokerage provides, local brokers have less, non-brokers the least. Here is the average idea value for the three categories of managers, the percentage of their ideas dismissed, and their average network-constraint score:

	Idea Value	Ideas Dismissed	Network Constraint
Enterprise Brokers	2.47	12.7%	38.4
Local Brokers	1.67	29.0%	58.2
Non-Brokers	1.48	41.7%	98.9

The enterprise brokers are more likely than the local brokers to have high-value ideas and less likely to have their ideas dismissed, but their lower level of network constraint shows that enterprise brokers are also exposed to a broader range of disconnected contacts. The three-category distinction between enterprise brokers, local brokers, and non-brokers has a statistically significant association with the value of a manager's idea and the probability of it being dismissed (24.4 F-test with 2 and 452 d.f. for predicting idea value, and 32.3 chi-square with 2 d.f. for predicting ideas dismissed), but the category distinctions disappear when I hold constant the continuous measure of network constraint (e.g., −4.3 test statistic for the log of network constraint predicting idea value, versus .9 and −1.1 test statistics for the categories distinguishing local and enterprise brokers). The same conclusion holds for the three categories predicting manager

with a college education or a graduate degree, but holding network constraint constant eliminates the association with education (Burt, 2004: 381).[13] Measuring work experience, age has no direct association with value, and a graph of idea value across age (not presented) is random showing no linear, curvilinear, or episodic association.[14]

2.2.3   Ideas Dismissed

Recall that the two senior managers judging value sometimes dismissed an idea without rating it. As one explained, "for ideas that were either too local in nature, incomprehensible, vague, or too whiny, I didn't rate them." Being dismissed was not a rare event. Almost three fourths of the ideas were dismissed by one or the other senior person evaluating ideas (71%). One in three ideas was dismissed by both judges (32%), which is the dashed line at the bottom of the right-hand graph in Figure 2.1. The positive association between network constraint and dismissed shows that managers in networks of densely interconnected discussion partners were less successful in communicating their idea to the senior managers judging value. Here again, the association

---

performance (Burt, 2004: 375 n.), so I have not discussed in the text the intuitive appealing distinction between local and enterprise brokers. Brokerage created a vision advantage in and beyond the manager's own business unit.

[13] Another measure of individual ability shows the same lack of direct association with value: 114 people in the study population graduated from the company's middle-manager leadership program. I have the grade on a four-point scale that each received in the program. Managers whose networks span structural holes did well in the program (-4.1 t-test for network constraint predicting grade), but the rated value of their idea for improving supply-chain operations is associated with their network, not their program grade (regressing value over program grade and network constraint yields a 0.3 t-test for grade and -3.3 for network constraint).

[14] Three additional bias effects are negligible. First, it seemed possible that value ratings would be higher for ideas offered with more explanation. Responses explaining ideas ranged from 13 to 1,897 characters (253 mean). However, there is no zero-order association with either judge's evaluation of value, nor in predicting idea value. Second, it seemed likely that judges would fatigue as they rated ideas so value would be lower for ideas later on the list presented to the judges. There is a negative zero-order association between value and sequential order, but the association is negligible when age and network constraint are held constant (Burt, 2004: 381). Chip Heath noted a third possible rating bias. The two senior managers, familiar with their own operations, might recognize and over-praise, or better understand, an idea from one of their subordinates. Rivalry is a related possibility. The two judges ran the two largest supply-chain operations in the company, so competition between them was inevitable. Feelings of competition might result in lower ratings for ideas from the rival organization. Neither bias was statistically significant in the ratings. I regressed ratings from each judge over two dummy variables (with controls for the rank of the respondent proposing an idea and the sequential order in which an idea was evaluated). One dummy variable identified respondents in the judge's own division. The other dummy variable distinguished respondents in the other judge's division. The reference group was respondents in neither division. Ratings were biased in the expected direction, but negligibly so.

with network constraint is nonlinear. The steepest increase in the odds of being dismissed happens with initial network constraint, in other words, when a manager first begins to rely on redundant discussion partners.

2.2.4   Ideas Discussed

At the same moment that good ideas emerge where bridge relations span holes in today's social structure, idea discussion shapes tomorrow's structure. Brokerage is again a correlate.

After explaining their idea, managers were asked whether they had discussed the idea with anyone in the company. If yes, they were asked to name the person with whom they had the most detailed discussion. A substantial minority of the supply-chain managers were dead-ends in the sense of never discussing their best idea (31%). A few said that they had discussed their idea, but were ambiguous about the discussion partner (7%; e.g., "everyone I can get to listen," "various," "other managers in supply chain"). The majority named a specific person with whom they had talked (67%), and some went on to name two or more discussion partners (14%).

Brokerage is the direct correlate of idea discussion. Regardless of idea quality, job rank, age, education, business unit, or region, people likely to discuss their idea were the people whose networks spanned structural holes (Burt, 2004: 381). More senior people were more likely to discuss their idea, but senior people more often bridged structural holes. A negligible association with job rank in the prediction model shows that idea discussion was correlated with bridging, not job rank.

Another way to look at idea discussion is to look at the other extreme of who chose not to offer an idea. Among the managers not responding to the survey were sixteen who entered their name in the survey website, then left before answering the question about their best idea. I have no way of knowing how many other potential respondents decided not to answer the survey after seeing the questions, but I do know which managers chose not to complete the survey. I predicted non-response with the idea predictors used above to see whether non-response was idea-related in the sense of having the same pattern of correlates as idea value and idea dismissal. Managers must have had various reasons for not responding to the survey, but the pattern of correlates predicting non-response looks exactly like the pattern predicting idea quality (Burt, 2004: 381): There is a strong association with brokerage and negligible associations with job rank, role, age, education, business unit, and location. The steep dashed line in Figure 2.1's right-hand graph shows the dramatic association with brokerage. Managers with networks that spanned structural holes were likely to express an idea (low .06 probability of non-response at 10 points of network constraint), while managers surrounded by densely interconnected discussion partners were unlikely to express an idea (.78 probability of non-response for 100 points of network constraint).

2.3　Corroboration

The supply-chain managers whose networks spanned structural holes were more likely to have a good idea, express their idea, and discuss their idea with colleagues. The evidence is attractive for its detail, but it comes from only one organization. It is therefore reassuring to see corroborating evidence, even if the corroboration is less detailed.

2.3.1　Cases in History

Anecdotal evidence for the hypothesized vision advantage of brokerage can be found in the remarks of prominent creatives quoted in Section 2.1, but archives on historical figures link brokerage and ideas in wider perspective.

For example, consider Eugene Stoner, father of the M-16 rifle and acclaimed genius in the world of small-arms experts:[15] "Eugene Stoner was a genius. An engineering genius of the first order." Says one expert. "Stoner was probably the most gifted small-arms designer since Browning," says another expert. Stoner's own explanation of his insight, however, makes clear how his creativity was an act of brokerage, moving knowledge familiar in one group to a second group in which the knowledge was a breakthrough idea. Stoner was an engineer with Fairchild Engine and Airplane Company when he entered the company's start-up prototype-gun division, ArmaLite. Before joining Fairchild, Stoner served in the Marines as an ordnance technician. Stoner's familiarity with ordnance and the use of plastics and aluminum in aircraft gave him an advantage in designing a radically new, ultra-light assault rifle, the AR-10. The novel rifle impressed Army observers in the 1955 trials to replace the World War II Garand rifle, which began a winding path that would lead to the AR-10's descendant, the M-16, being used across the American military services. As Stoner explains in a 1988 interview with the Smithsonian Institute, "I think my aircraft background and experience allowed me to get into some of these light-weight materials, for instance forged aluminum receivers, which were rather unknown at the time in weapons. But it was nothing particularly new to what I'd been doing all along in the aircraft equipment, in the fiberglass and all that."

The act of brokerage responsible for the creation of the M-16, recurs in history stories about "institutional entrepreneurs" (DiMaggio, 1988; Fligstein, 1997; and for broad review, Campbell, 2004). In politics, Greif (1994) describes how the position of *podestà* (a neutral third-party city manager) developed in Genoa through the twelfth and thirteenth centuries, bringing the city to its "golden age" of cooperative prosperity by playing the two quarreling elite factions against one another (p. 282, "By the 'threat' of assisting the other

---

[15] The quotes in this paragraph are taken from a video distributed through the History Channel ("Tales of the Gun: the M-16," 1998, A&E Television Networks). For more detail on Stoner's role in creating the M-16, I turned to Stevens and Ezell (1992).

faction he deterred each faction from attempting to take control over the city or acting 'illegally' "). Padgett and Ansell (1993) describe Cosimo de Medici's use of his contacts with opposing elite family factions to establish his Medicean political party in Renaissance Florence. Johansen (1982) argues that the novel form government took in the United States was a synthesis of European and Native American forms, a synthesis begun when Colonial envoys were sent to recruit the Iroquois as an ally for the British against the French. Eventually reflected in the young nation's Articles of Confederation, colonials, most notably Benjamin Franklin, found among the Iroquois a system of laws in which leaders served at the will of the people, tribes were made stronger by confederation, and life, liberty, and happiness were deemed a natural right of citizens. Jumping to more recent politics, Caro (1982: ch. 15) describes Lyndon Johnson's creation of a Washington power base in 1933 from the "Little Congress," through which he brokered connections between journalists and prominent people in government. In the arts, DiMaggio (1992, esp. pp. 129–130) describes Paul Sachs role as broker in establishing the Museum of Modern Art in New York; "Sachs could employ his talents precisely because his strong ties to sectors that had previously been only weakly connected–museums, universities, and finance–placed him at the center of structural holes that were critical to the art world of his time." In business, Dalzell (1987: Part I) describes Francis Lowell's role as broker in creating the American cotton industry. McGuire and Granovetter (2003) describe Samuel Insull's use of his contacts in finance, politics, and technology to shape the electric utility industry at the turn of the century (cf. Sediatis, 1998, especially pp. 373–374, on the greater flexibility, adaptability, and volume of business in Russian commodity markets created by organizers who had little previous contact with one another; Ellis, 2000 on Hong Kong toy companies using strong ties to enter foreign markets; Wong and Ellis, 2002, on Hong Kong companies using bridge ties to form joint ventures in China; Granovetter, 2002, on polycentric networks facilitating economic cooperation).

Providing a panoramic historical view, Collins (1998) offers sociograms of the intergenerational social networks among philosophers to show how the philosophers of greatest repute tend to be personal rivals representing conflicting schools of thought for their generation (Collins, 1998: 76); "The famous names, and the semi-famous ones as well who hold the stage less long, are those persons situated at just those points where the networks heat up the emotional energy to the highest pitch. Creativity is the friction of the attention space at the moments when the structural blocks are grinding against one another the hardest."

2.3.2   *Organizations*

There is related evidence at the aggregate level of organizations. In particular, it has been popular to study the ways in which technological change affects social structure at the same time that social structure affects technological advance (e.g., Barley, 1990: 92–95, provides crisp illustration with network data). Electronics and biotechnology have been favored research sites, with Walter Powell (e.g., Powell and Snellman, 2004) and Toby Stuart (Stuart, 1998) prominent ports of entry into the work. More generally, Kogut (2000) builds on a series of studies to propose a network theory of the firm in which value is derived from a firm's ability to create and lay claim to knowledge derived from its membership and participation in networks (cf. Nahapiet and Ghoshal, 1998, on social capital and knowledge; Powell and Smith-Doerr, 1994, on information issues in the economic sociology of networks, especially with respect to networks across organizations). These works develop a connection between an organization's bridges across structural holes and its capacity to learn—what Cohen and Levinthal (1990: 128) describe as an organization's absorptive capacity: "the ability of a firm to recognize the value of new, external information, assimilate it, and apply it to commercial ends," which can be studied in terms of industry factors that facilitate absorption and external networks that enhance absorptive capacity (e.g., Cockburn and Henderson, 1998; see Knoke, 2001: 362 ff. for review).

Organizations with management and collaboration networks that more often bridge structural holes in their markets learn faster and are more productively creative. Organizational learning and learning curves are discussed in Section 3.3.5, after the social capital of brokerage mixed with closure has been introduced. Meanwhile, there is evidence to consider on brokerage alone. For example, Lütz (1997) describes the integrative brokerage work of research institutes among rival German companies working to make their adhesive bonding a replacement for welding in automobile manufacturing (p. 225): "By informing each competing producer about the 'state of the art' of adhesive technology among the group of rivals, institutes created a state of almost perfect information—each competitor came to know about his rival's capacities to fulfil the requirements of the users from the automobile industry. . . . Linked by scientific intermediaries, a research group evolved, transcending well beyond the scope of conventional R&D projects." Sutton and Hargadon (1996) describe processes by which a firm, IDEO, uses brainstorming to create product designs, then clarify in Hargadon and Sutton (1997) the brokerage function served (see Hargadon, 2003; Sutton, 2002, for broader discussion). The firm's employees work for clients in diverse industries. In the brainstorming sessions, technological solutions from one industry are used to solve client issues in other industries where the solutions are rare or unknown. In other words, the firm profits from employee bridge relations, through which they brokered technology-flow between industries (cf. Allen and Cohen, 1969, on gatekeepers; Tushman and Scanlan, 1981b, on boundary-spanners). Fleming (2002) describes a similar process in Hewlett-Packard: policy was to move engineers between projects rather than having each project hire and fire individually. The result was that HP technologies were constantly being mixed in new combinations. As a senior engineer described the experience (Fleming, 2002: 1073): "I had to work in a single field for only two or three years and then like magic it was a whole new field; a paradise for creativity."

Drawing comparisons across companies, McEvily and Zaheer (1999) report greater access to competitive ideas for small manufacturers with more non-redundant sources of advice beyond the firm (and McEvily and Marcus, 2002, show lower absorptive capacity when the sales network is concentrated in a single customer). Stuart and Podolny (1999) report a higher probability of innovation from semiconductor firms that establish alliances with firms outside their own technological area. Comparing the biotechnology districts in Minneapolis and Philadelphia, Llobrera, Meyer, and Nammacher (2000) attribute the growth and adaptation of Philadelphia's district to its many overlapping but nonredundant networks around organizations in the district. Baum, Calabrese, and Silverman (2000) study Canadian companies in biotechnology for their growth in revenues, number of patents granted, and the extent to which a company had multiple kinds of alliance partners at start-up. Companies with a heterogeneous mix of alliance partners tended to enjoy faster revenue growth, and a dramatic advantage in obtaining patents. Koput and Powell (2003) report higher earnings and survival chances of biotechnology firms with more kinds of activities in alliances with more kinds of partner firms. Podolny (2001) describes venture-capital firms spanning structural holes by linking co-investors not otherwise investing together. Firms with a "deal-flow" network more often spanning structural holes more often invested in early product development—where the information benefits of spanning structural holes could be a competitive advantage in detecting potentially valuable ideas (cf. Beckman and Haunschild, 2002, on firms with more heterogeneous boards of directors paying lower premiums for acquisitions; Ruef, 2002, on the tendency for entrepreneurs "attempting to combine disparate ideas or routines" to discuss their venture with varied kinds of contacts; Shane and Cable, 2002, on early-stage investors using social networks to decide between ventures).

2.3.3   Origins in Personal Experience

Experience seems to be the answer to questions about how people learn to be network entrepreneurs. Lofstrom (2000) asked scientists, physicians, and engineers how much they learned from their firm's participation in an alliance intended to develop or extend a medical device technology. Individuals with more nonredundant contacts were more likely to report that they had "learned a great deal" in the alliance. Burt (2002) describes decay in banker networks over a four-year period. The rate of decay is high (nine out of ten disappear from one year to the next), but significantly lower for bankers who had more experience. In as much as bridges were social capital associated with bonus compensation, and bridge relations were less subject to decay when they involved people more experienced with bridges, social capital can be said to accrue to those bankers who already had it.

There is evidence from people learning social structures. Using DeSoto's (1960) experimental design for measuring the difficulty of learning a social structure, Freeman (1992) asked college students to learn the relationships in a small network that contained a structural hole. Errors occurred when students failed to recall a relationship that existed, but the most frequent error was to fill in the structural hole by saying that the two disconnected people were connected. Janicik (1998) used DeSoto's design but with older students and added a control for the network around each student in his or her most recent or current job. Students who held a job in which they were exposed to structural holes learned the network significantly faster, in particular because they quickly recognized the structural hole in the network (see Janicik and Larrick, 2005, for main results and refinements). If Freeman's undergraduates lived in small, dense friendship networks, as is typical of college students, then the summary conclusion from Freeman's and Janicik's experiments is that experience matters: People who live in a network that contains structural holes are more likely to recognize the holes in their next network.

From the other extreme, there is evidence of learning being difficult for people isolated from the diversity that brokerage provides. I develop this point in Chapter 4 when describing how closure locks people into ways of thinking and behaving. A quick example is Gargiulo and Benassi's (2000) description of managers in the research-consulting unit of a large Italian firm. They measure "coordination failure" as the extent to which a manager consults with people not relevant to his assigned projects. They show that coordination failures are significantly more likely for managers with small, dense networks. Weick (1996) makes a chilling analogy between jargon-bound academics and firefighters burned to death because they did not discard the heavy tools they were carrying. The analogy works, and generalizes to other kinds of people, because people so often identify themselves with the tools they employ in their work. People who cannot see clearly an alternative way to do their work are unlikely to give up the tools they have, and are likely to insist that others use the same tools. Recall the Planck quote in Section 2.1.2 on people blinded by the paradigm in which they rose to prominence: "a new scientific truth does not triumph by convincing its opponents and making them see the light, but rather because its opponents eventually die."

Brokerage can be a forcing function to strip away unproductive information. Creativity is as much about knowing where to focus as it is about knowing things to combine. Brokerage facilitates focus by highlighting what is uninteresting to target audiences. In crossing structural holes, mindful of Weick's (1996) advice, there is value to travelling light on full forage; eyes, ears, indeed all senses, on full alert. Jargon legitimating and useful in one context has to be translated into the local dialect to be useful in another context (recall the supply-chain "bad" ideas that were potentially good ideas buried in local

jargon). Re-reading Weick's (1996) editorial reminded me of a recent conversation with a consultant widely admired for his creative solutions. The consultant's academic training was impeccable, but there was little use of
academic concepts or tools in his work. He said he spends a long time listening
to a client; how they frame things, what seems to trouble them, then pitches a
solution for their troubles that comes from his academic training but uses
academic jargon only as the client wants an invocation of science to legitimate
the solution. A career of experience moving from one client to the next had
taught him how to deliver academic concepts and tools such that the solution
seemed to have been created from whole cloth, on the spot, in the language of
the client.

Whether bridging structural holes enhances an individual's ability to learn,
or more intelligent people learn faster and so better report holes in the social
structure around them, there is an association between structural holes and
learning. The implication is that the social capital of structural holes cumu-
lates over a career so it is useful to encounter holes early in the career
(cf. Sørensen, 2000, on the cumulative effects of social heterogeneity on
mobility). Managers with experience of structural holes are more likely to see
the holes in a new situation, and so enjoy the enhanced performance associated with spanning the holes, and so be promoted to more senior positions,
from which they have more opportunities to coordinate across holes.

2.4   Contagious Ideas

Research on the spread of ideas provides another corroborating view of the
vision mechanism. This research describes how a new belief or behavior (the
innovation) spreads from one person to the next (innovation adopters)
through a social system like the Figure 1.1 system of bridges and clusters.
Something about the network around two people makes one's ideas or behaviors contagious for the other.[16]

---

[16] The research literature is extensive. Rogers (1995) is the review and reference
standard (Valente, 1995, is a useful adjunct focused on networks). The interpersonal
processes by which cohesion and structural equivalence make one person's ideas or
behaviors contagious for another are reviewed with illustrative analysis in Burt (1982,
1987). Friedkin (1998) offers a more general model and in (2004) discusses groups in
terms of interpersonal cohesion (Cialdini and Goldstein, 2004, review work on the
psychology of conforming). It is difficult to get data on the interpersonal processes
when studying diffusion between organizations, so research is often based on joint-
involvement measures of probable connection such as serving on the same board of
directors or living in the same city (e.g., Davis and Greve, 1997; Westphal, Gulati and
Shortell, 1997; see Strang and Soule, 1998, for review). Bothner (2003) more precisely
defines structural equivalence in terms of organizations involved in the same sales
channels, and shows competition's role in contagion with evidence of organizations

The baseline assumption is that innovation spreads by word of mouth. In the decades around World War II, with the growth of mass media and development of social psychology, it became clear that social relations emerged from physical proximity, and shared opinion developed with social relations. Homans (1950) was a central theory (continued in Homans, 1961: 112–129). Festinger, Schachter, and Back's (1950) study of housing, friendship, and opinion was a much-cited source of evidence (Cartwright and Zander, 1968: 139 ff.). Building on Sherif's (1935) experimental studies of interpersonal influences created by physical proximity between socially similar people, Festinger et al. (1950) emphasized the causal force of arbitrary understandings created in informal social groups (cf. Homans, 1961: 120–125; Zucker, 1977; Friedkin, 2004: 414–420). The gist of the argument is that the cost and benefits of a new idea or practice are unclear. People get a handle on the unknown by asking friends and colleagues about it. As they talk to one another, people converge on a shared understanding of the new idea or practice. As Festinger and his colleagues (1950: 169) phrased their intuition: "The 'reality' which settles the question in the case of social attitudes and opinions is the degree to which others with whom one is in communication are believed to share these same attitudes and opinions." The prediction is that people connected by a strong relationship will have similar opinions about an innovation and follow one another quickly in adopting the innovation.

A widely cited source of evidence for the baseline prediction is Coleman, Katz, and Menzel's (1957, 1966) study of doctors prescribing a new antibiotic. The study was the first to combine mathematical models with extensive network data and a behavioral measure of adoption. The data are ancient history in terms of contemporary medicine, but the analysis serves as an exemplar for academic research and practitioners (e.g., Sawai, 1994), and has a continuing policy relevance (e.g., Carrin, 1987; Chow, 1998). An often-cited result from the study was the evidence of discussion partners beginning to prescribe the new drug at about the same time early in the diffusion process.[17]

---

under more intense competition (small and diversified) being more likely to imitate their structurally equivalent peers.

[17] The sentence in the text is correct, but there are multiple explanations for why it is correct. For Coleman, Katz and Menzel (1966: 114–130), doctors central in the discussion network were early adopters and socialized others, but it seems more likely that contagion was between structurally equivalent doctors regardless of direct contact (see Figure 2.2, and for more detail on the original Coleman, Katz, and Menzel evidence, see Burt, 1987: 1304–1306, 1313 n.). Either way, adoption was more determined by personal background than colleague behavior. The new drug spread without the slow-start period typical of early innovation (Burt, 1987: 1304–1306), and less variance in adoption dates was predicted by colleague adoptions than by characteristics of a doctor's background and practice (14% versus 26% respectively, Burt and Janicik, 1996: Fig. 3). Marsden and Podolny (1990) report no event-history evidence of contagion when they impute missing adoption dates from a doctor's personal background (see their appendix, pp. 210–211). The cross-sectional evidence of contagion in Burt (1987) also disappears

Citing the Festinger, Schachter, and Back study for precedent, the authors (1966: 118–119) reasoned that: "When a new drug appears, doctors who are in close interaction with their colleagues will similarly interpret for one another the new stimulus that has presented itself, and will arrive at some shared way of looking at it."

In fact, the association between diffusion and discussion is more complex than the baseline model predicts, and interestingly tied to brokerage. Figure 2.2 describes the association between diffusion and discussion, compiled across study populations. The populations are the Coleman, Katz, and Menzel (1966) doctors in American midwest cities in the 1950s, Minnesota corporate philanthropy officers in the early 1980s (Galaskiewicz, 1985, 1997; Galaskiewicz and Burt, 1991), and elite Washington D.C. lobbyists in the 1980s (Heinz, Laumann, Nelson, and Salisbury, 1993).

The horizontal axis is the strength of connection between two people. The strongest level of connection is when the two people cite one another as

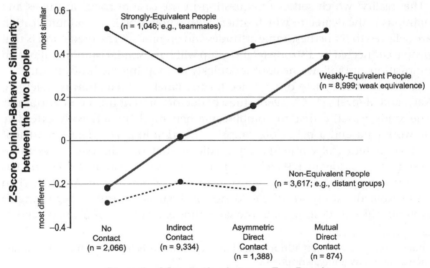

Fig. 2.2: Contagious ideas and brokerage

---

if missing adoption dates are imputed from a doctor's personal background. Strang and Tuma (1993: 633–634) report event-history evidence of contagion by equivalence (multiplying or adding to personal background) and cohesion (additive only), but in both cases, doctor background strongly predicts adoption date. In fact, just holding constant monthly advertising on the new drug in three magazines to the individual doctors can fully account for the evidence of contagion (Van den Bulte and Lilien, 2001). These re-analyses predict when a doctor begins prescribing the new drug. The evidence illustrated in Figure 2.2 of contagion by direct contact between pairs of doctors conditional on weak-equivalence would not be detected in the analyses.

colleagues with whom they discuss their work. The next lower level of connection is when one, but not both, cites the other. The next lower level is when they have no direct contact, but they discuss their work with people who know one another—there is *some* chain of intermediaries through whom information could get from one person to the other. The lowest level of connection is when the two people discuss their work with entirely separate groups of colleagues—there is *no* chain of intermediaries through whom information could get from one person to the other.

The vertical axis in Figure 2.2 is a z-score measure of opinion or behavior similarity. The score for a pair of *Medical Innovation* doctors, for example, is the (z-score) similarity between the dates when they began prescribing the new drug.[18] The score for each pair of corporate philanthropy officers is the z-score similarity in their evaluations of local non-profit organizations on which officer opinion differed sharply. The score for a pair of lobbyists is the z-score similarity between their beliefs about the American economy.

2.4.1   Discussion Irrelevant

Figure 2.2 shows that a strong connection between two people is irrelevant to contagion in two situations: within a group, and between distant groups. These are the nearly horizontal lines at the top and bottom of the graph.

Relations between people separated in distant groups are described by the horizontal dashed line at the bottom of the graph. Examples in Figure 1.1 would be anyone in Group A paired with anyone in Group D. The people in Group A talk to one another and somewhat to the people in Group B. People in Group D talk only to people in Group C. Each dot on the dash line in Figure 2.2 is the average opinion or behavior similarity between people at a level of connection. All of the dots on the dashed line are low in the graph showing that people in distant groups differ whether or not they talk to one another. On average, people in distant groups are $-.29$ standard deviations less similar than the average pair of people in a community. The lack of similarity remains if the two people have some chain of indirect connections through whom they could communicate ($-.20$ mean z-score), or one of them cites the other as a discussion partner ($-.23$ mean z-score). There is no mean reported in Figure 2.2 for "mutual citations" between distant groups on the dashed line because the "mutual" strength of connection did not occur between distant groups.

---

[18] One doctor began prescribing the new drug in month a and the other began in month b. The time between their adoptions (i.e., between a and b) is subtracted from the average difference for other pairs of doctors in their community and divided by its standard deviation to measure the extent to which the adoption difference between the two doctors was smaller than the average in their community (which would put the pair of doctors high in the graph) or larger than the average (which would put the pair low in the graph). For more detail on the dependent variables in the three populations see Burt and Janicik (1996), or Burt (1999*b*).

It might seem counter-intuitive to see that discussion is irrelevant to contagion inside a group. The horizontal line at the top of Figure 2.2 describes similarity in opinion or behavior between people who are structurally equivalent—which means that they talk to the same friends and colleagues.[19] Examples in Figure 1.1 would be a pair of people in Group A or a pair in Group C. Substantive examples would be two graduate students publishing the same kind of work and trained by the same professors, or two physicians in the same specialty trying to keep up with the rush of medical developments to live up to their image of a good physician and maintain their position in the hierarchy of medical advice and discussion, or two managers leading teams of engineers in the same company on similar products.

Structurally equivalent people do not have to talk to one another to stay aligned because peer pressure keeps them aligned. This is a central theme in Chapter 3. If you and I are structurally equivalent, my well-being is in some part dependent on how I stand relative to you with our shared constituency. I will monitor any shift in your opinion or behavior that makes you more attractive (a model describing the interpersonal comparison behind the peer pressure between structurally equivalent people is given in Burt, 1982: ch. 5, and abbreviated in Burt, 1987).

Peer pressure is especially interesting in the absence of direct connections between the peers. Cluster D in Figure 1.1 (white dots) is composed of structurally equivalent people who have no direct connections with one another. They are equivalent by dint of them all being tied to people in Group C. Group D is a satellite, or adjunct, status to Group C. These are the advisory or staff people who have in common their ties to line officers, their lack of ties with one another, and their invisibility to other groups. These are the people who claim close relations with popular people, but are not themselves the object of attention. Group D could be graduate students each working for a couple of the four professors in a dense-knit clique of experts on some topic. Each student will be familiar with achievements by the others.

The horizontal line at the top of Figure 2.2 shows that structurally equivalent people who talked to one another directly were similar in their opinions and adoption dates, but no more similar than structurally equivalent people who had no direct connection with one another.[20] Peer pressure between

---

[19] Scott (2000) and Kilduff and Tsai (2003) provide general introduction to measuring structural equivalence (or see Wasserman and Faust, 1994, for a more detailed introduction). For details on measuring structural equivalence in the three populations on which Figure 2.2 is based, see Burt and Janicik (1996) or Burt (1999b).

[20] Average z-scores are well above zero for structurally equivalent people regardless of direct connection (.51, .32, .43, and .50 for the four points on the horizontal line at the top of Figure 2.2). There is no statistically significant trend across the points (0.4 t-test adjusted for clustering between relations involving the same person, e.g., Kish and Frankel, 1974) and the mean of .47 for the people in direct contact is not significantly higher than the mean of .38 for the people with no direct contact to one another (1.4 t-test adjusted for clustering between relations involving the same person).

structurally equivalent people made them so alert to one another that they became similar to one another whether or not they spoke directly.[21]

2.4.2 Discussion Critical

Discussion is insufficient to overcome the differences between distant groups and superfluous to contagion within a group, but it is essential to contagion between adjacent groups. Weakly-equivalent people have some friends and colleagues in common, but more that are different. The weakly-equivalent are people who are nearly, but not really, peers. Weakly-equivalent people need not be aware of one another as near-peers until conversations between them reveal the partial equivalence of their positions with respect to people within the broader social structure. For example, sociologists and economists move in different academic circles but conversations between a sociologist and economist at the same university can reveal to each the many people they both know, admire, or disdain.

The upward-sloping bold line in Figure 2.2 shows that contagion between weakly-equivalent people depends on direct contact; the stronger the discussion contact, the more likely the contagion (see Brown and Reingen, 1987, for similar evidence; cf. Granovetter's, 1973: 1366, provocative argument about diffusion through weak ties between groups).

The bold line begins in the lower-left corner of Figure 2.2 with disconnected weakly-equivalent people being more different than the average pair of people in their community—the *Medical Innovation* doctors begin prescribing the new drug at different times, the elite lobbyists adhere to different beliefs about the American economy, the corporate philanthropy officers have different opinions about the relative merit of supporting certain non-profit organizations. The more they talk to one another, however, the more aware they become of what they have in common and the more they start to look like one another—sharing similar opinions and adopting innovations at about the same time. The average similarity indicated in Figure 2.2 by the dot for weakly-equivalent people who cite one another as discussion partners is statistically indistinguishable from the average similarity of people in the top horizontal line who

---

[21] One can see the future in early Bureau conclusions about evidence recognized thirty years later to be evidence of contagion by equivalence. Merton (1949: 465–466) concludes that "One gains the impression that although a relatively few people—the top influentials—exert influence upon people on all levels of the influence-structure, there occurs a secondary tendency for people to be otherwise most influenced by their peers in that structure. ... people in each influence stratum are more likely to be influenced by their peers in this structure than are people in the other strata." Katz and Lazarsfeld (1955: 331) conclude that "The flow of influence in this arena tends—as it does in every arena—to remain within the boundaries of each status level, but when it does cross status lines, there is no indication that the direction of flow is any more from high to low than it is from low to high."

are completely equivalent. In other words, discussion between people who have some contacts in common can overcome their many differences. Without the direct contact, these same people show no more belief or behavior similarity than people separated in distant groups—the effect of direct contact is the linear bold line that connects the top and bottom of the Z pattern in the graph. The Z pattern in Figure 2.2 can be seen in each of the populations when they are analyzed separately (Burt and Uchiyama, 1989; Burt and Janicik, 1996; Burt, 1999*b*).

2.4.3   *Opinion Leaders and Brokerage*

An early project at Columbia University's Bureau of Applied Social Research was a study of the 1940 presidential election, later published as *The People's Choice*. As so often quoted thereafter (Lazarsfeld, Berelson, and Gaudet, 1944: 151), the researchers were surprised to find little direct media effect on voters, instead finding "that ideas often *flow* from radio and print *to* opinion leaders and *from* these to the less active sections of the population." The role of opinion leaders in innovation diffusion was elaborated with Merton's (1949) contrast between cosmopolitan versus local leaders, and studied in subsequent Bureau projects, most notably Katz and Lazarsfeld's (1955) study of opinion leaders in consumer purchases (Rogers, 1997: 285–315). The "two-step flow" of communication—a process of information moving from the media to opinion leaders, and influence moving from opinion leaders to their followers—became a guiding theme for diffusion and marketing research (Katz and Lazarsfeld, 1955: 309 ff.; Rogers, 1995: 285; 1997: 308).

The results in Figure 2.2 show the brokerage role of opinion leaders. Opinion leaders are people whose discussions make innovations contagious for the people with whom they speak. Discussion is superfluous to contagion between people in the same group (strongly-equivalent people, the top of the Z pattern in Figure 2.2), and does not trigger contagion across the differences between people separated in distant groups (non-equivalent people, the bottom of the Z pattern). The place where discussion makes ideas contagious is where it connects near-peers in adjacent groups (weakly-equivalent people, the stem of the Z pattern in Figure 2.2). In other words, opinion leaders are brokers whose conversations trigger imitation across the social boundaries between groups.

These need not be leaders with superior authority, nor leaders in the sense of others wanting to imitate them. Defining opinion leaders by function (people whose conversations make innovations contagious) and structural location (people communicating with, and weakly-equivalent to, the individuals they influence) removes the vertical distinction implicit in the contrast between opinion leaders and followers (and sometimes explicit, e.g., Rogers, 1995: 291). In fact, the contagion associated with strong relations between weakly-equivalent people in Figure 2.2 is no greater if one of the people is socially prominent.[22] As King and Summers (1970: 44) summarize for a marketing audience, "In most contexts, the notion of an opinion leader dominating attitudes or behavior in his social network *overstates* the power of interpersonal communication." The opinion leaders more precisely identified as opinion brokers are active in their own group, but their adoption-eliciting influence is in adjacent groups. They are in some ways structurally similar to the people they influence, but in one important way distinct; they have strong connections to other groups. They are what Merton (1949) described as "cosmopolitans" (see Rogers, 1995: 294, for a similar conclusion, Rogers', 1995: 336 ff., discussion of change agents as linkers).[23]

Figure 1.1 is again useful illustration. Look at the figure as if it were a spatial map of structural equivalence distances in the sense that people closer together in the figure are more equivalent. Apply the three equivalence categories in Figure 2.2 to the people in Group A. Each person in the group is strongly-equivalent to the others in the group. The non-equivalence category contains James and those of his contacts on the far east side of the map. Everyone else is weakly-equivalent to Group A, which includes Robert and his contacts, and the people in Groups C and D. Most of these weakly-equivalent people have no direct connection with Group A, so they are unlikely sources of contagion for Group A (they would be in the lower-left of the Z pattern in Figure 2.2). Four of the weakly-equivalent people have direct connections to Group A. Those four are the people through whom contagion would occur; Robert, person 1, person 2, and the dot at the top of Group B. The four are the most likely opinion leaders through whom innovation comes to Group A. Their three contacts in A are the most likely early adopters in Group A.

So opinion "leaders," like Welch and Marcus at the top of the chapter, turn out to be more precisely opinion "brokers" who bear a striking resemblance to network entrepreneurs in social capital research. It is brokerage beyond a group that makes for opinion leadership within the group. The complementary content of diffusion and social capital research makes the analogy productive. Where diffusion research, in describing opinion leaders, describes the

---

[22] The bold diagonal line in Figure 2.2 describing contagion between weakly-equivalent people can be represented by a regression model predicting diffusion similarity from relationship strength. Adding covariates reveals no statistically significant change in the slope of the line for more or less prominent people. For example, there is no interaction with a binary variable distinguishing people cited by three or more colleagues (-1.5 t-test, three citations was the cut-off for prominence in Coleman, Katz and Menzel, 1966), and no interaction with a three-category prominence variable further distinguishing uncited people as the least prominent (1.8 t-test).

[23] The distinction illustrated by Robert and James is analogous to an early distinction between cosmopolitan and local leaders, crisply summarized as follows on a dimension relevant to social capital (Merton, 1949: 457): "The cosmopolitan influential has a following because *he knows*; the local influential because, because *he understands*. The one is sought out for his specialized skills and experience; the other, for his intimate appreciation of intangible but affectively significant details."

substantive details of people brokering information flow between groups, social capital research describes the competitive advantage that results. Corroboration for the analogy comes from research showing that opinion leaders tend to have the correlates of social capital, namely, higher levels of education, higher incomes, and greater mobility (Gatignon and Robertson, 1985; Rogers, 1995: 293–299, 335–370).

2.5 Adaptive Implementation

In addition to their advantage in detecting opportunities, people rich in structural holes have an advantage in seeing ways to launch projects that take advantage of the opportunities. Established ideas have constituency and budget. New ideas typically have neither. Implementing a new idea involves mobilizing support from people who will benefit from the idea such that they shift budget currently allocated to other tasks. Network entrepreneurs are a budget reallocation mechanism, mobilizing support to shift resources to new applications where the resources would be more productive.[24]

Brokerage offers an advantage in seeing who to contact for support, how to connect them, and when. Networks across structural holes (*a*) provide a broad base of referrals to customers, suppliers, alliances, and employees for a project, (*b*) improve due diligence on potential customers, suppliers, alliances, employees, financing, and alternative organization models, (*c*) increase the probability of knowing which of alternative ways to pitch the project will most appeal to specific potential customers, suppliers, or other sources of support, and (*d*), the projects they launch are more likely to reach fruition because network

---

[24] The advantage that brokerage creates for detecting and developing good ideas creates some level of correlation between the two activities: network entrepreneurs seeming creative in detecting good ideas will also seem creative for their adaptive implementation of ideas. For the purposes of this book on network models, there would appear to be little reason to separate the detection and development of ideas. I separate them for two reasons: One is that the distinction between seeing and doing has significance in studies of entrepreneurship, which in essence is about brokerage (e.g., Schumpeter, 1934 [1911*b*]: 88; cf. 1947: 152: "Economic leadership in particular must hence be distinguished from 'invention.' As long as they are not carried into practice, inventions are economically irrelevant. And to carry any improvement into effect is a task entirely different from the inventing of it, and a task, moreover, requiring entirely different kinds of aptitudes. Although entrepreneurs of course may be inventors just as they may be capitalists, they are inventors not by nature of their function but by coincidence and vice versa"). Second, returns to brokerage can occur for either seeing or developing good ideas, so the two activities are correlated but distinct manifestations of the vision advantage of brokerage. The point is illustrated by the supply-chain managers discussed in this and the preceding chapter. Salary, promotion, and positive performance evaluations were associated with bridges and good ideas (Figures 1.5A, 1.5B, and 2.1) but little effort went into implementing the ideas (Section 5.2.2).

entrepreneurs are more likely to anticipate and adapt to the problems that will inevitably arise. They are aware of trouble sooner, more flexible in reshaping a project to adapt to exogenous change,[25] and more able to control the interpretations others give to the project by tailoring solutions to the specific individuals brought together for the project. In contrast to ideas imposed by bureaucratic authority, the adaptive implementation of ideas is responsive to uncertain and changing circumstances.[26]

Evidence on adaptive implementation is primarily in the form of anecdotes, in part because the processes by which people bridge structural holes are so varied and sensitive to context. Case materials developed for business education can be a rich and readily available source because so much of business leadership is about bringing together ill-connected functions, organizations, or market segments—in other words, building bridges across structural holes. For example, Harvard Business School's John Clendenin case describes a manager making more efficient the flow of components between Xerox's regional operations in the late 1980s (Eisenstat, 1993). Regional operations had evolved independently such that each region had its own inventory systems. The independence made sense in Xerox's early days. By the time of the case, logistics technology had progressed to the point were it would be more efficient to ship components in a just-in-time production system rather than leave components on shelves as inventory. There was now value to bridging the structural holes between the regional operations. The problem was that regional leaders had good reasons to prefer the status quo. The case is about how Clendenin overcame resistance to bridge the disconnected regional operations, adding substantial value to Xerox and growing his group in proportion.

---

[25] This is vividly illustrated by networks of illegal activity subject to sudden exogenous shocks such as drug trafficking (see Williams, 1998; Klerks, 2001; Morselli, 2001, 2003; van Meter, 2001, esp. pp. 76–77), and makes the people bridging structural holes a productive target for destabilizing a criminal network (Klerks', 2001, "social bridge builders" and "criminal contact brokers"; and Carley, Lee, and Krackhardt, 2001, on destabilizing networks more generallly).

[26] Adaptive implementation refers to personal qualities that can be discussed more broadly as social skills. For example, Baron and Markman (2003) distinguish social skills from social capital, saying that entrepreneurs can learn of an opportunity or get an initial interview through social capital, but moving beyond that point requires social skills, which include things such as the ability to read others accurately, make a good first impression, adapt to diverse social situations, and be persuasive. Baron and Markmen are undeniably correct in highlighting the importance of what they discuss as social skills. Two points are explicit in this section: First, the social skills involved in adaptively implementing new projects are integral to the documented aggregate association between brokerage and performance. Second, the social skills are themselves a function of social capital. Brokers sharpen their social skills by negotiating between the conflicting perspectives and practices of their contacts (illustrated in Fligstein's, 1997, discussion of the social skills required to be an institutional entrepreneur, and Pollock, Porac, and Wade's, 2004, discussion of lead-underwriter motivations in assembling an IPO deal network).

Brokerage processes in larger organizational perspective are described in a complement of INSEAD cases on strategic alliances involving the visionary biochemist, Alejandro Zaffaroni. The earlier of the two cases describes interests over the course of the 1977–1982 alliance between Swiss pharmaceutical giant, Ciba-Geigy, and California company, ALZA, that Zaffaroni founded in 1968 to develop products involving controlled-release drug delivery (Doz and Angelmar, 1991; also see Doz, 1988; Doz and Hamel, 1998). The more recent case consists of videotaped interviews with key people in the California company, Affymax, founded by Zaffaroni in 1988 to develop products to accelerate the drug-discovery process, and British pharmaceutical giant, Glaxo-Wellcome, that purchased Affymax in 1995 (case still in production when this chapter was written). In both cases, Zaffaroni's small, thriving, entrepreneurial company was to create new products, and the large, bureaucratic partner was to commercialize; Ciba-Geigy doing clinical tests and marketing for ALZA drugs, Glaxo-Wellcome integrating Affymax discovery products into large-scale drug development.

One of the Affymax leaders in the video case describes Zaffaroni's value to the enterprise as a network entrepreneur: "he [Zaffaroni] is reading and thinking very widely. He is totally unafraid of any new technology in any area of human creativity. He has wonderful contacts with people in many different areas, so he sees the bridges between otherwise disparate fields. Then he places them in front of you. The way he works is to give it to you—and instantly you can see what he is driving at; there is some potential technology synergy or some business opportunity. Then he leaves it with you. He trusts, the wonderful thing I like about him, is that he trusts you to see whether there is value or not. He delegates responsibility, scientific and managerial, to people. You know that he has picked you. You know that he trusts you, he has picked you to have certain qualities, and he is not going to second-guess you." Zaffaroni institutionalizes his bridges with interdisciplinary workshops involving prominent outsiders, and his own reputation for success and high moral standard in bringing people together. In fact, one of the Affymax leaders praises Zaffaroni precisely as a source of instruction on adaptive implementation: "So, at a personal level, he [Zaffaroni] is very good to be around, because you learn how to deal with people, get the best out of them, and how to deal with problems when they inevitably arise."

The question remains of how to generalize across the cases. Ellis (2003) and Hargadon (2003) offer frameworks using a network metaphor. See Aldrich (1999: ch. 4) and Thornton (1999) for broad review, Aldrich in particular for intuitions about the changing role of networks over the course of a venture (cf. Doz and Hamel, 1998; Van de Ven et al., 1999; Steier and Greenwood, 2000, with respect to structural holes; Podolny, 2001, for results across cases). Archives on historical figures are informative for their diversity. Several were cited in Section 2.3 on famous creatives, with a broader set available on adaptive implementation. An example to which I often return is Barkey's

(1991, 1994) comparative analysis of brokerage and control in France versus the Ottoman Empire (cf Simmel, 1902: 185 186, on the Incas and Venetians). Although an obvious site for research on social capital, research on the role of social networks in entrepreneurship has been limited by idiosyncratic events and rudimentary data (with rare exceptions such as Stuart, Hoang, and Hybels, 1999, on affiliations speeding a venture's time to Initial Placement Offering (IPO), or Higgins and Gulati, 2003, on affiliations increasing the probability that a venture's IPO is sponsored by a prominent investment bank).[27] With widespread substantive interest in entrepreneurship, and the intimate link

---

[27] I discuss elsewhere the potential value and shortcomings of network data in research on entrepreneurs (Burt, 2000*b*: 370–372). Two examples are sufficient to illustrate the point. Birley (1985) is a pioneering study in the genre. Focusing on businesses created between 1977 and 1982 in the county surrounding the city of South Bend in Indiana, Birley (1985: 107–108) showed that: "the main sources of help in assembling the resources of raw materials, supplies, equipment, space, employees, and orders were the informal contacts of family, friends, and colleagues. The only institution that was mentioned with any regularity was the bank, which was approached towards the end of the process when many of the resources were assembled and the elements of the business set in the entrepreneur's mind." Network data here are ratings of kinds of contacts (Birley, 1985: 113): "Available sources of help were listed and respondents were asked to rank the value of that source in assembling the resources of the firm. No rating for a category indicated that as far as the entrepreneur was concerned, no help was received."

Similar network data were used in what could be the most authoritative study of networks in entrepreneurship. Brüderl and Preisendörfer (1998) interviewed in 1990 a random sample of 1,700 entrepreneurs who had started five years earlier a business in Upper Bavaria, Germany. The network data were ratings of kinds of contacts (Brüderl and Preisendörfer, 1998: 217): "To get an impression about the role of social contacts in the start-up period of new businesses, participants of our study were asked on a scale ranging from 1 (no support) to 5 (full support) whether they received any support from different kinds of people." With separate measures of active and emotional support from the entrepreneur's spouse, the network data were analyzed as levels of support from two broad categories of people; weak ties (defined as business partners, acquaintances, former employers, or former coworkers), and strong ties (spouse/life-partner, parents, friends, or relatives). Brüderl and Preisendörfer report that entrepreneurs whose business had survived the five years to the survey were more likely than nonsurvivors to give credit to their spouse and strong ties for support.

These two studies are leading examples of the interesting and productive work that has been done on networks and entrepreneurship, but they reveal little about the association between network structure and entrepreneurship. The studies do not include data on the variable strengths of an entrepreneur's relations with individual contacts, and the variable strengths of connections between pairs of contacts. Ratings of support from, or acquaintance with, broad categories of contacts leave unknown the network structure variables that measure an entrepreneur's social capital. Approximations can be made from the distribution of contacts across categories typically separate in social structure. This is the intuition behind Lin's (2002) positional measurement of social capital (see Lin, Fu and Hsung, 2001, for quick introduction; Erickson, 1996, for widely cited application). Renzulli et al. (2000) is a recent illustration in entrepreneurship. They report on the discussion contacts of men and women in the Chapel Hill area of North Carolina who are thinking about starting a business. Renzulli et al. do not have data on

between network structure and entrepreneurship, the emerging sophistication of network argument and evidence in entrepreneurship is promising. For example, Nicolaou and Birley (2003*a*) distinguish three kinds of university spin-outs in terms of network structure, and Nicolaou and Birley (2003*b*) provide evidence of strong, nonredundant discussion relations predicting which university employees leave to join a spinout. Johnson (2004) reasons explicitly from the perspective of the structural hole spanned, distinguishing kinds of factors affecting success in the emergence, maintenance, and dissolution stages of bridging a structural hole (there are two helpful summary tables on pp. 222–223). Pollock, Porac, and Wade (2004) offer an especially fertile discussion of the process of choices and considerations through which the lead underwriter assembling an IPO deal network acts as a "network architect" whose selection of partners for a deal "creates and manages structural holes" in the capital market. I return to the entrepreneurial function of brokerage in Chapter 5.

2.6 Conclusions

This and the preceding chapter establish a performance association with the social capital of structural holes. The conclusion from Chapter 1 was that people and teams bridging structural holes have a social-capital advantage evident in their more positive evaluations, more likely promotion, and higher compensation relative to peers. This chapter was about the mechanism responsible for the performance association. The hypothesis for this chapter was that people who live in the intersection of social worlds are at higher risk of having good ideas. Qualifications come immediately to mind, but the gist of the hypothesis is familiar in sociology and makes intuitive sense: Ways of thinking and behaving are more homogeneous within than between groups, so people connected to otherwise segregated groups are more likely to be familiar with alternative ways of thinking and behaving, which gives them the option of selecting and synthesizing alternatives. Vision is the active ingredient in brokerage. Like adding radar to aircraft, or an MRI to medical care, brokerage reveals conditions and possibilities not otherwise visible. It exposes you to variation; variation in your own work, and variation in related kinds of work. With early access to diverse information, beliefs, and behavior,

---

relations between contacts, but they know the sector from which each contact was drawn (family, friends, business associates, etc.), so they compute a measure of the extent to which all of a person's contacts come from the same sector. Consistent with the brokerage argument, Renzulli et al. (2000: Table 4) report that the people who actually do start a business were more likely to draw their contacts from multiple sectors. Entrepreneurship is inherently an exercise in brokerage. It is an area ripe for study with advances in network theory and analysis.

people whose networks span structural holes can expect to find themselves moving ideas from one group to another, proposing ideas that are new to the recipient group, and so seeming within the recipient group to be gifted with creativity.

Brokerage is associated with good ideas. The evidence came in four parts. First, there is anecdotal and aggregate evidence of the association. Second, the association is apparent at the level of individuals in the example supply-chain organization. Managers whose networks more often spanned structural holes were more likely to express their ideas, less likely to have their ideas dismissed by senior management, and more likely to have their ideas evaluated as valuable (Figure 2.1).

Third, bridge relations are the channels through which discussion changes opinions and behavior (Figure 2.2). Ideas are more contagious across bridge relations than they are through relations inside a group (peer pressure within the group makes ideas contagious whether or not peers talk directly to one another). The two-step flow of communication familiar from early diffusion research is a compound of two different network mechanisms; contagion by discussion with opinion leaders gets information into a group, contagion by structural equivalence peer pressure drives diffusion within the group. Opinion "leaders," like Welch and Marcus at the top of the chapter, turn out to be more precisely opinion "brokers" who bear a striking resemblance to the network entrepreneurs in social capital research. It is brokerage beyond a group that makes for opinion leadership within the group.

Fourth, brokerage can facilitate adaptive implementation. Established ideas have constituency and budget. New ideas typically have neither. Implementing a new idea involves mobilizing support from people who will benefit from the idea despite those people having allocated their budget to other tasks. In this, network entrepreneurs are a budget reallocation mechanism, mobilizing support to shift budget to new applications where it now can be seen to be more productive. In contrast to ideas imposed by bureaucratic authority, the adaptive implementation of ideas is responsive to uncertain and changing circumstances—and is inherently an act of brokerage. Evidence on brokerage facilitating adaptive implementation is primarily in the form of anecdotes, in part because the processes by which people bridge structural holes are so varied and sensitive to context, but the available evidence is suggestive of general processes, and consistent with other evidence of value created by brokerage across structural holes.

Figure 2.3 is a summary representation of the evidence. Network constraint is on the horizontal axis, idea value on the vertical. The data in Figure 2.3 are pooled from the graphs in Figure 2.1.[28] The graph shows good ideas associated

---

[28] Figure 2.3 was constructed in the same way as Figure 1.8 and with the same heuristic intent. I computed three measures of idea value for each of the supply-chain managers: a six-point rating by one judge (1 to 5 with 0 for not rated), the rating by the other judge, and a three-category variable distinguishing (3) ideas not dismissed by

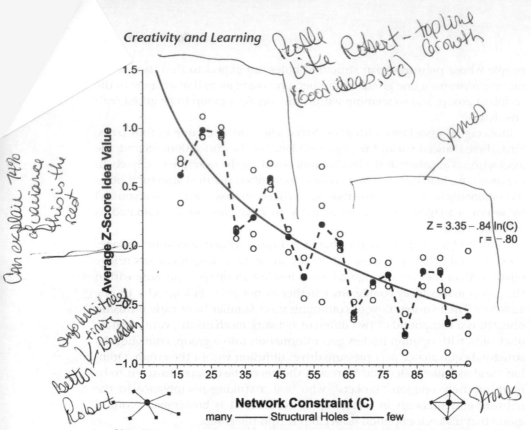

Note: Circles are average z-score ratings of value of a best idea (Z) for a five-point interval of network constraint (C). Dashed line goes through mean values of Z for intervals of C. Bold line is performance predicted by the natural logarithm of C.

Fig. 2.3: Good ideas are associated with brokerage, especially at high levels of brokerage (stylized fact #2).

with brokerage, especially at high levels of brokerage (i.e., low levels of network constraint). The nonlinear, negative association with good ideas in Figure 2.3 looks like the association in Figure 1.8 between network constraint and performance. Initial increments of constraint are more destructive than incremental additions to already high levels of constraint. The implication is that good ideas are more likely in more complex social environments, especially complex ones. More, the similar associations that network constraint has with performance in Figure 1.8 and good ideas in Figure 2.3 is an element of construct validity for the argument that they both reflect the social capital of bridging structural holes.

---

either judge, from (2) ideas dismissed by either judge, from (1) ideas dismissed by both judges. I standardized scores to zero mean and unit variance to remove intercept differences between the judges. Each dot in Figure 2.3 is an average score on the vertical axis within a five-point interval of network constraint. Dots are positioned on the horizontal axis by the average constraint score within a five-point interval. Three dots over a five-point interval correspond to the three measures of idea value.

THREE

Closure, Trust, and Reputation

TRUST remains an unresolved concern. The problem is illustrated in Figure 3.1. In situation A, network entrepreneur Robert has initiated a bridge relation with Jessica, a person in another group. He is asking Jessica to join him in supporting an idea. The idea looks good, but costs and benefits are not clear. Indeed, they cannot be clear. The idea is new. It has no concrete precedent in the company. That means Jessica's peers share no experience in terms of which Jessica can explain her support of Robert. More, she has no history with Robert, so she has no precedent establishing the quality of his thinking or his ability to deliver. The lack of social and personal precedent means that there is a risk in supporting Robert.[1] Robert's request for Jessica's support is a request for trust.

The concept of trust can trigger strong emotions and has alternative meanings, so let me pause to define its use here: You trust someone when you commit to a relationship before you know how the other person will behave. Distrust is a reluctance to commit without guarantees about the other person's behavior. The two definitional qualities are that trust is a relationship with someone (or something if the object of trust is a group, organization, or social category) in which contractual terms are incompletely specified. The more unspecified, taken-for-granted, the terms, the more that trust is involved. You anticipate cooperation from the other person, but you commit to the relationship before you know how the other person will behave. When you exchange sensitive information with someone, trust is implicit in the risk you now face that the other person might leak the information. When you enter a group effort, you trust the other people to contribute their share. A university faculty

---

[1] I focus in Chapters 1 and 2 on positive returns to brokerage. The returns can be less attractive, such as organized crime (Williams 1998; Morselli, 2003), fraud (Tillman and Indergaard, 1999), or corporate misgovernance (Mitchell, 2003: 54 ff., on Enron and Worldcom). Morselli and Tremblay (2004) surveyed prison inmates, measuring the structural holes in their networks and their earnings from criminal activity. Replicating results in Chapter 1, Morselli reports positive associations between earnings and structural holes for inmates involved in market offenses ("drug dealing, fencing, smuggling, loansharking, sex peddling, illegal gambling operating and other supply-related offenses"). The point here is that brokerage is a mechanism for re-allocating resources. The reallocation can be constructive, irrelevant, or corrosive. The risk of corrosive warrants caution.

granting tenure to a professor trusts the professor to continue to be productive. A faculty committee allocating a fellowship to a graduate student trusts the student to work toward the degree. Anticipated cooperation is a narrow slice of the spectrum of concepts spanned by richer images such as Barber's (1983) distinctions between trust as moral order, competence, and obligation (Levi, 2001, provides a succinct overview of trust concepts). However, anticipated cooperation is much of the trust required for brokerage. Morality and integrity are implicit in the definition. The central issue is flexible cooperation. As Macauley (1963: 61) quotes one of his local Wisconsin purchasing agents; "If something comes up, you get the other man on the telephone and deal with the problem. You don't read legalistic contract clauses at each other if you ever want to do business again. One doesn't run to lawyers if he wants to stay in business because one must behave decently." Ellickson (1991: 57) describes a live-and-let-live norm used to informally resolve cattle trespass problems between landowners in Shasta County, a rural California area just south of the Oregon border: "Not only are most trespass disputes ... resolved according to extralegal rules, but most enforcement actions are also extralegal." Resorting to legal remedies tars the reputation of both parties. Referring to two prominent legal disputes between landowners, local residents described to Ellickson (1991: 64) the people on both sides of the "two claims as 'bad apples,' 'odd ducks,' or otherwise as people not aware of the natural working order. Ordinary people, it seems do not often turn to attorneys to help resolve disputes." In the same vein, one of Uzzi's (1996: 678) New York garment district managers explained: "With people you trust, you know that if they have a problem with a fabric they're just not going to say, 'I won't pay' or 'take it back.' If they did then we would have to pay for the loss. This way maybe the manufacturer will say, 'Hey, OK so I'll make a dress out of it. Or I can cut it and make a short jacket instead of a long jacket.'" Macauley (1963: 61) offers a nice summary quote from another local businessman; "You can settle any dispute if you keep the lawyers and accountants out of it. They just do not understand the give-and-take needed in business."

In fact, trust is likely to be more critical where brokerage is more valuable. The value of brokerage increases with task ambiguity. The less clear the job, the more valuable it is to know how other people view or do the job (see Section 3.3.6). Two factors define a course of action: data and colleagues. The data are what you know. The colleagues are who you know. Where a task is ambiguous, what you know is out of date or of unclear relevance. Who you know is the available path to stable certainty. You and I have a relationship. Whatever else comes up, you are someone I feel I can trust. This image of finding stability in core relationships is nicely illustrated in a quote prominently displayed in Finlay and Coverdill's (2002: 24) description of the role that "headhunters" play in executive recruitment (also see the argument and evidence in the next chapter):

[A headhunter] needs to be a true broker. A true middleman. ... oftentimes when I've made initial contact with people that maybe are at a controller level or a VP of finance, we'll be talking for ten or fifteen minutes, and they'll say, "I'm not sure why you're calling. Are you looking at me as a candidate or are you looking at me as a potential customer?" And I'll say, "I'm the middleman. I'm looking at developing a relationship with you, and I'm sure something will fall, one side or the other, if I'm successful at developing that relationship."

Note the unspecific, long-term goal. Brokerage is often discussed in terms of a concrete, short-term goal. Network entrepreneurs are described—as I am describing Robert in Figure 3.1—as asking themselves, "Who are the people I should involve in this venture, this project, this career action?" In contrast, the above quote shows the broker more clear about the person than the venture. The relationship could turn into an opportunity to place someone or recruit the person with whom the headhunter is talking, but either way, this relationship feels to the headhunter like it is a productive relationship to establish and maintain. That sense of investing in people with whom you think good things could happen before you are sure what those things are captures the essence of brokerage and the critical role that trust plays in brokerage. This is not to say that every person in a venture will be a trusted contact; only that a venture without trusted contacts is qualitatively different, and at higher risk of discontinuation, from a venture that involves one or more trusted contacts. In short, people often decide on colleagues before they decide on ventures: I build this relationship to put myself at increased risk of productive accident.

Returning to Robert soliciting Jessica's support, situation B adds a strong history between Robert and Jessica. She knows and has confidence in Robert. Jessica's history with Robert can lower her uncertainty about supporting his current proposal. Risk is further reduced in situation C. Robert and Jessica have strong ties to mutual colleagues. The relationship between Robert and Jessica in situation C is what was termed a "bond" in Section 1.1.5. Not only does Jessica know Robert, she knows that he will be embarrassed in front of their mutual friends if he acts in some way to violate Jessica's trust. Bad behavior could cost Robert his sense of self and social standing in the group. Jessica can factor that cost into the risk of supporting Robert's proposal. This is the gist of the closure argument. Closed networks—that is to say networks in which people are connected such that no behavior goes unnoticed—create advantage by decreasing risks that would otherwise inhibit trust.

The tension between brokerage and closure is illustrated in Figure 3.1. The trust required to make the bridge in situation A work is ensured by the closed network in situation C, but the Robert–Jessica connection is no longer a bridge in situation C. It is just another redundant connection within a group. More generally, the tension is that the social capital of structural holes depends on trust—in as much as the value created by brokers involves new, and so incompletely understood, combinations of previously disconnected

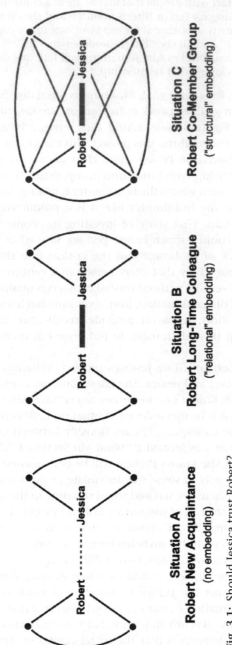

Situation A
Robert New Acquaintance
(no embedding)

Situation B
Robert Long-Time Colleague
("relational" embedding)

Situation C
Robert Co-Member Group
("structural" embedding)

Fig. 3.1: Should Jessica trust Robert?

ideas—but trust is a feature of closed networks, precisely the condition that brokers rise above.

This chapter is about the trust needed to realize the value of bridging a structural hole and the network closure needed to ensure the trust. Sections 3.1 and 3.2 provide argument and evidence for closure lowering the risk of trust. The more closed the network, the more likely that misbehavior will be detected and punished. Not wishing to lose reputation accumulated in a long-term relationship, or built up within a group of colleagues, people cooperate with other people in the network. There is clear evidence of trust being more likely in a strong than in a weak relationship, especially if the strong relationship is embedded in a closed network. Section 3.3 is about the social capital defined by mixtures of brokerage and closure. Brokerage is about coordinating people between whom it would be valuable, but risky, to trust. Closure is about making it safe to trust. The key to creating value is to put the two together, building closure around valuable bridge relations. Closure is valuable when it spans a structural hole. I illustrate with evidence on closure-related variable returns to brokerage for people, teams, and markets.

3.1   Closure and Embedding

It will be convenient to refer to Robert and Jessica in a more general way. Let ego refer to the person being asked to trust. Alter is the person to be trusted. In the discussion of Figure 3.1, Jessica and Robert were respectively ego and alter. There is some strength of relationship between the two people (discussed in Sections 1.1.5 and 1.5), and surrounding them are friends, colleagues, acquaintances, and enemies. These other people are third parties to the relationship. Dots in Figure 3.1 indicate third parties to the relationship between Robert and Jessica. Where ego and alter are connected to the same third party, there is an indirect connection through a third party, or more simply, there is a third-party tie between ego and alter. The stronger the third-party ties connecting two people, the more closed the network around them.

3.1.1   Trust in Strong Ties

Begin with the relationship between two people under study, ego and alter, ignoring for the moment the social setting in which they come together. Trust between ego and alter is twice created by repeated interaction, from the past and from the future.[2]

---

[2] This image of trust between two people isolated from the rest of the world is the setting for much of exchange theory predicting trust as a result of repeated contact. Two prominent examples are Homans' (1961) analysis of social behavior and Blau's (1964)

Cumulative Build

From the past, repeated cooperation from alter makes ego more confident in alter's tendency to cooperate. Some tit-for-tat share of the cumulative process can be cast as a statistical decision problem in which ego becomes more certain of alter across repeated samples of alter behavior.[3] The repetition of

---

analysis of social exchange. See Ekeh (1974: 81–187) for historical exegesis of the individualistic British–American version of exchange theory contrasted with the French collectivist variant from Durkheim and Levi-Strauss, and Blau (1994: 152–172) for Blau's later view, especially pages 156–158, explaining his continued focus on dyadic exchange. With respect to trust, the gist of the theory is that trust and distrust develop because relationships involve unspecified obligations for which no binding contract can be written (Blau, 1964: 112–113). Putting aside moral obligation to focus on parameters of cost–benefit calculation (cf. Ekeh, 1974: 175), the trust definition in the text is based on Coleman's (1990: ch. 5) succinct definition for systems of two-party exchange.

[3] In preparation for the discussion of network closure as bandwidth and echo, I find it helpful to think about the repeated exchange imagery in terms of a statistical decision model. The model is in a footnote because the text alone has been preferable and sufficient for many readers. Ego is a person having to decide whether to trust a colleague, alter. Through whatever time period is relevant, ego has had some number of direct personal experiences with alter. Let each personal experience be a game. Given ego's N games with alter, each with an outcome g (from 1 when alter fully cooperated, to −1 when alter defected on ego's cooperation; let g be continuous for the purposes here), ego's best guess of alter in the next game is the average $\bar{g}_n$ across prior games. The mean is a best guess about alter, but a guess nonetheless. The uncertainty in ego's guess is a function of two information variables, volume and consistency. Ego can be more certain about alter if there has been a long history of exchanges (N large) or alter behaved consistently in the exchanges (low variance in g). Ego cannot be certain about alter if they have little history together (N small) or alter's behavior has been erratic (high variance in g). Given the variance in ego's experience of alter behavior,

$$(1) \qquad\qquad s_n^2 = \sum^N (g - \bar{g}_n)^2 / (N - 1),$$

the standard error of the mean provides a test statistic for ego's decision (mean alter behavior in prior games, $\bar{g}_n$, divided by the standard error of the mean):

$$(2) \qquad\qquad (\bar{g}_n)\sqrt{N}/s_n.$$

Larger values of the test statistic (more positive or more negative) are defined by a longer history of games (larger N) or more consistent alter behavior (smaller s_n). A large positive value means that ego can be certain alter will cooperate, so alter can be trusted. A large negative value means that ego can be certain alter will not cooperate, so alter should be distrusted. With respect to the baseline prediction in the text, a strong relationship between ego and alter implies a history of positive games (large N, high $\bar{g}_n$, low s_r), which means a large positive value of the test statistic, and so a high probability of ego trusting alter.

Statistical inference is only a metaphor for the argument, but there is virtue in making three assumptions explicit. I am grateful to my colleague Al Madansky for suggesting improved language for the metaphor, and for convincing me that leaving the assumptions implicit could obscure the argument. (1) There is a zero implicit in the test statistic. The test-statistic ratio of the mean to its standard error is implicitly a ratio of the mean minus zero, quantity divided by its standard error. The question for ego is whether the cooperative exchange promotes trust. More generally, the cumulation involves escalation. From tentative initial exchanges, people move to familiarity, and from there to more significant exchanges (Cross and Parker, 2004: 98–104, offer concrete steps for starting the process). The gradual expansion of exchanges promotes the trust necessary for them. Blau (1968: 454) summarizes the process as follows: "social exchange relations evolve in a slow process, starting with minor transactions in which little trust is required because little risk is involved and in which both partners can prove their trustworthiness, enabling them to expand their relation and engage in major transactions. Thus, the process of social exchange leads to the trust required for it in a self-governing fashion."

The cumulative build is fueled in part by people coming to know one another such that they can better predict probable behavior, not just whether the other person will cooperate, but whether a specific proposal is something the other person is especially likely to push to fruition. Granovetter (1992: 42) succinctly summarizes the information benefits of this "relational" embeddedness (cf. Granovetter, 1985: 490): "That trustworthy behavior may be a regularized part of a personal relationship reflects one of the typically direct effects of relational embeddedness and explains the widespread preference of all economic actors to deal with those they have dealt with before. Our information about such partners is cheap, richly detailed, and probably accurate." Geertz (1978: 30–31) describes as "clientelization" people managing information difficulties in a Moroccan bazaar by focusing on repeated exchange with known customers or suppliers. The information advantage is illustrated by quotes from Uzzi's fieldwork on relational embedding in apparel (Uzzi, 1996), banking (Uzzi, 1999; Uzzi and Gillespie, 2002), and law (Uzzi and Lancaster, 2004). Levin and Cross (2004) report a survey of managers in three organizations who felt that they received useful information from people

expected value represented by the mean of g is clearly above zero (trust alter) or below zero (distrust alter). (2) The N in the denominator of the standard error is a count of prior games as independent events. To the extent that games are interdependent, the denominator is less than N, thus increasing the standard error because ego has fewer than N independent bits of information with which to estimate the expected value of a game with alter. Having no data on this issue, and no incentive to introduce the complexity of interdependence into the argument, I put the issue aside by leaving in general form the function aggregating ego's experience with alter. In empirical research testing for third-party effects, I use the current strength of ego's relation with alter as a control for however many games have been played sufficient to bring ego to his or her current strength of relation with alter. (3) Similarly, the T in the denominator below in n. 9 is based on an assumption that ego's T vicarious games with alter are independent games. Count T is never set equal to the number of third parties, nor to the number of third-party stories that ego hears. It is a general function of ego's exposure to gossip through third parties (as N is a general function of ego's personal exposure to alter). All that is necessary to predict the third-party effects on trust is that T increases with the strength of third-party connections. The issue of how T varies with the strength of third-party connection is left undefined as a task for future research.

working on their project, providing personal experience not available in written documentation, who the respondent perceived would look out for the respondent's interests (see Cross et al., 2001, for a more ethnographic look at these themes; Cross and Parker, 2004, for elaboration). Jensen (2003) reports on commercial banks crossing into investment banking. The odds of a firm first using a commercial bank to serve as lead investment bank is significantly increased by previous use of the bank's commercial banking services. Baker and Faulkner (2004) conclude that investors in a fraudulent oil company were less likely to lose their "entire investment" if they invested because of a prior relationship with one of the firm's principles, agents, or employees. Explicitly concerned with brokerage, Windolf and Schief (1999) describe West German managers as information brokers between the East German companies on whose boards the West Germans sit, Ellis (2000) describes the tendency for Hong Kong toy companies entering foreign markets to rely on market information from prior business associates rather than third-party market research, and Wong and Ellis (2002) describe the tendency for Hong Kong companies entering China to more quickly decide between alternative venture partners when their information comes from family or close friends rather than casual friends or acquaintances. As one respondent explained his selection of venture partner (Wong and Ellis, 2002: 284): "It is hard to say whether you can trust anybody unless you have had the experience of working with him. We had not worked together before. I think that trust is based on the fact that we are [come] from the same village. But more important is that I had known him for over two years before we established this joint venture. After two years of observation, I felt comfortable that I had a good understanding of him."

Reputation also builds in the relationship. Reputation is behavior expected of you. Over the course of repeated exchanges, two people build a sense of who they are in the relationship, a sense of what to expect from the other person as well as themselves. This was a central point in Blau's social exchange theory. Krackhardt (1992) provides another view of such relations when he describes patterns of strong friendship in a small organization: "philos" relations connect people who interact, have a history with one another, and have come to feel emotional affection for one another. In economic theory, reputation is typically defined with an eye to the future: the reputation accumulated in a relationship can be lost if either party behaves so as to erode the relationship (e.g., Tullock, 1985; Kreps, 1990; Gibbons, 1992: 88 ff.; Milgrom and Roberts, 1992: 257–269). Where reputation is an asset, people can be expected to behave in prescribed ways to protect their reputation. There is also the question of identity. Granovetter (1992: 44) highlights identity in discussing relational embeddedness: "I may deal fairly with you not only because it is in my interest, ... but because we have been close for so long that we expect this of one another, and I would be mortified and distressed to have cheated you *even if you did not find out* (though all the more so if you did)." One does not wish to be the kind of person who betrays old friends—even if they never find out about it. A relationship can be destroyed at either end. The other person can withdraw. Or you can behave in such a way that the relationship loses what it once meant to you. Either way, the expectation that misbehavior could destroy a relationship can result in cooperation even if defection would be more profitable in the short run.

In sum, past cooperation is a basis for future cooperation such that trust is correlated with the strength of a relationship.[4] A history of repeated cooperation between two people strengthens their relationship, increasing the probability that they trust one another. If people have an erratic history of cooperation mixed with exploitation, or a consistent history of failure to cooperate, they will distrust one another, avoiding collaborative endeavors without guarantees on the other's behavior. The preceding two sentences are a verbal statement of the statistical decision model in footnote 3. In fact, the correlation between trust and relation strength is such that trust is sometimes used to define strong relations (for example, note the "mutual confiding" and "reciprocal services" in Granovetter's, 1973: 1361, widely cited definition of strong ties in Section 1.1.5), creating an element of tautology in the claim that a strong relationship yesterday predicts trust today. Tautology notwithstanding, the predicted correlation between trust and relationship strength is a useful baseline for measuring the effect of network context on trust.

Illustrative Evidence

Figure 3.2 contains illustrative evidence of trust increasing over time in three of the populations discussed in Chapter 1. The three populations are presented

---

[4] There is diverse work on this point. For example, see Zucker (1986) on process-based trust, Staw and Ross (1987) on commitment escalation, Stinchcombe (1990: 164–165) on the information advantages of current suppliers for building trust, Kramer (1999) on history-based trust, Kollock (1994) for illustrative laboratory evidence. Widely cited evidence of autocorrelation in organization relations is provided by Gulati (1995; Gulati and Gargiulo, 1999) and Uzzi (1996, 1999; Uzzi and Gillespie, 2002; Uzzi and Lancaster, 2004). Illustrative related bits of evidence are the tendency for joint ventures to survive longer when between firms that have had other business together (Kogut, 1989), and the tendency for later contracts between two organizations to be more flexible than initial contracts (Raider, 2003). There are also computer simulations showing how trust between two people might build across repeated exchange (e.g., Axelrod, 1984; Bendor, Kramer and Stout, 1991; especially Bendor, Kramer and Swistak, 1996, for review; Roberts and Sherratt, 1998, for simulations close to the original exchange formulation by Homans and Blau in that the optimum strategy is to begin with small acts of cooperation and "raise the stakes" with repeated cooperation from alter). There is research to be done on the amount of cooperation to offer at each stage of a relationship's development, the relative weight to be given to dimensions of relational strength, or their impact on trust relative to the level of risk in a proposed collaborative effort (e.g., Kollock, 1994; Roberts and Sherratt, 1998; Snijders and Raub, 1998; Buskens and Weesie, 2000), but it is sufficient here to take as a baseline that trust is a correlate of relational strength.

together because similar questionnaires were used to obtain network data in the three populations. The senior managers in panel A are a benchmark because of published research on the network structure of their social capital. The staff officers and managers in panels B and C are included for corroboration. Trust is indicated by a manager citing a colleague as someone with whom he or she would discuss potentially damaging personal information, and the increasing bold lines in Figure 3.2 show that older relationships are more likely to be cited for trust. Distrust is indicated by a manager citing someone as a most difficult colleague, and the decreasing dashed lines show that recent relationships are more likely to be cited for distrust. Most cited relations were cited for neither trust nor distrust (69%, 4,831 of 6,995 cited contacts).[5]

For example, the first graph in Figure 3.2 describes trust and distrust across 3,015 relations cited by 284 senior managers in a large American computer manufacturer. Managers cited colleagues they deemed to be key contacts for information, personal advice, and political support within the organization. Brokerage among these contacts is associated with early promotion to senior rank (Figure 1.5D). More specifically, the first column in Figure 3.2A summarizes 378 new contacts, colleagues cited who had been known for a year or less. Of the 378, 9% were cited as people the manager trusted and 11% were cited as people the manager did not trust. The other 80% were cited for neither trust nor distrust. Over the next five years, managers move more contacts into trust or distrust. By the fifth year, 15% of colleagues were cited for trust and another 15% were cited for distrust. Colleagues seem to be sorted into two groups after five years (a period about equal to two job assignments in this firm); those you

---

[5] Details on sampling and surveying the senior managers are available elsewhere (Burt, 1992, 1997b, on their networks as social capital; Burt and Knez, 1995; Krackhardt, 1996, on trust and distrust of colleagues). The managers and staff officers answered a series of sociometric questions asking them to name (a) people with whom they most often discussed important personal matters, (b) the people with whom they most often spent free time, (c) the person to whom they report, (d) their most promising subordinate, (e) their most valued contacts in the firm, (f) the people they would name as essential sources of buy-in to their replacement if they were promoted to a new job, (g) the contact most important for their continued success in the firm, (h) their most difficult contact, and (i) the people with whom they would discuss moving to a new job in another firm. The staff-officer data are not as well documented in published research. The staff officers are a saturation sample in the sense that all human-resource employees in two firms were mailed a network questionnaire, of whom 218 in one firm returned the questionnaire (65% response rate; see Burt, Jannotta, and Mahoney, 1998) and 99 in the other firm (40% response rate). Respondents were representative on various dimensions including rank, age, salary, gender, and geography, except that employees in senior ranks of the first firm were more likely to return the questionnaire. I combine the respondents as a single study population because their work is so similar, and so different from work in the other two study populations. There are no significant differences between the two staff-officer samples in the number of colleagues cited (13.1 average in one firm, 12.4 in the other, 1.6 t-test, P = .10), or the sociometric results (0.9 z-statistic for a company dummy added to predict trust, 0.03 for distrust, P > .3).

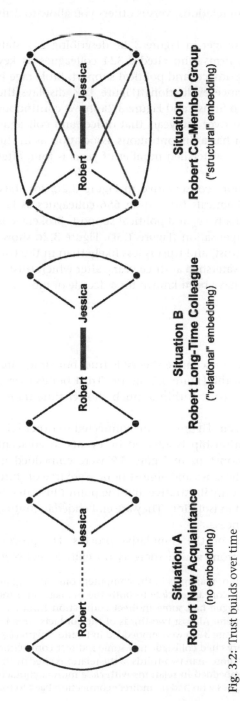

Fig. 3.2: Trust builds over time

trust and with whom you maintain relations, versus others you allow to drift away.

The association with time is stronger in Figure 3.2B, describing 217 staff officers in two financial services firms who cited 3,324 colleagues as key contacts for information, personal advice, and political support. Brokerage is associated with positive performance evaluations (Figure 1.5C displays the association for the larger of the two firms), and Figure 3.2B shows continuous increase in the probability of trust over the years that officer and colleague have known one another. Distrust has a discontinuous association as in the computer company except that the watershed number of years is four, after which distrust is much less likely.

The association with time is more conservative in Figure 3.2C, for sixty senior managers in the French chemicals firm citing 656 colleagues as key contacts for information, personal advice, and political support. Brokerage is associated with high relative compensation (Figure 1.5F). Figure 3.2C shows distrust initially more likely than trust, and trust is less likely than in the two American populations. There is a watershed at three years, after which trust is more likely (especially when they have been known for a decade or more).

Slow, Rare, and Dangerous

The cumulative process described in exchange theory is true, but slow, rare, and dangerous. Slow is implicit in the Figure 3.2 metric: Trust builds over a period of years. Brokerage requires trust within a much shorter time frame: months, weeks, even minutes.

Second, the cumulating relations in Figure 3.2 are connected to other relations. What happens in one relationship is affected by events in adjacent relations. Two-thirds of the relationships in Figure 3.2 were embedded in connections with close mutual colleagues and almost none were free of third parties.[6] The data in Figure 3.2 are only illustrative, but the point illustrated is a familiar one: relations rarely exist in isolation. They are embedded in mutual friends, colleagues, and acquaintances.

Then there is the risk of relying on the cumulative process. The process works most reliably in relations from which there is no exit, as between

---

[6] Two-thirds of relations cited by senior managers in the computer company (Figure 3.2A) were embedded in relations with colleagues *close* to both the manager and the colleague (65%), and every cited colleague had some indirect connection through a mutual friend to the manager citing them. Almost two-thirds of the contacts cited by the staff officers in financial services (Figure 3.2B) were embedded in relations with *close* mutual contacts (64%), and again, every cited colleague had some indirect connection back to the officer citing them. Slightly more than two-thirds of the relations cited by the French managers (Figure 3.2C) were embedded in relations with *close* mutual contacts (68%), but there were nine (2%) colleagues who had no indirect connection back to the manager citing them.

parents and children forced to live together, husband and wife where divorce is not an option, or two countries locked in a long-term struggle. The cumulative build can be illustrated with computer simulations (Axelrod, 1984). Allow any possibility of exit from difficult relations, however, and the same computer simulations show that the people who thrive are the ones who exploit the initial trust that people show them (Burt, 1999c). Abusive people experience frequent rejection, but they simply move on to abuse new contacts. Over time, abusive people dominate.

3.1.2   Trust in Closed Networks

What protects the innocent are friends and colleagues providing scarecrow warning about abusive people. Within a closed network, warning comes reliably early and at low cost so that abusive people can be squeezed out of the network.

Bandwidth

Imagine a network of interconnected people telling stories; not stories in the sense of deception, just stories in the sense of personal accounts about people; in other words, gossip. Rosnow and Fine (1976: 87) offer what I have in mind when they "broadly define gossip as nonessential (often trivial) news about someone." Merry (1984: 275) provides more detail: "Gossip is informal, private communication between an individual and a small, selected audience concerning the conduct of absent persons or events. Gossip thrives when the facts are uncertain, neither publicly known nor easily discovered. Gossip generally contains some element of evaluation or interpretation of the event or person, but it may be implicit or unstated." Gossip is the sharing of news, the catching up, through which we build and maintain relations (Gambetta, 1994).

The network around each person is like a broadcast system transmitting stories to a colleague audience of armchair quarterbacks in vicarious game play with the person. Signal about personal behavior multiplies as it spreads in stories. In your relationship with a contact isolated from the rest of the world, there is only the information you and the other person display to one another. Put that same behavior in a network of third parties, and the other person receives repeated signals about you from vicarious game play in the stories that third parties tell about their interpretation of you and interpretations they have heard from others.[7] Jessica in Figure 3.1 has two sources of information

---

[7] I am excluding third parties strategically inserted between two people to strengthen or weaken their relationship, such as third-party facilitators and positions of authority in a corporate or legal hierarchy (e.g., Coleman, 1990: 43–44, on complex relations; Black and Baumgartner, 1983; Shapiro, 1984, 1987; Black, 1993: ch. 6, on third parties in the legal process; Morrill, 1995: 92–140, for ethnographic illustration of the Black and

about Robert: One is her own direct experience of Robert. The other is her vicarious experience of Robert in the stories she has heard from third parties, where the volume of stories she hears increases with the strength of third-party ties that surround the two people.

The stronger the third-party ties between ego and alter, the more closed the network around them and the greater their vicarious experience of one another.[8] Alternative, redundant communication channels let numerous tellings of a story get around quickly. Further, ego learns from stories repeated by different observers a richly detailed account of alter behavior. The more consistent the stories ego hears about alter, the more certain ego can be about trusting alter.[9] What was a problem in Chapter 1 is here an asset. The benefit of brokerage came from seeing variation in belief and practice across groups.

Baumgartner view applied to managers). The third parties put aside would also include what Fine (1996) describes as "reputational entrepreneurs," people working to enhance or destroy the reputation of a targeted reputation. These instrumental third parties surely make use of closure's reputation mechanism, but I put them aside because adding them requires a consideration of the case-specific motives for their presence. This chapter, and the next, are about what could be termed "natural" third-party effects in casual conversations. "Gossip does not work well if the receiver suspects ulterior motives behind the transmitter's story" (Gambetta, 1994: 11).

[8] The assumption that third parties enhance information flow can be found in laboratory experiments controlling interpersonal contact (e.g., Bavelas, 1950; Cook et al., 1983), metaphorical images of actual organization (e.g., the image of Playco in Morrill, 1995), or theoretical images of organization (e.g., Bendor and Mookherjee, 1990: 38, on third-party effects where "the actions of every member with respect to all other members are observable without error to the entire group"). The assumption is particularly clear in computer simulations because simulating information flow requires an explicit decision about closure's effect on flow. For example, Carley (1986, 1991) simulates networks in which connected people share facts drawn at random from what they know, so more contact between people results in each knowing what the other knows. Baker and Iyer (1992) run simulations to show that markets with networks of more direct connections could improve communication between producers, which would stabilize prices, a central finding in Baker's (1984) analysis of a securities exchange. Raub and Weesie (1990) use simulations to describe how reputation effects could vary with the speed with which third-party disclosures reach people (cf. Yamaguchi, 1994; Buskens, 1998; DeCanio and Watkins, 1998; Buskins and Yamaguchi, 1999). Macy and Skvoretz (1998: esp. fig. 4) run simulations to describe how trust could be more likely between people in a small network of frequent interaction.

[9] Continuing with the statistical decision model in n. 3, ego's information on alter is now a composite of two kinds of information: information gained from personal contact with alter in N games, and information gleaned from T games played vicariously in third-party stories about alter. Gossip increases the volume of ego's information on alter; (N+T) is higher than N. The magnitude of T varies with the strength of ego's third-party connection to alter, but it is sufficient for the moment to say that T varies from zero to some positive number with the volume of third-party stories relayed to ego. If closure creates bandwidth, then third parties offer a broader sample across the population of data on alter and ego's inference is made more accurate and more efficient in the same way that parameters estimated from a large sample are more precise than estimates from a small sample.

Redundant contacts were inefficient. Closure is about monitoring to detect misbehavior. Redundant contacts ensure reliable, early warning. A closed network provides wide bandwidth for the flow of stories as packets of people data. Detection is the trust-relevant feature of the flow. The omnipresent hydra-eyes of a closed network makes it difficult for misbehavior to escape detection. The more closed the network, the more penetrating the detection.

Control

There is an element of evaluation in the stories people hear. Ego learns from the tone of repeated stories how people in the network feel about the behavior discussed. Does the story behavior reflect a belief shared within the network such that telling the story is a form of witnessing the teller's own commitment to the belief? Did the behavior offend? Evaluation communicated in a story lets ego infer the politically correct interpretation of the story behavior. The more you are discussed as illustrative of shared beliefs, the higher your social standing. The more a person is predicted to behave in a way consistent with shared beliefs, the less risky it is to trust the person. A reputation for being trustworthy can make it possible to build bridges that would otherwise be too risky. People celebrated for exhibiting shared beliefs have an incentive to be still more consistent with shared beliefs so as to maintain and build reputation. At the other extreme, there is an incentive to avoid misbehavior knowing it is sure to be detected to the detriment of one's reputation. It is in the protection of reputation that we work to behave well, with or without formal controls, and sometimes despite them. You might not care much about the job, or your boss, but you do the right thing because that is the right thing to do—and if you don't, there will surely be a story about it haunting you into the future. In as much as public declaration of shared belief occurs in telling stories, subsequent stories can be expected to become more normatively clear than preceding ones.[10] Adverbs and adjectives, then verbs and nouns, can be expected to escalate across repeated tellings. Thus heroes and heroines are born. This is a theme developed in the next chapter (Section 4.1).

Social obligation and identity are defined with reputation. To the extent that you are defined by the people with whom you affiliate, two people affiliated with the same contacts have structurally equivalent identities. In other words, people strongly connected through third parties share some element of identity. They are, to a degree, the same kind of person. Undercutting, or otherwise failing to cooperate with your own kind is a betrayal viewed

---

[10] For examples of opinion polarizing to extremes within closed networks, see Laumann (1973: 126), Myers and Lamm (1976), Isenberg (1986); Lamm (1988); Bienenstock, Bonacich and Oliver (1990), Williams and Taormina (1992); Brauer, Judd and Gliner (1995); Baron et al. (1996). Friedkin (1999) brings this work together in a network process underlying group polarization.

with suspicion by observers debating trust. More, you have reputation in each group with which you are affiliated, or more precisely, in which you are discussed. The more groups with which you are affiliated, the more alternative reputations you have, the more you realize that you have some say in which you take to heart (Simmel, 1955 [1922]; Merton, 1957), and the more unique and alone you are in your identity (Durkheim, 1951 [1897]; Coser, 1975). A person affiliated with only one group—for example, their family, a team, or a neighborhood group—has only one reputation, which must necessarily be their social identity. Lose the group and you lose your identity. There is more here than strong relations between people in a closed network; there is a lack of choice. A person strongly connected into two groups is less constrained than a person similarly connected to only one of the groups. Closure means closed to alternatives. To the extent that reputation-protection is a motivation, people in a closed network have a single source of reputation and can be expected to protect it.

Frank Ellis is an instructive example. Ellis was one of the largest landowners in Ellickson's (1991) study of disputes resolved informally through social norms. He was a rancher and real estate broker in his late fifties when he bought his large tract of land in Shasta County. Ellis had risen to prosperity outside Shasta County. He stands out in Ellickson's analysis for his immunity to the reputation mechanism by which Shasta County landowners resolved disputes. The area (Ellickson, 1991: 57): "... remains distinctly rural in atmosphere. People tend to know one another, and they value their reputations in the community. Some ranching families have lived in the area for several generations and include members who plan to stay indefinitely. Members of these families seem particularly intent on maintaining their reputations as good neighbors." Residents (p. 57) "seem quite conscious of the role of gossip in their system of social control. One longtime resident, who had also lived for many years in a suburb of a major California urban area, observed that people in the Oak Run area 'gossip all the time,' much more than in the urban area. Another reported intentionally using gossip to sanction a traditionalist who had been 'impolite' when coming to pick up some stray mountain cattle; he reported that application of this self-help device produced an apology, an outcome itself presumably circulated through the gossip system." Returning to Frank Ellis (p. 58): "The ranchette residents who were particularly bothered by Ellis' cattle could see that he was utterly indifferent to his reputation among them. They thought, however, that as a major rancher, Ellis would worry about his reputation among the large cattle operations in the county. They therefore reported Ellis' activities to the Board of Directors of the Shasta County Cattlemen's Association. This move proved unrewarding, for Ellis was also surprisingly indifferent to his reputation among the cattlemen."

The idea of control eroded by connections to multiple groups is exactly as discussed in Chapter 1 with respect to brokerage, but it is here viewed from the other side of control. Brokerage is about seeing variation by escaping the constraint of one group. Closure is about subjecting a person to control to lower the risk of trusting the person. Reputation is the active ingredient in that control. Reputations are defined by people monitoring and discussing individual behavior, and by so doing, mutual friends and colleagues constitute an adaptive control on behavior.[11] This is the reputation mechanism by which closure lowers risk that would otherwise inhibit trust. Where that trust is an advantage, closure is social capital.

For example, Coleman (1988: S102–103; 1990: 306–307) discusses reputation and closure with respect to rotating-credit associations: "These associations are groups of friends and neighbors who typically meet monthly, each person contributing to a central fund that is then given to one of the members (through bidding or by lot), until, after a number of months, each of the *n* persons has made *n* contributions and received one payout." The associations are a strategy for raising investment capital (see Biggart, 2001, for a closer look at how such associations operate; Carr and Tong, 2002, on the microfinance movement in which loans to the poorest of people are managed through reputation rather than property). Network closure is essential (Coleman, 1988: S103): "without a high degree of trustworthiness among the members of the group, the institution could not exist—for a person who receives a payout early in the sequence of meetings could abscond and leave the others with a loss. For example, one could not imagine a rotating-credit association operating successfully in urban areas marked by a high degree of social disorganization—or, in other words, by a lack of social capital." With respect to norms and effective sanctions, Coleman (1990: 310–311; cf. 1988: S104) says: "When an effective norm does exist, it constitutes a powerful, but sometimes fragile, form of social capital. ... Norms in a community that support and provide effective rewards for high achievement in school greatly facilitate the school's task." He (1988: S107–S108) summarizes: "The consequence of this closure is, as in the case of the wholesale diamond market or in other similar communities, a set of effective sanctions that can monitor and guide behavior. Reputation cannot arise in an open structure, and collective sanctions that would ensure trustworthiness cannot be applied."

---

[11] Notice how simply this eliminates the monitoring problem that Hechter (1987; 1990: 243–244) uses to motivate his argument about dependence and formal control being necessary conditions for cooperation in large groups. Hechter (1987: 73–77) takes issue with Axelrod's (1984: ch. 4) use of the live-and-let-live system of trench warfare to illustrate the point that cooperation emerges in difficult circumstances if people anticipate future interaction with one another. Hechter stresses the implicit monitoring necessary to the live-and-let-live system, the difficulty of monitoring even between the two armies which is analogous to a two-player game, and the implausibility of that monitoring (without formal controls) in games of more than two players (see Macy, 1991: 827–829, for illustration with simulated prisoner's dilemma games; Knez and Camerer, 1994, for laboratory illustration with weakest-link coordination games). In short, cooperation is more difficult in larger groups. Hechter's argument presumes that everyone monitors everyone else; whereupon monitoring is more difficult in larger groups because there are more people to monitor. The closure argument reduces the monitoring problem to realistic proportions. Overlapping networks of third parties do the monitoring, one relationship at a time (e.g., see the Polanyi quote on p. 135).

Coleman's closure argument is prominent with respect to social capital, but it is not alone in predicting that closure facilitates trust. The trust associated with closure corresponds to Heider's (1958) balance theory in psychology: ego and alter connected positively to the same third parties should have a positive connection with each other.[12] There is an analogous closure argument in economics in which mutual acquaintances make behavior more public, creating an incentive for good behavior to maintain reputation, which decreases the risk associated with trust between ego and alter, and so increases the probability of trust (e.g., Tullock, 1985; Grief, 1989). Taking an economic perspective on law enforcement, Ellickson (1991: 177–183) explains how "close-knit social groups" facilitated the enforcement of norms among Shasta County landowners (p. 181): "First, these cross-cutting relationships help members maintain a gossip network through which to pass information about how particular members acted in the past in particular social interactions. Second, these interlinkages help members share information about previous consensual economic and social exchanges, and thus to develop the objective valuation system they need to assess the welfare-enhancing tendencies of various norms. Third, because cross-cutting ties facilitate the identification and rewarding of 'champions of the public,' they enhance the possibility that a third-party Good Samaritan will exercise vicarious self-help to enforce norms." Anthropologists have long reported on gossip in small communities. Merry (1984) offers a review and ethnographic illustration that foreshadows Coleman's closure argument. She presents gossip as a reputation-production mechanism (Merry, 1984: 277, "Gossip is about reptuation, particularly lapses between claims to reputation and reports of actual behavior. ... One does not gossip about a prostitute who turns 'tricks,' but one does gossip about the respectable matron who is observed with men sneaking into her house day and night") and concludes that gossip's social-control potential is highest in what Coleman describes as a closed network (Merry, 1984: 277 and 296, "close-knit, highly connected social networks," and "bounded social systems in which the costs of desertion or expulsion are higher and the availability of alternative social relationships less").

Sociology is rich in closure arguments.[13] Granovetter's (1985, 1992) embeddedness metaphor is particularly well known. Trust is more likely

---

[12] Based on Heider's (1958) initial work, network balance and its extension, transitivity, was a popular application of cognitive consistency to social structure (e.g., Davis, 1970). Later work was primarily methodological, but balance continues to be discussed as an equilibrium of consistency between adjacent relations in a network (for review, see Burt, 1982: 55–60, 71–73; Wasserman and Faust, 1994: ch. 14; Doreian et al., 1996; Scott, 2000: 13–16; Doreian and Krackhardt, 2001; Kilduff and Tsai, 2003: 42–49, 70–75).

[13] For example, Gambetta (1988b), Bradach and Eccles (1989), Nohria and Eccles (1992), Swedberg (1993), several handbook chapters in Smelser and Swedberg (1994, esp. Powell and Smith-Doerr, 1994), and for empirical evidence Brass, Butterfield and Skaggs (1998), DiMaggio and Louch (1998), Gulati and Gargiulo (1999), Buskens and

between people with mutual friends ("structural" embeddedness, Granovetter, 1992: 44): "My mortification at cheating a friend of long standing may be substantial even when undiscovered. It may increase when the friend becomes aware of it. But it may become even more unbearable when our mutual friends uncover the deceit and tell one another." Trust was less of an issue in classical sociology, perhaps because roles were less ambiguously defined at the end of the nineteenth century, but network closure was a prominent theme. For example, Simmel (1902) described how relations were strengthened and empowered when embedded in third parties. The mere presence of a third party can calm disagreement (p. 170): "a gesture, a way of listening, the quality of feeling which proceeds from a person, suffices to give to this dissent between two others a direction toward consensus." And the dissent at issue is no more than the usual day-to-day frictions (p. 170): "The issue need by no means be a real strife or struggle. It is rather the thousand easy varieties of opinion, the jarring of an antagonism of natures, the emergence of quite momentary antitheses of interest or feeling, which color the fluctuating form of every association, and is constantly modified in its course by the presence of the third party." Krackhardt pursued Simmel's intuitions in empirical work, showing that embedded strong relations—termed "Simmelian ties"—are more stable than unembedded relations (Krackhardt, 1998) and more associated with opinion and behavior similarity between the connected people (Krackhardt, 1999; Krackhardt and Kilduf, 2002; cf. the discussion in Section 2.4 of ideas more contagious between people who are structurally equivalent). From another direction, Durkheim (1951 [1897]) argued in his influential empirical work on suicide for the importance of being surrounded by a dense network precisely for the regulation it provides on what would otherwise be unquenchable, and so maddening, desires.[14]

Weesie (2000). Lawler and Yoon (e.g. 1993, 1998) propose a "theory of relational cohesion" that stands uniquely intermediate between the arguments in Sections 3.1.1 and 3.1.2. Consistent with the cumulative build in social exchange theory (Section 3.1.1), Lawler and Yoon predict that trust and commitment emerge from escalating exchanges, emphasizing the "emotional buzz" associated with positive exchange. They go on to predict where certain relations develop and others do not as a function of location in network structure. Where the structure of alternative contacts in a system of peers makes certain pairs of people more likely to have positive initial exchanges with one another, that likelihood, however slight, encourages further exchange, which can be expected to create clusters of dense, positive relations (cf. Feld, 1981, on social foci).

[14] One of Durkheim's illustrations is the contrast between Protestants and Catholics, and his use of the two religions as social types corresponds to the comparison in Figure 1.1 between Robert and James respectively (Durkheim, 1951 [1897]: 158): "The only essential difference between Catholicism and Protestantism is that the second permits free inquiry to a far greater degree than the first ... the Catholic accepts his faith ready made, without scrutiny... A whole hierarchical system of authority is devised, with marvelous ingenuity, to render tradition invariable. All variation is abhorrent to Catholic thought. The Protestant is far more the author of his faith." Durkheim argues that

3.2   Evidence of Trust

The hypothesis for this section is that strong and positive third-party ties between two people invoke closure's reputation mechanism, which lowers the risk for either person trusting the other, making trust more likely.[15] Mizruchi (1992: ch. 4) offers a thorough review toward the conclusion that density needs to be distinguished from business unity, but it is more usual to see network density, or network closure more generally, cited as an antecedent to trust and cooperation.

3.2.1   *Anecdotal Evidence*

There is abundant anecdotal evidence of trust associated with closure. The speed, saturation, evaluation, and reputation-definition associated with closure are discussed under labels such as cohesive groups, strong cultures, teams,

---

the higher suicide rates among Protestants can be attributed to the lack of regulation that their religion provides. Religion can resolve unanswerable questions through social consensus, but religion's social authority is less where individuals are in some significant way free to craft their own religion. A consequential line of future research would be to see how the network constraint associated with lack of success is associated with mental health. A beginning point is that the coordination required by brokerage subjects network entrepreneurs to high stress (e.g., divorce, heart attack) but success and engagement in work is emotionally positive; living well at higher velocity (e.g., Sieber, 1974; Coser, 1975; Marks, 1977).

[15] Conversely, the more negative third-party ties—in which the people you trust distrust the other person and people close to the other person distrust you—the more likely you will be distrusted. Closure predicts who is distrusted as well as who is trusted, but research has focused on the trust-inducing effect of closure so that is my focus in this chapter. The negative side is addressed in the next chapter. I mention negative ties here because closure evidence of balance in relations can be stronger for positive than negative third-party ties. If the reputation advantages of treating friends well is matched by advantages from abusing enemies, then sanctions discouraging abusive behavior between colleagues with mutual friends could exist along with sanctions encouraging abuse of people distrusted by one's friends—as is explicit in Greif's (1989: 868) analysis of the Maghribi traders who felt free to cheat ostracized traders. But the Maghribi had a relatively stable boundary between insiders and outsiders. Consider a structure in which boundaries change, as is typical of the boundaries between groups in an organization. A colleague capable of abusing someone today who is not "one of us," is capable of abusing you tomorrow if you are no longer one of us. The more complex and dynamic an environment, the more likely that social boundaries between us and them change. The result of abusive behavior, even if consistent with group values today, is that the abuser acquires a reputation for being someone capable of abuse. Abusive behavior, even if directed toward today's legitimate targets, has ambiguous signal value in terms of reputation (see Gambetta, 1993, on "endogenous distrust" created by the Mafia making it honorable to abuse people not under the Mafia's protection, thereby weakening reputation as a control mechanism for the market as a whole). The one unambiguous prediction from the reputation mechanism in closure is that positive third-party ties increase the probability of cooperative behavior.

and cults. The discussions are alike in describing a closed network within which reputation is controlled such that individuals can be trusted to collaborate within the group.

For example, I begin my class on the closure argument with a video of people from a successful team discussing their work together. I use a video segment on the Data General team under Tom West that produced the Eclipse minicomputer in 1980 (described for a general audience by Kidder, 1981, and see the retrospectives in Ratliff, 2000; Peters, 2002), or a video segment on the Apple Computer team under Steve Jobs that produced the Macintosh microcomputer in 1984 ("In Search of Excellence" video, 1988, illustrating Peters and Waterman, 1982). The task put to viewers is to look for qualities of the people and their conversations that indicate membership in a strong team.

To guard against learning resistance because people on the videotaped teams are so young and the computer industry unique, I offer examples of similar group dynamics in different settings. The interpersonal dynamics of closed networks transcend time and task (but video coverage is spotty). There are local contemporary examples in a recent newspaper or magazine of basketball teams, elite business clubs, fire-fighting teams, movie-production teams, navy seal teams, race-car pit crews, or string quartets. There are also examples in academic discussions of closure such as Coleman's above-cited discussions of rotating credit associations and the Jewish diamond exchange. Back in time, there are examples in other industries such as the Ericsson team sequestered in Lund, Sweden away from company headquarters to develop the company's first hand-held mobile phone in 1987 (Meurling and Jeans, 1997); or the Lockheed skunk works in Burbank, California, responsible in 1944 for America's first jet fighter, America's famous spy planes, the U-2 and SR-71 Blackbird, and the F-117A stealth fighter in 1982 (Rich and Janos, 1994). Further back in time are the Bolsheviks under Lenin in the 1910s, the Jesuits under St. Ignatius and the subsequent itinerant integration of Jesuit schools by Nadal in the 1500s (Coser, 1973; O'Malley, 1993), or the Maghribi traders in the 1000s Mediterranean (Greif, 1989). Connecting into the academic literature on organizations, Barker (1993) provides a succinctly rich ethnographic account of closure in operation (for a broad overview, see O'Reilly and Chatman, 1996: 174–187). He describes the emergence of a new control system as a small (150 employees) manufacturing company moved in 1988 from a traditional bureaucratic chain of command to greater self-management within production teams. Barker's (1993: 418) orienting question to employees asks how control practices in the new environment are different from the practices in place before the change to teams. One employee complained that (Barker, 1993: 408), "he felt more closely watched now than when he worked under the company's old bureaucratic system. He said that while his old supervisor might tolerate someone coming in a few minutes late, for example, his team had adopted a 'no tolerance' policy on tardiness and that members monitored their own behaviors carefully." As the employee summarized (Barker, 1993:

408): "Now the whole team is around me and the whole team is observing what I'm doing."

Following the video, what emerges in discussion is a list of qualities describing closure-enforced control through reputation (Morris and Marsh, 1988, offer compelling photo illustration to display as points are raised). The qualities are alike in indicating a strong beetle-like shell around the group, a boundary between insiders and outsiders. This is evident, in a general way, from the lack of concrete knowledge, or the abundance of stereotypical knowledge, that insiders have about the outside world. "One of us" is an oft-heard term of endearment. Trust is strong and widely distributed inside the group, but markedly absent outside the group.

A quality always mentioned early in discussion of video evidence is the enthusiastic group alignment around a goal not appreciated outside the group. People are enthusiastic. They describe sharing a common goal. In fact, sharing their goal was a feature of being on the team. As one misty-eyed Macintosh person explains, "There is nothing like a group effort toward a common goal to unite people. That was the deal."

More than sharing a goal, there is a sense of mission. The group is after a transcendental goal bigger than everyday life. "I'm not doing this for the money." "I'm not doing this for Steve Jobs." "This is a chance to change something, really, honestly, truly, for the better." "And everybody just wanted to work; not because it was work that had to be done, but because it was something we really believed in, that was just going to really make a difference. And that's what kept the whole thing going." The sense of importance is explicit when Tom West invites a marketing manager to explain to the Eclipse team that their project is going to be worth a billion dollars a year to the company.

The sense of importance has a personal side heard in statements about the opportunities people had to do things in the group that they would not have been able to do in the outside world. An Eclipse person explained that work on the project was also a question of personal survival. With the concentration of company resources in an alternative project in North Carolina, "The company had seemed to say that you're just going to do diddly stuff. You know, you're not going to do anything important to DG [Data General]. There was an element of, we've got to prove, to the company, that we can do very important work, and the company's going to have to depend on us." A Macintosh person who had been elevated to a position of significant responsibility explained, "There's no way, in the world, that anybody would give me this chance to run this kind of operation. I don't kid myself about that. This is an incredibly high risk, both for myself personally and professionally, and for Apple as a company, to put a person like myself in this job." "This is a place where people were afforded incredibly unique opportunities that they could do; they could write the book again."

Remarks about personal importance continue into personal ownership and responsibility for the project. This is manifest in statements about "that's mine," or "I did that," but integrity of ownership in a group project is contributing your share. As one Eclipse person explained: "Since Jim is killing himself; I mean he's here every night until three in the morning. I'd almost feel guilty if I wasn't working so hard. I want it to be as much my project as much as it is his." A manufacturing person in Barker's (1993: 422) study feels guilty about an incomplete shipment: "I feel bad, believe it or not. Last Friday, we missed a shipment. I feel like I missed the shipment since I'm the last person that sees what goes to ship." Another employee comments (Barker, 1993: 422): "Under the old system, who gave a hoot if the boards shipped today or not? We just did our jobs. Now, we have more buy-in by the team members. We feel more personal responsibly for the product."

Peer pressure and stronger corrective action is there if you don't feel guilty (Hackman, 1976). Another of Barker's (1993: 425) people explained: "If you notice that somebody's not getting anything done, then we can bring it up at a [team] meeting, you know, and ask them what the problem is, what's causing them not to be able to get their work done." As Jobs describes his Macintosh team: "The greatest people are self-managing. They don't need to be managed. Once they know what to do, they'll go figure out how to do it. They don't need to be managed at all." If peer pressure is not enough, the team can remove the problematic person, as one sympathetic co-worker sighed to Barker while her team was meeting to fire someone caught loafing (Barker, 1993: 427): "They're back there, judge, jury, and executioners."

The peer pressure can be stressful. This is closure's counterpart to the brokerage tension of coordinating divergent interests. A manufacturing person in Barker's (1993: 432) study expressed it well: "After you've been here awhile, you're gonna get super-involved, then you're gonna get burned out. I see this with person after person. You get really involved, you take it home with you, you eat with it, you sleep with it. You work 12, 16-hour days and you just burn out. You may step out just a bit, let someone else get supper-involved for awhile, then you'll pick it up again. But you won't have that enthusiasm anymore."

The sense of mission is defined in part by powerful, threatening forces outside the group. DEC was a cited threat to the Data General team, whose goal was to build a "VAX killer." IBM was a cited threat for the Macintosh team, whose goal was to build a microcomputer for "the rest of us." Those are death-dealing external threats. Then there is the closer-to-home threat of colleagues who "don't get it." For the Eclipse team it was company bureaucrats focused on an alternative effort in North Carolina. Tom West asked people on the team not to discuss their work outside the team in the hope that the secrecy would promote their interdependence and avert intervention by senior company officials intent on focusing company resources on the effort in North Carolina. For the Macintosh team it was Apple bureaucrats enjoying ample revenues from their current machines such that they did not understand the critical importance of Apple developing the Macintosh to counter IBM's entry into the microcomputer market. Steve Jobs is cited by one Macintosh team member for "giving us space" and "sheltering us from the corporate noise." For the Jesuits, the problematic colleagues were the monks, well-established across Europe but too withdrawn from the world to effectively counter the Protestant threat (Coser, 1973).

A strong boundary between inside and outside is also indicated by special treatment given to things that cross the boundary. The stronger the boundary around a group, the more likely the group has rite of passage to mark the transition from being a heathen outsider to saved insider (Gennep, 1960 [1908]). For the Eclipse and Macintosh teams, the rite of passage was an arduous recruitment ritual (arduous, not rigorous). As Jobs described the Macintosh team: "When you get a core group of ah, ten great people, it becomes self-policing as to who they let into that group." Examples are the hazing that precedes entry to a fraternity, the process of losing ribbons of shame in company executive education programs, the more-rigorous training required to enter elite corps, the circumcision or other scarring required to claim adult membership in a group, or the process by which food is certified as appropriate for insiders to eat.

More generally, the group has symbols of its identity separate from the outside world. This can be as simple as a separate physical location, such as the basement corner occupied by the Eclipse team, the Macintosh building across the street from Apple headquarters, IBM's microcomputer group in Florida distant from company headquarters in New York, or the Lund cell phone group distant from Ericsson headquarters in Stockholm. The separation can be more symbolic, such as the pirate flag that the Macintosh team flew over its building to indicate that they were running across the grain of corporate America and the Apple bureaucracy across the street (Apple employees were the people most exposed to the pirate flag). Dress code is a related symbol of separate identity. Examples are the casual dress among Apple employees, the formal dress in old IBM, Yakuza tattoos, the plain look of the Amish, the specialized look of Orthodox groups, the Shriner *fez*, or the theme shirts worn by people attending the same event.

More symbolic still is the language used at work. The word "shibboleth" refers to a catchword or slogan used by insiders but regarded by outsiders as meaningless. The term comes from a biblical story in which members of the Ephraimites tribe could not pronounce shibboleth (no "h") so an opposing tribe that could pronounce the word used it as a password to identify and kill Ephraimites. A common shibboleth is the elevation of the group leader to charismatic status with well-rehearsed insider stories about his or her behavior. The video evidence includes drab stories drawing appreciative eye contact between team members (e.g., a laughter-inducing story in the Eclipse video about Tom West being upset when he heard team members discussing the project on their CB radios). Contemporary shibboleths include academic jargon, repetition within the group of jokes not funny outside the group, the use of simple codes such as Pig Latin or the acronyms referencing programs and technologies, or the use of work concepts to describe behavior outside work as "I applied an ECO to my love life" (Engineering Change Order). The shibboleths are signals of whole stories for insiders, encoded experiences that mark insiders from outsiders.

Knowledge is its own category of shibboleth because of its implications for brokerage. As people work together, they accumulate experience about the work. Some of that experience is recorded in published records. Much remains in stories and assumptions. People develop what Weick and Roberts (1993) describe as a "group mind" in which individuals know their role in the group. Role is something more than task. Experienced people of a group mind certainly know the task they are assigned to do, but what is more, they know how their assigned task affects tasks assigned to other people, and they adjust to coordinate with the others. To see group mind at work, Weick and Roberts go to a setting in which it would be dangerous for people not to function as an integrated group. They study coordination on an aircraft-carrier flight deck, a setting described by an insider as follows (Rochlin, LaPorte, and Roberts, 1987: 78):

imagine that it's a busy day, and you shrink San Francisco Airport down to only one short runway and one ramp and one gate. Make planes take off and land at the same time, at half the present time interval, rock the runway from side to side, and require that everyone who leaves in the morning returns that same day. Make sure the equipment is so close to the edge of the envelope that it's fragile. Then turn off the radar to avoid detection, impose strict controls on radios, fuel the aircraft in place with their engines running, put an enemy in the air, and scatter live bombs and rockets around. Now wet the whole thing down with sea water and oil, and man it with 20-year-olds, half of whom have never seen an airplane close-up. Oh and by the way, try not to kill anyone.

Action in this setting is a coordinated effort. For example, Weick and Roberts (1993) explain that planes do not land on an aircraft carrier, they are recovered: "And recovery is a set of interrelated activities among air traffic controllers, landing signal officers, the control tower, navigators, deck hands, the helmsman driving the ship, etc. As the recovery of a single aircraft nears completion in the form of a successful trap, nine to ten people on the landing signal officer's platform, up to fifteen more people in the tower, and two to three more people on the bridge observe the recovery and can wave the aircraft off if there is a problem." Weick and Roberts (1993) argue that the pressure to coordinate gives rise to a group mind among experienced people. People who work on a flight deck must surely feel distinguished from people who have never had the experience. More generally, we are brought together by any group experience we have that is not shared by the outsiders we meet. Where experience distinguishes insiders from outsiders, it is likely to be encoded in a story that insiders share with one another and with newcomers to revel in their separate identity. Examples would be stories about a dangerous event that the insiders escaped, or a breakthrough victory for the group, especially if it involved great good luck, or a display of outsider dismay or foolishness. Other shared experience remains unstated, taken for granted (the deepest kind of blinder to alternative beliefs and practice). Examples would be the boundary conditions at which a model breaks down such as a degree of cold, miles of height, or level of debris. There are often elements in an otherwise functional model that are especially sensitive to alternative model specifications. There are tolerances that one metal press can handle better than an adjacent press. There is one sales agent you can trust more than your others on a certain kind of client call. These are unwritten bits of knowledge accumulated while working together. Whether experience is encoded in a symbolic story or left as an assumption about work inside the network, the encoded experience is tacit knowledge that is especially difficult to coordinate between groups. Moving such knowledge is a task for which the vision advantage of brokerage is especially valuable (discussed in Section 3.3).

In discussing the anecdotal video evidence, viewers get a feel for the way closure works and can offer sensible illustrations from their own experience. They can cite examples of people trusting one another and spot indicators of closure facilitating the trust. However, their instances of trust occurring with closure are not evidence of trust associated with closure. For that, they need to see how the probability of trust changes with levels of network closure.

3.2.2   Comparative Evidence

The results in Figure 3.3 show trust associated with closure in two populations. The left-hand graph describes trust and closure around the senior managers introduced in Figure 3.2A. The graph to the right describes the staff officers in two financial firms introduced in Figure 3.2B. As in Figure 3.2, the vertical axis in Figure 3.3 measures the percentage of column contacts cited for trust. The horizontal axis distinguishes contacts by their strength of connection with the survey respondent. After naming key contacts for information, advice, and political support, respondents were asked to distinguish contacts with whom they felt "especially close," "close," "less close," or "distant." For Figure 3.3, the "especially close" contacts are strong ties. The "less close" and "distant" contacts are weak ties. Trust is clearly a correlate of relationship strength, especially in the strongest relationships.[16] Trust is more likely in close relations

---

[16] Statistical tests for alternative specifications are reported elsewhere (Burt and Knez, 1995; Burt, 2001). Logit regression models show very strong associations between trust and relation strength in Figure 3.3; 16.54 z-score for the senior managers, 15.30 z-score for the staff officers, and 18.38 z-score for the bankers to be presented in Figure 3.4. Test statistics are corrected for autocorrelation between relations cited by the same person (e.g., Kish and Frankel, 1974).

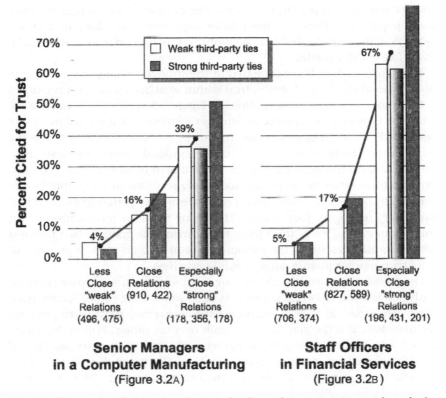

**Senior Managers
in a Computer Manufacturing**
(Figure 3.2A)

**Staff Officers
in Financial Services**
(Figure 3.2B)

Fig. 3.3: Trust amplified in closed networks. Parentheses contain number of relations embedded in (weak, strong) third-party ties

than in weak ones (16% versus 4% respectively for the managers, 17% and 5% for the staff officers), but it is much more likely in especially close relations, increasing to 39% among the managers and 67% for the officers.

Gray and white bars in Figure 3.3 show the increment of trust associated with closing the network around a relationship. Closure is measured here by the strength of indirect connection between two people through colleagues as third parties.[17] Gray bars refer to relationships in which respondent and

---

[17] The indirect connection between manager i and contact j through third-party k is the product of two relations (these are symmetric network data): the link between i and k, and the link between k and j. Let z_{jk} be a measure of the strength of the relationship between j and k. The managers and staff officers were asked to indicate the strength of connection between their contacts. Contacts could be "especially close" in the sense that they communicated often enough to be familiar with one another's operations, "distant" in the sense that the contacts were total strangers or would rather not spend time together, or "other" in the sense of being somewhere between the extremes of "especially close" and "distant." The response data for relations were scaled 1.0 for

contact were connected through third parties more than average for their study population. These are the relationships more embedded in a closed network. Call them "embedded" relations. White bars refer to relations relatively free of third parties.

The network effect is concentrated in the strongest relationships. Closure does not increase the probably of trust within weak relations. Trust is cited in 3.4% of the embedded weak relations in Figure 3.3 versus 4% of other weak relations. Closure matters more for stronger relations. Trust is cited in 21% of embedded "close" relations versus 16% of other "close" relations. The big jump in trust happens when third parties surround "especially close" relations.[18] Because the network effect is concentrated in strong relations, I distinguish three levels of closure around strong relations in the graphs: white bars describe the strong relations relatively free of third parties (bottom 25% of third-party ties), gray bars describe the strong relations most embedded in third parties (top 75% of third-party ties), leaving the gradient bars between white and gray describing the relations embedded in an average presence of third parties (interquartile range of third-party ties).

The probability of trust within strong relations does not increase continuously across levels of closure. Trust is as likely in the least embedded relationships (white bar) as it is in relations with an average third-party presence (gradient bar). It is the gray bar that stands over the others. Half of the strong embedded relations among the managers were cited for trust (versus 36% of their less-embedded strong relations) and three-fourths of the strong embedded relations among the officers were cited for trust (versus 62% of their less-embedded strong relations).

I see in Figure 3.3 three categories of relationship with respect to trust. For each category, Table 3.1 lists the probability of trust. Trust is unlikely in weak relations whether they are embedded or not (first row of Table 3.1). The probability increases substantially in a strong relationship even if there is a weak or average third-party presence around the relationship (second row). The probability increases again if the strong relation is embedded in a strong third-party presence (third row). Relations in the third row are what Krackhardt (1998, 1999) terms "Simmelian ties" to highlight the stability and

---

"especially close", 0.0 for "distant," and .34 estimated for "other" (Burt, 1992: 287–288). The strength of third-party connection between i and j is the sum of indirect connections through third-parties k, $\Sigma_k z_{jk} z_{ki}$, $i \neq k \neq j$. Gray bars in Figure 3.3 refer to relations embedded in third-party connections higher than average for their study population.

[18] My qualitative statements about negligible and large effects here are based on statistical tests for increases in trust. The difference between the gray and white bars over weak relations in Figure 3.3 is statistically negligible (-1.17 z-score with a control for difference between the managers and officers, P = .22). The association between trust and closure across "close" relations is statistically significant (2.76 z-score, P < .01), but much less than the association between trust and closure across "especially close" relations (5.86 z-score, P < .001).

Table 3.1: Percent of relationships cited for trust (number of relations at risk of citation are given in parentheses corresponding to Figures 3.3 and 3.4)

Direct Connection	Indirect Connection	Senior Managers	Staff Officers	Bankers
Weak or Average	Weak or Strong	11.3%	11.9%	25.9%
		(2,303)	(2,496)	(11,311)
Strong	Weak or Average	36.0%	62.2%	60.5%
		(534)	(627)	(989)
Strong	Strong	51.1%	82.6%	75.8%
		(178)	(201)	(355)
	Total	18.0%	25.6%	30.0%
		(3,015)	(3,324)	(12,655)

influence created when a strong relationship is embedded in mutual friends, colleagues, and acquaintances as third parties to the relationship. Compare rows in Table 3.1 to determine the relative importance of relational and structural embedding. Differences between the rows are all statistically significant, but the magnitude of increase associated with closure around a strong relationship is about half the increase associated with having a strong relationship.[19] This harks back to Granovetter's (1985: 490) observation that relational embedding is preferred to structural in that better information comes "from one's own past dealings" with a person.

A drawback to the evidence in Figure 3.3 is that relation strength is measured at the same time as trust. With trust sometimes used to define strong relations, the association between trust and relation strength in Figure 3.3 could be dismissed as no more than respondent consistency.[20]

---

[19] For the managers in Table 3.1, the second row is 25 points higher than the first, and the third is 15 points higher than the second. The increment for embedding strong relations is 60% of the strong-tie increment (15 is 60% of 25). For the staff officers, the embedding increment is 40% of the strong-tie increment (20 points versus 50). For the bankers, the embedding increment is 43% of the strong-tie increment (15 points versus 35). Chi-square tests for differences across the rows in Table 3.1 are 250.50 for the managers, 386.09 for the officers, and 325.10 for the bankers, all of which clearly reject the hypothesis of trust independent of the rows (P < .001, 2 d.f., statistics adjusted down for autocorrelation between relations cited by the same survey respondent).

[20] I made an effort to hold constant the history of relationships by holding constant the duration and frequency of contact. Respondents were asked about duration ("How long have you known each person?") and frequency ("On average, how often do you talk to each?"). Consistent with social exchange theory (Section 3.1.1) and the results in Figure 3.2, stronger relations occur between people who often talk to one another or have known one another for a long time, but the effects displayed in Figure 3.3 are robust to controls for frequency and duration (see Burt, 2001). Frequency has no direct association with trust when added to the statistical models predicting trust or distrust. Duration has a direct association with trust, but the key trust associations with strong ties and third parties remain strong. The trust effects of frequency and duration are entirely or largely mediated through their association with relation strength measured by emotional closeness, which is associated with trust as illustrated in Figure 3.3.

Therefore, the results in Figure 3.4 are useful for two reasons. First, trust is measured a year after the network data used to measure closure, so there is a proper sequence to the data. Time order is not causal order, but it is reassuring to see the Figure 3.3 results with cross-sectional data reappear in Figure 3.4 where there is a proper sequence to the data. Second, the data in Figure 3.4 make it possible to see a more continuous representation of the association between trust and closure.

The data in Figure 3.4 come from two annual surveys within the investment division of a large financial organization. The respondents, whom I will discuss as "bankers," include senior people responsible for making and closing deals, as well as people in administrative positions who manage bankers in lower ranks, or manage analysts who service the bankers. These are the bankers in Figure 1.5E, which shows the brokerage association with relative bonus compensation. The two surveys providing network data were annual peer evaluations in which employee named colleagues with whom they had frequent and substantial business in the preceding year. There are 345 "bankers" citing colleagues in their own and other divisions of the organization. A total of 12,655 relationships were cited.[21] Bankers were asked to make a summary evaluation of their cited colleagues as *poor* (persons receiving multiple poor evaluations were encouraged in the company to look for a different line of work), *adequate* (a negative evaluation akin to the grade of C in graduate school), *good*, or *outstanding*. Poor to outstanding are my synonyms for the words actually used in the peer evaluations. To compute measures of direct and indirect connection, I assembled the contact network around each banker by searching through the peer evaluations for the banker's cited contacts, contacts citing the banker, and peer evaluations between the contacts.[22]

---

[21] The 12,655 cited relations are 8,298 to colleagues in the division (insiders) and 4,357 to colleagues in other divisions of the company (outsiders). Trust and distrust are similarly associated with third parties within and beyond the division (Burt, 2001: 66–67).

[22] I assigned to the banker data arbitrary quantitative scores consistent with opinion in the organization: 1.0 for a maximum evaluation (outstanding), .5 for middle evaluations (.5 for good, −.5 for adequate), and −1.0 for the minimum (poor), leaving zero for disconnections between colleagues who do not cite one another. For the purposes of this section, I measure banker third-party ties in terms of their absolute magnitude (i.e., third-party connection between i and j is $\sum_k |z_{ik} z_{kj}|$ across all colleagues k, excluding i and j themselves), postponing directed ties to the next chapter. The choice between direction and magnitude is only a choice in the banker networks (network data on the other two study populations only describe variably positive connections between contacts), and results on directed ties in the next chapter show that the banker relations are balanced in intensity not direction (Figure 4.3), so absolute magnitude is the appropriate measure of third-party ties in this section.

Consistent with descriptions of investment banking in the business press (e.g., Eccles and Crane, 1988; Lewis, 1989), the image I infer from the network data is a social system loosely integrated at the macro level but tightly integrated at the micro level. Most of a banker's colleagues do not cite one another. Citation density varies across time and bankers from zero up to 84.4%, around an average of 27.3%. The 27.3% average means that one in four pairs of colleagues are connected by a citation. The organization is too large for every person to have frequent and substantial business contact every year with every other person. More importantly, redundant communication channels and peer pressure enforcing social norms do not require global density if there are overlapping spheres of local density. Although most of a banker's colleagues do not cite one another, almost every relationship with a colleague is embedded in third-party ties. In fact, the average banker–colleague relationship is embedded in eight third-party ties, five of them positive. Density is low within the banker networks, but almost every banker relation with a colleague exists in a social setting of third parties.

In addition to a summary evaluation, bankers evaluated colleagues for specific qualities. Trust was one of the qualities. Figure 3.4 shows how the probability of a colleague being cited for trust this year varies with the strength of the banker–colleague relationship last year. Trust here means that the colleague was given the most positive evaluation for *cooperation* in reaching collective goals, and *integrity* in sharing information and responsibility for disappointing results (again, cooperation and integrity are my synonyms for the terms actually used in the peer evaluations).

The graph to the left in Figure 3.4 looks just like the two graphs in Figure 3.3, except now the outcome happens a year after the predictor. Trust this year increases systematically with the strength of the relationship in place last year. The several thousand relations new this year are a mixture of strengths. They are cited for trust more often than last year's negative relations, about the same as last year's "good" relations, and much less than "outstanding" relations. The probability of trust increases disproportionately in relations that were "outstanding" last year. Trust increases with closure around last year's relationship, especially in an "outstanding" relationship. The third column in Table 3.1, summarizing the left-graph in Figure 3.4, shows a pattern of trust similar to the patterns in the first two columns, summarizing Figure 3.3.

Graphs such as Figure 3.3 and the one to the left in Figure 3.4 show closure associated with trust within existing relations. But what of relations with colleagues who were not cited as the most frequent and substantial business contacts? Analysis of existing relations under-represents situations in which closure occurs without producing trust.

The graph to the right in Figure 3.4 is a more thorough test of the closure argument—and it yields results consistent with the results already reported. The data are all possible relations among the bankers, that is 118,680 relations from one banker to another (345 bankers times 344 other bankers as potential

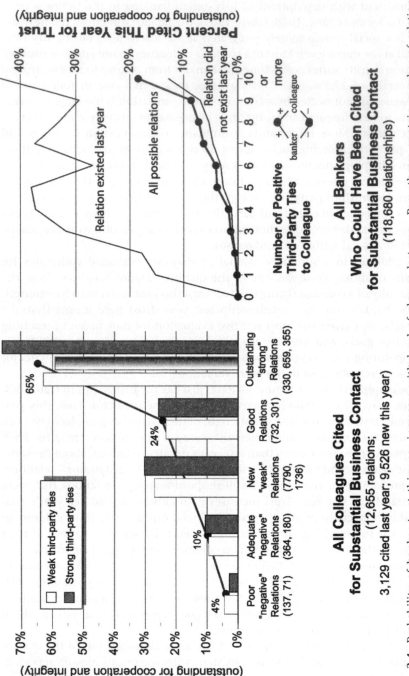

**All Colleagues Cited
for Substantial Business Contact**
(12,655 relations;
3,129 cited last year; 9,526 new this year)

**All Bankers
Who Could Have Been Cited
for Substantial Business Contact**
(118,680 relationships)

Fig. 3.4: Probability of banker trust this year increases with level of closure last year. Parentheses contain number of relations embedded in (weak, strong) third-party ties

colleagues).[23] The horizontal axis in the graph shows the number of positive third-party ties connecting each pair of bankers, as illustrated in the sociogram below the horizontal axis. A positive third-party tie between banker and colleague occurs in either of two ways: the banker made a positive evaluation of someone who made a positive evaluation of the colleague (a friend of a friend is a friend), or the banker made a negative evaluation of someone who made a negative evaluation of the colleague (an enemy of a friend is an enemy).[24]

The bold line in the graph shows trust increasing with the number of third parties connecting banker and colleague. The other two lines show how closure interacts with a pre-existing relationship. Most pairs of bankers in year two did not have extensive work together in the previous year, so the aggregate (bold) line in the graph looks like the thin line below it describing trust in relations that were not cited last year. Trust in a colleague not cited last year increases slowly with closure. However, if the banker did have extensive work with the colleague last year, the thin line at the top of the graph shows a dramatic increase in the probability of trust with one, two, and three mutual contacts. After three mutual contacts, trust is already high and increases only slightly.[25] The difference between the two thin lines in the graph shows how closure works with a pre-existing relationship. Embedding a new relationship in mutual contacts increases the probability of trust within the relationship (lower thin line in the graph), but the effect is dramatically higher and faster if the relationship is on-going (upper thin line). This is a detailed view of the gray

---

[23] The graph to the left in Figure 3.4 shows the 12,655 relations cited by the bankers. Of the 118,680 relationships in the right-hand graph that could have been cited, 8,298 were (7% density). The other 4,357 banker citations were to colleagues elsewhere in the organization. I do not know the density of citations to other divisions because I do not know the number of colleagues at risk of being cited. However, I know that 431 colleagues were cited in other divisions. There are 148,695 possible relations from the 345 bankers to the 431 outsiders, of which 4,357 were cited, defining a 3% density of citations to outsiders. The 3% is higher than the true density because there are more than 431 colleagues in other divisions who could have been cited, but 3% is significantly lower than the 7% density among the bankers so I feel comfortable focusing on relations within the division (−21.3 logit z-score). Note that this kind of analysis is not possible in the two Figure 3.3 populations, as in most survey network studies, because I do not have data on relations between contacts cited by different survey respondents.

[24] The association with trust is strong for both kinds of positive third-party ties, though stronger for friends of friends than for enemies of enemies. Statistical results are available elsewhere (Burt, 2001: 59) holding constant last year's relationship and the number of third parties available to a banker as possible indirect ties to colleagues.

[25] Logit models predicting a banker–colleague trust citation from the number of mutual contacts between them show statistically significant association for relations embedded in zero to three third parties (17.26 z-score, with adjustment for autocorrelation between relations involving the same banker) and for relations embedded in four or more third parties (23.96 z-score). However, the slope of association is much steeper for the initial interval; 1.08 logit coefficient for zero to three mutual contacts versus .39 after three mutual contacts.

bar being so much higher than the other two bars over "especially close" relations in Figure 3.3 and the graph to the left in Figure 3.4.

The evidence seems sufficient to conclude that trust is associated with closure. This is not to say that closure is a guarantee of trust or safety. In Figures 3.3 and 3.4, there are many people connected by strong relations embedded in closed networks who did not cite one another for trust.[26] Granovetter (1985: 487–493; 1992: 43–47) stresses the lack of guarantee in his embeddedness argument: "the trust engendered by personal relations presents, by its very existence, enhanced opportunity for malfeasance" (1992: 43). The point can be illustrated with examples of trust violated (e.g., almost half of fraud cases involve victims who had a prior relationship with the offender),[27] or it can be illustrated by bonds of collaborative malfeasance broken (e.g., cracking price-fixing cartels by creating a law by which there is a promise not to prosecute the cartel firm that first reports the other firms in the cartel, Spratling, 2001). The point is also illustrated by the difficulty of collective action against deviant members, such that a higher power is often invoked to enforce the action and prevent defectors to the collective action (e.g., employees calling on a higher-rank person to fire a disruptive colleague, Greif's, 1989: 863, Maghribi traders appealing to the broader Jewish community to impose social sanctions against another trader, or Platteau's, 1994, examples for his broader argument that the higher power, not closure, is the critical factor responsible for trust in closed networks, p. 564: "Private and public order institutions are required and recourse to coercive power cannot be escaped"). In sum, the argument linking trust and closure is that closure creates a reputation cost for bad behavior, which decreases, without eliminating, risks that would otherwise inhibit trust. Available anecdotal and comparative evidence supports the argument.

3.3 Evidence of Social Capital

In a sense, the case for network closure being social capital has just been made. If it is an advantage to live among friends engaged in a society of trust, and network closure increases the probability of such a life, closure is social

---

[26] Subtract from 100% the gray bar over "strong" relations in each graph. That is 49% of the strong senior-manager relations embedded in strong third-party ties, 17% of the strong staff-officer relations embedded in strong third-party ties, and 24% of the strong banker relations embedded in strong third-party ties.

[27] The percentage is from Shapiro's (1984: 34–35) exceptional access to files of the Securities and Exchange Commission (cited by Granovetter, 1992: 43, to illustrate limits to embedding; also see footnote one to this chapter). The exact percentages that Shapiro reports for prior relationship between victim and perpetrator are 40% strangers, 12% some kind of relationship, 10% professional relationship, 9% friends or family, and 29% prior relationship could not be determined. "Almost half" in the text refers to 46% of cases in which a prior relationship is known or ruled out.

capital. Though legitimate, such a conclusion is unproductive because it segregates closure from brokerage. Closure provides a reputation mechanism associated with happy and safe, while brokerage provides a vision mechanism associated with achievement and rewards. To get to the foundation for integrating closure with brokerage, trace closure to the benefits it provides beyond trust. By lowering the risk associated with trust, closure leads to advantages that would otherwise be unlikely or impossible, and in providing those advantages closure is social capital.

3.3.1   *Three Examples*

There is a large literature on the social capital of closure, but for a moment consider three early and widely-known contributions.

Coleman and the High-School Students

Coleman (1988) promulgated the concept of social capital to explain network effects in his research on educational achievement. For students at risk of dropping out, there can be a free-rider problem among adults in that parents rely on teachers to keep the student in school, teachers rely on parents to motivate the student to stay in school, and neighbors can ignore the whole issue with a simple "he's not my kid." When the adults in a child's life are connected with one another, each reinforces the others in pushing the child to complete his or her education.

Coleman (1988; 1990: 590–597) presents three bits of evidence to show that children living within closed networks of adults are less likely to drop out of high school: First, children in families with two parents and few children are less likely to drop out of high school. Two parents living together can more effectively than two parents living apart collaborate in the supervision of a child. Second, children who have lived in the same neighborhood all their lives are less likely to drop out of high school. Parents, teachers, and other people in the neighborhood are more likely to know one another and collaborate in the supervision of a child than can parents new to the neighborhood. Third, children in Catholic and other religious private schools are less likely to drop out. Parents, teachers, and parents of the child's friends at the private schools are more likely, relative to adults in the same roles in a public school, to know one another and collaborate in the supervision of a child.

Greif and the Maghribi Traders

At the time that Coleman was studying the high-school students, a graduate student in economics was finishing what was to become a celebrated dissertation on closure and reputation. Greif (1989) describes how closure operated among the eleventh-century Maghribi traders. The Maghribi were middle-class Jews in North Africa whose trade by boat and caravan spanned the Mediterranean. Business was risky in that sale prices and dates were unknown at the time that a merchant invested in a shipment. Greif (1989: 860) notes:

A journey from Egypt to Sicily, for example, could take 13 to 50 days, and ships did not always reach their destination. Within the ship the goods were not well sheltered and were often damaged in transit. Furthermore, as the captain of the ship was not responsible for packing, loading, and unloading the goods, there was always the possibility that he or the crew would pilfer the goods.

Merchants developed a system to manage the delivery and sale of goods (Greif, 1993: 528):

Agency relations among the Maghribis were extremely flexible, as merchants operated through several agents at the same time and even at the same trade center and seem to have been at ease initiating and canceling agency relations ... Agency relations enabled the Maghribi traders to reduce the cost of trade by better allocating risk through diversification, by benefiting from agents' expertise, and by shifting trade activities across trade centers, goods, and time.

With investment separated from return by a logistics nightmare, the flexible agency relations required trust because of the incentives for dishonesty. An agent could sell your shipment at a good price, then give you a fraction of your share of the profits explaining that another boat arrived before yours, lowering the price for your shipment.

Network closure could make trust practical. Active correspondence between trade centers enabled traders to monitor behavior. Traders only employed other Maghribi as agents (excluding, for example, potentially lucrative agency relations with Italian Jews), and acted in concert to exclude traders found to be abusive. Maghribi letters illustrate the closure argument.[28] Greif (1993: 530)

---

[28] The custom was to deposit documents that contained the name of God in a special chamber in the synagogue—the geniza—so that they could be disposed of with special rites, and so eliminate the risk of accidentally desecrating any written form of God's name. Most documents of the time, certainly descriptions of risky business, contained a sacred invocation that destined the document to the geniza. Every synagogue in the Middle East once had a geniza that was regularly emptied and its contents buried. However, the geniza of the synagogue in Fustat (old Cairo) was renovated in 1025 and accumulated documents for centuries without being emptied. This changed in 1866 when a collector of Jewish antiquities alerted European interests to the two and a half stories of largely medieval books, letters, and other documents he found in the Fustat geniza. Documents were spirited away over the next decades to be sold to collectors. Greif's description of the Maghribi traders is based on approximately 250 documents from diverse collections (Greif, 1989: 859 n.; see Greif, 1989, for citations to scholarly writing on the documents; Goitein, 1967, for authoritative description of the documents on business activities). There is no census of the original

cites an example of punishment and restitution: "Around 1055 it became known in Fustat that Abun ben Zedaka, an agent who lived in Jerusalem, embezzled the money of a Maghribi trader. The response of the Maghribi traders was to cease any commercial relations with him. His bitter letter indicates that merchants as far away as Sicily had ostracized him. Only after a compromise was achieved and he had compensated the offended merchant were commercial relations with him resumed." There is more to the system than avoiding punishment. Traders acted to protect reputation. Greif (1993: 531) describes the instance of a trader managing the sale of two loads of pepper, one his own and the other owned by another merchant. In a letter to the other merchant, the trader explained that he received the other's pepper and waited for the price to improve. "However, the slump got worse. Then I was afraid that suspicion might arise against me and I sold your pepper to Spanish merchants for 133." That night new buyers arrived, the price went up, and the trader sold his own pepper at 140–142. He explains to the other merchant: "But brother, I would not like to take the profit for myself. Therefore, I transferred the entire sale to our partnership." To avoid reputation damage, the trader sells the other's pepper early, but to protect his positive reputation, he shares with the other higher profits obtained from the sale of his own pepper. Significantly (Greif, 1993: 531), "He did not behave this way ... out of concern for his future relations with that specific merchant. His letter is explicit about his desire not to serve as an agent for this merchant in the future." His concern was his reputation in the broader network of traders.

Putnam and the Italian Communities

Putnam (1993) reported what was to become the most influential study of closure as social capital (Tarrow, 1996, offers a succinctly enthusiastic exegesis). Putnam, Leonardi, Nanetti, and Pavoncello (1983) summarize their then ten-year study of successful local government in fifteen regions in Italy. Success was measured on eight dimensions (coalition stability, budget promptness, spending capacity, law-passage rate, legislative innovation, regional planning, reform legislation, and an independent assessment of local planning for housing and urban development; Putnam et al., 1983: 59–60; cf. Clark and Ferguson, 1983, on American cities). Regional differences in success could be traced to three factors, discussed in the 1983 paper as ecological factors: socioeconomic development in the region, demographic stability, and "civic culture" (a contrast between political cultures that were "participant and sociable" versus "passive and parochial" as measured by three indicators:

---

documents, so the layers of sampling bias in any selection of the documents is unknown. Representation aside, Greif (1989, 1993) provides clear and substantively rich illustration of the closure argument.

voter turnout, newspaper readership, and trade-union membership; Putnam et al., 1983: 63–67).

Greater breadth of vision is displayed in Putnam's (1993) later report, focusing on the social capital inherent in "civic culture," and closing with the book title (p. 185): "Building social capital will not be easy, but it is the key to making democracy work." Putnam (1993: 115) makes a broad distinction between "civic" versus "uncivic" regions:

Some regions of Italy have many choral societies and soccer teams and bird-watching clubs and Rotary clubs. Most citizens in those regions read eagerly about community affairs in the daily press. They are engaged by public issues, but not by personalistic or patron–client politics. Inhabitants trust one another to act fairly and to obey the law. Leaders in these regions are relatively honest. They believe in popular government, and they are predisposed to compromise with their political adversaries. Both citizens and leaders here find equality congenial. Social and political networks are organized horizontally, not hierarchically. The community values solidarity, civic engagement, cooperation and honesty. Government works.

In the contrasting "uncivic" regions, public life (p. 115):

is organized hierarchically, rather than horizontally. The very concept of "citizen" here is stunted. From the point of view of the individual inhabitant, public affairs is the business of somebody else—*i notabili*, "the bosses," "the politicians"—but not me. Few people aspire to partake in deliberations about the commonweal, and few such opportunities present themselves. Political participation is triggered by personal dependency or private greed, not by collective purpose. Engagement in social and cultural associations is meager. Private piety stands in for public purpose. Corruption is widely regarded as the norm, even by politicians themselves, and they are cynical about democratic principles. "Compromise" has only negative overtones. Laws (almost everyone agrees) are made to be broken, but fearing others' lawlessness, people demand sterner discipline. Trapped in these interlocking vicious circles, nearly everyone feels powerless, exploited, and unhappy.

Putnam (1993) finds the image of social capital apt in distinguishing the two kinds of regions. He explains what he means by social capital (p. 167): "Social capital here refers to features of social organizations, such as trust, norms, and networks, that can improve the efficiency of society by facilitating coordinated actions," then follows with quotes from Coleman's (1990: 302 ff.) definition of social capital. The networks were voluntary associations such as neighborhood associations, cooperatives, sports clubs, and political parties (Putnam, 1993: 173): "Networks of civic engagement are an essential form of social capital: The denser such networks in a community, the more likely that its citizens will be able to cooperate for mutual benefit." Closure's reputation mechanism is the reason why (Putnam, 1993: 173–174): Dense networks increase the potential costs to a defector in any individual transaction, foster norms of reciprocity, improve the flow of information about the trustworthiness of individuals, and embody past collaborative successes that can serve as a template for future collaboration.

3.3.2   Closure and Brokerage

The three examples differ on economic, political, and social dimensions, but they have two things in common.

Most obviously, the examples show people advantaged by closure's reputation mechanism.

Second, the advantage they describe concerns brokerage. All three examples are instances of closure facilitating coordination across a structural hole. For Coleman, the hole is the generation gap between high-school students and their parents. Network closure across teachers, parents, and parents of friends enables coordination across the generation gap. The evidence is not about children doing well in school; it is about enforcing adult interests in keeping a child enrolled who would otherwise be at risk of dropping out.[29]

For Greif, the structural holes bridged are the geographic separations between cities in which the Maghribi traded. Maghribi network closure across the cities allows coordinated trade between the cities. Greif, Milgrom, and Weingast (1994) similarly describe medieval merchant guilds and the expansion of trade otherwise inhibited by incentives for opportunistic behavior (see Fenster and Smail, 2003, on gossip and reputation more generally in medieval Europe). Kock and Guillén (2001) describe the role of government protectionism for the growth of business groups within late-developing economies. Casella and Rauch (2002) describe information benefits of ethnic networks for international trade, capturing an insider-trading advantage for people in the network, like the information advantage that Ellis (2000) describes for leaders of Hong Kong companies talking to old contacts before entering foreign markets, or the information advantage that Sorenson and Stuart (2001) describe for syndicates of venture-capital firms coordinating expertise across otherwise segregated industry and regional markets.

For Putnam, the structural holes being bridged are the political differences inevitable between interest groups. The network closure provided by voluntary associations cuts across the interest groups, creating a sense of community and allowing coordinated action. Putnam's image of closure as social capital is starkly illustrated where the lack of bridge relations renders a community unable to take coordinated action to save itself, or the presence of bridges prevents structural holes from dividing a community.

---

[29] A closure effect on "dropping out" need not generalize to "doing well." Closure empowers parental control over the child, but a diversity of contacts is more likely to encourage the child's intellectual development (for the reasons given in Chapter 2). For example, analyzing data on mathematics achievement from the National Education Longitudinal Study survey of 9,241 students in 898 high schools, Morgan and Sørensen (1999: 674) question the value of network closure [brackets inserted]: "In contrast to his [Coleman's] basic hypotheses, our findings lead us to conclude that the benefits offered by the typical network configurations of horizon-expanding schools outweigh those of norm-enforcing schools."

Illustrating the first point, the Italian community in 1950s Boston's West-End did not prevent the destruction of their active community, and their failure to act can be attributed to the lack of bridge relations between the dense social clusters in which they lived (see Granovetter, 1973: 1373–1376).[30]

Illustrating the second point, Locke (1995: Chap. 4) describes labor relations correlated with social capital (see Granovetter, 2002: 51, for quick summary of Locke's Turin–Milan contrast in terms of cross-cutting associations). Milan and Turin are central cities in adjacent northern regions high on Putnam's civic community measures of social capital, with Milan in the more civic (e.g., Putnam, 1993: 150). Fiat operates in Turin, with conflicting labor and management factors. Alfa Romeo operates in Milan, with less confrontational labor relations. Locke's (1995: 125) sociogram of Fiat's situation shows a structural hole between Fiat and its allies on one side versus the company unions and their interconnected allies on the other side. The sociogram of Alfa Romeo's situation shows Alfa and its unions connected with many of the same allies, and those allies interconnected, such that the bridge between management and labor is embedded in a closed network.

Illustrating the second point at the other extreme of social capital, Sicily was the third-lowest of the twenty regions on Putnam's performance and civic community measures (e.g., Putnam, 1993: 98). The coordination that social capital could provide is instead purchased from a private contractor. Gambetta (1993) interprets the Mafia's prominence in Sicily in terms of its operations as a

---

[30] See Just et al. (2004) for an analogous argument, backed by MRI evidence, in which autism is attributed to a lack of bridge relations between clusters in the brains of autistic people. Going further back into Boston's history, Han (2004) describes the brokerage role that Paul Revere played with his historic ride. Revere was a member in three of the five principal social clubs in Boston, and in his craft as silversmith enjoyed connections to upper- and lower-class groups. Revere exercised a unique brokerage role in mobilizing leaders to whom he was attached in separate groups. In fact, Revere was only one of two people who set off to mobilize the community against the British on that April, 1775 night. The other rider, William Dawes, rode off into anonymity. Dawes made his ride to Lexington alerting whomever he bumped into. Revere rode to local community leaders with whom he was familiar, who in turn alerted local citizens. Fischer (1994: 141–142) describes the difference as follows: "Revere's ride to Lexington covered nearly thirteen miles in less than two hours. His circuit was a broad arc north and west of Boston. In every town along that route Paul Revere met with Whig leaders—Richard Devens in Charlestown, Isaac Hall in Medford, probably Ebenezer Stedman in Cambridge, Benjamin Locke and Solomon Bowman in Menotomy. William Dawes traveled a longer distance on a slower horse—nearly seventeen miles in about three hours. . . . No evidence exists that he spoke with anyone before he reached the Clarke house in Lexington. It is difficult to believe that he did not talk with at least a few people on the road, but in many hundreds of accounts of the Lexington alarm, only one person remembered meeting him that night—Lexington's Sergeant Munroe, who was unable to recollect his name." In terms of coordinating across structural holes in the community, Dawes stood as James in Figure 1.1 to Revere as Robert.

third party facilitating transactions otherwise inhibited by opportunism and distrust.[31]

Whether the lack of civic community manifests as responsibility deferred to government, or a private contractor such as the Mafia, it is distinct from the active involvement of citizens in the "civic" regions. Putnam's social-capital distinction drew particular interest in the United States when he (2000) later showed that the United States looked more like the "uncivic" Italian communities, with the contemporary lack of civic participation tracing back across a thirty-year decline.

Other Corroboration

Consider other instances in which closure's reputation mechanism provides an advantage.[32] For example, rating systems are a ubiquitous feature of contemporary life: J. D. Power ratings of customer satisfaction, eBay ratings of user satisfaction with trade partners, or magazine ratings of business schools. These ratings improve coordination across the structural holes between buyers and sellers in a world of strangers. I have seen how carefully manufacturers and service providers adjust to the J. D. Power ratings. Transactions have occurred

---

[31] Recall Putnam's focus on hierarchy in the less-civic regions, where people defer governance to "i notabilli," the bosses. Putnam (1993: 146) cites Gambetta (1988a), both of whom cite an 1876 social travelogue by a civic-minded Tuscan landowner, Fanchetti, attributing the prominence of the Mafia in Sicily to two factors: an ineffective system of justice and law enforcement, and a culture of mistrust. Both factors can be traced over a centuries-long history of divide-and-conquer rule (Pagden, 1988). Gambetta (1988a: 162) succinctly summarizes: "the unpredictability of sanctions generates uncertainty in agreements, stagnation in commerce and industry, and a general reluctance towards impersonal and extensive forms of cooperation. Sicilians—as everyone knows—do not trust the state: beyond the boundaries of limited clusters, they often end up distrusting one another as well," and goes on (Gambetta, 1993) to offer a compelling account of the Mafia as a third-party alternative to the state protecting rights in business transactions. He opens his market interpretation of the Mafia with a quote from a local cattle-breeder (Gambetta, 1993: 15): "When the butcher comes to me to buy an animal, he knows that I want to cheat him. But I know that he wants to cheat me. Thus we need, say, Peppe [that is, a third party] to make us agree. And we both pay Peppe a percentage of the deal." The Mafia grows as a third party facilitating transactions otherwise inhibited by opportunism and distrust.

[32] For broad review of closure providing social capital, see for example, Portes (1998); Cohen and Pruzak (2001); Woolcock and Narayan (2001). Portes and Mooney (2002) compare three communities to illustrate how the social capital of closure can be contingent on local material and institutional resources. Taylor and Doerfel (2003) discuss Croatian civic society in terms of nongovernment organizations coordinating across structural holes in an election campaign. Putnam and Feldstein (2003) describe a variety of programs intended to re-establish the participation-benefits of network closure in local communities. The website of the World Bank is a rich source for projects applying closure (www.worldbank.org).

on eBay because the seller has a good reputation from previous business. Much-desired transactions have not happened because the eBay buyer or seller has insufficient positive reputation within the system. I lived through a fundamental transformation of the University of Chicago Graduate School of Business in response to low initial ratings in the first business-school ratings. I can think of no student or alumni group, and I know there was no internal group, that could have triggered the kind of changes in the Chicago GSB that those business-school ratings triggered by publicly raising questions about reputational standing among peers.

For a more specific example, consider the issue of how to price the risk of an institution's debt. Gorton (1996) uses Diamond's (1989) reputation argument to describe the value of reputation to banks created during the 1838 to 1860 Free Banking Era in the United States. To put the argument in its original vernacular (Diamond, 1991: 690): "Reputation effects eliminate the need for monitoring when the value of future profits lost because of the information revealed by defaulting on debt is large. Borrowers with higher credit ratings have a lower cost of capital, and such a rating needs to be maintained to retain this source of higher present value of future profits." Gorton shows that the debt of new banks is discounted more heavily than otherwise similar banks, and the discount declines over time as the new banks become reputable.[33] Podolny (1993) uses a status metaphor to describe a similar reputation effect among investment banks. Reasoning that "tombstone" advertisements display more prominently the higher status banks involved in an offering, Podolny measures relative status by the frequency with which bank A is displayed higher and in larger print, than bank B. More reputable (higher status) investment banks can raise capital at lower cost, and Podolny argues (p. 848) that: "higher-status banks should take advantage of their lower cost to underbid their competitors for the bonds that they wish to underwrite." He shows for several thousand investment grade offerings in the 1980s that higher status banks enjoy lower costs.[34]

---

[33] "Otherwise similar" is measured by same period and location (Gorton, 1996: 367–369), and on the second point, see Gorton's distinction between "good" and "bad" banks where a good (reputable) bank is one for which the initial discount on its debt decreases to the market average within 13 months after the bank's formation.

[34] Lower cost is inferred from higher-status banks having smaller "spread" between the dollar amount the client pays the bank for the offering and the dollar amount for which the bank sells the offering (Podolny, 1993: 848–853; cf. Carter and Manaster, 1990; Carter, Dark, and Singh, 1998, on underwriter position in advertising tombstones as a measure of reputation). Where Gorton (1996) describes perceived risk decreasing with time in the market, and Podolny describes perceived risk decreasing with prominence in a status ordering, Zuckerman (1999) reports on the cost of looking risky. Zuckerman describes the buying and selling of corporate stock as a market mediated by stock analysts as "product critics" whose recommendations and endorsements enforce conformity within industries by depressing demand for the stock of companies that do not conform. Other factors held constant, Zuckerman (1999: 1405) argues that: "a product

Similar words describe the role of closure's reputation mechanism in science. Here is Polanyi (1983 [1966]: 70–72, also pp. 83–84), in his book on tacit knowledge, explaining how the myriad explorations of scientists are aligned by what is now discussed as reputation:

Research is pursued by thousands of independent scientists all over the planet, each of whom really knows only a tiny part of science. How do the results of these inquiries, each conducted largely in ignorance of the others' work, sustain the systematic unity of science? And how can many thousands of scientists, each of whom has detailed knowledge of only a very small fraction of science, jointly impose equal standards on the whole range of vastly different sciences? ... It is done by applying a principle that I have not seen described elsewhere, although it is used in various fields; I would call it the *principle of mutual control*. It consists, in the present case, of the simple fact that scientists keep watch over each other. Each scientist is both subject to criticism by all others and encouraged by their appreciation of him.... It is clear that only fellow scientists working in closely related fields are competent to exercise direct authority over each other; but their personal fields will form chains of overlapping neighborhoods."

The image of scientists concerned about their reputations and reputations defined by evaluative adjacent scientists is the backbone for Kuhn's (1970 [1962], 2000) influential work on paradigms and their enforcement (cf., Shils and Janowitz, 1948, on why the German Wehrmacht continued to function toward the end of World War II despite repeated defeats; monitoring was between buddies in the squad, and the army was a system of interlocked squads; Marshall, 1978 [1947]: ch. 9, on the corresponding effect of "tactical cohesion" in the American forces).

For a more concrete example, DiMaggio and Louch (1998) describe consumer purchases using the 1996 General Social Survey of a national probability sample of adult Americans. They report (p. 623): "Almost one-half of all used-car purchases from individuals (46.0 percent) and home purchases where no agent is used (46.8 percent) are transactions between relatives, friends, or acquaintances." Let "insider" refer to family, friends, and acquaintances (versus strangers). Let a "risky product" be something purchased infrequently where cost can greatly exceed value (e.g., used car or home versus bedroom furniture or home maintenance). DiMaggio and Louch (1998) describe buyers preferring to buy risky products from insiders because of assurances it provides, and sellers preferring not to sell to insiders because of obligations it entails. For example (p. 632), 50% of people buying a used car would prefer to

---

experiences weaker demand to the extent that it does not attract reviews from the critics who specialize in the category in which it is marketed." Zuckerman (1999: 1422–1424) shows a statistically significant discount in the stock price of a company not well covered by the analysts for the company's industry ("not well covered" is based on a ratio of industry analysts covering the firm divided by the largest number of analysts covering a firm in the industry).

buy from an insider (versus 21% who would prefer to buy from a stranger), and 19% of people selling a used car would prefer to sell to an insider (versus 31% who would prefer a stranger). Of the people who purchased a used car from an insider (p. 633), 55% were "extremely satisfied" and 5% were "not so satisfied," versus 43% and 15% for people who purchased from a stranger. DiMaggio and Louch (1998: 633) conclude: "These patterns reflect a widespread perception that persons in one's social network are constrained to treat one more generously and honorably than are strangers."

Consider the practice of washing your hands. A recent health-policy study reported that about two million people admitted to hospitals acquire an infection there (McGuckin et al., 1999). The infections cause nearly 20,000 deaths and cost an estimated $4.5 billion to treat. Handwashing is the single most effective measure for preventing hospital-acquired infections, but health-care workers wash their hands in less than half of the instances in which it is indicated. People know that they are supposed to wash their hands. Studies of bathroom behavior show that almost everyone (about 95%) say that they wash their hands, but direct observation reveals that about two-thirds of adults, and a miserly one in five college students, actually do.[35] Policy-makers are not blind to the potential of closure's reputation mechanism. The McGucklin study tested a program that used patients to remind health-care workers to wash. Within 24 hours of admission, patients were visited by a health educator explaining how handwashing can prevent infections and pointing out occasions when handwashing was indicated. Patients were encouraged to ask health-care workers "Did you wash your hands?" Patients were given a "tiny furry creature" for their gown that held a banner reading "Did you wash your hands?" The program ran for six weeks in four hospitals and involved 441 patients. Staff handwashing was measured by soap usage. Soap use increased during the program by a substantial 34%, which was projected to eliminate 10% of preventable infections for a hospital cost saving of $80,000 per year.

Consider closure's effect on people who are not strangers, but who work in separate groups such that trust could be problematic. The peer (360) evaluations widespread in contemporary organizations are an illustration. As companies at the end of the last century took layers out of their hierarchy to cut costs, vertical chains of command became less clear. People reported to someone they rarely saw. People reported in a matrix organization to multiple supervisors. In all, supervisors became less familiar with the behavior of their

---

[35] This statement is based on an unattributed study reported in O'Reilly (1989: 19), an unpublished 2000 survey by Wirthlin Worldwide for the American Society for Microbiology, and an unpublished 2003 survey reported on the Wirthlin Worldwide website (www.wirthlin.com). Actual wash rates are estimated by having an observer in a restroom stall or hair combing for a long time. The two Wirthlin surveys involved observing 7,836 and 7,541 adults. Toronto was an exception in that 96% of people were observed to wash their hands during the 2003 SARS outbreak.

direct reports, making supervisors less able to provide annual evaluations. The new supervision task was to monitor employee behavior that crossed the structural holes between organization silos. In a 360 evaluation system, evaluations are obtained from everyone with whom an employee has substantial contact; subordinates, peers, people in other divisions, and people higher in the organization (thus the 360, for 360 degrees). Knowing they will be evaluated by the people with whom they work, employees are expected to behave in a way that will not damage their evaluations, to the detriment of their compensation and promotion chances. Thus, closure's reputation mechanism is intended to enhance coordination between employees otherwise segregated in separate organization silos.

The reputation mechanism does not require a formal peer evaluation system. Lazega (2001: ch. 4) describes a three-city corporate law firm in which thirty-six partners and thirty-five associates specialized in niches among which cooperation was required to meet client needs. Lazega (2001: 138) explains that individuals had an incentive to free-ride on others and "the firm did not have many formal ways of dealing with free-loading," a concern voiced by one of the managing partners: "There are people who ... may wind up resting on their laurels, sitting on their hands, whatever euphemism you want to come up with for being lazy both intellectually and how much they are willing to work." Using network data identifying colleagues with whom partners and associates most often worked and to whom they turned for advice, Lazega computes the network constraint index on each attorney as a measure of network closure. The more closed the co-worker network around an attorney, the more likely that he or she put in extra hours keeping up with colleagues and participating in colleague cases. Lazega (2001: 141) concludes: "attorneys who were informally sought out for advice and for collaboration by many others tended to bill and collect more than others. . . . This confirms our expectations: members with a constraining co-workers' network put in more time, collected more hours, and collected more money."

Moving to the detail of comparative data on individual relationships, Reagans and McEvily (2003) describe the tendency for knowledge, especially complex tacit knowledge, to move between people who are part of a cohesive network with extensive range. Seidel, Polzer, and Stewart (2000) report that people hired by a mid-size high-technology firm are offered larger salary incentives when they have a friend in the organization. Peterson, Saporta and Seidel (2000: 781 n.) dig further into the hiring process with data on the hires studied by Seidel et al. augmented by data on the people not hired. Having a friend in the organization starts what Peterson, Saporta and Seidel (2000: 809) describe as a causal chain: the friend's referral affects the place of first interview, which affects the probability of a second interview, which has an effect on whether an offer is made. Especially consequential are the relations that span the customer interface. Uzzi and Lancaster (2004: 325) quote the client of a large law firm: "If we work with a law firm for two years it is a pretty sure bet we have a trust relationship because it means we've renewed with them, we're not negotiating a new contract, and have a pattern of comfort in interaction." The relational embedding of a continuing relationship lowers coordination risk and cost such that sellers can enjoy good margins while giving clients lower interest rates on bank loans (Uzzi, 1999; Uzzi and Gillespie, 2002) and lower rates for the legal advice of partners in large law firms (Uzzi and Lancaster, 2004). Using exceptional data on commercial real estate transactions, Garmaise and Moskowitz (2003) show that a broker is more likely to get bank financing for a transaction when the broker has a history of dealing with a bank and has concentrated his or her past business in a small number of banks. Kadushin (1995) and Frank and Yasumoto (1998) describe a network of coordinating ties across organizations and subgroups among French financial elites. Lütz (1997) describes closure and collaboration emerging among rival German automobile suppliers from the integrative brokerage work of research institutes. Lincoln and Gerlach (2004) provide an overview of closure's often-reported governance effects in the Japanese economy. Dyer and Nobeoka (2000) and Dyer and Hatch (2004) describe closure in the supplier network of a prominent Japanese firm, Toyota. The Bluegrass Automotive Manufacturers Association facilitates exchanges between Toyota's suppliers in the United States. Toyota has consulting teams that move among suppliers to replicate best practice across the network. The Association and consulting teams strengthen collaboration within Toyota's supplier network. Suppliers feel that they share with one another a lot of information about their Toyota production, especially relative to the little sharing they do about their production for large American car producers. There is more here than encouraging suppliers to share. Toyota's suppliers often produce for large American car producers. Why should Toyota improve supplier production, just to have suppliers use that knowledge to more efficiently produce parts for the large American car producers? The Toyota production system is sufficiently different that suppliers cannot move their Toyota-learned production efficiencies to the production of parts for American competitors. Even holding constant supplier reputation costs, the switching costs would make parts too expensive. "Without a wholesale adoption of the Toyota production system, GM cannot allow individual suppliers to expropriate Toyota's knowledge" (Dyer and Hatch, 2004: 5). The result is that a single supplier produces parts for Toyota at a lower cost and higher quality than it can produce similar kinds of parts for its largest American customer. Uzzi and Lancaster (2004: 340) offer a general conclusion for the above work: "embedded ties lower transaction costs, which opens up opportunities for price reduction. ... the types of relationships that form between producers and consumers can significantly affect prices, especially the pricing of goods where high trust can reduce the transaction costs typically viewed as irreducible through contracts."

Structural Autonomy

If closure can secure a bridge over which brokerage creates value, there should be systematic variation in returns to brokerage. Returns should be higher where closure works with brokerage to enhance coordination across structural holes that could be closed to advantage. Returns should be lower where closure works against brokerage to coordinate across structural holes better left open.

Figure 3.5 illustrates the social capital that closure provides when combined with brokerage. Alternative networks are presented for a group of three people in the table at the lower-left in Figure 3.5. The illustrative groups I have in mind are defined by the two network criteria that define information redundancy (cohesion and structural equivalence in Figure 1.2), but it is just as well to have in mind more colloquial definitions of group: family, team, neighborhood, ethnicity, or industry.

The table columns distinguish conditions of low and high closure within the group, corresponding to Putnam's (1993) distinction between "uncivic" and "civic" communities. The two sociograms to the right of the table show the group with all three people connected. Network closure is high.[36] Trust and

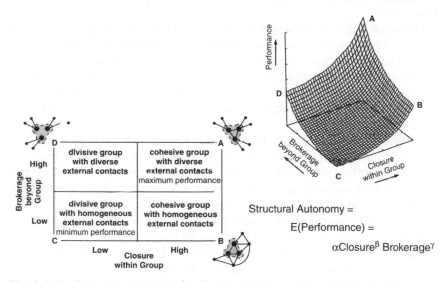

Fig. 3.5: Performance is highest for closure within a group combined with brokerage beyond the group (stylized fact #3)

---

[36] The closure can exist as density or hierarchy, both of which increase network constraint within a group (Section 1.2.2). There is some evidence that hierarchy is a more usual form of closure. Examples are Crane (1972) on the center-periphery structure of invisible colleges, Greif's (1989: 862–863) observation that the Maghribi traders

cooperation are expected. The sociogram to the left of the table shows the group with no connections within the group. Structural holes stand in the way of communication and coordination within the group, which weakens group ability to take advantage of brokerage opportunities beyond the group. Distrust, indifference, and coordination problems are expected.

The table rows distinguish conditions of low and high brokerage beyond the group, corresponding to the Figure 1.1 distinction between James and Robert, or more appropriately, the comparison of TQM teams in Figure 1.5H. The upper row of the table in Figure 3.5 shows each person in the group with non-redundant contacts beyond the team. In spanning structural holes beyond the team, their networks reached a diverse set of perspectives, skills, or resources. They correspond to the low-constraint TQM teams, to the left in Figure 1.5H, which were composed of employees with many non-redundant contacts beyond their team and deemed the high-performance teams in the company. The sociogram at the bottom of Figure 3.5 shows the group connected to four interconnected, and so redundant, contacts outside the group. Such a team has access to a single set of perspectives, skills, or resources, and is expected not to see or successfully implement new solutions, as illustrated by the low performance of high-constraint teams in the lower-right corner of Figure 1.5H.

The graph in Figure 3.5 shows how the group is expected to perform across the cells of the table. Performance here refers to innovation, positive evaluation, early promotion, compensation, and profit. The graph shows a non-linear association between performance and social capital in the form of closure within the group and brokerage beyond the group. Points A, B, C, and D at the corners of the table in Figure 3.5 correspond to the same points in the graph.

Performance is highest at the back of the graph (quadrant A), where network closure is high within the group (one clear leader or a dense network connecting people in the group), and the group's external network bridges structural holes in the surrounding environment (member networks into the surrounding organization are rich in diverse perspectives, skills, and resources). This is the quadrant for stories about closure providing social capital. The sociogram next to A could be three Maghribi traders anchored in separate cities, representatives of three leading institutions in one of Putnam's "civic" communities, or three people joined in a rotating-credit association running businesses in separate industries. This is also the quadrant described by the concept of

---

sanctioned not through their dense network with one another but through "a public appeal to the Jewish communities" in which they were embedded, Provan and Milward (1995) observation that higher performing mental health systems have a hierarchical, rather than a dense, network structure, or Koza and Lewin's (1999: 648–649) description of coordination problems that arise if there is only density without hierarchy. A leader with strong relations to all members of the team improves communication and coordination despite coalitions or factions separated by holes within the team.

structural autonomy, from which the structural hole argument in Chapter 1 developed (Burt, 1980; 1982; 1992: 38–45). A structurally autonomous group consists of people strongly connected to one another, with extensive bridge relations beyond the group. Stated in terms from the last two chapters, a structurally autonomous group has a strong reputation mechanism aligning people inside the group, and a strong vision advantage from brokerage outside the group. They have a creative view of valuable projects, who to involve, and they work together to make it happen.

Performance is lowest at the front of the graph (quadrant C), where network closure is low within the group (members spend their time bickering with one another about what to do and how to proceed) and redundant contacts beyond the group offer few brokerage opportunities (members are limited to similar perspectives, skills, and resources). This is the quadrant of minimum structural autonomy. People come to the group knowing the same things, so there is little to be gained from their assembly beyond sharing workload. Sharing involves coordination, so bickering within the group limits even that. In quadrant C are the teams that began with little potential and delivered only irritation.

The shape of the performance surface is nonlinear in two ways. First, the direct association with brokerage and closure is nonlinear. Performance decreases more with initial erosions of high brokerage or high closure than it does with the same increment of structural change at already low levels of brokerage or closure (cf. Figures 1.8 and 2.3). Second, there is an interaction between brokerage and closure. Performance at a high level of brokerage and closure is more than the sum of the performance expected from high brokerage alone plus high closure alone. In other words, point A in the graph is higher than the sum of performance at points B and D.

3.3.3 Markets

Figure 3.5 is my inference from four bits of evidence. First, the functional form of the performance surface in Figure 3.5 comes from research with census data describing the association between industry profits and market structure. The performance surface in Figure 3.5 resembles the graph to the left in Figure 3.6, which describes how industry profit margins (specifically, price–cost margins) vary with network structure in and beyond aggregate American industries.[37]

---

[37] The surface in Figure 3.5 is defined in terms of industry variables as follows (see Burt et al. 2002: 178, for details): $P = \alpha(1-\text{Con})^\beta(\text{C})^\gamma$, where P is the price–cost margin for an industry, Con is the four-firm concentration ratio for the industry (so $1-\text{Con}$ is a measure of competitive constraint within the industry), and C is network constraint defined by industry buying and selling with concentrated supplier and customer sectors (C measures supplier–customer constraint on the industry). Estimates of β and γ are negative describing how price–cost margins decrease with increasing constraint. Statistical tests for the association β, between intra-industry constraint, $1-\text{Con}$, and profit

Over the high-closure, high-brokerage point at the back of the graph, an industry providing structural autonomy is one in which there is low competition between industry producers dealing with disorganized suppliers and customers.

The analogy with market structure research is productive in two ways. First, the market results are based on a census of market conditions, so they include data on the performance-network association at extremes not present in most samples of managers. Second, in spanning a broader range of network conditions, the market results show more clearly the nonlinear form of returns to network structure. The strongest network effects occur with structural change that erodes maximum closure or brokerage. With respect to closure within a group, in other words, performance should be weakened more by the first significant structural hole in the group than by another hole emerging within an already disorganized group. With respect to brokerage beyond the group, performance should be weakened more by the entry of one strong perspective, or skill, or resource in the surrounding organization than it would be by the entry of another external pressure on a group already frozen by external pressures.

The Figure 3.6 axis measuring closure within an industry is based on industry concentration ratios, the proportion of industry output that comes from the four largest competitors in the industry. The evidence of profit margins increasing with industry closure is no more than the familiar idea that monopolists do well and crowding lowers margins.

The association with brokerage is less widely familiar. The Figure 3.6 axis measuring brokerage beyond an industry is based on the network constraint index in Chapter 1. The index is here adapted to measure the extent to which industry producers face coordinated supplier and customer markets.[38] There are scattered papers on the association between industry margins and structural holes among suppliers and customers (see Chapter 1 n. 22), but Saxenian (1994) provides a richly detailed illustration. She compares two regional high-technology economies: Silicon Valley, south of San Francisco, and Route 128, a region along the north and west of the beltway around Boston. Silicon Valley is marked by its success over time. Route 128 is not. Saxenian's question is why.

---

margin, range from −4.8 to −9.9 across 1963 to 1992 (Burt et al., 2002: 190). Statistical tests for the association γ, between supplier-customer constraint (C) and industry profit margin, range from −4.1 to −9.3 across 1963 to 1992 (Burt et al., 2002: 190). I discuss the performance surface in Figure 3.5 in terms of closure and brokerage, rather than internal and external constraint, to make the discussion consistent with the other examples here.

[38] The index is computed from concentration within supplier-customer markets and trade data from aggregate buying and selling between markets (e.g., Burt 1992: ch. 2; Burt et al., 2002: 175). With respect to the network constraint index in Section 1.1.5, network relationship z_{ij} is the dollars of goods that establishments in industry i sold to establishments in industry j, and each contact-specific constraint coefficient, c_{ij}, is multiplied by the level of concentration in supplier–customer market j.

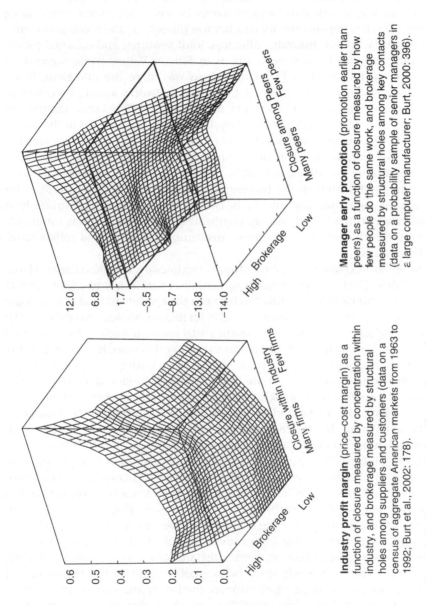

Industry profit margin (price–cost margin) as a function of closure measured by concentration within industry, and brokerage measured by structural holes among suppliers and customers (data on a census of aggregate American markets from 1963 to 1992; Burt et al., 2002: 178).

Manager early promotion (promotion earlier than peers) as a function of closure measured by how few people do the same work, and brokerage measured by structural holes among key contacts (data on a probability sample of senior managers in a large computer manufacturer; Burt, 2000: 396).

Fig. 3.6: Performance surface for markets and managers

Saxenian begins by describing how technology in Route 128 was organized in terms of large, vertically-integrated, firms while Silicon Valley remained a population of specialists coordinating across firms. For example, there was status in Silicon Valley to frequent moves between companies, while along Route 128, leaving one firm for another was infrequent and taken as evidence of dissatisfaction or disloyalty. Alliances, joint ventures, and informal collaboration between firms were common in Silicon Valley, while segregation between secretive and self-contained firms was more the rule along Route 128 (see Fleming et al., 2004, on the denser networks among inventors in Silicon Valley). There are elements of Putnam's (1993) "civic culture" in Saxenian's description of Silicon Valley. Like other organizations in the Valley, venture-capital firms were knitted together by informal socializing and frequent collaborative investments. Venture capital in Route 128 was less available and more exclusive (see Castilla, 2003, on network connections among venture-capital firms in the two regions). The leading local universities for engineers played different roles in the two regions, MIT finding it unseemly to participate in the risk of start-up companies, while Stanford was intimately involved with continuing education, institutional support, and collaborative relationships.

Saxenian's explanation, informed by the flexible-specialization thesis in Piore and Sabel (1992), is that integrating specialists within a single firm inhibits variation and flexible coordination between the specialists. That is why Route 128 failed to adapt to the changing market for high technology. Saxenian (1994: 161) concludes: "Silicon Valley continues to reinvent itself as its specialized producers learn collectively and adjust to one another's needs through shifting patterns of competition and collaboration. The separate and self-sufficient organizational structures of Route 128, in contrast, hinder adaptation by isolating the process of technological change within corporate boundaries."

Saxenian's instructive contrast should not be taken too far. She focuses on DEC to represent Route 128 firms, with corroborative mention of other local firms such as Data General, Raytheon, Honeywell, RCA, and Sylvania. She portrays Silicon Valley with a more diffuse combination of firms, though HP and Fairchild SemiConductor are often mentioned. A cross-section of senior manager networks in DEC shows that people often knew their key contacts in the firm many years before they joined the firm (Burt, Hogarth, and Michaud, 2000: 137). The image of segregated bastion does not accurately depict DEC. Second, vertical integration was an advantage for DEC in the early years when it was battling IBM (Robertson, 1995). DEC should not be criticized for having a wrong strategy so much as for being unable to adapt its once-successful strategy to the faster-paced electronics market at the end of the century (see Markusen, 1996, on successful industrial districts organized as a "hub-and-spoke" network around one or a few large firms).

These cautions said, there is a replicable contrast in Saxenian's analysis. The contrast Saxenian develops between Silicon Valley firms illustrated by HP versus Route 128 firms illustrated by DEC could be developed equally well by comparing CISCO's ecosystem of loosely affiliated companies thriving in competition against large, vertically integrated competitors such as Alcatel, Lucent, and Nortel (e.g., Ferrary, 2003). The gist of either contrast is coordination via a "new" economy network of adaptive, flexible connections versus coordination via an "old" economy bureaucratic authority structure.

In terms of social capital, Route 128 suffered because large firms coordinated across structural holes that produced productive variation between specialists (*le vide* cited by the Rhône-Poulenc CEO in Section 2.1). With respect to Figure 1.1, every social system is a balance between specialization within the clusters and integration between the clusters. Saxenian's analysis says that Route 128 put too much emphasis on integrating the clusters.

Consider the situation of a group of people, a handful or a hundred, working in a small firm that specializes in some technology. The specialist firm corresponds to one of the clusters in Figure 1.1. The firm buys supplies from upstream specialists and sells to downstream specialists.

There are two familiar ways (on a continuum from one to the other) to think about coordinating relations between the specialist firm, its suppliers, and its customers. The market solution is to focus on specialization within clusters and let the market coordinate between clusters. The bureaucratic solution is to create a vertically integrated organization, purchasing the specialist firm along with selected suppliers and customers so that the flow of goods from supplier through producer and on to customer can be managed with an eye to efficient scale, accurate and reliable information, and cooperation induced by mutual interest in the health of the shared enterprise (ignoring the fact that it is often easier in large bureaucracies to deal with suppliers and partners outside the firm).

Saxenian's analysis shows how integration within a single firm does the things that closed networks are predicted to do: First, it homogenizes belief and behavior differences that would otherwise develop between the firms as separate entities. People within the vertically integrated enterprise can become blind to alternatives. The vision advantage, described in Chapter 2 as the mechanism by which brokerage provides advantage, is lost when corporate process homogenizes belief and practice across specialists. This point is engagingly illustrated in Peterson and Berger's (1975) influential analysis of diversity in the popular music industry. There are cycles of market concentration in the industry. Periods when the largest firms hold a large share of industry output are followed by periods in which their market share is eroded by smaller competitors. When production is more concentrated in the largest firms, the music produced is more homogeneous (cf. Lee, 2004).

Second, vertical integration creates obligations to existing plans and partners, even if partners in other firms would be better (as you would expect friends to support you even if someone else were preferable). The commitment point is nicely illustrated in Kogut and Zander's (2000) report on a natural experiment in flexible specialization. The German optics firm, Carl Zeiss, was divided at the end of World War II into a West German organization (Zeiss Oberkochen) separate from an East German organization (Zeiss Jena). Kogut and Zander (2000) trace patent activity by the two organizations from 1950 through 1990. They conclude (p. 184) that Zeiss Jena in East Germany suffered from a lack of "close contact with advanced consumers and suppliers in many areas," as expected in a vertically integrated enterprise, perhaps especially in this case of a vertically integrated enterprise operated by the government. Whatever limitations were imposed by the lack of "close contact," however, Zeiss Jena remained innovative, even exceeding Zeiss Oberkochen, in terms of a diverse patent portfolio. What hurt Zeiss Jena was being locked into poor investments (pp. 182–184):

The historical evidence from the archival investigation illuminates the negative effects of political decisions on Jena's research policies, the constraints of having to innovate by plan, and the pressures to supply a wide range of "customers." Zeiss Jena during the 1950s and 1970s displayed a much more diversified patent portfolio than did West German Zeiss. ... But it was hampered by a system of central planning that dissipated innovative resources in accordance with planned targets. ... Zeiss [Jena] suffered because of the Plan's refusal to permit experimentation in any sector of the economy to fail. This meant that the firm could not rely on the emergence of external innovations. As a consequence, Zeiss [Jena] was forced, by plan, to try to succeed in areas in which it knew it had already failed.

Exit is the key to an expression popular in Silicon Valley: "Fail often to succeed sooner." As much as social capital is about coordinating previously disconnected operations, it is about getting out of coordination efforts that have proven to be unproductive.

3.3.4 Teams

A second source of evidence for the integration in Figure 3.5 comes from research on team performance as a function of network closure in and beyond a team.

Suggestive results came from research in which networks beyond a team are inferred from the demography of the people within the team. Ancona and Caldwell (1992a) provide a study of this type describing 409 individuals from 45 new-product teams in five high-technology companies. Teams were distinguished by managerial ratings of innovation, member reports on the volume of communication outside the team (Ancona and Caldwell, 1992b, distinguish types of communication), functional diversity (members from multiple functions) and tenure diversity (members vary in their length of time with the firm). Structural holes are implicit in the boundaries between corporate divisions and the boundaries between cohorts of employees in that each division or cohort is presumed to have its own unique perspectives, skills, or resources. A team composed of people from diverse corporate functions spans more structural holes in the firm, and so has faster access to more diverse information and more control over the meaning of the information, than a team composed of people from a single function. For tenure diversity, replace the timing and control advantages of access to more functionally diverse information with the same advantages stemming from access to information that differs between employees long with the firm who are familiar with how things have worked before and newer employees more familiar with procedures and techniques outside the firm.

For the reasons discussed in Chapter 2, innovative solutions are expected from teams with brokerage relations across divisions, and Ancona and Caldwell report higher managerial ratings of innovation for teams with more external communication, and more external communication by teams drawn from diverse functions.

Tenure diversity has the opposite effect. Ancona and Caldwell report some benefits of tenure diversity associated with higher evaluations of team performance, but the aggregate direct effect of tenure diversity is lower performance. Presumably, people drawn from widely separate employee cohorts have more difficulty with communication and coordination within the team.

The conflicting results were brought together in a productive way by Reagans and Zuckerman (2001) in their study of performance in 223 corporate R&D units within 29 major American firms in eight industries. They report higher levels of output from units in which scientists were drawn from widely separate employee cohorts (implying that their networks reached diverse perspectives, skills and resources outside the team) *and* there is a dense communication network within the unit (see Reagans, Zuckerman, and McEvily, 2004, for stronger results when network diversity beyond the team is measured directly rather than with a demographic-diversity proxy). In other words, the negative association between performance and tenure diversity reported by Ancona and Caldwell could have been positive if the density of communication within the team had been held constant. Tenure diversity (or other kinds of diversity, see Williams and O'Reilly, 1998) can be disruptive because of the difficulties associated with communicating and coordinating across different perspectives—but when communication is successful (as implied by a dense communication network within the team), team performance is enhanced by the timing and control advantages of the team having access to more diverse information.

This is as Ancona and Caldwell initially predicted, and it is a productive interpretation of Reagans and Zuckerman's analysis because team networks and performance can be linked with the performance effects of structural holes in market networks. The aggregate profit margin for a market increases with the organization of producers in the market and the disorganization of suppliers and customers. The market model applied to team performance predicts that high-performance teams will be those in which member networks beyond the team span structural holes (giving the team access to diverse perspectives, skills and resources), and strong relations within the team provide communication and coordination (so the team can take advantage of its access to diverse perspectives, skills and resources). The high-performing R&D units in Reagans and Zuckerman's analysis are in quadrant A of the table in Figure 3.5, where structural autonomy is highest.

Brainstorming groups offer another view of brokerage interacting with closure to define team performance, specifically as brokerage is associated with creativity. Laboratory and field studies of brainstorming groups show two things: Groups generate fewer, and fewer high-quality, ideas than the same number of people working separately, but people in the studies nevertheless report that groups generate more ideas and as individuals report higher personal performance within groups (e.g., Diehl and Stroebe, 1987; Mullen, Johnson, and Salas, 1991, for review; Paulus, Larey, and Ortega, 1995, for field illustration in an organization). The connection with social capital is that performance is significantly improved if individuals come to the brainstorming group from heterogeneous backgrounds (Stroebe and Diehl, 1994: 293–297). In other words, the value of group brainstorming is a function of the group facilitating the exchange of ideas across structural holes that separate members in the absence of the group. This is a useful analogy because (*a*) it fits with Reagans and Zuckerman's story about the social capital of groups increasing as a function of network density inside the group combined with bridge relationships spanning structural holes outside the group, and (*b*) it means that the brainstorming studies which analyze group process can be used to better understand the process of brokerage. For example, Sutton and Hargadon (1996) and Hargadon and Sutton (1997) describe processes by which a firm, IDEO, uses brainstorming to create product designs, creating a status auction within the firm (see Lazega, 2001, on coordinated relations used to manage status auctions in brainstorming sessions in a corporate law firm). IDEO's employees work for clients in diverse industries. In the brainstorming sessions, technological solutions from one industry are used to solve client issues in other industries where the solutions are rare or unknown. The firm profits, in other words, from employee bridge relations through which they broker the flow of technology between industries.

3.3.5   *Learning Curves*

A third source of evidence for the integration in Figure 3.5 comes from research that links group productivity to closure's reputation mechanism. The reputation mechanism can create economic value in two ways. One is decreased labor cost. The more closed the network, the higher the quality and quantity of labor available at a given price in the network. This is illustrated by the Section 3.2.1 anecdotal evidence on teams. Recall the transcendental sense of the shared goal. A person on the Macintosh team explained: "everybody just wanted to work; not because it was work that had to be done, but because it was something we really believed in, that was just going to really make a difference. And that's what kept the whole thing going." Recall the work ethic. A person on the Data General team that created the Eclipse computer was quoted: "Since Jim is killing himself; I mean he's here every night until three in the morning. I'd almost feel guilty if I wasn't working so hard. I want it to be my project as much as it is his." Peer pressure ensures the guilt. A person on a manufacturing team recently converted to team governance explained: "If you notice that somebody's not getting anything done, then we can bring it up at a [team] meeting, you know, and ask them what the problem is, what's causing them not to be able to get their work done." Between feeling obligation to do your fair share, avoiding the embarrassment of public inquiry, and the feeling that this is an important project on which you don't want to be a problem, people put in extra hours getting it done right. Further, closure reduces coordination time and cost so projects move to completion more quickly. The concern about reputation that elicits labor quality and quantity elicits it in coordination with other people in the network. As Jobs described his Macintosh team: "The greatest people are self-managing. They don't need to be managed. Once they know what to do, they'll go figure out how to do it. They don't need to be managed at all."

By lowering labor cost, making a team self-aligning, and so shortening time to completion, closure's reputation mechanism can yield dramatic improvements in productivity—and little things can trigger it. For example, Ulrich, Zenger, and Smallwood (1999: 184) offer an unattributed story about Charles Schwab (the industrialist, not the stockbroker): "while one day visiting one of his steel mills as the day shift was leaving, [Schwab] took a piece of chalk and wrote on the floor the number of steel ingots that shift had produced. The night shift, seeing the number, took it as a challenge and proceeded to produce more ingots than the day shift and wrote the number in chalk on the floor. As days went by, productivity escalated shift by shift—simply because Schwab had written a number in chalk on the plant floor."

Consider the design and production of the Tu-4, the first Soviet Union strategic bomber.[39] Toward the end of World War II, the Soviet Union had voluminous tactical aircraft, but their strategic aircraft had been destroyed early in the war, they had no concrete plans for producing such aircraft, and their requests to allies for strategic bombers such as the B-17 Flying Fortress, B-24 Liberator, and B-29 Super Fortress went unanswered (in part because of the kind of engagements the Soviet Union was fighting). Then came the opportunity. Three B-29s were forced in the Summer and Autumn of 1944 to land in Siberia after operations in the Pacific. The Soviet Union was not at war with Japan, so the planes were impounded. This gave the Soviet engineers the

---

[39] With a recent release of documents, the story of Andrey Tupolev and his Tu-4 is available in print (Gordon and Rigmant, 2002) and video ("Stealing the Superfortress," 2001, A&E Television Networks).

opportunity to copy, rivet for rivet, the Wichita-built B-29. One of the three B-29s was disassembled to reverse engineer the plane. One was kept whole for reference. The third was used for training and performance tests. The clone Soviet aircraft was named the Tu-4, a mirror image of the B-29, even down to a quick surface repair that had been made to the copied B-29. The Tu-4s that flew in the August 1947 Air Fleet celebration stunned the world. No one thought that the Soviet Union had such capabilities.

The closure story lies in how the Soviets managed to so quickly and accurately copy the B-29. The program manager was famed engineer, Andrey Tupolev, given carte blanche support by Stalin, including whatever use he needed of Beria's enforcement organization—which gave the term "deadline" real meaning. But you cannot shoot everyone, and the complexity of the task made coordination a staggering problem that had to be solved quickly to meet Stalin's two-year timeline for the project. The technology was new, and based on American rather than Soviet production processes—and components ended up distributed across 900 separate subcontractors, none of whom understood how their piece of the puzzle fit with the others. Gordon and Rigmant (2002: 24) explain: "The leaders of some design bureaux responsible for various units and systems persistently sought to be exempted from copying the American prototypes, claiming that the equipment developed in their OKBs [design department] was in no way inferior and was already series-produced into the bargain." Subcontractors usually have something on the shelf that meets "almost exactly" a customer order. The problem in this case was that small deviations in items not well understood, especially with the tendency for the Soviet options to be heavier than the new American counterparts, would add up to a plane that would not fly. To drive alignment, (Gordon and Rigmant, 2002: 24), "Tupolev resorted to an unusual step: at his initiative an exhibition was arranged in the mock-up hall on the fifth floor of this design bureau, presenting virtually all the units and equipment items of the aircraft. They were accompanied by notice boards specifying the ministries, enterprises, stipulated delivery dates and names of the officials directly responsible for the item. Members of the Politbureau, ministers, chief designers and factory directors were invited to the exhibition. It became a peculiar kind of tool for putting pressure on the enterprises responsible for the equipment, making it possible to take expeditious administrative measures against those chief designers or factory directors who displayed negligence or reluctance." Production relative to schedule was on constant display for each subcontractor relative to the other subcontractors. Variation in subcontractor production shrank dramatically. The display created a reputation cost for delay, a cost under Stalin that could be physically dangerous to a subcontractor. Equipment deliveries "were made on schedule and, most importantly, the home-produced sub-assemblies and equipment items were not overweight compared to their American prototypes" (Gordon and Rigmant, 2002: 24).

On the other side of the world, another dramatic production story was slowing down, a story on which there are better data. America produced almost three thousand Liberty Ships during World War II, the most ships of one design ever launched.[40] America's pre-war support of Britain required merchant ships. German submarines were sinking merchant ships three times faster than Britain could build them. Ships needed to be produced at a faster rate, said President Roosevelt, to ensure that Europe had "food, fuel, weapons, even liberty itself." To construct these "liberty ships," the U.S. Maritime Commission turned to established shipbuilders such as Bethlehem Steel on the East Coast, and on the West Coast, to Henry Kaiser, a man who had never built a ship in his life, but under whose superb program-management skills the construction of Hoover Dam had been completed two years ahead of schedule. Kaiser looked at the production process with the eyes of a network entrepreneur, cutting corners by integrating production steps traditionally seen as separate. Welding was faster than riveting, and whole bows, sterns, and deck houses were produced as pre-fabricated subassemblies, cut when necessary into parts for delivery, then welded back together at the ship. Shipyards changed from a custom shop in which ships were built one at a time from the keel up, to an assembly line in which parts were pre-fabricated in convenient locations and delivered to the ship when needed.

Productivity soared. The first Liberty Ship, launched in September of 1941, was constructed in 244 days. Across subsequent ships the construction time dropped to the 140 days targeted by the U.S. Maritime Commission, and kept dropping to 72 days by May of 1942, then 46 days by August. Figure 3.7 contains production data for seven of the shipyards; Kaiser's Richmond, California and his Portland, Oregon yards so often mentioned in stories about the Liberty Ships, two yards on the East Coast run by established shipbuilders (the Fairfield yard set up by Bethlehem Steel in Baltimore, Maryland and the Portland, Maine yard run by New England Shipbuilding), and three shipyards in the South later brought in to expand production (St. Johns River Shipbuilding in Florida, Southeastern Shipbuilding in Georgia, and Todd Houston Shipbuilding in Texas). These seven shipyards account for 2,053 of the 2,778 Victory Ships built. The graph to the left in Figure 3.7 illustrates the point

---

[40] Lane (2001 [1951]) describes the Liberty Ship production in the context of other programs managed at the time by the U.S. Maritime Commission. Adams (1997) describes Henry Kaiser's career leading up to, and subsequent to, the Liberty Ships. There is also an engaging video available on the Liberty Ships that illustrates the reputation effects on productivity ("Victory at Sea," 1997, A&E Television Networks, for their "Empires of American Industry" series). In the course of obtaining more precise estimates of capital-cost effects and quality in ship production, Thompson (2001) obtained production data on individual Liberty Ships, which he generously made available on his university website. The number of Liberty Ships produced differs across reports depending on how one codes variations on the basic design and initial ships produced with the British. My numbers of 2,778 ships produced, of which 2,053 were produced in the seven Figure 3.7 yards, are based on Thompson's (2001) data.

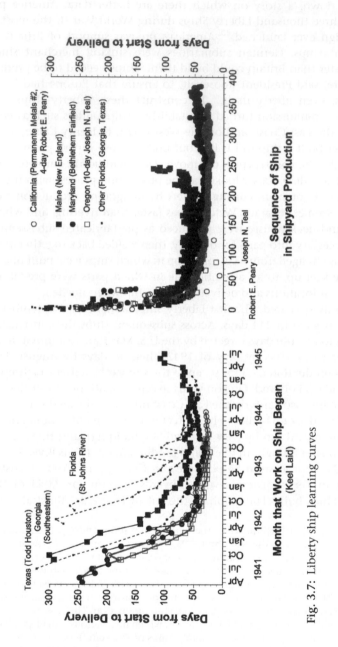

Fig. 3.7: Liberty ship learning curves

emphasized in academic papers on the data: people learned by doing (Rapping, 1965; Argote, 1999: 41–51; Thompson, 2001). Production times dropped sharply in each shipyard, but the first ships built by every shipyard took a long time. Holding constant the date at which a shipyard began building, the graph to the right in Figure 3.7 shows how production times plummeted across the first fifty ships a yard built. The downward-sloping curve in the graph is discussed as a "learning curve" in which cost decreases by a fixed percent with each doubling of cumulative volume. Estimates of the percent vary between kinds of production, but are often 20% to 30% (e.g., what costs a dollar a unit in the first batch produced, drops by 20% to 80 cents in the second batch, then another 20% to 64 cents in the fourth batch, then another 20% to 51 cents in the eighth batch, and so on).[41] Costs decrease most sharply through the first few batches, then decrease less across subsequent batches as people settle into a production process.

Closure's reputation mechanism played a role in the Liberty Ship productivity improvements. Passive learning because you have been through the process before is one thing. Learning because your reputation depends on it is another. For example, to recruit workers for whom the arduous work on the Liberty Ships would be a life improvement, Kaiser sent recruiting trains to Texas, Oklahoma, and Arkansas where people were especially hard-hit during the Depression. As in the Schwab and Tupolev examples above, public displays of production fostered competition to be best among peers. In a 1942 speech to workers in his Richmond, California yard, Kaiser said (Adams, 1997: 115): "A Liberty Ship was launched [yesterday at the Oregon yard] in record time of 26 days. Today you have broken that record and have established a new one of

---

[41] Learning curves have long been familiar in individual learning (e.g., Thurstone, 1919), but the first estimate of an organization's learning with cumulative production experience (Wright, 1936) drew little academic attention until production data on the Liberty Ships so reliably showed the curves (Searle, 1945; Rapping, 1965; Yelle, 1979). Dutton and Thomas (1984) compare 108 learning curves in 22 field studies (a large majority showing 10% to 30% gain for every doubling of cumulative output, see p. 238). Henderson's discussion of such curves as "experience curves" in his influential consulting practice had an impact on how the curves were used in business strategy (Sterns and Stalk, 1998: 12–17). In her review of organization learning, Argote (1999) offers numerous examples and thorough discussion of the learning involved in a group moving down a learning curve. Thompson (2001) reports lower estimates of learning in the Liberty Ship production than earlier studies when he holds constant capital costs and production quality, but still reports a significant effect of experience. Cappelli (2004) offers evidence from a different angle. If the social capital created in moving down a learning curve is valued by a company, it should react to a drop in demand by re-training employees for other jobs rather than laying them off or firing them (see Argote, 1999: 37–41, on the learning-curve loss created at Lockheed when an increase in oil prices depressed demand for the L-1011). Cappellli (2004: 440) uses U.S. Bureau of the Census survey with a national probability sample of businesses to show that re-training is significantly more likely in businesses that rely on employees to coordinate with one another within teams or across flexible working hours.

24 days. Today's record will be short-lived for I am told by our boys that tomorrow's record of less than 18 days will be established within the next few months." In the following month, the Oregon yard completed a Liberty Ship in 10 days (the Joseph N. Teal in Figure 3.7). Two months later, the Richmond yard completed a Liberty Ship in the astounding time of 4 days, 15 hours, and 26 minutes (the Robert E. Peary in Figure 3.7). The fact that the time is known in minutes signals the reputation mechanism at work. These record-breaking production times required specialized supply chains with back-up workers for the three shifts per day, so some of the effort that went into these ships was an extravagance. They lie well below the bulk of the production data in Figure 3.7. Regardless, Kaiser called them "incentive ships" because he saw them as a motivation for his workers (Adams, 1997: 115). Similarly, the person to whom Kaiser reported, Admiral Vickery, used stories in the national media to keep pressure on the East Coast shipyards by comparing their performance to Kaiser benchmarks set on the West Coast.

More systematic evidence of reputation is available on the seven shipyards in Figure 3.7. The above illustrates Kaiser's use of reputation to drive his employees. His two West Coast shipyards in Figure 3.7 stand in contrast to the East Coast yards of Bethlehem Steel and New England Shipbuilding. The learning curve evident in the graph to the right in Figure 3.7 is substantially faster for the West Coast yards, where Kaiser most ardently drove reputation, average for the three Southern yards, and substantially slower for the two East Coast yards with their established traditional production processes.[42] Another indicator concerns two production intervals, differently linked with reputation. The time interval from laying the keel to launching the ship was the focus of media attention and Kaiser's exhortations to employees. There was less attention to a second interval, when the floating ship was "outfitted" for delivery. For example, the four days, 15 hours, and 26 minutes required to

---

[42] Figure 3.7 displays total production times, from keel laid to delivery. I regressed the log of a ship's production time across the log of the sequence of the ship in its yard's production (first Liberty Ship built, tenth, fiftieth, etc.). A dummy variable distinguished ships produced in the two West Coast yards. Another distinguished ships produced in the two East Coast yards. With no other adjustments (so this exercise is solely for illustration), the results are a $-.38$ coefficient and -67.9 t-test for the shorter time required to build later ships, a $.15$ coefficient and 9.4 t-test for the longer times in the East Coast yards, and a $-.25$ coefficient and -16.3 t-test for the faster times in the West Coast yards. These differences are inflated by times increasing as it became clear that the war was ending. The association between production time and sequence position is negative across the horizontal axis in Figure 3.7, but it is positive after Paris was liberated in August, 1944 (4.9 t-test), still positive back to the June invasion at Normandy (3.6 t-test), and does not become significantly negative until the series is extended back to March, 1944 (-4.2 t-test). Looking only at production times up through the invasion of Italy in January, 1944, the negative association with sequence is strong ($-.44$ coefficient), and there remains faster production in the two West Coast yards ($-.16$ coefficient, -8.5 t-test) and slower production in the two East Coast yards (.10 coefficient, 5.1 t-test).

build the Robert E. Peary was the time from laying the keel to launching the ship. It took another three days to outfit the ship before it was ready for delivery. Differences between the shipyards are especially sharp on the time interval used to fuel the reputation mechanism. On the keel-to-launch interval, the focus of public attention, the two West Coast yards in Figure 3.7 were significantly faster than the three Southern yards, and the two East Coast yards were significantly slower. On the less-attended-to outfitting interval, there are no statistically significant differences between the yards though they all learned to outfit the ships more quickly as they became more experienced.[43]

To study behavioral and cognitive correlates of the learning curve, Adler (1990) reports on qualitative fieldwork describing production in an electronic equipment manufacturer with plants in the U.S., Europe, and Asia. The company shows productivity gains with cumulative experience in eight organization units over the course of work on a "new-generation device" (Adler, 1990: 940–948), and the gains are higher where changes are made to improve coordination between departments (Adler, 1990: 948–954). To improve coordination between the Development and Manufacturing departments, for example, part of Manufacturing Engineering was shifted to Development, and a Development team was physically sited next to the Manufacturing people with whom they were to coordinate. To improve coordination between primary and secondary manufacturing sites, differences between their production practices were made explicit (versus tacit knowledge) so that a "start-up" team motivated by international competitive pressure could focus on elements to coordinate that would be valuable (avoiding unproductive coordination that might otherwise have been mandated by corporate headquarters). Adler and Clark (1991) offer corroborating evidence when they obtain higher estimates of productivity gains by holding constant what they interpret to be organizational disruptions created by change to prior production practice (cf. Hatch and Mowery, 1998, on new processes disrupting the gains otherwise associated with cumulative engineering experience).

With respect to Figure 3.5, note the evidence of brokerage and closure in these examples. Tupolev had to align otherwise reluctant and segregated subcontractors. Kaiser had to take cycles out of tasks segregated in the established process of producing ships. Both used closure's reputation mechanism to drive alignment. From his observation of learning in progress, Adler (1991:

---

[43] Production time in the Figure 3.7 yards was on average 42.4 days of keel-to-launch and 13.9 days of outfitting. Estimating the model in the preceding note—excluding ships produced after the January, 1944 invasion of Italy—the keel-to-launch period decreased sharply with experience ($-.46$ coefficient, -73.6 t-test), especially in the two West Coast yards ($-.23$ coefficient, -11.7 t-test), more slowly in the two East Coast yards (.10 coefficient, 4.9 t-test). The outfitting period, which received less public scrutiny, also decreased significantly with experience ($-.37$ coefficient, -39.2 t-test), but neither faster in the West Coast yards (.01 coefficient, 0.5 t-test) nor more slowly in the East Coast yards (.06 coefficient, 1.8 t-test).

954) concludes that company barriers to organization learning had been "primarily organizational culture and the associated status hierarchy—rather than any individual cognitive limitations."

3.3.6   Contingency Functions

A fourth source of evidence for the integration in Figure 3.5 comes from research showing that brokerage is more valuable in less routine work. Recall the program manager quoted in Section 2.3 who "did not want my people even thinking about alternatives." His opinion reflected the kind of work he was supervising. His program was based on well-understood technology, in a company with a long history in the technology. He was hiring people to do work that he had done at one time. He just wanted people to do the jobs for which he had hired them. "Good enough and on time" were his quoted objectives.

Work Uncertainty and Number of Peers

The quoted manager supervised what can be termed "routine" work in the sense that there was a preferred or prescribed way to do the work. The more routine the work, the less valuable brokerage will be for its introduction of alternatives, and the more valuable closure can be for its capacity to align people in the known way of executing the work. The creativity and learning associated with brokerage can be valuable to breaking out of prescribed routines, or obtaining a new job that involves less routine work, but brokerage is not likely to be appreciated by people such as the quoted manager responsible for delivering routine work. The less routine the task, the more uncertain the work, the more valuable brokerage can be because a "good" completion will require decoding and negotiating the interests of constituencies who will judge the worth of the completed work.

There is evidence of brokerage more valuable for less routine, more uncertain, work. Marsden (2001; Marsden and Gorman, 1999) shows with a national probability sample that informal, social capital, search strategies are more likely to be used to fill vacancies for jobs that involve complex work and require autonomous decision-making. Further down the organization hierarchy, Flap and Boxman (2001) show a similar result for employers evaluating college graduates applying for their first full-time job. At a more aggregate level, Hansen, Podolny, and Pfeffer (2001) report task contingency for new-product teams in a leading electronics firm (also see Hansen, 1999, in Section 1.3.3). They find that teams composed of people with more nonredundant contacts beyond the team complete their assigned task more quickly—for teams working on a new product for an unfamiliar market or a new product involving unfamiliar technology. If the team was working on a new product based on a familiar technology for a familiar market, however, the network effect is negligible. Engineers in routine jobs were more likely to be assigned to the new-product teams working with familiar technologies for familiar markets.[44] At a still more aggregate level, Podolny (2001) describes the contingent value to venture-capital firms of a co-investment network that spans structural holes. Firms with a network bridging structural holes do a large proportion of their investments in ventures at an early stage of development (where uncertainty is highest about the market potential of a venture). In short, the social capital of bridging structural holes is more of an advantage in more uncertain ventures.

There is ample precedent for measuring the extent to which work is non-routine in the sense that people have to figure out how best to perform it (e.g., Kohn and Schooler, 1983), but ecology offers a simple, concrete metric—the number of people, call them peers, doing the same kind of work. A manager could have many peers, a few, or none if no one else is doing the same work.

More peers mean more routine, less uncertain work because peer behavior is a frame of reference defining how to proceed. Competition keeps each manager tuned to peer performances and organizations define work processes and templates for jobs held by many employees. Further, legitimacy is established by many people doing the same work. The way a job is performed can be legitimate not because of content or quality, but because many people perform it that way (e.g., economists in a business school, or the old saying, "you don't get fired for buying IBM," or the more recent, "you don't get fired for buying Cisco").

The conditions are reversed for a manager who has few peers. There is no competitive frame of reference: no peers for informal guidance, and it would be inefficient for the firm to define a job specific to only a few employees. The manager has to figure out for herself how best to perform the job. Further, legitimacy does not come with the job; it has to be established. With few people doing the work, establishing the legitimacy of a job performance depends on getting others to accept your definition of the job (e.g., sociologists in a business school).

As brokerage is more valuable in the completion of less routine work, it should be more valuable to managers with few peers. Managers assigned to more unique tasks face more uncertainty in how to do the tasks. The vision

---

[44] A related study yields a slightly different result. Mizruchi and Sterns (2001) analyze network effects on loan decisions in a commercial bank. The people to whom a loan officer went to get approval for a loan is the officer's approval network. Loan uncertainty in the form of a complex deal lowers the probability of a loan being approved, but officers with approval networks that span structural holes in the bank are more likely to have their loans approved (Mizruchi and Sterns, 2001: 664). The network and uncertainty effects are additive in the published paper. With brokerage more valuable for less routine work, the network effect on loan approval should be higher for loans that are more uncertain. Instead, the network effect is constant across levels of uncertainty (Mizruchi, private communication, 3/18/03). I take this to mean that all loans are uncertain to an extent that makes it wise to build an approval network that spans structural holes.

advantage of bridging structural holes puts a manager in a position to better read diverse interests to define needed policy and to know better who can be brought together productively to implement policy. Such information has little value to the manager whose work is defined by corporate convention or the boss. The contingency argument is that peers erode the value of brokerage to the extent that disorganization among peers intensifies competition between the peers and elicits behavioral guidelines from higher authority.[45]

Closure and Contingency

Curves in Figure 3.8 describe how the value of brokerage is contingent on number of peers, and so work uncertainty. I discuss the curves as contingency functions. The vertical axis in Figure 3.8 measures the value of brokerage using the magnitude of correlation between performance and network constraint, from a strong association at the top of the graph to no association at the bottom. Inset graphs to the left of the vertical axis display heuristic performance associations with constraint. The top graph shows a .96 correlation, which is stronger than any displayed in Chapter 1 (where correlation magnitude varies from .30 for the bankers in Figure 1.5E to .79 for the TQM teams in Figure 1.5H).

The horizontal axis in Figure 3.8 is number of peers and the contingent value of brokerage is a power function of peers: $v = \alpha(N)^\beta$, where v is the magnitude of correlation between performance and network constraint for a job category, and N is the number of people in the category (Burt, 1997a, reports tests against job rank and alternative functional forms). Coefficients α and β are parameters describing how brokerage value varies with peers. Contingency functions A and B in Figure 3.8 describe the association between network constraint and early promotion for senior managers in a large computer manufacturer (Figure 1.5D). Function C describes the association between network constraint and compensation for the supply-chain managers in a large electronics company (Figure 1.5A).[46]

Estimates of coefficient β are negative, describing the rate at which brokerage value decreases with an increasing number of peers. The rate at which peers erode value is steepest for small numbers of peers, to the left in the graph,

---

[45] The contingency argument is analogous to organizational ecology arguments in network analysis describing the competition and legitimacy that result from an increasing number of organizations in a market (Burt, 1992: 215 ff.; Han, 1993, 1994; cf. Hannan and Freeman, 1989: 131–141), and ecological reasoning applied to organization demography (Pfeffer, 1983; Haveman and Cohen, 1994).

[46] Analysis leading to contingency functions for the senior managers is available in Burt (1997a). To get the illustrative contingency function for the supply-chain managers, I estimated the correlation between performance and network constraint for each of their five job grades, holding constant the background variables held constant for Figures 1.5A and 2.1 (listed in Burt, 2004: Table 1), then fit a contingency function, $v = \alpha(N)^\beta$, through the five correlations (v) and the number of supply-chain managers (N) in each job rank.

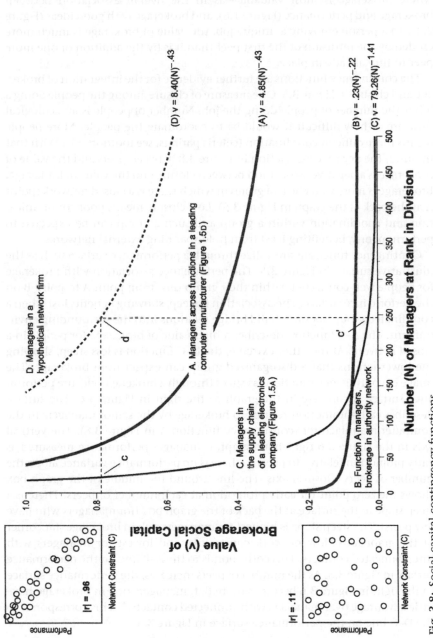

Fig. 3.8: Social capital contingency functions

where brokerage is most valuable—as in the overall association between brokerage and performance (Figure 1.8), and brokerage with good ideas (Figure 2.3). To a person enjoying a unique job, the value of brokerage is much more eroded by the intrusion of the first peer than it is by the addition of one more peer to fifty already in place.

The contingency functions are further evidence for the integration of broker-age and closure in Figure 3.5. One measure of closure among the people doing a job is the number of people doing the job. Number of people is an ecological measure of how difficult it would be to coordinate the people. More people means more difficult coordination (ceteris paribus, see footnote 11). With that in mind, the negative association in Figure 3.8 between peers and the value of brokerage is a negative association between closure and the value of brokerage. Brokerage is more valuable to a group in which there is a closed network (point A at the back of the graph in Figure 3.5). Low closure means poor communica-tion and coordination within a group and such a group can be expected to perform poorly, benefiting least from hole-spanning external networks.

Contingency functions are a slice through a performance surface such as the illustrative surface in Figure 3.5. The performance association with brokerage for people well-connected within their group runs from point A to point B on the performance surface. The association is steep, showing benefits lost when a coordinated group does not build bridge relations into the surrounding envir-onment. The A–B function describes a high value of brokerage for people in a closed network. At the other extreme, the D–C function is less steep, showing the lower returns that a disorganized group can expect from brokerage. The image of contingency functions as slices through a brokerage–closure perform-ance surface is concrete in the graph to the right in Figure 3.6. The surface describes early-promotion returns to brokerage by the senior managers in the computer manufacturer (contingency function A in Figure 3.8). The vertical axis in the Figure 3.6 right-hand graph is manager performance measured as early promotion relative to peers so there is no performance variance along the number of peers (closure) axis. The line around the middle of the graph box shows the zero point for early promotion at each number of peers. There is a steep slope to the surface at the back of the graph box (for managers who have few peers). The steep slope is highest for managers rich in brokerage (far corner of the graph box, low network constraint), and lowest for managers with interconnected contacts. This corresponds to the A–B line on the performance surface in Figure 3.5. As the number of peers increases, the performance surface to the right in Figure 3.6 becomes more flat; managers rich in brokerage have little advantage over managers with connected contacts.[47] This corresponds to the D–C line on the performance surface in Figure 3.5.

---

[47] Statistical tests show that only the slope of the surface is changing. Average pro-motion date and average intensity of network constraint are the same for managers with few or many peers. Early promotion and network constraint are equally varied for

Virtual Monopoly

A manager for whom N equals 1 has no peers and so has a monopoly over the kind of work she does. Her work is unique, perhaps as the chief executive officer, chairman of the board, or the one company representative to an unusual market. A monopoly manager's success depends on coordination with people doing other kinds of work—which means that the information access and control benefits of brokerage can be valuable. How valuable is defined by the first parameter in a contingency function. Coefficient α is the expected correlation between network constraint and performance for managers with a monopoly on their job. When N equals 1, v equals α.

A near-zero estimate of α means that brokerage has no value. For example, contingency function B in Figure 3.8 describes the value of brokerage in authority relations for the senior managers in computer manufacturing. The authority network contains the manager's subordinates, boss, and cited key sources of buy-in. Function A shows that brokerage in the authority network provided little social capital (Section 1.5.2). The expected correlation between early promotion and authority-network constraint is consistently low, regardless of peers. The correlation is only .23 even at the extreme of monopoly ($\alpha = .23$), implying that there are no circumstances for these managers in which brokerage limited to authority relations generates social capital.

An estimate of α larger than 1 means that managers with one or more peers enjoy a virtual monopoly over their work. In a large organization, two managers can do the same work but be so segregated from one another that each has a virtual monopoly over his or her work. Examples could be the head of the Asia division versus the head of European operations, or heads of human resources in separate business units in a bureaucratic organization. Virtual monopoly can occur with different numbers of peers depending on the way that managers doing their kind of work are scattered through an organization. The criterion number is defined by the contingency function. Solving for N when v equals 1, defines the number of peers at which virtual monopoly exists: virtual monopoly $N = (1/\alpha)^{1/\beta}$.

For example, contingency function A in Figure 3.8 describes the value of brokerage in discussion relations among the senior managers in computer manufacturing. The function says that their organization was segmented to such an extent that a manager who was one of less than 40 people doing the same kind of work had a virtual monopoly ($[1/4.85]^{-1/.43} = 39.4$). At N equal to 39.4, function A crosses the upper boundary of v equal to 1. This was a company in which senior people had substantial job autonomy.

---

managers with few or many peers. What is different across numbers of peers is the extent to which early promotion is correlated with network constraint—strong for managers with few peers, weak for managers with many peers.

Other contingency functions in Figure 3.8 illustrate lower and higher thresholds for virtual monopoly. In contrast to the computer managers who had a virtual monopoly if they were one of less than 40 peers, contingency function C shows that the supply-chain managers lose a virtual monopoly facing half as many peers ($[1/79.26]^{-1/1.41} = 22.2$). The implication is that the supply-chain managers had less job autonomy than the senior managers in the computer company. Virtual monopoly is readily available to managers described by contingency function D, a hypothetical function included here as a heuristic device. I expect functions like D in highly differentiated organizations such as a large consulting firm or law practice containing many partners who are located in many cities and have diverse expertise. A manager has only to be one of less than 143 managers doing the same work to enjoy a virtual monopoly: ($[1/8.40]^{-1/.43} = 142.6$).

3.4   Conclusions

This chapter has been an introduction to the reputation mechanism by which closure provides trust, and a resolution to the social-capital tension between brokerage and closure. Trust is the Achilles heel to the brokerage argument. You trust someone when you commit to a relationship before you know how the other person will behave. The more unspecified, take-for-granted, the terms of a relationship, the more trust is involved. The social capital of structural holes depends on trust in as much as the value created by brokers involves new, and so incompletely understood, combinations of previously disconnected ideas. The trust issue is moot if brokers confine themselves to trusted contacts, but that would limit brokerage to long-standing networks, which would leave the bulk of brokerage value untapped.

So I began with the etiology of trust and the reputation mechanism by which closure provides it. The network around two people is closed to the extent that both have strong relationships to mutual contacts. Those mutual contacts—friends, colleagues, acquaintances, or other contacts—are third parties to the relationship. With respect to network constraint in Chapter 1, closure is manifest as a dense network (in which the two people are surrounded by interconnected third parties) or a hierarchical network (in which the two people share a strong connection with the same central figures, see the discussion of network constraint in Section 1.1.5). The more closed the network, the more likely that misbehavior will be detected and punished. Not wishing to lose reputation accumulated in a long-term relationship, or built up within a group of colleagues, people cooperate with other people in the network. Their reputation incentive to cooperate lowers the risk otherwise associated with trust, and so increases the probability of trust. Trust is more likely in a strong than a weak relationship, especially if the strong relationship is embedded in a closed network (Figures 3.3 and 3.4, Table 3.1). There is potential economic value. People in a closed network can be expected to work harder, longer, and at higher quality. More, they are self-policing about what needs to be done. Teams finish more quickly, at higher quality, with less cost. Savings in labor and coordination translate into efficiency, evident in learning curves describing productivity improvement as people acquire experience with a task (Figure 3.7).

3.4.1   Brokerage–Closure Tension

Closure is at once contradictory to, and interdependent with, brokerage. The social capital of structural holes depends on trust, but trust is a feature of closed networks, precisely the condition that brokers rise above. There are three elements to the brokerage–closure tension. With respect to network structure, brokerage and closure contradict one another in the role third parties play in social capital. In closure's reputation mechanism, third parties create social capital by improving information flow, making it possible to detect and punish bad behavior, thereby facilitating trust. In brokerage, social capital is created by bridge relations that coordinate across groups with complementary resources, knowledge, or practice. Network bridges are defined by the lack of third parties. Third parties need not erode the brokerage potential of a relationship, but they are an indicator that the relation provides information redundant to what is available through other sources.

With respect to network content, the information that flows through social structure plays different roles in the two mechanisms. Brokerage creates value by exposing people to variation in information. Closure's value comes from driving variation out of the closed network. In the brokerage argument, information is valuable when it is nonredundant. That is what constitutes access to variation. In the closure argument, information is valuable when it is redundant. Closure links reputation to prescribed behavior by increasing the probability of reputation-eroding behavior being detected within the closed network.

Third, with respect to the person affected, the two mechanisms have different targets. In brokerage, the object of action is you, improving your vision and helping you escape the demands of other people. Brokerage forces you to see alternatives by exposing you to the diversity of opinion and practice across groups. The conflicting demands of multiple groups frees you from excessive demands in any one group. Closure, on the other hand, is about forcing other people to behave in prescribed ways. Closure's control potential is the reason for closure's use in contemporary organizations as a replacement for, or complement to, traditional vertical chains of command in a bureaucracy. Network closure forces people to collaborate by linking reputation to alignment with others in the network.

3.4.2 Tension Resolved

One way to deal with the brokerage–closure tension is to reject the mechanism less supported by empirical evidence. The results and review in Chapters 1 and 2 support brokerage over closure as social capital. Networks that span structural holes are associated with good ideas, positive job evaluations, likely promotion, and compensation significantly higher than peers.

Even if structural holes are the source of advantage, however, they need not be the proximate cause. Where a set of people are cross-cut by numerous differences, any of which could function as a structural hole, closure could give them an advantage in coordinating despite their differences, whereupon closure would be the proximate cause of advantage—even though the substance of the advantage is closure's bridge across the pre-existing structural holes. More, when two old friends from separate groups decide to collaborate, they begin introducing trusted colleagues in their group to people in the other group. The initial bridge relation begins to be embedded in third parties. For these newly connected people, emerging closure is the proximate cause of advantage—even though the source of advantage is the structural hole they are working to span. In terms of proximate cause, closure can be the more accurate definition of social capital, so it would be inaccurate to reject closure in favor of brokerage.

A second option is to hide from the brokerage–closure tension by segregating the mechanisms, saying that they are equally valid but different. For example, one could say that closure defines when it is safe to trust, while brokerage defines when it is valuable to trust. Or, closure is about driving out variation in favor of people adhering to accepted standards, while brokerage is about introducing variation to identify more rewarding standards. Segregation is a safe option—and a popular option judging from the closed networks of scholars that have sprung up devoted to brokerage or closure but not both. Safety and popularity notwithstanding, the segregation option is in its own way inaccurate in light of evidence supporting a third option.

A third option is to integrate the mechanisms in a broader model, which is the option proposed in the concept of structural autonomy (Figure 3.5). Brokerage is about coordinating people between whom it would be valuable, but risky, to trust. Closure is about making it safe to trust. The key to creating value is to put the two together. Bridging a structural hole can create value, but delivering the value requires the closed network of a cohesive team around the bridge. In Figure 1.1, for example, one could argue that James' social capital does not come directly from the closed network among his contacts, but from that closure around James as a bridge coordinating the southern and northern factions within group B. Network entrepreneurs identify rewarding structural holes in a market or organization, and have an advantage in managing the work of bridging the hole, but a closed network is the organizational suture that tightens coordination across the hole. Section 3.3 contains evidence on people, teams, and markets regarding the structural-autonomy trade off between brokerage and closure. A structurally autonomous group consists of people strongly connected to one another, with extensive bridge relations beyond the group. Stated in terms from the last two chapters, a structurally autonomous group has a strong reputation mechanism aligning people inside the group, and a strong vision advantage from brokerage outside the group. They have a creative view of valuable projects, who to involve, and they work together to make it happen.

3.4.3 Research Cumulates

Brokerage and closure combined in structural autonomy are a foundation for cumulating research results across studies. Figure 3.8 depicts contingency functions running along the surface of the graph in Figure 3.5. In the absence of such contingency functions, research will be aggregated across studies as if any study were a replicate test of the same proposition. Interventions will be designed as if any population were an equally suitable site in which to enhance social capital. A naive observer can be expected to summarize research by stating the proportion of studies that report a strong performance association with social capital.

Figure 3.5 shows how a study can report exclusive evidence of social capital from network closure or brokerage without calling either argument into question. Estimated effects depend on the shape of the underlying contingency function and where along the function managers were selected for study.[48] For example, the contingency function in Figure 3.8 for the supply-chain managers in Chapters 1 and 2 shows that brokerage provided no compensation benefits for those in jobs with numerous peers (point c' on the contingency function, see Burt, 2004: Table 1, for evidence of negligible returns to brokerage). A sample of the supply-chain managers in junior ranks would show no association between salary and brokerage. At the same time, a sample of managers with unique jobs in the same population would show a strong social-capital effect (point c on the contingency function, with evidence in Figure 1.5A showing high returns to brokerage).

More generally, Figure 3.5 helps cumulate research efforts by more clearly locating study populations relative to one another: Relative to the ideal mix of closure and brokerage in structural autonomy (quadrant A; high-performing R&D teams in Reagans and Zuckerman, 2001), closure within a team can fail to improve performance (quadrant B; Sparrow et al., 2001), while structural holes inside the team can erode performance (quadrant D; Sparrow et al., 2001;

---

[48] The expected magnitude of correlation between performance and network constraint, $E(v)$, is the sum of where sample managers i exist on a contingency function, v_i, and the probability, p_i, with which managers at that point are sampled for study: $E(v) = \Sigma_i p_i v_i$.

Cummings and Cross, 2003) at the same time that a lack of structural holes in the external network erodes performance (quadrants B and C; see Section 1.3.3 for references). In an environment rich in diverse perspectives, skills, and resources, group performance depends on people overcoming their differences to operate as a group. Group performance will vary with in-group closure, not brokerage, because brokerage opportunities beyond the group are for everyone abundant. This is the Figure 3.5 surface from point A to point D. Greif (1989) and Putnam (1993) are example studies on that segment of the Figure 3.5 surface. Rosenthal's (1996) study of TQM teams illustrates the other extreme. People on the teams had been trained to act as a team and there was enthusiasm for TQM in the firm—so the teams did not differ greatly in closure. Closure was high in all of them. Team performance therefore varied with a team's external network. If a cohesive team can see a good idea, it can act on it. With all teams cohesive, performance variance increases with brokerage beyond the team (this is the Figure 3.5 surface from point A to point B). In Section 1.3.3, I discussed studies reporting high performance for groups with external networks that spanned structural holes. With Figure 3.5 in mind, these studies tell me not that the closure argument is in error so much as they tell me that closure within the groups was less problematic than brokerage beyond the groups.

I closed Chapters 1 and 2 with a summarizing stylized fact: the performance association with brokerage in Figure 1.8, the creativity association with brokerage in Figure 2.3. My stylized fact for this chapter is the performance surface in Figure 3.5 describing structural autonomy defined by mixtures of brokerage and closure. The trust association with closure is another candidate for summary, but summary would be premature. The association is more complex than implied by the closure argument in Section 3.1 and more complex than the evidence displayed in Figures 3.3 and 3.4. The stories that sustain closure's reputation mechanism need not be entirely true, which has demonstrable implications for people distorting one another's reputations. That is the subject of the next chapter.

FOUR

Closure, Echo, and Rigidity

ON July 14, 2004, the British House of Commons printed a report entitled *Review of Intelligence on Weapons of Mass Destruction*. There had been concerns about Britain's alignment with the United States in the invasion of Iraq. Among the stated goals of the invasion was removing weapons of mass destruction threatening the region and the world at large. Failure to find the weapons, and judicious reflection after the invasion, supported the conclusion that the information provided by intelligence agencies was not used appropriately to inform policy decisions. Among the report's strong and weak points is a wise observation concerning the limitations of intelligence (p. 14, brackets added):

A hidden limitation of intelligence is its inability to transform a mystery into a secret. In principle, intelligence can be expected to uncover secrets. The enemy's order of battle may not be known, but it is knowable. The enemy's intentions may not be known, but they are knowable. But mysteries are essentially unknowable; what a leader *truly* believes, or what his reaction would be in certain circumstances, cannot be known, but can only be judged. JIC [Joint Intelligence Committee] judgements have to cover both secrets and mysteries. Judgement must still be informed by the best available information, which often means a contribution from intelligence. But it cannot import certainty.

This chapter is about where people find the certainty. Certainty does not come from data. Data are exogenous. Certainty is endogenous. People find it in one another.

The trust association with closure is more complex, more powerful, and decidedly less salutary, than argued in the previous chapter. Deeper understanding of closure comes from asking about the motives of third parties relaying information. Third parties had no motives in Chapter 3. Networks were like a plumbing system through which information moved; more pipe meant better access. The more closed the network, the more likely that everyone in the network had full information on network-relevant behavior. Such a connection between closure and information can be termed a "bandwidth" hypothesis: strong, redundant connections ensure a reliable flow of data so that everyone in the network is informed about behavior that enhances or erodes reputation.

Bandwidth is a special case of a broader "echo" hypothesis based on the social psychology of selective disclosure in informal conversations. In contrast to the full information communicated by third parties in Chapter 3, the assumption in this chapter is that third parties communicate a sample of what they know, a sample defined by etiquette such that people hear predispositions echoed by colleagues and treat the echo as data. Allowing third parties to be polite has dramatic implications. The resulting echo hypothesis says that closed networks do not enhance information flow so much as they reinforce predispositions. Information obtained in casual conversations is more redundant than personal experience but not properly discounted, which creates an erroneous sense of certainty. Interpersonal evaluations are amplified to positive and negative extremes. Favorable opinion is amplified into trust. Doubt is amplified into distrust. Echo does not differ from bandwidth on the enforcement potential of network closure. It differs on the information closure provides. Closure as bandwidth enhances access so people in the network are better informed. Echo says that the access is to a biased sample.

I present evidence of echo being more accurate than bandwidth in predicting trust, but predicting trust is not my primary goal for this chapter. My goal is to describe how the reputation mechanism for control in a closed network reinforces a network, making it rigid, resistant to change. I use data on network stability for evidence of the rigidity associated with closure, but I wish to keep rigidity separate from stability. Stability covers a broader set of issues addressed in the next chapter. Rigidity can result in network stability, but it can also result in the dissolution of a network. Where stability refers to what actually happens (a network continues over time), rigidity refers only to internal forces that would preserve the network over time in the absence of other forces. Rigidity carries an implication of stability, and I will show evidence of closure associated with stability, but rigidity also implies crystalline fragility and an inability to adapt.

The chapter is in five sections: After the idea of network echo is contrasted with bandwidth in Section 4.1, Chapter 3's evidence of bandwidth is shown in Section 4.2 to be a subset of broader evidence that supports echo over bandwidth. The shift to echo continues in Section 4.3 with data on the language used to describe relations. Amplified feelings of trust and distrust should be evident in the language people use to describe their relationships. The evidence in Section 4.3 shows people in closed networks using inflammatory language and blaming difficult relations on their colleague's character. Section 4.4 is about resistance to change. Feelings of trust and distrust amplified to extremes do not change easily, especially when embedded in adjacent strong relations. The evidence in Section 4.4 shows closure increasing via echo the stability over time of relations, people, and their relative standing. The stylized fact for this chapter, in Section 4.5, is that closure reinforces network structure; slowing decay and amplifying relations to extremes of trust and distrust.

The evidence in this chapter supporting echo over bandwidth does not reject the evidence presented in Chapter 3. Trust is associated with closure as illustrated in Section 3.2. Closure mixes with brokerage to define the social capital of structural autonomy as illustrated in Figure 3.5.

What echo does in this chapter is expand the effects in Chapter 3 to recognize closure as a more powerful, more dangerous, source of control because control no longer depends on information being consistent across a network, or accurate anywhere in the network. Closure's reputation mechanism is now free to reproduce, in fine detail, the clusters and holes in an existing social structure. Network closure does not facilitate trust so much as it amplifies predispositions to extremes of trust and distrust, creating an arthritis in which people cannot learn what they do not already know—thereby deepening the structural holes that segregate groups and allowing legacy organizations to survive in spirit long past the formal organization in which they developed.

4.1. Bandwidth and Echo

The sociogram in Figure 4.1 will be useful for distinguishing echo from bandwidth. Dots in Figure 4.1 are people. Lines indicate relations; solid line for a strong positive relationship, dashed line for a weak relation, wavy dashed line for a strong negative relationship. Jessica in Figure 4.1 has strong positive relations with three contacts (1, 2, 3), weak relations with two (4, 5), and strong negative relations with two (6, 7). The baseline prediction from Blau's social exchange theory or Granovetter's image of relational embedding (Section 3.1.1) is that Jessica asked to name the people she trusts would name contacts 1, 2, or 3. Predictions are listed to the left in Figure 4.1. She would be

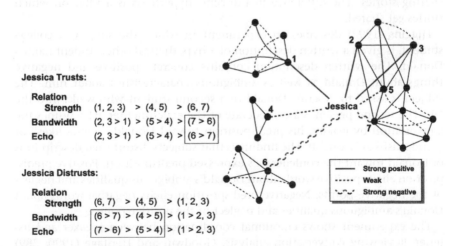

Jessica Trusts:

Relation			
Strength	(1, 2, 3)	> (4, 5)	> (6, 7)
Bandwidth	(2, 3 > 1)	> (5 > 4)	> (7 > 6)
Echo	(2, 3 > 1)	> (5 > 4)	> (6 > 7)

Jessica Distrusts:

Relation			
Strength	(6, 7)	> (4, 5)	> (1, 2, 3)
Bandwidth	(6 > 7)	> (4 > 5)	> (1 > 2, 3)
Echo	(7 > 6)	> (5 > 4)	> (1 > 2, 3)

Strong positive ——
Weak ·····
Strong negative ‿‿

Fig. 4.1: Who does Jessica trust?

less likely to name contacts 4 or 5, and unlikely to name contacts 6 or 7. If Jessica were asked to name the people she distrusts (where distrust is not the complement to trust so much as an opposite extreme separated in the middle by contacts a person neither trusts nor distrusts), she would be expected to name contacts 6 or 7. She would be less likely to name contacts 4 or 5, and unlikely to name contacts 1, 2, or 3.

The bandwidth hypothesis extends reputation to the surrounding network of friends, colleagues, and acquaintances. Two people embedded in a network of interconnected mutual friends and colleagues are more likely to trust one another (Section 3.1.2). Among Jessica's close contacts (1, 2, 3), trust is less likely with contact 1 because there are no third parties to the relationship (her relation with contact 2 is embedded in a positive third-party tie through contact 3, and vice-versa). Between her weak contacts (4 and 5), Jessica is less likely to trust contact 4 because there are no third parties to the relationship. Jessica's relationship with contact 5 is complicated by 5's close relationship with 7, with whom Jessica has a strong negative relationship, but ensured by 5's close relationship with a mutual friend, contact 2. To the extent that Jessica trusts either of her negative contacts (6 and 7), it would be 7 because she has some guarantees on 7's behavior from 7's embedding in third-party ties through contact 2, and 2's friend 5.

4.1.1 Etiquette Creates an Echo

Looking more closely at the social psychology of conversation, there is reason to question bandwidth in favor of what can be termed an echo hypothesis. As in the previous chapter, people are sharing stories about people and events of mutual interest, and people in closed networks have wider bandwidth for sharing stories. The difference in the echo hypothesis is a filter on which stories get shared.

Higgins (1992) describes an experiment in which the subject, a college student, is given a written description of a hypothetical other student named Donald. The written description contains concrete positive and negative things about Donald as well as ambiguous characteristics about him. The subject is asked to describe Donald to a second student who walks into the lab. The second person is a confederate of the experimenter, who primes the conversation by leaking his predisposition toward Donald ("kinda likes" or "kinda dislikes" Donald). The finding is that subjects distort their descriptions of Donald toward the confederate's expressed predisposition. Positive predisposition elicits positive words about Donald's ambiguous qualities and neglect of the negative points. Negative predisposition elicits negative words about Donald's ambiguous qualities and neglect of the positive points.

The experiment shows emotional coordination between speaker and listener. Reviewing conversation analysis, Goodwin and Heritage (1990: 289) emphasize the path-dependent evolution of a conversation: "every action is simultaneously *context shaped* (in that the framework of action from which it emerges provides primary organization for its production and interpretation) and *context renewing* (in that it now helps constitute the frame of relevance that will shape subsequent action)." Etiquette facilitates the emotional coordination that sustains conversation. Just as there is form and content to a network (Section 1.4), there is form and content to conversations about the network. Etiquette in conversation form defines things such as turn taking (Goodwin and Heritage, 1990). For example, Gibson (2003: 1349; 2004: Table 2), observing conversations in scheduled meetings of managers, reports that the person (target) addressed by the last speaker is typically the next speaker (especially in adjacency pairs such as questions–answers between job ranks), and targets of the current speaker tend to be the prior speaker, prior target, or whole group.

In this chapter, I draw on a central point of etiquette in conversation content: It is rude to contradict the tone of the conversation. It is polite to raise topics on which speakers are likely to agree, and avoid topics that would erode the social standing of the other speaker (discussed as not embarrassing the other speaker or causing a loss of face, Grice, 1975; Goody, 1978; Brown and Levinson, 1987). For example, Fine (1986: 409) summarizes his analysis of teenager gossip as follows: "Teenagers must present actions which are susceptible to several possible interpretations in ways which are likely to be supported by other speakers, either through ratification utterances or by story-chaining. The audience members actively or tacitly ratify the speaker's remarks, even if they disagree with the talk in principle. Interactants have techniques by which they can express their disagreement—through later contrary examples (which, too, are usually not disagreed with) or by audience role distance through joking interjections." Building on Fine's work, using Heise's (1979) sequential representation of conversation, Eder and Enke (1991) analyze language sequence in teenager gossip to highlight the importance of initial expressions for the subsequent course of the conversation (cf. Robinson and Smith-Lovin, 2001, on the use of jokes to mark status early in conversations among college students).

The emotional coordination enabled by etiquette highlights a quality of social structure left implicit in the earlier chapters. I left implicit the assumption, naive but widely invoked, that a strong relation between two people means they share what they know. So viewed, networks are a plumbing system in which strong connection between two people is pipe through which information flows.

More often than not, people share a sample of what they know. What a third party knows about you is their population of data, from which they draw a sample to disclose in any specific conversation. Subjects in the Higgins experiment had the initial sheet of information on Donald from which they drew a sample to share with the second student in the experiment. If the sample to be shared had been drawn at random, conversations aggregated across people and time would provide an unbiased picture of Donald. But a random sample would be rude, or at best socially inept. It is polite in casual conversation to go along with the flow of sentiment being shared. Data are sampled not for population representation, but for emotional coordination.

The tone of the conversation is apparent from a variety of cues ranging from the subtle nuance of a raised eyebrow or a skeptical tone of voice, to the blatant signal of expressing a positive or negative opinion. Skill in reading a social situation is manifest as an individual ability (e.g., the human capital of "emotional intelligence," Goleman, 1995; or a "sixth sense," Hogarth, 2001). As illustrated by the high-performance teams discussed in the previous chapter, however, the skill is probably more developed between people who have spent group time with one another such that individual ability to "read emotional cues" increases with network closure (see Elfenbein, Polzer, and Ambady, 2004, for argument and illustration).

The result is an echo. Speakers, tuned to one another's emotions, share story data-samples consistent with predispositions. We share in conversation those of our facts consistent with the perceived dispositions of the people with whom we speak, and facts shared are facts more likely to be remembered. As Fine (1996: 1170) so nicely phrased it in his discussion of people whose stories shape the reputations of others ("reputational entrepreneurs"): "We remember our history, not through the details of events, but through labels that characterize and summarize these events." Of the positive and negative data available to share in a conversation, the datum actually shared depends on the tone of the conversation. If people in a conversation seem to feel good about you, the third party relays a story in which you were a good colleague. It would be rude to bring up that embezzlement charge a couple years ago. If people seem to feel uncomfortable about you, the third party relays a story in which you were less than a good colleague. It would be rude to bring up that award for excellence you received a couple years ago. Having shared a story featuring certain of your behaviors, people are thereafter more likely to think of you in terms of the behaviors discussed (e.g., Fine, 1986, on exaggerated opinions in which some teenagers can "do no wrong," while others can "do no right").[1] Etiquette does not affect every conversation equally, and people are not everywhere polite, but allow that etiquette sometimes prevails. The more polite the society, the more likely the echo. The more closed the network, the louder the echo.

4.1.2 Motives

People are more likely to follow the rules of etiquette in a formal setting than in an informal discussion with colleagues. If etiquette biases what is shared in

---

[1] For generalization and evidence, see Brown and Levinson (1987), Stirling (1956), Rosen and Tesser (1970), Drew and Heritage (1992), Klayman (1995: 393–401), Backbier, Hoogstraten, and Terwogt-Kouwenhoven (1997), and Higgins (1999). Etiquette is an element in the broader process of people defining one another as a by-product of the stories they share (e.g., Cialdini, 1989; Tilly, 1998b).

informal discussion, the bias has to be in the interest of both parties to the discussion, the third party relaying a story, and the person listening to the story. These are questions about motive. Why would third parties echo the listener's predisposition regardless of the third-party's own opinion? For a third party displeased with someone, gossip is an opportunity to get even (e.g., Black, 1995: 855 n.; "gossip is the handling of a grievance by an informal hearing in absentia—in the absence of the alleged offender"). On the other side, we have all been in the role of third party sharing a story that fit the tone of a conversation. Given a known etiquette bias in third-party information, why don't people discount what third parties say?

Motive is clear from the ends served. Gossip in not about information. It is not about accurate portrayal of the people and events discussed. People who share our gossip with the person discussed are troublemakers (Goodwin, 1982). Gossip is about connecting the two people sharing a story. Emotional coordination in gossip serves a relationship-building function for people similar to grooming between primates. As primates signal attachment and hierarchy by picking bugs off one another, we signal by telling stories about the people and events around us (see Dunbar, 1996, for the analogy; Cialdini and Goldstein, 2004, on compliance and conformity resulting from a desire for affiliation and positive self-concept). As Merry (1984: 276–277) phrases the "grooming" dimension: "Gossip is a form of private information that symbolizes intimacy. It is a social statement that the recipient of gossip is as socially close or closer to the speaker as is the subject of the gossip. To the audience, gossip is a confidence, a sign of trust and closeness. As gossip becomes more judgmental, it becomes a more powerful statement of social intimacy and trust." Given the heterogeneous interests of the people around us, the way we build relationships with one another—for economic, political, social, or other reasons—is to focus on what we have in common. The most obvious cue to common interests is the tone of the conversation. It is rude to bring up data inconsistent with the tone of what has just been said. The only people who insist on telling us everything they know on a topic are teenagers exercising Montessori independence from adults (Fine's work certainly shows etiquette in their discussions with one another)—which goes a long way to explaining why we'd rather not hang out with them. In the succinct phrasing of Fran Lebowitz (1981: 14): "Spilling your guts is just exactly as charming as it sounds." A further problem with full disclosure is that third parties far apart in social structure can relay inconsistent stories. Etiquette simplifies decisions about people by protecting us from data on the full range of their behavior, and allows people of diverse interests to ignore differences that would otherwise inhibit conversation (e.g., Nyberg, 1993; Kuran, 1997, on the need for deception in everyday life). Finally, as much as etiquette facilitates the formation of relations despite our differences, it facilitates disengaging from a conversation without insulting the other person. Corroborating a predisposition ends discussion without seeming rude, and information consistent with what the other person already knows is more likely to be accepted and less likely to provoke disagreement (e.g., Ross and Anderson, 1982, on attribution errors; Klayman, 1995, on people more likely to see data consistent with their beliefs; and Simons and Chabris, 1999, on people unlikely to see strikingly obvious new data while they are focused on other data).

Building their relationship shades into a sense of social identity for speaker and listener. Gossip is about creating and maintaining relationships, especially between socially similar people, people "of our kind." Beyond the immediate conversation, etiquette highlights structural equivalence with respect to the discussed events and people of mutual interest. When you and I discuss our views of John, we reinforce our relationship with one another and narrow the confidence interval around our joint opinion of John. There is a scene in *Annie Hall*, a movie popular with my generation of Americans, in which the hero and heroine are sitting in Central Park making fun of people who walk by. With each whispered, patronizing characterization and resulting shared giggle, the man and woman are connected as co-conspirators against concrete points of reference in the surrounding environment. For more live data, listen to conversations between men and women meeting one another in a recreation facility intended to promote matching—a singles bar, a dance, et cetera: You like that music, I like that music. You like that author, I like that author. You disdain that person, I disdain that person. The more points of similarity, the more that the two people are the same kind of person; the more reasonable that they should be friends.

The people and events we jointly disdain have a special importance. Who we are is in some measure defined by who we are not (e.g., Gluckman, 1963; Elias and Scotson, 1994 [1965]: ch. 7; Erikson, 1966; Wittek and Wielers, 1998). That is the foundation for Durkheim's intuition about the social value of criminals (Durkheim, 1933 [1893]: 102; cf. Erikson, 1966: 4):

Of course, we always love the company of those who feel and think as we do, but it is with passion, and no longer solely with pleasure, that we seek it immediately after discussions where our common beliefs have been greatly combated. Crime brings together upright consciences and concentrates them. We have only to notice what happens, particularly in a small town, when some moral scandal has just been committed. They stop each other on the street, they visit each other, they seek to come together to talk of the event and to wax indignant in common. From all the similar impressions which are exchanged, from all the temper that gets itself expressed, there emerges a unique temper, more or less determinate according to the circumstances, which is everybody's without being anybody's in particular.

Hoffer (1951: 91) strips away the academic tone: "Mass movements can rise and spread without belief in a God, but never without belief in a devil. Usually the strength of a mass movement is proportionate to the vividness and tangibility of its devil." As we build images of the people and events around us, we construct their reputation at the same time that we construct a sense of ourselves, making claims to a reputation of our own. This is consequential because it interlocks reputations, making them more difficult to change. Changing the reputation of the principle person or group in a popular story can affect the reputation of people drawn together by sharing the story (see Section 4.5.2 on reputation ownership).

Building relations and reputations has value, but it would be naive to assume that these motives are responsible for listeners believing the stories they hear. We know from our own experience that speakers are polite. With a known etiquette filter on casual conversation, people should discount the information content of gossip about colleagues.

That is, unless there is no meaningful point estimate of a colleague. To say third parties lie when they obey the etiquette filter in sampling data to share assumes that there is a truth they are not sharing. But what if there is more than one truth? We each behave well with some people and not with others. For example, suppose you had productive exchanges with a new colleague Susan, and related your experiences to a friend who corroborated your positive experience. With positive personal and third-party opinion established, you are on a path to trusting Susan. But your trusted secretary of many years turns out to be a close friend of Susan's secretary, through whom you learn about Susan's abuse of a former colleague. The truth about Susan, as with most people, is context and partner specific. Point estimates of a person being good or bad is a small fraction of variance in colleague evaluations. The point is illustrated by two features of banker–colleague evaluations discussed in the next section (Figure 4.3). Positive and negative evaluations increase together, not in opposition. The more often a banker is evaluated, the more often he or she receives positive and negative evaluations.[2] Second, analysis of variance shows that a banker's evaluation of a colleague is more a function of the specific banker–colleague pair than either the banker or the colleague as individuals.[3]

In other words, a decision about someone's trustworthiness is an evaluation made without a concrete empirical referent, and there is ample evidence that such evaluations are shaped by discussion with peers. Recall the discussion of small worlds and the research in social psychology showing that people in the

---

[2] The number of evaluations a banker receives is correlated .91 with the number of positive evaluations received, and .80 with the number of negative evaluations. Similarly, Sparrowe et al. (2001: 321) report evaluations increasing with employee centrality in the network of advice relations and the network of hindrance relations.

[3] Regress banker i's evaluation of colleague j across the mean evaluation made by banker i and the mean evaluation received by colleague j. Of the variance across 31,394 evaluations, analysis of variance shows that 26% measures differences between respondents (some bankers give higher ratings on average), 15% measures differences between subjects (some bankers receive higher ratings on average), and the remaining 59% of the variance measures qualities specific to the respondent-subject pair of bankers. In other words, the distinction between positive and negative relations is a function of the two people involved more than either person individually (see Kenny and Albright, 1987: 399, for a similar result describing relations between college students).

same social cluster tend to have redundant information, beliefs, and behaviors (Sections 1.1 and 2.4). As Coleman, Katz and Menzel (1966: 118–119) adapted the research to study doctors prescribing a new drug: "When a new drug appears, doctors who are in close interaction with their colleagues will similarly interpret for one another the new stimulus that has presented itself, and will arrive at some shared way of looking at it." Friends discussing ambiguous items socialize one another into a shared perception. That is echo. Those socializing discussions are the gossip responsible for the echo effects in this chapter. The socializing is confined to ambiguous items. It does not happen on questions of fact. To borrow the original example in Festinger, Schachter, and Back (1950), the claim that a road is a dead-end can be checked with empirical data. Travel down the road to find out for yourself. Office gossip typically concerns ambiguous items, topics of conversation about which colleagues are uncertain. There are no concrete data against which one can check the accuracy of a claim that appointing James to the job would be a dead-end. The claim feels as true as there are colleagues who agree with it. If someone seems predisposed to trust you, perhaps the person is one of the people who will get along with you, and it is not surprising that their friends relay stories about you consistent with the positive predisposition. On the other hand, if the person seems predisposed to distrust you, perhaps the person is one of the people who will not get along with you, so it is not surprising that the person's friends offer stories about you consistent with the negative predisposition. Gossip is not about truth, it is about sociability (e.g., Gambetta, 1994: 13; "Plausibility is more relevant than truth. A convincing story gets repeated because of its appeal not its truthfulness."). A by-product of that sociability is that predispositions are reinforced—intensely positive in some clusters and intensely negative in others, depending on cluster predispositions.[4]

---

[4] An implication is that certain people are more susceptible to control by gossip. People unclear about their social standing will find it in the conversations around them, and so be more susceptible to control by gossip. Merry (1984: 282–284, 286–288) talks about people of very high, or very low, status being immune to control by gossip. Phillips and Zuckerman (2001) provide argument and corroborating evidence. Conformity is highest among people in the middle of a status order; where status is most ambiguous, making them more "status conscious." Reasoning backward from the fact that people assert their insider status when they relay stories as the arbiters of others' reputations (e.g., Erikson, 1966, on the Salem witch hysteria, and Boyer and Nissenbaum, 1976, on the specific individuals who identified witches), it is likely that people in the middle of a status order are also more often the "reputational entrepreneurs" to whom Fine (1996) attributes the creation and destruction of reputations. It is tempting to think about gossip becoming more important with the increasingly ambiguous definitions of jobs in flattened-down organizations, but gossip and reputation have been important social forces for a long time (e.g., Grief, 1989, on communication and reputation in the medieval Mediterranean; Fenster and Smail, 2003, on gossip and reputation, "fama," in medieval Europe). I prefer Durkheim's nineteenth-century intuition quoted in the text—when people feel a threat to their social standing, they find

Here again, social-capital implications are more by-product than goal. The immediate goal is building the relationship between two people. A by-product is more certain opinion about a colleague. There is no intention on a listener's part to over-react to incomplete information, but third-party gossip creates a feeling of having more information than is the case. Echo is an unintended consequence of purposive social action. Merton (1936) drew attention to this class of explanations, later developing the theme with review of illustrative work in his contrast between manifest and latent functions, and his discussion of the self-fulfilling prophecy (see Merton, 1968, esp. 105n, 114 ff., 182, 475 ff.). The third-party effects of gossip need not be exclusively an unintended consequence of purposive action, but they are often unintended.[5] The recognition is productive in two ways: First, it focuses analytical attention (cf. Merton, 1968: 119–124). Recognizing the unintended consequences of gossip is a prophylactic against wasting analytical time on reasons why listeners fail to discount gossip. Attention is focused instead on the ways in which interaction for other reasons with third parties creates a vicarious feeling of repeated interaction with a discussed colleague, and from there a false sense of

---

affirmation in social contact with one another, identifying people on the periphery of their group who are clearly not "us" and celebrating heroes who embody what we would like "us" to look like. The people most susceptible to, and involved in, social control by gossip are the people most insecure about their place among the people around them. This status insecurity could be treated as low self-esteem and people with low self-esteem are more susceptible to peer pressure, but focusing on status ambiguity allows that person can be more or less susceptible to gossip in different situations. A person clear about his social standing on one project could appear to have high self-esteem and be indifferent to gossip at the same time that he appears on another project to have low self-esteem where his ambiguous status leaves him sensitive to colleague stories about his behavior.

[5] In this, I am stopping short of Elster's (1983: 43–85) analysis of by-products. Elster focuses on conditions that occur *only* as a by-product of action directed toward other goals. The predicted effects of third-party gossip are probably more often than not by-products in Elster's sense. The amplified certainty created by gossip is an over-reaction to information, and that seems an unlikely intentional goal. There are occasions, however, on which such an unlikely goal could be sought. On the positive side, ego doesn't know alter, is assigned to work with alter, so positive third-party gossip can make ego feel more comfortable with alter. Even between friends there are times when a positive third-party story is a welcome aid to one friend trying to overlook an unpleasant act by the other. On the negative side, ego doesn't know alter, is uncomfortable working with new people, so negative third-party gossip is an excuse not to trust alter. Still, there is a difference between seeking an outcome, and feeling comfortable with the outcome. Ego afraid of trusting alter might find comfort in negative third-party gossip that provides ostensibly objective grounds for not trusting alter. But that is not the same as consciously looking for negative gossip, or announcing to friends that one is looking for negative gossip. These examples are (interesting) pathological third-party effects in which ego defensively induces a third-party effect to resolve the tension of having to decide whether to trust alter. Such behavior is an issue for subsequent work on echo as a function of listener motives.

certainty about the colleague. Second, recognition clarifies the analysis of seemingly irrational social patterns, and so lays a foundation for replacing morality judgments with analytical understanding (Merton, 1968: 118–119, 124 ff.). The gossip argument offers a reason why reasonable people do not always act so; for example, enthusiastically endorsing a colleague's competence beyond levels warranted by the facts as you see them, or deriding a colleague's character to an extreme. This is neither stupidity, nor immaturity, but rather an expression of certainty appropriate to the person's felt level of information, a level amplified by gossip beyond the sensibilities of a neutral observer. What was a glimmer of insight can become irrefutable fact with sufficient echo.

In sum, the motives responsible for echo in closed networks are not about why speakers lie or listeners are naive. Such framing implies a distinction between social exchange and the truth. The motive is speakers and listeners working to better establish their standing with each other, and together defining the truth by discussing it.

4.1.3   Echo and Reputation

Contradictory predictions by bandwidth and echo makes it possible to test them against one another. The bandwidth hypothesis in Chapter 3 is concerned with positive third-party ties, illustrated in the lower-right corner of Figure 3.4. A positive third-party tie exists between two people with strong positive connections to a mutual friend, and it exists between two people with strong disdain for the same colleague. The trust predicted in relations embedded in positive third-party ties is predicted by bandwidth to be distrust where there are strong negative third-party ties. The forms are ego and alter where ego thinks well of colleagues who disdain alter or alter thinks well of colleagues who disdain ego. Treating ego badly is prescribed behavior in alter's group. Treating alter badly is prescribed behavior in ego's group. Ego and alter would be wise to distrust one another. The bandwidth prediction is that trust within the relationship between two people builds in the direction of the third-party opinion in which it is embedded. Generalizing beyond recent discussions of trust, the idea that direct connections should be consistent with indirect connections through third parties has long been discussed in sociology as balance theory, an import from cognitive consistency theory in psychology (Doreian et al., 1996; see Kilduff and Krackhardt, 1994, for balance applied to reputation in a work group).

Echo is a local production process in which inconsistent relations can develop next to one another. Etiquette makes it possible for information to vary between adjacent relationships because the information disclosed by third parties will depend on their perception of preferences within each relationship. Echo does not require that people recall the individuals from whom specific stories were heard (so many stories begin with the line; "I can't recall where I heard it, but I heard recently that ...''). Opinion differences between neighbors can continue unspoken. Strong positive relationships can exist next to strong negative ones. The bandwidth prediction of correlation between third-party opinion and the trust between two people is limited under echo to opinion intensity: The echo prediction is that stronger third-party ties foster more intense opinion such that relations adjacent in a network need not be balanced in their direction (I trust friends of my friends), so much as their intensity (I have an opinion, positive or negative, of my friends' friends).[6] Thus, where the bandwidth hypothesis predicts the direction of sentiment, echo predicts the intensity or certainty of the sentiment.

---

[6] The hypothesis can be stated more precisely in terms of the statistical decision model in Ch. 3 nn. 3 and 9. Ego has $(N+T)$ game outcomes g, N outcomes in ego's personal experience with alter and T outcomes in stories ego has heard about alter. The sum of squared deviations in ego's N personal experiences is: $\Sigma^N[g - \bar{g}]^2 = \Sigma^N[(g - \bar{g}_n) - (\bar{g} - \bar{g}_n)]^2$, where $\bar{g}$ is the grand mean across all $(N+T)$ games, and $\bar{g}_n$ is the mean of ego's N experiences. Squaring the expression and summing components yields: $\Sigma^N(g - \bar{g}_n)^2 + \Sigma^N(\bar{g} - \bar{g}_n)^2 - 2(\bar{g} - \bar{g}_n)[\Sigma^N(g - \bar{g}_n)]$, where the third term is zero because the sum of deviations around their mean (the term in brackets) is zero. Do the same accounting to get the corresponding variance terms for ego's T vicarious games with alter in third-party stories: $\Sigma^T(g - \bar{g}_t)^2 + \Sigma^T(\bar{g} - g_t)^2 - 2(\bar{g} - \bar{g}_t)[\Sigma^T(g - \bar{g}_t)]$, where $\bar{g}_t$ is the mean of the T vicarious games, and the third term is again zero because deviations around the mean sum to zero. Thus, there are three components in the variance in ego's data on alter behavior: variance across the N personal experiences (s_n^2), variance across the T vicarious games (s_t^2), and variance created by discrepancy between ego's personal and vicarious experiences :

$$(3) \qquad s^2 = \frac{\Sigma^N(g - \bar{g}_n)^2 + \Sigma^T(g - \bar{g}_t)^2 + [\Sigma^N(\bar{g}_n - \bar{g})^2 + \Sigma^T(\bar{g}_t - \bar{g})^2]}{N + T - 1},$$

which can be analyzed, at a level of precision appropriate to the measurement available, in terms of the following expression (B for bias variance).

$$\frac{(N)s_n^2 + (T)s_t^2 + [B]}{N + T}.$$

Third parties guided by etiquette expose ego to stories that reinforce ego's predisposition, so $(N+T)$ increases relative to s_t^2 faster than N increases relative to s_n^2. The result is a standard error of ego's combined information on alter (Eq. 3 divided by $N+T$) smaller than the standard error of personal experience (Eq. 2),

$$(4) \qquad s_n^2 \frac{(N + T)}{N} > \frac{(N)s_n^2 + (T)s_t^2 + [B]}{N + T}$$

If ego and alter are in a context free of third parties, the bias term (B) is zero, vicarious games (T) are zero, and the variance in Eq. (3) equals the variance in ego's personal experience (Eq. 1 in ch. 3 n. 3)—so Eq. (4) is an equality. There is no third-party effect. In the presence of third parties guided by etiquette, the bias term (B) approaches zero, the sum of experiences exceeds ego's personal experience ($N + T > N$), and variance in third-party accounts (s_t^2) approaches zero, which means the standard error of ego's information on alter approaches zero—so the inequality in equation (4) is large, generating the predicted third-party effect of ego more certain in his or her evaluation of alter.

Illustrative Predictions

The evidence of trust in the previous chapter (Figures 3.3 and 3.4) is consistent with bandwidth and echo. Trust is expected in strong relationships, especially when they are embedded in strong third-party ties. This is the prediction if third parties are neutral conduits for information (bandwidth). It is the prediction if third parties are an etiquette-biased source of corroborating information (echo). The way to test bandwidth against echo is to look for situations in which third-party ties in one direction generate trust in the other direction (illustrated below). Bandwidth predicts that such situations should not occur. Echo predicts that they can.

Using Figure 4.1 for illustration, bandwidth and echo are indistinguishable in predicting who Jessica trusts. The hypotheses differ at the extreme of predicting trust within Jessica's negative relationships to contacts 6 and 7 (thus the box in Figure 4.1 around the predictions), but the probability of trust is so low in negative relations that this will be a difficult difference to measure with available research instruments.

Distrust is more interesting. The bandwidth hypothesis predicts that Jessica is more likely to distrust contact 6 than 7 because there are no third parties to her relationship with 6 and so no reputation costs to 6 for misbehavior toward Jessica. The echo hypothesis predicts that Jessica is more likely to distrust contact 7 because that relationship is embedded in third-party ties through contacts 2 and 5, both of whom will offer stories about contact 7 to Jessica that corroborate Jessica's negative relationship with 7. Similarly for Jessica's weak relationships, bandwidth predicts that Jessica is more likely to distrust contact 4 than 5 because there are no third parties to her relation with 4 and so no reputation costs to 4 for misbehavior toward Jessica. The prediction is complicated by Jessica's negative relation with contact 7, who could be expected to tell to both Jessica and contact 5 negative stories about the other so that a negative relationship develops between them consistent with the negative indirect relationship through contact 7. Cutting against that complication is 7's strong, positive connection with contacts 5 and 2, and the strong, positive third-party tie between Jessica and 5 via contact 2. With positive balance of

---

More specifically, to better distinguish echo from bandwidth, let t_{ea} be a measure of ego's trust in alter, a variable that ranges from negative one if ego definitely distrusts alter, up to one if ego definitely trusts alter, with neutral zero indicating that ego neither trusts nor distrusts alter. Let z_{ea} be a measure of the strength of ego's relationship with alter, a variable that ranges from negative one for a strong, negative ego–alter relationship, up to one for a strong, positive relationship, with a neutral zero indicating no prior relationship. Bandwidth predicts that ego's trust in alter, t_{ea}, increases with the sum of indirect connections to alter through third parties k ($\Sigma_k z_{ek}z_{ka}$, $e \neq k \neq a$). In other words, the direction of ego's opinion is correlated with third-party opinion. Echo predicts that ego's certainty about alter, $|t_{ea}|$, increases with the absolute value of indirect connections to alter through third parties ($\Sigma_k |z_{ek}z_{ka}|$, $e \neq k \neq a$). In other words, the intensity of ego's opinion increases with the intensity of third-party ties.

indirect connections between Jessica and contact 5, and Jessica's relation with contact 4 embedded in no third-party ties, Jessica is more likely to distrust 4 than 5 under the bandwidth hypothesis. Echo reverses the bandwidth prediction. Distrust is more likely with contact 5 than 4 because the relation with 5 is embedded in third-party ties through contacts 2 and 7. Jessica's weak relationships with contacts 4 and 5 are both subject to the inevitable doubts about trusting someone with whom one has only a weak relationship, but third-party gossip is expected to amplify those doubts more with contact 5. Contact 7 would find it especially easy to be polite in reinforcing anything negative that Jessica or contact 5 had to say about one another.

Echo-Affected Relations Define Reputation

Reputations are typically measured as an average evaluation. These are the 360 evaluations discussed in Section 3.3.2 (and below in Section 4.4) along with other reputation measures such as mean evaluations of cars, traders on eBay, professors, and so on. Someone receiving an average evaluation of 1.5 on a five-point scale is an employee not well appreciated by colleagues. An average evaluation of 4.5 indicates positive colleague opinion. The first employee has a weak reputation, the second a strong, positive reputation.

It is a short step to factor in the uncertainty of a reputation. If the 1.5 average evaluation were based on two evaluations, while the 4.5 was based on many, there would be less uncertainty in the second average. Reasoning from the standard error of the mean, uncertainty increases when data are few and contradictory.

Gossip reduces uncertainty in each evaluation. Echo-amplified evaluations aggregate to define echo-amplified reputations. Let ego be someone evaluating a colleague, alter. As third-party gossip amplifies ego's opinion of alter, it aggregates across egos to amplify alter's reputation. People more certain in their trust of alter define a more certainly positive reputation for alter. However many people admire alter, the positive reputation they generate increases with third-party connections through which admirers share stories that reinforce one another's opinion of alter. At the other extreme, detractors are more dangerous for alter's reputation when they have extensive third-party connections because the detractors will be more certain of alter's faults than would be the case if they were socially isolated from one another. Reputations embedded in dense third-party connections are amplified. More certain admirers and detractors mean stronger reputation effects as people respond to alter's more clearly positive or negative reputation.[7]

---

[7] An alternative explanation for the amplified opinions is that people are misled by lower quality information in gossip. For example, Gilovich (1987) showed undergraduates a video of a person describing "something you are not too proud of," then asked subjects to describe the person on audio tape, and rate his culpability for his bad

4.2 Evidence of Distrust

My evidence of echo describes third parties associated with colleagues cited for distrust, the language used to explain difficult relationships, and network stability over time. Figure 4.2 begins with colleagues cited for distrust. The people citing colleagues for distrust are the senior managers, staff officers, and bankers who cited colleagues for trust in Figures 3.3 and 3.4. For the bankers, a colleague is cited for distrust when, in the annual peer evaluations, the banker gave the colleague minimum ratings for integrity and teamwork. For the managers and staff officers, it is indicated by a sociometric citation for most difficult colleague: "Of your colleagues, who has made it the most difficult for you to carry out your job responsibilities?" The citation is open to alternative interpretations since it does not ask about distrust explicitly (Krackhardt, 1996), but when respondents were asked to explain why they cited the person they did, their explanations indicated distrust (Section 4.2). Of all the colleagues cited as important work contacts, few were cited for distrust (9% of the senior-manager contacts, 12% of the staff-officer contacts, 8% of the banker contacts).

The most obvious association in Figure 4.2 is the baseline association between distrust and relation strength. The weaker the relationship, the more likely it is cited for distrust. Further replicating the results of the previous chapter, the association is nonlinear. Distrust in Figure 4.2 is concentrated in the least positive category of relations in each study population—just as trust in Figures 3.3 and 3.4 is concentrated in the most positive relations in each study population.[8]

---

behavior. A second subject then listens to the audio tape, and rates the person's culpability. Evaluations by the students with second-hand knowledge from audio tape are more extreme in blaming the person for his bad behavior. Gilovich argues that second-hand accounts elicit more extreme evaluations because the second-hand accounts leave out mitigating circumstances and situational constraints. That reduces the accounts to "cheap talk" which should be discounted (e.g., Gibbons, 1992: 210 ff., on cheap-talk games). But why should people believe a story stripped of situational details? Echo does not require people to be so naive. Third-party accounts are accurate, but not representative. Other things being equal, each third party has positive and negative stories about you. People receive complete stories, but not a representative set of stories. A person cannot know whether he or she is getting a subset of information biased toward the positive (or negative) because they do not know the scope of each third party's information on you.

[8] Statistical tests for alternative specifications are reported elsewhere (Burt and Knez, 1995; Burt, 2001). Logit regression models show strong negative associations between distrust and relation strength in Figure 4.2; -12.17 z-score for the senior managers, -12.78 z-score for the staff officers, and -6.27 z-score for the bankers. Test statistics are corrected for autocorrelation between relations cited by the same person (e.g., Kish and Frankel, 1974).

4.2.1 Distrust Associated with Third Parties

The data in Figure 4.2 are useful because distrust can be studied for the extent to which it is embedded in strong third-party ties. The network measure of indirect connection through third parties is taken from the previous chapter (footnotes 17 and 22). Grey bars distinguish relations embedded in strong third-party ties (indirect connection between respondent and colleague is stronger than average for their study population). White bars describe relations comparatively free of third parties.

If network closure were only providing bandwidth for information, then distrust would be less likely in relations embedded in positive third-party ties. Just the opposite is true. The odds of distrust increase when weak or negative relations are embedded in strong third-party ties. Consider the senior managers. Distrust is concentrated in weak relationships as expected under bandwidth and echo. It is in these relations that distrust variance is richest, so I distinguish three categories of third-party tie strength to see how embedding is associated with distrust (weakest 25% is white, 25–75% is gradient, strongest 25% is gray). On average, senior managers cited 24% of their weakest relations for distrust. The average drops to 9% for weak relations free of third parties (white bar to the left in Figure 4.2). The average increases to 39% for weak relations embedded in strong third-party ties.

This is precisely what should happen when network closure produces echo. When manager and colleague have mutual close contacts, the colleague often comes up in the manager's discussions with the contacts. Etiquette means that the manager hears stories, or shadings of stories, consistent with his opinion of the colleague, making the manager more certain in his opinion. Doubts, to be expected in a weak relationship, get amplified into distrust. In all three populations, the bankers, staff officers, and senior managers, distrust is concentrated in the weakest relations embedded in strong third-party ties. That is the same concentration pattern observed in Figures 3.3 and 3.4 for third-party effects facilitating trust.[9]

---

[9] Here again, statistical tests for alternative specifications are reported elsewhere (Burt and Knez, 1995; Burt, 2001). With respect to Figure 4.2, a logit regression model predicting distrust from relation strength (as in the previous footnote)—from the binary distinction in Figure 4.2 between strong and weak third-party ties, and a dummy variable distinguishing the weakest category relations embedded in strong third-party ties— shows statistically significant associations corresponding to the points made in the text. Respective test statistics of −7.11, 1.85, and 3.02 for the senior managers show distrust concentrated in weak relations, especially the ones embedded in strong third-party ties. Test statistics of −9.85, −.22, and 2.58 show the same thing for the staff officers. Test statistics of −6.92, 2.39, and 2.13 also show for the bankers the association between distrust and third parties.

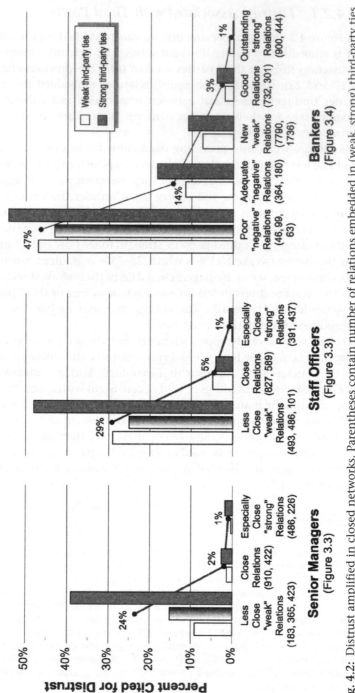

Fig. 4.2: Distrust amplified in closed networks. Parentheses contain number of relations embedded in (weak, strong) third-party ties

4.2.2   *Balance in Intensity Not Direction*

Figure 4.3 contains evidence on the bankers that more precisely supports echo over bandwidth. I am limited to the bankers because I do not have data on relations beyond each survey respondent's contacts in the other two populations. The relations described in Figure 4.3 are all 118,680 possible between the 345 bankers. These are the relations introduced in the previous chapter for the right-hand graph in Figure 3.4.

Relationships are sorted on the horizontal axis of Figure 4.3 with respect to third-party ties. In the left graph, relations vary from zero negative third-party ties up to ten or more. Evaluations of poor or adequate are treated as negative, evaluations of good or outstanding as positive (as in Figure 4.2). Illustrated at the bottom of Figure 4.3, a negative third-party tie between banker and colleague could occur in either of two ways: the banker made a positive evaluation of someone who made a negative evaluation of the colleague, or the banker made a negative evaluation of someone who made a positive evaluation of the colleague. In the right graph, corresponding to the right-hand

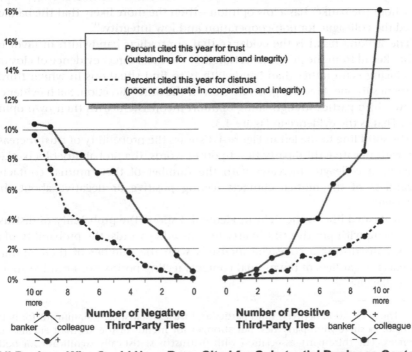

All Bankers Who Could Have Been Cited for Substantial Business Contact
(118,680 relationships)

Fig. 4.3: Closure last year is associated with trust and distrust this year

graph in Figure 4.3, relations vary from zero positive third-party ties up to ten or more. Illustrated at the bottom of the graph, a positive third-party tie between banker and colleague occurred when the banker made a positive evaluation of someone who made a positive evaluation of the colleague (a friend of my friend is my friend), or the banker made a negative evaluation of someone who made a negative evaluation of the colleague (enemy of my enemy is my friend).

This graph illustrates the way that bandwidth is a special case of echo. Two lines plotted in Figure 4.3 support bandwidth (and echo), one of which was presented in the previous chapter as evidence of closure's association with trust (bold line in the graph to the right in Figure 3.4). The solid line to the right in Figure 4.3 shows the probability of trust increasing with the number of positive third-party ties. The more mutual friends and mutual enemies a banker and colleague share, the more likely that the banker will cite the colleague for outstanding cooperation and integrity. Also consistent with both bandwidth and echo, the dashed line to the left in Figure 4.3 shows the probability of distrust increasing with negative third-parties. The more often that banker and colleague had separate constituencies—the banker's contacts having a low opinion of the colleague, or the colleague's contacts being people of whom the banker has a low opinion—then the more likely that the banker cited the colleague for non-cooperation and low integrity.[10]

The striking result is the evidence that contradicts bandwidth in favor of echo. Recall from the previous section that the most direct evidence of closure producing echo rather than bandwidth is to find situations in which third-party ties in one direction generate trust in the other direction. Such evidence shows third parties strengthening opinion inconsistent with their own opinion. That is the evidence in Figure 4.3:

The solid line to the left in Figure 4.3 shows the probability of trust increasing with negative third-party ties. In other words, the probability of a banker trusting a colleague increases with the number of their mutual contacts, regardless of the mutual contacts feeling positive or negative about the colleague.

The dashed line to the right in Figure 4.3 shows the probability of distrust increasing with positive third-party ties. In other words, the probability of a banker distrusting a colleague increases with the number of their mutual contacts, regardless of the mutual contacts feeling positive or negative about the colleague.

---

[10] The association between third parties and trust is statistically significant for both forms of positive third-party ties, but stronger for friends of friends than enemies of enemies. The third-party association with distrust is statistically significant for both forms of negative third-party ties, though stronger for enemies of friends than friends of enemies. Statistical tests are reported elsewhere (Burt, 2001: Table 2) holding constant last year's relationship and the number of third parties available to a banker as possible indirect ties to colleagues.

In other words, the banker–colleague relations are balanced in intensity, not direction. Strong relations facilitate strong adjacent relations, positive and negative. In fact, the probability of banker trust is associated more closely with total third-party ties than the balance toward positive third-party ties. The probability of distrust is associated more closely with total third-party ties than with a balance toward negative third-party ties.[11]

A skeptical reader might want to attribute the results in Figure 4.3 to something unusual in investment banking, but the results are more likely typical of medium to large organizations. For example, see Coles, Harris, and Dickson (2003) for illustration of conflict and cooperation coexisting over time in the joint-venture network between two defense contractors, one in the U.S. and the other in the U.K. The results in Figure 4.3 could seem unusual because sociometric choices in survey network data are not usually analyzed with respect to the population of relations that could have been cited. Here, the survey network data are analyzed in conjunction with a roster of people in the study population who could have been cited. Another generic feature of the results in Figure 4.3 is their consistency with a common finding in network analysis—relationships develop in clusters to form a small world (illustrated in Figure 1.1). As the number of third-party ties between two people increase, it becomes increasingly likely that the two people know about, and have an opinion of, one another. When completing their annual peer evaluations, bankers were more likely to remember work with colleagues with whom they had mutual friends, acquaintances, or enemies.

The central point is the empirical support for echo over bandwidth. Bandwidth predicts balance between adjacent relationships, my friend's friend is my friend, my friend's enemy is my enemy. That prediction is clearly contradicted in Figure 4.3 by trust associated with negative third-party ties, and distrust associated with positive third-party ties. Figure 4.3 is precisely the pattern predicted by echo. With gossip pandering to predispositions, strong positive relations can develop next to strong negative relations. What is balanced by etiquette-filtered gossip is the intensity of adjacent relations, not their direction. Strong third-party ties mean a high volume of gossip, from which strong relations emerge, either positive or negative, depending on predispositions.

---

[11] See Burt (2001: Table 2) for statistical tests showing significant increases in trust, and significant increases in distrust, with each kind of positive and negative third-party tie. The closing statement to the paragraph is based on logit models predicting trust and distrust from strength of last year's relationship and number of colleagues cited, then adding to the predictors the total number of third parties to the relationship and the extent to which positive exceed negative third parties. The logit z-score test statistics are 19.9 and 9.9 for the third-party sum and balance respectively in predicting trust, 21.9 and −4.8 respectively in predicting distrust (Burt, 2001: Table 2). A balance toward positive third parties increases the probability of trust and decreases the probability of distrust, but both effects are weaker than the increased probability of trust and distrust with the sum of positive and negative third-party ties.

4.3   Character Assassination

Where relations are predicted by network structure to be more intense, language describing the relations should be more extreme and personal. For example, gossip-amplified feelings of trust would be manifest in effusive and heroic language (e.g., see Khurana, 2002, on charismatic leaders, esp. pp. 170 ff. on able candidates coming to be recognized as charismatic leaders). At the other extreme, stories we share about disreputable colleagues are a bond between us, an assertion of what is reputable, and a warning of what happens to unscrupulous people. The sociology of the situation is that if we didn't have an occasional unscrupulous colleague, we would have to make him up (see the discussion of motives in Section 4.1.2).

This section elaborates on the distrust associated with third parties in Section 4.2 by looking at the language used to describe difficult relationships. When the senior managers and staff officers in Figure 4.2 cited their most difficult colleague, they were asked to explain in a phrase or two why the colleague was so difficult. It is clear from Figure 4.2 that third parties around weak relations are associated with distrust, but language could be a different dimension. Where a manager and colleague have close, mutual friends, the manager might avoid extreme language. Closure increases the odds of a colleague hearing about your derogatory remarks. To avoid embarrassment, and any stigma attached to being negative about insiders, managers in a closed network might temper extreme language they would otherwise use to vent frustration with a difficult relationship. If closure tempers extreme language, closure slows the escalation of distrust—and so operates to facilitate trust. On the other hand, if the echo hypothesis is correct, then third parties relay stories that corroborate our suspicions of difficult colleagues, which would inflame difficult relations. Where echo is at work, difficult colleagues are described using extreme and personal language reflecting the speaker's amplified certainty about the colleague.[12]

Blame is a prominent feature in the manager and officer explanations of difficult relations. Some explanations blame the colleague, others blame the situation.[13] *Situational* attributions cite organizational issues ("conflict of

---

[12] I am concerned here with a person expressing disparaging remarks about a colleague. This leaves aside the question of whether the remarks stick, creating a negative reputation about the discussed colleague. Feeling that a person's character is flawed is distinct from converting a public to that feeling. The latter is a political campaign of supporters being quiet while detractors distribute catchy stories in support of their view. This is the work of what Fine (1996) describes as "reputational entrepreneurs," which he illustrates with the destruction of Warren G. Hardings' positive reputation within six months of Hardings' death (one of several "difficult reputations" described in Fine, 2001). My question for this section is less grand. I merely want to know whether people in closed networks show the effects of echo in their opinions of colleagues.

[13] This is a familiar dimension of difficult relationships. See Rodin (1985: 825–834), Ross and Fletcher (1985), and Blount (1995) for reviews of Heider's (1958) distinction between personal versus situational attribution.

goals; what was good for him was bad for my group," "personally we got along wonderfully, but people in her organization have a difficult style"), or the vicissitudes of global business ("language barrier was very difficult"), or the colleague's situation ("she is under a lot of pressure and it spills over to the people around her"). Personal attributions were more numerous and complex. In reading through the explanations, I distinguished two kinds of personal attributions:[14] *Competence* attributions are neutral about the colleague's character, citing things like the colleague being "too emotional and immature to manage his organization," or "promoted too high, too fast; beyond her level of experience," or simply "does not understand his functional area." Then there were managers who attributed the difficulty to a flaw in the colleague's *character*, explaining that the colleague was "dishonest; self-serving, no integrity," or an "egotistical, self-oriented liar; worst manager I have ever met," or "not trustworthy, a back-stabber," or simply a "nasty, ill-tempered bitch."

There are items to note in the explanations (for example, character attributions are more likely in the financial services firm), but I begin with the progression implicit in moving from blaming a difficult situation, to blaming colleague competence, to *ad hominem* remarks about the colleague's character. Repeated difficulty identifies a disreputable colleague: Your initial meetings with John are difficult. You have little experience with John, so the difficulty of your initial meetings could be explained in multiple ways—the problem could have been peculiar to those meetings (you caught John at a bad time, or you were a little more difficult than usual), or a function of the situation in which

---

[14] A selection of illustrative explanations from each category are given elsewhere (Burt, 1999a: Table 1). To analyze the explanations, I prepared a list of explanations in random order and went down the list circling the category that best described each explanation. I checked the reliability of the coding by asking a colleague, Joseph E. Jannotta, Jr., to go through the same list. Mr. Jannotta was the president and founder of Jannotta/Bray and Associates, selling it in 1995 to a large Philadelphia firm looking to establish operations in Chicago. The company operates in a variety of businesses related to the outplacement of senior employees. Mr. Jannotta has heard a rich diversity of senior manager explanations about relationships gone wrong. Here is the tabulation of my coding (in the rows) against Mr. Jannotta's (columns):

42	20	1
23	68	12
3	27	60

in the order of situation, competence, and character. A loglinear model of the table shows only two significant positive interactions; tendencies to agree on situational explanations and explanations blaming the other person's character (5.8 and 6.7 loglinear z-scores respectively, $P < .001$). The only two significant negative interactions are tendencies not to confuse situational and character explanations (-3.6 z-score in the upper right cell, -5.5 in the lower left, $P < .001$). All other interactions are negligible (largest is 1.3 z-score for the middle cell, where Mr. Jannotta and I agree on competence explanations). So, the situation and character categories of explanation in Figure 4.4 are the most reliable. Fortunately, these are the categories most important to the third-party effects, and the third-party effects are statistically significant with either coding.

you had to deal with John (the issue under discussion was complex and ambiguous, the interests of his and your organizations do not align easily, etc.). As you have repeated contact with John, all of it difficult, you realize that the problem isn't you or the situation. The problem is John.

Character assassination is a useful image here. It is a person telling a story in which someone behaved disreputably. It is not enough that the colleague was disreputable in a difficult situation, a situation in which anyone might behave poorly. Character assassination is best served in a reluctant tone of moral indignation. "It is not I who was wronged by the manager's behavior; it is any right-thinking person; it is people like us." Character assassination involves severe and personal language (e.g., Van Maanen, 1978, on "assholes").

Echo can give people that feeling of self-righteous indignation even if they have had little direct contact with the person being assassinated. In the push and shove of negotiating contradictory interests, it is easy for discussion to escalate from arguments about the facts, to arguments about the character of people whose views differ from your own. Gossip encourages the escalation. People more exposed to gossip have a vicarious feeling of repeated interaction such that they are more certain in their trust or distrust of a colleague. Go back to the situation-to-person progression for attributing blame. Managers more exposed to gossip are more likely to interpret difficult relations in terms of the colleague's personality because they have corroborating stories about the colleague. They are more certain that the colleague, not the situation, is the problem. To some extent, voicing an emotion makes it more real. Hearing the emotion echoed by trusted colleagues makes it more real. A more certain manager is more likely to use strong words to express his or her certainty.

4.3.1 Third Parties and Linguistic Inflammation

There is evidence of third parties associated with linguistic inflammation. The point is illustrated in Figure 4.4. Explanations by the senior managers are sorted on the vertical axis of Figure 4.4 into the three kinds (blame the situation, blame the colleague's competence, or blame the colleague's character), then sorted within each kind by the strength of third-party ties in which the explained difficult relationship was embedded. Gray bars refer to difficult relations embedded in strong third-party ties. White bars refer to relations relatively free of third parties.

The graph to the left in Figure 4.4 shows that relations blamed on a difficult situation are typically free of third parties (white bar is 79%). At the other extreme, almost all difficult relations blamed on the colleague's character were embedded in strong third-party ties (gray bar is 96%). The third-party association with character assassination is visible, statistically significant, and even stronger for managers whose other colleagues form a closed network around

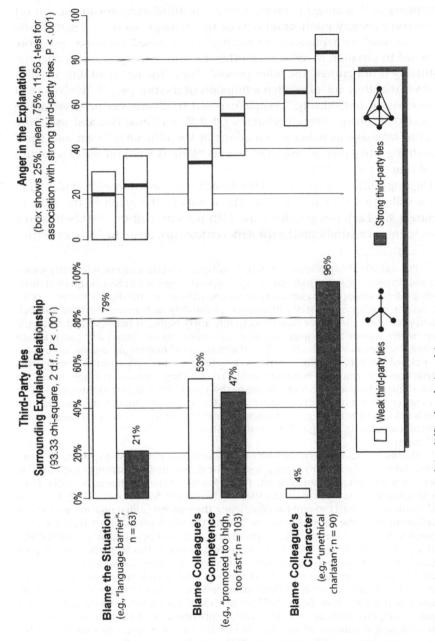

Fig. 4.4: Senior managers explain difficult relationships

the manager.[15] A closed network is awash in third-party gossip and cut off from contradictory information outside the network, so echo is particularly loud. Network entrepreneurs, in cutting across closed networks, are more exposed to variation in opinion and therefore more likely to realize that the difficulty is not entirely the other person's fault. The reality of difficult relations is that they are more often a function of the two people involved than either person individually.[16] People exposed to diverse perspectives can be expected to blame difficult relations on difficult situations and use more neutral language in public explanations of the difficulty: "John and I just couldn't get together on that one" (versus "John is a moron" or "I wouldn't trust him to carry spit").

Digging a little deeper, I coded the hostility expressed in each explanation on a scale from 0 to 100 and plot the results in the graph to the right in Figure 4.4.[17] Each box goes from the 25th percentile of the distribution in a row, to the mean (indicated by the dark vertical bar), up to the 75th percentile.

---

[15] The statistically significant test statistic in Figure 4.4 is less strong, but clearly rejects the null hypothesis, in the staff-officer explanations. There is a 21.88 chi-square statistic with 2 d.f. for character assassination associated with strong third-party ties (P < .001). Across the managers and staff officers, the probability of blaming the most difficult relation on the colleague's character is significantly higher if manager and colleague have many friends and acquaintances in common (strong third-party tie; 8.1 logit z-score test statistic), and higher still if the manager's contacts are densely connected in a closed network (2.6 logit z-score test statistic for network constraint measuring interconnection among a manager's contacts). Holding constant the boss being the most difficult contact does not eliminate the effects from strong third-party ties or network constraint (test statistics of 8.8 and 2.6 respectively), though it is true that the boss is unlikely to be the target of character assassination even if he or she is cited as most difficult colleague (−3.0 logit z-score test statistic).

[16] See n. 3.

[17] Hostility scores are given elsewhere for a selection of illustrative explanations (Burt, 1999a: Table 1). The hostility score is a semantic differential evaluation of each explanation (Osgood, Suci and Tannenbaum, 1957). My use of the differential is similar to its use in empirical tests of affect control theory (Heise, 1979; Smith-Lovin, 1987; Robinson and Smith-Lovin, 2001), except I am predicting the semantic differential evaluation of a relationship from the network structure around the relationship, rather than the prior emotions in the relationship. If I had panel data or time-series on manager emotions, I would be using them. The affect control research makes it clear that emotions are path dependent. The hostility generated by a difficult relationship, for example, is probably more intense for a manager who enters the relationship anticipating cooperation and success. Returning to the cross-sectional data, the score plotted in Figure 4.4 is an average across repeated codings of the level of hostility implicit in each manager's explanation. I wrote a computer program to display each explanation on the screen, then ask for a three-category evaluation of whether or not the manager seems hostile toward the other person; (0) no, (50) maybe, or (100) yes. The explanations are presented at random and the 256 evaluations are recorded. I use three categories because my initial use of five categories left me too often feeling that I was making arbitrary distinctions between categories. The three-category distinction felt more reliable. I use repeated measures to get more precise distinctions between managers. I completed the computer

The least anger is expressed in explanations blaming a difficult situation (for example, the explanation "conflict of goals; what was good for him was bad for my group" received an average rating of 0 for anger). There is more anger when dealing with an incompetent colleague ("too emotional and immature to manage his organization" received an average anger score of 75), and there is extreme anger when the difficulty was a disreputable colleague (e.g., "nasty, ill-tempered bitch" was consistently rated as angry). The anger expressed in an explanation is greater when the difficult relation is embedded in strong third-party ties, significantly so when the colleague's competence or character was blamed for the difficulty, and even more so when the explanation came from a manager embedded in a closed network.[18]

Another indicator of emotional intensity is the effort a respondent expends to get his or her point across. The respondents under study are explaining to me, a professor, why they had difficulty working with someone. Why bother? Nothing is gained by getting the explanation right—except the emotional release of venting frustration to convince a neutral third-party. Viewed as an exercise in venting frustration, explanations that show more effort indicate more intense manager emotion. Explanations can be compared in terms of a simple count of words or phrases.[19] Some people offered one thought, such as

---

questionnaire once a day for four days. The data plotted in Figure 4.4 are averages of my four successive evaluations. Reliability is an issue in the sense that occasionally cryptic explanations are not coded into to the same content categories every day. Here are the test–retest covariances for the four days (correlations in the upper diagonals):

1391.5	(.799)	(.775)	(.774)
1087.9	1333.2	(.822)	(.785)
1076.3	1116.6	1384.7	(.779)
1066.2	1057.6	1069.9	1362.7

The four evaluations are not identical, but they covary on a single dimension. The first principal component describes 84% of the variance in the four evaluations (second component describes 6%).

[18] The statistically significant test statistic in Figure 4.4 is less strong, but clearly rejects the null hypothesis, in the staff-officer explanations. There is a 5.13 t-test statistic for the hostile phrasing associated with strong third-party ties (P < .001). Across the senior managers and staff officers, the anger expressed in explaining the difficult colleague is significantly higher if manager and colleague have many friends and acquaintances in common (strong third-party tie; 10.7 t-test test statistic), and higher still if the manager's contacts are densely connected in a closed network (3.3 t-test for network constraint measuring interconnection among a manager's contacts). Holding constant the boss being the most difficult contact does not eliminate the effects from strong third-party ties or network constraint (test statistics of 10.8 and 3.3 respectively), though there is significantly less anger in explanations of the boss being one's most difficult colleague (−2.1 t-test). Holding constant the greater anger expressed in explanations blaming the colleague's character (anger bars in Figure 4.4 drift to the right, 22.0 t-test) does not eliminate the anger association with strong third-party ties (5.0 t-test) nor the association with network constraint (2.3 t-test).

[19] Sociolinguistic analysis compares the frequency of linguistic elements in text from different speakers to compare social influences on the speakers. Counts of elements that

"managed a parallel sales organization with a different philosophy," or "preferred to push her own agenda instead of the group's." The other people begin with one thought, then offer a further reason for the relationship being difficult, and some continue with additional reasons. Thoughts are separated in the written explanations by commas, colons, semi-colons, new lines, spaces, or dashes. For example; "manipulative; insensitive to people; dishonest" (three thoughts), or "I do not know the answer; most likely an understanding of the work I do rather than him personally" (two thoughts). The respondent begins writing something, then adds another thought as if to say "and another thing . . ." In keeping with the results in Figure 4.4, the explanations that contain more than one thought more often come from people embedded in closed networks describing difficult relationships embedded in strong third-party ties.[20]

4.3.2 Angry Words

Figure 4.5 contains the frequencies with which specific words were used by the senior managers to explain difficult relationships. The seventy-eight words

occur "relatively frequently" and are "relatively easy to identify" offer more reliable and informative data (Hudson, 1980: 140 ff.). I discuss phrase counts in the text because phrases were easy to identify, indicate effort, and have the expected association with third-party connections. I began with word counts, which are even easier to identify than phrase counts. The initial idea was that more words written about a difficult relationship could indicate more effort in describing the relationship. The average explanation contained 9.2 words. The longest contained 41 words. The shortest (other than ignoring the question) contained only one word ("incompetent" was a favorite). Words, however, seem to be a function of the manager's impulse to vocalize rather than a function of the relationship they describe. The number of words in an explanation is independent of structural context (-1.6 t-test for the association with strong third-party ties, 0.2 for the association with network constraint). Holding constant the difference between the two study populations (staff officers gave shorter explanations), the number of phrases in an explanation was significantly higher if the explained relationship was embedded in a strong third-party tie (2.4 t-test for the association with third-party ties) or the speaker was embedded in a closed network (2.5 t-test for network constraint).

[20] Topper and Carley (1999) illustrate another source of evidence on network echo. The structure of attention in a continuing media story should take on a center-periphery pattern. Topper and Carley (1999) analyze newspaper stories (and Coast Guard reports) filed in the first 14 days of the Exxon Valdez oil spill. They distinguish 46 organization actors involved in the oil spill and for each of the 14 days they infer a (46, 46) network in which two actors are connected on a specific day if a "working relationship" between the two actors was mentioned in a story that day. Topper and Carley (1999: 86) show the network becoming increasingly centralized, with Exxon and the Coast Guard the most central actors. Network data have long been inferred from joint involvement in media accounts (e.g., Davis, Gardner, and Gardner, 1941; Burt and Lin, 1977), but Topper and Carley differ in tracking a specific story over a short period of time. The centralization that Topper and Carley report is exactly what should happen if journalists and officials reporting on the story were affected by echo. Gossip among interested parties would focus attention on certain actors whose reputations as protagonists would be amplified

mentioned more than five times are listed.[21] Height in the graph indicates the frequency with which a word is used. The words most often used are generic (my, to, the, of, and), though the frequent use of "not" means that managers were stating attractive qualities then saying the difficult relationship/colleague did not have such qualities. Words are arranged on the horizontal axis in ascending order of their use in explanations embedded in strong third-party ties. For example, "self" was used in twelve explanations. It appears to the far right of the graph, at 100%, because all twelve of its uses were to describe relations embedded in strong third-party ties.

The word frequencies corroborate the third-party association in Figure 4.4 with blaming difficulty on colleagues. To the far-left in Figure 4.5 are the words most often used to describe difficult relations relatively free of third parties. The words are about difficulties in an organization. The word used most often is "support"; the other person did not, or could not, or will not provide support. The broader situation issue is the "organization" and general "man-

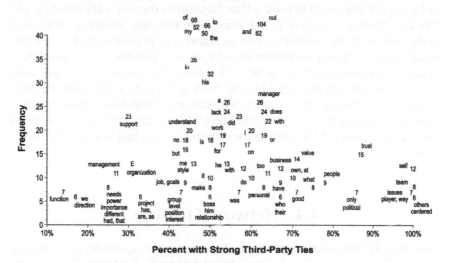

Fig. 4.5: Words used to explain difficult relationships. Words are sorted left to right in order of their use to describe relations embedded in strong third-party ties

---

to extremes, and subsequent stories would be about other actors as they relate to the main protagonists, in this case Exxon and the Coast Guard. The echo hypothesis for media accounts more generally is that the more closed the social network among people reporting on an event, the more quickly story rhetoric will escalate and stories will center on a few protagonists. The more rich in structural holes the network among people reporting on an event, the more neutral the tone of stories and the more likely that alternative perspectives will add alternative protagonists.

[21] To make words consistent across managers for the word count, I edited the explanations in three ways. I converted contractions to full words (e.g., "didn't" becomes "did

agement." Related words are "we" "had" "different" opinions about the "importance" of the "goals" or "direction" of the "job," "position," "needs," "function," or "project."

To the far-right of Figure 4.5 are the words used to describe difficult relations embedded in an audience of third parties. The words are about the other person putting self before others. Such words likely to get the attention of colleagues because stories containing these words are safeguard colleagues against being burned by disreputable people. The most often mentioned words to the right in Figure 4.5 are "trust" and "value," as in you cannot trust the other person, he doesn't value the right things. The other person's focus on self ("self," "centered," "player," "only," "own," "way," and "political") is contrasted with the proper focus which is other people (e.g., the respondent manager: "team," "people," "others," and "business").

Notice that the contrast is not between self and the firm; it is between self and other people. Words about the firm ("organization," "management," "functions," etc.) are used in situational explanations and appear to the left in Figure 4.5. The words beyond self to the right in the graph are about people ("team," "people," "others"). The association between "business" and third parties (67% on the horizontal axis in Figure 4.5) is interesting because the word "business" is not as obvious an indicator of reputation-talk as words like "trust," "self-centered," or "team." "Knowing the business" is a manager phrase akin to the fighter-pilot phrase "having the right stuff." Generic difficulties of commercial life are discussed with antiseptic words about "organization," "management," and "functions." When talk shifts to reputations and the interpersonal foundation for commercial life, talk is about the "business."

4.4   Network Stability

The control potential of closure depends on reputation spanning projects. You do some work in one project group. Word gets around defining your reputation, which you carry into your next project group. If reputation were to begin anew with each project there would be no reputation cost to proscribed behavior.

Bandwidth and echo are processes by which closure can carry reputation across projects. Bandwidth ensures that people in the new project group are informed about you, so you construct an identity as you work that will be with

---

not" and "I've" becomes "I have"). I converted abbreviations to full words (e.g., "/" and "&" become "and" and "mgr." becomes "manager"). I converted tense or plurals to match majority use (e.g., two managers mentioned "goal" and seven mentioned "goals," so I converted "goal" to "goals" in the first two explanations and report nine mentions of "goals" in Figure 4.5).

you across projects, which is expected to make you careful about your behavior. Echo ensures that people in the new project group hear stories about you, positive stories if the new group is predisposed toward you, negative otherwise. Reputation is beginning anew in the sense that the new group affects what they hear, but more specifically, there will be a social construction of you that begins with an uninformed audience reacting from their predispositions to the stories that most often circulate about you. You enter a project saying hello to strangers who feel they know you.

The evidence in Figure 4.6 shows echo more responsible than bandwidth for reputation stability in that stability reflects relations balanced in their intensity, not their direction. The three panels of evidence describe stability in the banker population previously discussed in Figure 1.5E for returns to brokerage, in Figure 3.4 for network bandwidth and trust, and in Figure 4.3 for network echo and trust. The horizontal axis in each graph is the number of third-party ties connecting a banker and colleague in this year's annual peer evaluations. There is a third-party tie between banker and colleague for each mutual contact with whom they both had frequent and substantial business in the year preceding the annual evaluations.

4.4.1 *Same Relations*

Other things equal, relationships weaken over time such that some observed today are gone tomorrow. The tendency for relations to weaken and disappear I will discuss as decay. Functions describing the rate of decay over time I will discuss as decay functions, and variables in the functions I will discuss as decay factors.[22]

The Liability of Newness

There is reason to expect a "liability of newness" like the phenomenon in population ecology models of organizations (Hannan and Freeman, 1989: 80). Relations decay over time, but more slowly in surviving relations.

---

[22] Decay is not exactly the right word here. The word is appropriate to my data in that citations disappear at a "decay" rate that can be estimated. The word is not appropriate to the relationship underlying the data. When events pull friends apart—they graduate to positions in different cities, or they marry into different social circles—the friendship is not destroyed so much as it goes into remission. It lies there inactive waiting to be revived when occasion permits. Relationships do not die unless we behave badly in the leaving them. Leave a relationship with a good exit impression and gossip-borne echo will amplify your positive reputation. Leave badly, and echo will spin up a negative image of you that will be difficult to change later. I cannot say how much social capital is about the strategic maintenance of relationships or the strategic distribution of relationships left behind. I do know that too little attention is given to the latter (illustrated by this remark appearing in a footnote).

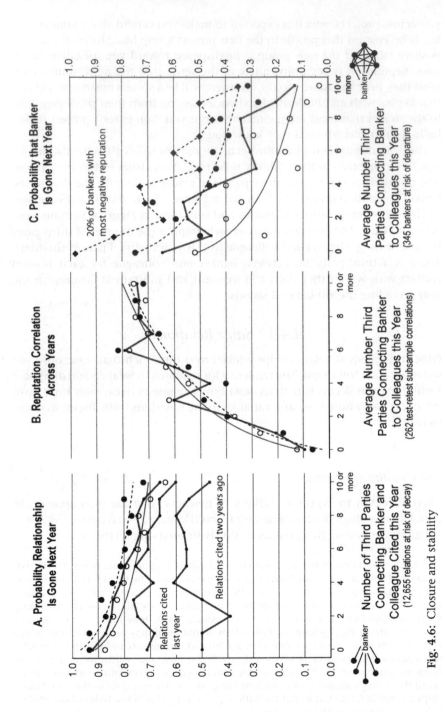

Fig. 4.6: Closure and stability

The decay process begins with people becoming acquainted as a function of random chance and exogenous factors. People who would not otherwise seek one another out can find themselves neighbors, colleagues in the same company, assigned to the same project team, or seated next to one another. It is rude not to strike up a relationship (Blau, 1977, on the opportunities and constraints that social structures create for relations to emerge, Feld, 1981, on the social foci from which relations emerge). The relations can be bridges to other groups when they result from events that bring people together from separate groups, events such as cross-functional teams, inter-department committees, or inter-organizational conventions and professional meetings. People in these relationships often discover that they do not enjoy one another, or cannot work well together, so they disengage in favor of more compatible contacts. The selection process in which new (hoped to be) compatible contacts replace existing (known to be) incompatible ones means that relations on average weaken and decay over time. There is a liability of newness because the longer a relationship has survived, the more likely that it connects people who have learned to appreciate one another, which increases the probability of the relationship continuing into the future.

Learning is more than an accompanist to selection processes. There is also learning from your current relationships to identify kinds of people with whom you are likely to be compatible. Whatever the average probability of a new relationship disappearing next year, that probability should be lower for people more experienced in the study population because experienced people have learned to identify partners with whom they can be compatible.

In sum, there are two kinds of aging responsible for a liability of newness. One is the age of a relationship, call it tie age, for which the liability of newness is evident from slower decay in older relationships. Second is the time that the person citing a relationship has spent in the study population (or in a specific role within the study population), call it node age, for which the liability of newness is evident from slower decay in relations cited by people with more experience.

Closure and Decay

The social capital benefits of bridge relationships are an incentive to build them, but maintaining them is another matter. Consider Robert's relationship with contact 6, which gives him access to group C in Figure 1.1. If not contact 6, then some other contact in the group could provide access. The benefit for Robert continuing with contact 6 is that a history of interaction can decrease the cost of a relationship while increasing trust and reliability within the relationship (relational embedding). On the other hand, there is no evidence that social capital is limited to bridges that continue over time. People involved in bridge relations could derive their advantage simply from being more exposed to contradictory information—which can happen with short-term or long-term bridges—from which people become adept at synthesizing and communicating ideas across contradictory views as discussed in Chapter 2.

A further complication is that bridges are in two ways more costly to maintain. First, the cost is shared by fewer people. The cost of maintaining a bridge is borne entirely by the two parties to the bridge, e.g., Robert and contact 6 in Figure 1.1. In contrast, the relationship between James and contact 4 is in some part maintained by their three mutual friends. Second, bridges are more expensive because they have no immediate precedent. Strong relations are observed more often between people similar on socially significant attributes such as location, socioeconomic status, gender, and age (discussed in Sections 1.1 and 2.4). The tendency for people to have relations with people like themselves implies that bridges require special effort. As Grabowski (1999: 707) summarizes the precedent-breaking costs of establishing a bridge relation:

Middlemen in the process of bridging structural gaps face significant difficulties. They must establish social links across a chasm of ignorance. In order to do this the middleman must bear a significant amount of fixed cost, since he must gather much information on the size, composition, and organization of social networks he is trying to link. In addition, information must be gathered on the reputation of the members (or at least the most important members) of each of the two networks to be integrated. Modern versions of gift exchange between middlemen and leaders of the social networks involved may also have to take place. This might involve the provision of valuable information at no cost, the provision of critical resources, and so on.

The trust associated with closure adds another layer. For the reasons of information flow and enforceable social norms discussed in this and the preceding chapter, relations embedded in dense networks are more likely to be strong. As closure facilitates the development of strong relationships, it can be expected to slow decay (making relations "sticky," Krackhardt, 1998).

Decay Observed

The first graph in Figure 4.6 shows closure slowing decay in the banker relations. Decay is measured on the vertical axis by the proportion of colleagues cited this year who are not cited next year. The horizontal axis indicates the number of mutual contacts between banker and colleague. At the top of the graph, positive relations (solid thin line) are less subject to decay than are negative relations (dashed thin line), but the downward-sloping thin lines in Figure 4.6A show that both positive and negative relations are less likely to decay in a closed network and the association is robust to controls for alternative decay factors (Burt, 2002). Causal order is not implied. It is equally accurate to say that people who continue to work together accumulate mutual contacts. The slower decay in embedded relations is consistent with other studies. Feld (1997) analyzes network data on 152 students enrolled in a small college at the beginning and end of their freshman year. Of 5,345 initial sociometric citations for recognition, 54% were observed again in the second survey, but the percentage increases significantly with mutual acquaintances. Krackhardt (1998) analyzes network data gathered over a semester on 17 sophomore college students living together. He too finds that a relationship is more likely to continue when the two students have mutual friends.

The point supporting echo over bandwidth is that closure preserves relations similarly for positive and negative relations—and Figure 4.3 documented the preservation even when third parties disagree with the banker's opinion of the colleague. Positive relations are less subject to decay when embedded in negative third-party ties, and negative relations are less subject to decay when embedded in positive third-party ties. The more closed the network around banker and colleague this year, the more likely they will acknowledge working together next year.[23]

As relations age, they become self-sustaining. I have data on four years of the banker relations so I can distinguish relations that are one, two, or three years old. Some relations are older still, but I do not know when each relationship started. Fortunately, relations change so quickly in this population that "this year" is the first year for most colleague relationships. The bold line labeled "Relations cited last year" in Figure 4.6A describes decay in relations that were two years old when they were at risk of decay. Even if there are no third parties to the two-year old relations (over the "0"), they are as protected from decay by their age as a first-year relationship embedded in ten or more third parties (over the "10 or more", about 70% decay for each). Decay is much less likely in relations that make it to three years (described by the bold line labeled

---

[23] Statistical tests for trust and distrust were given with the results in Figure 4.3 (n. 11). Here are z-score test statistics for logit regressions predicting decay from the log count of third-party ties this year (TP stands for third party and test statistics have been adjusted down for autocorrelation between relations cited by the same banker):

	All Relations	Negative Relations	Positive Relations
Log all TP ties	−7.40	—	—
Log positive TP ties	—	−4.93	—
Log negative TP ties	—	—	−5.55
Evaluation this year	−6.26	1.65	−4.48
Marginals next year	−5.03	−4.55	−6.37

The first column predicts decay in a relation with the total number of third-party ties between banker and colleague. Column two predicts decay in relations that were rated "poor" or "adequate" this year (dashed line in Figure 4.6A). Column three predicts decay in relations that were rated "good" or "outstanding" this year (solid thin line in Figure 4.6A). The controls show that decay is less likely in a relationship more positive this year (−6.26 z-score) and less likely between a banker and colleague who send or receive many citations (−5.03).

"Relations cited two years ago" in Figure 4.6A). No amount of closure around first-year relations brings them down to this low rate of decay (50% is low for this banker population). The decay rates show that closure primarily protects new relations. As the lines drop down in Figure 4.6A, indicating lower rates of decay, they become more flat, indicating less decay-protection from closure. Closure slows the decay of two-year old relations, but the association is only statistically significant for positive third-party ties. Closure has no association with decay in three-year old relationships.[24] In short, closure primarily slows decay by carrying relations through the initial period of a relationship, when the risk of decay is highest (cf. Hite and Hesterly, 2001, on closed networks around new firms).

The declining risk of decay as relations age can be seen in the limited data available on other networks. Averaging results across the studies reviewed in Burt (2000a: fig. 1), 61% of friendships and support relationships outside the family survive the first year, and 18% are cited again ten years later. If the initial decay rate were constant, less than one percent would have survived the decade. Stronger relationships are less subject to decay: 72% of social support relations with family survive the first year, and 33% are cited again ten years later (your sister continues to be your sister, but you need not

---

[24] These conclusions are based on logit models predicting decay in two- and three-year old relations. Decay in 4,674 two-year old relations decreases with the number of positive third-party ties in which the relationship is embedded (-5.23 logit z-score) but has no association with negative third-party ties (0.68 z-score). Decay in 883 three-year old relations has no association with positive or negative third-party ties ($-.71$ z-score for positive, -1.11 for negative). Most readers will not be troubled by the new data introduced in this paragraph, but for those who are, here are the decay data (see Burt, 2002: 345, for details):

Years Observed (T)	First Panel (P)	At Risk	Decay	Decay Rate
1	1	12655	9526	.75
2	1	3129	2246	.72
3	1	883	467	.53
1	2	3835	3173	.83
2	2	662	398	.60
1	3	1545	865	.56

The first row contains the 12,655 relations analyzed in Figures 3.4 and 4.3. Of the 12,665 relations at risk of decay, 9,526 were not cited in the next year, defining a .75 decay rate. The remaining 3,129 relations were at risk of decay in the second annual survey, of which 2,246 were not cited, leaving 883 relations at risk of decay in the third annual survey. New relations are added each year. There are 3,835 relations added in the second survey, of which 3,173 decayed, and so on. A logit model predicting decay in the above table (with test statistics adjusted down for autocorrelation between relations cited by the same banker) shows decay decreasing as a relationship ages (-6.71 z-score for T, years observed) and as the banker becomes more experienced (-3.78 z-score for P, the panel in which a relationship is first cited by the continuing bankers). Controls for additional decay factors leave these two liability-of-newness effects strong (Burt, 2002: 336, 352).

continue to cite her as a source of social support). If the initial decay rate were constant, only 3.7% would have survived the decade.

Kinked Decay

Figure 4.6A shows a decreasing probability of decay as a relation matures. The liability of newness is especially pronounced in bridge decay—the relations over "0" on the horizontal axis. Decay is highest in new relations (92%), lower in two-year old bridge relations (71%), and lowest in three-year old bridge relations (50%). A continuous decay function can be drawn through these data (Burt, 2002: fig. 2), but there is evidence that bridge decay is kinked rather than continuous.

The evidence of kinked decay comes not from relations known to be bridges, but from certain kinds of relations that are probably bridges. For example, marriage can be a bridge relationship between the network around the husband and the network around the wife. Employment can be a bridge relationship for the employee linking the network inside a firm with her network outside. Relations between organization can be bridges for people in an organization connected to people in another organization. Whether any such relation is a bridge depends on the surrounding network structure. One of the classic network studies, Bott (1957), is about the degree to which a marriage is a bridge (when the husbands network does not overlap with the wife's, their marriage is a bridge across the two networks), and the segregated sex roles that develop in bridge marriages (see Burt, 1992: 255–260, for an interpretation in terms of bridges and structural holes). Douthit (2000) finds the same pattern in employment. Segregated work roles are more likely when supervision is a bridge relationship in that the boss' contacts do not overlap with the employee's.

Regardless of whether they are network bridges *per se*, relations such as marriage, employment, and organizational relations are bridge-like in spanning a social boundary: Marriage spans gender and kinship boundaries. Employment and relations between organizations span the boundary around an organization.

The bridge-like quality of these relationships is useful to note because they do not show a continuously declining decay function. They instead show kinked decay functions as illustrated in Figure 4.7. The "Probability of Switching Auditor" line in Figure 4.7 is from Levinthal and Fichman's (1988: fig. 1) study of auditor–client relationships. Decay is measured by the probability that a company switches from its current accounting firm to a new one. The companies include all major publicly traded corporations in the U.S. (excluding financial firms), along with many smaller ones, and most do not switch auditors over the fourteen years studied (low probabilities of decay in Figure 4.7). The probability of switching in Figure 4.7 increases through the first few years with a new auditor, peaks at four years, then decreases. Baker, Faulkner, and Fisher (1998: 165) run a similar analysis of relations with advertising agencies. Over the twenty three years studied, the average relationship is about five years. The risk of a company discontinuing the relationship with a new agency increases through an initial period of years, after which the relationship is decreasingly subject to decay. Kogut (1989: 184) runs a related analysis on a selection of joint ventures, and finds the risk of dissolution increasing for the first three years of a venture (cf. Deeds and Hill, 1998: 156–157, who find increasing risk of decay in the first five years of biotechnology research alliances, using perceived opportunism as a measure of decay). Japanese joint ventures in the U.S., which can be expected to have stronger pre-contract endowments as discussed below, have a longer initial period of low risk that lasts beyond a decade (Hennart, Kim and Zeng, 1998: 389).

The "Probability of Leaving Employer" line in Figure 4.7 is from Brüderl (2000: fig. 2) and shows the probability of a blue-collar worker in a West German manufacturing plant quitting given his or her time on the job. The risk of quitting increases for a few months, peaks at about five months, and decreases thereafter (Farber, 1994, reports a peak for young American workers at about three months). Brüderl (2000: fig. 1) reports a decay function for cohabitation in West Germany that increases sharply to its peak at two to

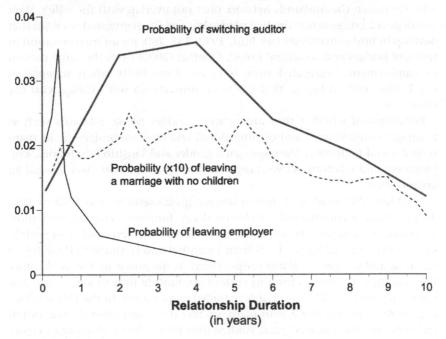

Fig. 4.7: Kinked decay functions

three years, then decreases as the couple continues to live together (Brüderl and Kalter, 2001, report another analysis of the data showing the negative association between divorce and marriage duration). The peak is two to three years later for the probability of marriage ending in divorce, illustrated by the dashed line in Figure 4.7, which is taken from Heaton's (1990: 59) graph of divorce rates estimated from a national probability sample of Americans (cf. Diekmann and Mitter, 1984; Brüderl and Diekmann, 1995).

Kinked decay functions are evidence of a liability of adolescence, distinct from the continuously decreasing decay functions familiar as evidence of a liability of newness (Levinthal and Fichman, 1988; Brüderl and Schüssler, 1990; Fichman and Levinthal, 1991). The initial period of low, increasing decay risk is discussed as a honeymoon, after which decay follows its usual course of decreasing in more mature relationships, leaving a peak risk in the "adolescence" of the relationship life course.

Kink-Producing Endowments

Endowments are the initial stock of assets with which relations begin (Fichman and Levinthal, 1991: 443–444): "we suggest that relationships can start with some initial stock of assets, which (depending on the particular context) can include favorable prior beliefs, trust, goodwill, financial resources, or psychological commitment. We propose that if a relationship starts with an initial stock of assets, the risk of the relationship dissolving at its inception is reduced, even if the initial outcomes of the relationship are unfavorable." Kinked decay functions happen when an endowed relationship's decay risk is low initially because of an immunity created by the endowment, increases as the immunity ends, then decreases with further duration (Hannan, 1998: 142).

Two kinds of endowments are relevant to the lack of kinked decay in the decay of the banker relations. Exit barriers are one. Barriers would include investments that cannot be moved to a new relationship, reputation costs of being seen by potential new partners as unable to make relationships work, costs created by allies of the erstwhile partner, or legal regulations intended to slow exit. For example, a divorce settlement is required to exit marriage (cohabitation involves less formal, but still unpleasant, decisions about who gets what from the joint household), and conditions that clarify life after divorce lower the barrier to leaving a marriage (dual careers, available alternative partners, previous experience with divorce, no-fault divorce, lack of children; e.g., see White, 1990). Changing employers involves a variety of costs created by the loss of close colleagues, the search for new employment, the inconveniences of geographical mobility, learning the operations of a new company, and building relations with new colleagues. Switching to a new supplier involves all of the above plus the costs of lost financial, human, and social capital invested or created to make the prior relationship work. Exclusive contracts indicate a lack of alternatives, and exclusive contracts with advertising agencies show less decay, especially if the agency is in-house (Baker, Faulkner, and Fisher, 1998). Scale and complexity are barriers to switching suppliers because a large, complex company requires more investment in helping a supplier understand company operations and the investment is not easily transferred to a new supplier—and large, complex companies are less likely to discontinue their relationship with a supplier (Levinthal and Fichman, 1988; Baker, Faulkner, and Fisher, 1998).

Maturity is a second endowment. Contractual relations—such as marriage, employment, or relations between organizations—are by some unknown amount older than the time that has passed since the contract began. Whatever learning occurred in the pre-contract period is an endowment lowering the risk of decay during the contract. Consider marriage. As of the wedding day, a marriage contract begins that is at some risk over time of ending in divorce or separation. You are not officially at risk of divorce until the day you marry, so marriage date is an appropriate start-point for duration. With respect to network decay, however, the relationship terminated by divorce did not begin on the wedding day. The relationship began when the couple first met and liked one another, which put them in the risk set for marriage and divorce. Some people marry soon after they meet. Others date for a while, then live together, and eventually marry. Many relationships expire before marriage. In other words, marriage is a contractual phase in a longer-running relationship. Preceding the marriage is a function describing decay in the relations which did not survive to a marriage contract (cf. Fichman and Levinthal, 1991: 452).

Similarly, a relationship between two organizations does not begin on the day a contract is signed. The contract was preceded by people discussing a link between the organizations. Preceding the decay function for the contractual relation between the organizations is a steeper function describing decay in interpersonal relations with representatives of alternative vendors with whom contracts were never signed. In fact, the interpersonal backbone for interorganizational relations is highlighted in a follow-up study of the auditor–client relations in Figure 4.7. Seabright, Levinthal, and Fichman (1992) report that company time with an auditor is negligible in predicting the switch to a new auditor. The key variable is the tenure of the Chief Financial Officer (or the average tenure of the audit committee). Change the senior executive who reports the audit, and the company is more likely to switch to a new auditor regardless of company time with the current auditor.

Some amount of the learning acquired during a pre-contract relationship falls out of date or is rendered irrelevant by exogenous change—which creates a kink in the decay function. You knew her well when you lived together, but career, cash, and children took the two of you in different directions that led to divorce. Our previous advertising agency was perfect for our position in the market, but the market changed and with it our advertising department, which led us to our new agency. When the endowment expires, risk of decay increases to a point (the peak in the decay function), after which decay risk decreases as usual with age.

Three implications follow. One is that measures of pre-contract connection are important control variables when predicting decay in contractual relations.[25] Two, exit barriers and pre-contract endowments mean that contractual relationships show decay rates lower than the rates for otherwise similar relationships. The rates for employment, marriage, and auditor–client relations are well under .05 in Figure 4.7. These contractual relations were preceded by friendship, social support, and colleague relations for which decay is a much higher risk. The average one-year decay rate is .39 in friendship and social support beyond the family (Burt, 2000a: Table 1), which is an underestimate of decay in new relations because the rate is an average across all relations cited in an initial survey, including long-term relations in which decay is unlikely.

A third implication is that if control variables could be found sufficient to hold constant variation in endowments, then the low risk of decay during a honeymoon period would increase, and the peak risk during adolescence would move forward, such that decay would show the continuously decreasing decay that is the liability of newness. Levinthal and Fichman (1988: 362–365) come close to the ideal with their analysis of audit qualifications. Auditors, like other providers of professional service, depend on reputation. When an auditor feels that a report does not conform to generally accepted accounting practices, the auditor can protect its reputation by putting qualifications on the report. Putting qualifications on an audit is an indicator of exit-barrier and pre-contract endowments expiring within a relationship, or as Levinthal and Fichman (1988: 364) put it: "Our interpretation is that a qualified opinion is an indicator of conflict within the auditor–client relationship." Holding constant the timing of audit qualifications takes the kink out of the auditor

---

[25] Interpretation problems with the control variables can be anticipated, as illustrated by research on the link between cohabitation and divorce (see Smock, 2000: 6–7, for review). Cohabitation preceding marriage was initially understood to be a period in which two people could get to know one another and so make a better-informed decision about whether they were a good match for marriage. Cohabitation turned out to increase the risk of divorce. Current understanding is that people who cohabit are a kind of person more prone to divorce. The cohabitation preceding marriage is no longer interpreted as a period of due diligence so much as revealed preference. The same conundrum can be anticipated for any measure of the endowment provided by a pre-contract relationship. For example, imagine a control variable that measures a company's due diligence on suppliers before signing with one. If the control variable has a negative association with decay in the subsequent supplier relationship, then the variable could be interpreted as an endowment improving the quality of the match between company and supplier. If the association turns out to be positive, the variable could be interpreted equally well as an indicator of the kind of people running the company—perhaps overly cautious people stuck in bureaucratic due-diligence processes, so of course they have trouble dealing with other organizations.

decay function (Levinthal and Fichman, 1988: 365): "When we controlled for the effect of qualifications, the hazard rate decreased monotonically with time."

I find no evidence of kinked decay in the banker relationships (Burt, 2002: 357–358), but the kink in such fast-decaying relations could have occurred during the first year, before the second panel of data. More importantly, all relations have some period in which you cannot disengage. At minimum, etiquette is a kink-producing endowment common to interpersonal relationships. Remember that cocktail conversation in which you were trapped for what seemed like eternity. When two people are introduced, there is some initial period during which it would be rude to break away. To be sure, etiquette is not a long-suffering endowment. The honeymoon could be no more than the time it takes for the person to say hello. It could be no more than the duration of the program or seminar in which you meet one another. It could be the duration of the project in which you are both involved. Whatever the relationship, there is some initial period of time for which the risk of decay is zero. Therefore, all relationship decay must be kinked and my stylized fact in Figure 4.8 assumes kinked decay.

4.4.2 Same Relative Standing

As closure slows change in relations, its effects should aggregate across relations to slow change in banker reputations. There is evidence of reputations continuing from one year to the next: The mean evaluation of a banker this year is correlated .68 with the mean evaluation next year. The high correlation is surprising because so much reputation variance is specific to banker–colleague pairs (n. 3), and there is such high turnover in relations from one year to the next. Note the high rate of network decay just discussed: Most relations do not recur next year. Of 12,655 relations cited this year, only 25% are cited again next year.

Over a drink with the head of a company division, I asked about the stable reputations despite relational chaos. He took on a puzzled look, then patiently explained to me that "of course" the evaluations are stable. They are the company's market index of banker quality. A good banker this year is a good banker next year, whether he works with the same people each year, or different people. Scores go up and down a little depending on personalities and banker opportunities, but good people continue to be good people, and weak people are weeded out.

The division head understood peer evaluations to be data on human capital. The evaluations are also data on social capital if, beyond quality of work observed, colleagues were affected by stories they heard about the banker's work.

The human-capital and social-capital interpretations can be tested against one another. If individual ability is the reason for reputation stability over time, then stability should be independent of connections among the people evaluating a banker. A good banker should receive a good average evaluation whether the people making the evaluations work together or are drawn from separate parts of the organization. If reputation stability depends on colleagues discussing the banker, on the other hand, then stability should increase with connections between the people evaluating a banker.

And that is what Figure 4.6B shows: The stability of a banker's reputation from one year to the next increases with the strength of connections among colleagues evaluating the banker.[26] The horizontal axis is the average number of third parties connecting a banker with a colleague who cited the banker. Bankers over the "0" on the horizontal axis were complete brokers in the sense that they worked with colleagues with whom they had no mutual contacts. Bankers over the "1" had an average of one mutual contact per colleague. The vertical axis in Figure 4.6B is a correlation between banker reputations in adjacent years. Reputation stability is clearly not independent of network closure. The correlation between reputations in adjacent years increases from a .10 correlation for bankers whose colleagues do not work together, up to a .74 correlation for bankers whose relations are embedded in an average of 10 or more third parties. Where colleagues evaluating a banker are densely connected, the banker's reputation continues over time. Where the evaluating colleagues are not connected, reputation is quickly forgotten.

Consider two hypothetical bankers who worked well with ten colleagues last year. One of the bankers worked with colleagues segregated in the organization so they did not cite one another in the annual peer evaluations (illustrated by the sociogram to the lower-left in Figure 4.6). That banker would be over the "0" on the horizontal axes in Figure 4.6. The second banker worked with five colleagues who worked together in one division and another five who worked together in a second division (sociogram to the lower-right in Figure 4.6). The second banker would be over the "4" on the horizontal axes.

Both bankers did good work, but it is the second banker's work that will be remembered. The solid thin line in Figure 4.6B shows that a banker doing good

---

[26] The vertical axis is the correlation within a subsample around each banker. Finifter (1972) is a good introduction to the subsampling strategy. Rank order the bankers present in both years by their average number of third-party connections with colleagues (the horizontal axis of Figure 4.6B before averages are converted to the integer values reported in the figure). The six bankers above and below banker i on the list are drawn as a subsample around banker i. Banker i's score on the vertical axis in Figure 4.6B is the correlation for the 13 people in the subsample between reputation this year and next year. I settled on subsamples of a dozen colleagues after testing alternatives. The association with closure in Figure 4.6B increases sharply through subsamples of size 4, 6, and 8 colleagues (decreasing sampling error), more slowly through subsamples of 10 and 12 colleagues, then little for larger subsamples. I took 12 as the inflection point. With subsamples of 13, I lose the first six and last six bankers in the rank order, along with the 71 bankers who left before the second annual peer evaluations, which leaves 262 subsample correlations on which Figure 4.6B is based.

work for colleagues not connected with each other can expect to be forgotten. The exact correlation expected between the banker's reputation this year and next year is given by the level of the solid thin line over the "0" on the horizontal axis. The correlation is indistinguishable from random noise. The bankers work with so many new contacts each year that their work is quickly forgotten—unless the people with whom they work talk to each other. For the second banker, the one who worked with two groups of connected colleagues, reputation has an expected correlation of .57 over time. What carries a banker's reputation into the future is people talking about the banker.

More specifically, if bandwidth were the process through which stories circulate, then negative stories would be more likely to pass through negative third-party ties and positive stories would be more likely to pass through positive third-party ties. If echo is the process, then the difference between positive and negative third-party ties is irrelevant. Strong third-party ties in either direction would increase the flow of stories sympathetic to predispositions such that reputations become more stable.

The evidence of echo over bandwidth is that reputation stability is associated with closure even when reputation is inconsistent with the third-party ties in which it is embedded. The solid thin line in Figure 4.6B (positive reputation stability) is higher than the dashed line (negative reputation stability), but not by much, and the two lines increase similarly with network closure. More, stability comes from positive and negative third-party ties. The horizontal axis in Figure 4.6B (positive reputation stability) counts all third-party ties, but I get the same result of closure stabilizing reputation if I predict the stability of

---

[27] Here are ordinary least squares t-test statistics for regression models predicting the reputation-stability correlation in the subsample around a banker (vertical axis in Figure 4.6B, see previous footnote) with various controls (TP stands for third party):

	All Bankers	Negative Rep Bankers	Positive Rep Bankers
Log all TP ties	14.14	—	—
Log positive TP ties	—	8.06	—
Log negative TP ties	—	—	6.92
Banker age (in years)	−2.27	−1.67	−1.14
Rank (six job ranks)	.90	−.25	1.04
Relative bonus (z-score)	−.08	−.49	.80
Average evaluation	.66	.77	—
|Z-score average evaluation|	2.24	.79	1.89
Number evaluations	.42	1.29	−.78

The first column predicts stability for all 262 bankers using the average total number of third-party ties to the banker's colleagues. Column two predicts stability for bankers with below-average evaluations (dashed line in Figure 4.6B). Column three predicts stability for the bankers with average or higher evaluations (solid thin line in Figure 4.6B). The control variables do not matter as much here as they do for the other two graphs in Figure 4.6. Age matters some (−2.3 t-test; reputation is less stable in a banker's later

positive reputations from counts of negative third-party ties, or if I predict the stability of negative reputations from counts of positive third-party ties.[27]

There is a normative inference to be drawn. The organization and individual bankers on average benefit from the stability closure provides. Bankers have to trust one another on new projects without personal experience of one another. They have to rely on vicarious experience from stories they have heard. Third-party gossip carries positive reputations from one year to next. Bankers can move from project to project as trusted insiders. There is also a dark side. It is dangerous to have detractors with extensive third-party connections because they will be more certain of a banker's faults than would be the case if the detractors were socially isolated from one another. Third-party gossip carries negative reputations from one year to the next, so bankers join projects preceded by gossip about deals gone bad. They have an incentive to avoid risky projects because mistakes are not soon forgotten. Bankers deemed suspect can expect to be ostracized from productive relations, even driven from the firm by character assassination in third-party gossip.

4.4.3 Same People

The third graph, Figure 4.6c, shows the rates at which bankers in different network positions leave the organization. The vertical axis is the probability that a banker leaves before the next annual evaluations. As in Figure 4.6B, the horizontal axis is the average number of mutual contacts shared by banker and colleague. The main point in the graph is that bankers in closed networks are less likely to leave the organization. Over the "0" on the horizontal axis, the bold line in Figure 4.6c shows that two-thirds of bankers leave who have colleagues with whom they share no mutual contacts (65%). Over the "10 or more" third-parties per colleague, one in ten bankers leave who are embedded in a closed network of colleagues (13%). The bold line shows how the probability of banker exit decreases with increasing network closure around the banker.

---

years). Extremely negative or extremely positive reputations are slightly more stable than neutral reputations (2.2 t-test, the control variable is the absolute value of the average evaluation of a banker converted to a z-score). Stability is overwhelmingly a function of embedding relations in third parties. The above results show in a familiar way that the curves in Figure 4.6B are robust to controls for basic factors that could account for reputation stability, but the statistical results should not be interpreted literally because the dependent variable is a moving average across observations. Here is a more routine test: $E2 = .01 - .06\text{Closed} + (.58 + .38\text{Closed})E1$, where E1 and E2 are average colleague evaluations of a banker in the first and second year, and "Closed" is a dummy variable equal to 1 if the banker's relations with colleagues are more embedded in third parties than the average banker. The coefficients are least-squares estimates across the 274 continuing bankers. The respective t-test statistics are -1.4, 7.5, and 3.7. The equation shows no significant difference in the reputations of bankers in open or closed networks (-1.4 t-test) but more stable reputations in closed networks (3.7 t-test).

Banker reputation in this organization is measured by the average colleague evaluation received from bonus-eligible employees. In the annual performance evaluations, bankers who received positive colleague evaluations are more likely to be promoted and receive high bonuses. The hollow dots in Figure 4.6C are exit rates for bankers with average-or-better colleague evaluations. The thin, solid regression line through these positive-reputation bankers is at the bottom of the graph, which shows that bankers with positive reputations are less likely to leave, and the downward slope of the line shows that the positive-reputation bankers least likely to leave are the ones embedded in a closed network. The less-likely exit of positive-reputation bankers in closed networks is consistent with bandwidth and echo. Colleagues in a closed network of positive relations inform and reinforce one another's positive opinion of other people in the network.

I infer that closure has its effect through echo rather than bandwidth because closure keeps everyone in the organization—regardless of positive or negative closure, and regardless of the banker's reputation. The horizontal axis in Figure 4.6C counts the total number of third-party ties, but I get the same result of closure inhibiting exit if I use only positive or only negative third-party ties.[28] If bandwidth were responsible for employee retention, then

---

[28] Exit is measured over three years. The vertical axis in Figure 4.6C corresponds to an exit variable coded across the 345 initial bankers as 1 for the 71 bankers who leave next year, .5 for the 60 who leave the year after that, and 0 for those who stayed with the firm. Means on this variable are presented in Figure 4.6C. Here are z-score test statistics for ordinal logit regressions predicting the three categories of exit from the log count of third-party ties (for the nonlinear curves in Figure 4.6C) with various controls (TP stands for third party):

	All Bankers	Negative Rep	Most Neg Rep	Positive Rep
Log all TP ties	−5.23	—	−3.02	—
Log positive TP ties	—	−3.23	—	—
Log negative TP ties	—	—	—	−3.92
Banker age (years)	3.68	3.55	1.18	2.06
Rank (six job ranks)	−3.32	−2.54	−1.67	−3.29
Relative bonus (z-score)	−3.40	−4.71	−3.04	−0.68
Average evaluation	−5.50	−2.59	−0.73	−3.17
Number of evaluations	−.41	−1.23	1.08	.91

The first column predicts exit by any of the 345 bankers using the average total number of third-party ties to the banker's colleagues. Column two predicts exit by the bankers with below-average evaluations (dashed line in Figure 4.6C). Column three predicts exit by bankers whose reputations are at the bottom 20% of bankers (dashed line through the diamonds in Figure 4.6C). Column four predicts exit by the bankers with average or higher evaluations (solid thin line in Figure 4.6C). The control variables matter. Bankers are less likely to leave the firm if they are young, hold higher job rank, received a higher bonus than their peers (relative bonus is the vertical axis in Figure 1.5E), or received an enthusiastic evaluation from colleagues. The number of colleagues evaluating the banker did not affect exit (see Lin, Dean, and Ensel, 1986, on the critical importance

people with bad reputations would be less trusted in the organization and more the object of character assassination in gossip, which would make them less productive bankers, so they would be wise to leave the organization to begin anew elsewhere. Instead, the dashed regression line through the solid dots in Figure 4.6c show that closure retains bankers with below-average colleague evaluations. To be sure, the dashed line through the solid dots is higher than the solid line through the hollow dots; in other words, bankers with below-average reputations are more likely to leave the organization.[29] However, the two regression lines are almost parallel, each showing closure's effect of retaining bankers in the organization. In fact, I looked at closure effects on exit by the least attractive bankers—the bottom 20% of the reputation distribution. Their average exit rates are indicated by the dashed line through diamonds in Figure 4.6c. These bankers with the most negative reputations are most likely to leave. In the upper-left of Figure 4.6c, ninety percent of them leave next year if the colleagues giving them the negative evaluations are little connected with one another. But look at the exit rate drop when those colleagues are connected: Only a third of the least-attractive bankers leave when their colleagues are strongly connected (over "10 or more mutual contacts") and the statistical association between closure and exit remains strong.[30]

In sum, bankers rated attractive or unattractive by colleagues this year are more likely to be with the firm next year if they are embedded in a closed network. Closed networks retain bankers, whether or not there are colleagues who think ill of the banker. Bankers leave when they fail to find a network of connected colleagues.

The three graphs in Figure 4.6 show closure slowing network change by increasing the probability that next year's organization contains the same people, in the same relations, with the same reputations.

4.5 Conclusions

This chapter has been about the reputation mechanism through which people are controlled in a closed network. I framed the discussion in terms of two

---

for mental health of having one close contact, and the marginal value of an increasing number of them). The point across the columns is that closure reduces the probability of exit regardless of the direction of relations defining closure. The three counts of third-party ties are too highly correlated to enter in the same prediction, but I get the closure effect if the count of just negative third-parties replaces all TP ties in the first column (-5.45 z-score) or if the count of just positive third-party ties replaces all TP ties in the first column (-5.70).

[29] This is the effect of "average evaluation" in n. 28.
[30] This is the "most neg rep" regression model in n. 28.

hypotheses about the way that information circulates to create reputation. The bandwidth hypothesis—assumed in closure models of social capital and related work such as models of reputation in economics—says that closed networks enhance information flow by providing multiple communication channels (deviants will be discovered). The echo hypothesis—based on the social psychology of selective disclosure in informal conversations—says that closed networks do not enhance information flow so much as they amplify existing opinion.

The bandwidth and echo hypotheses are difficult to separate in past research because research has so often described situations in which the hypotheses make identical predictions: We know that distrust is more likely in negative relationships. We know that trust is more likely in positive relations embedded in closed networks of positive relations. These results are consistent with both bandwidth and echo. Figures 3.3 and 4.2 provide illustrative evidence (and see Friedkin's, 1999, model of the network process underlying group polarization).

Evidence across a broader range of network conditions, in particular where the two hypotheses contradict one another, supports echo over bandwidth. Positive relations with mutual colleagues do not alleviate distrust within difficult relations. They are associated with amplified distrust and angry character assassination (Figures 4.2 and 4.4). Bandwidth is more explicitly rejected in favor of echo by the fact that relationships are balanced in their intensity, not their direction (Figure 4.3). With an etiquette filter on the information that passes between people, strong connections mean more conversations in which initial opinions are corroborated so people come to more certain, more intense, opinions.

My conclusion from the evidence presented is that there is significant echo in the bandwidth created by network closure—to such an extent that echo is the more accurate model of information flow.

4.5.1   Reinforced Networks

The stylized fact for this chapter, illustrated in Figure 4.8, is that closure's reputation mechanism reinforces the status quo. Strong relations between friends of friends are amplified in intensity through friends gossiping. New relations between friends of friends are protected from decay. With strong relations less subject to decay, and new relations between friends of friends more likely to survive to maturity, the existing structure is reinforced, increasing density within clusters and deepening the holes between clusters.

The graph to the left in Figure 4.8 illustrates the closure association with trust. Gossiping third parties echo opinions within the closed network, amplifying positive predisposition into trust, doubt into distrust. To create the graph, I aggregated the network data analyzed in this chapter on managers, officers, and bankers to describe, in a rough summary way, the amplification associated with closure. Trust is concentrated in the most positive relations embedded in the strongest third-party ties (cf. Figures 3.3 and 3.4) and distrust is concentrated in the least positive relations embedded in the strongest third-party ties (cf. Figures 4.2 and 4.3).

Note the relative effects of direct versus indirect connection, what Granovetter (1992) distinguished as relational versus structural embedding. The bars in Figure 4.8 differ more across strengths of relationship than across strengths of third-party ties. In other words, the majority of variance in trust and distrust is predicted by relational embedding. To put a rough number on the difference, relation strength accounts for 85% to 98% of the explained variance in trust and distrust. There is a statistically significant association with structural embedding, but the association is only 2% to 15% of explained trust variance.[31]

Three considerations dampen the implied greater consequence of relational embedding. First, some amount of the relational embedding effect is tautological, as mentioned earlier, in that trust is an element in the definition of strong relations. Second, the tautology issue is moot when trust has to be decided before two people have spent the years together required to build trust. It is often, if not typically, the case that trust cannot wait for years, whereupon the few points of variance explained by bringing in third parties is the best security available. If we were to count up the number of times that people depend on relational versus structural embedding, my guess is that the percentages would flip to the majority depending on structural embedding because that was the best security available. These situations of risky action having to precede trust are rewarding sites for the research strategy of estimating returns to brokerage in terms of benefits to people connected by brokers (see Section 1.1.5).

Third, structural embedding plays a unique role in protecting new relations from decay, which gives new relations in closed networks a survival advantage in becoming self-sustaining strong relations. My evidence for this point

---

[31] This sentence is based on a regression model estimated across all 18,994 relations in the manager, officer, and banker populations: $Y = a + bZ + cC + dZC$, where Y is three categories of trust (1 if the survey respondent cited the colleague for trust, -1 for a distrust citation, 0 otherwise), Z is the three levels of relationship strength in Figure 4.8 (1 for positive, -1 for negative, 0 otherwise), and C is the three levels of third-party ties in Figure 4.8 (1 for strong, -1 for weak, 0 otherwise). Ordinal logit test statistics (adjusted down for autocorrelation between relations cited by the same respondent) for the three effect coefficients are a z-score of 35.8 for b, the association between trust and relation strength, 0.30 for c, the direct effect of embedding the relationship in third parties, and 5.03 for d, the amplified trust and distrust in extreme relations embedded in strong third-party ties. Using ordinary least squares to predict Y as a continuous variable yields t-tests of the same relative magnitude, 40.9, 0.16, and 4.9 for coefficients b, c, d respectively. Of the predicted variance in continuous Y, 85% is predicted by Z for the senior managers, 96% is predicted by Z for the staff officers, and 98% is predicted by Z for the bankers.

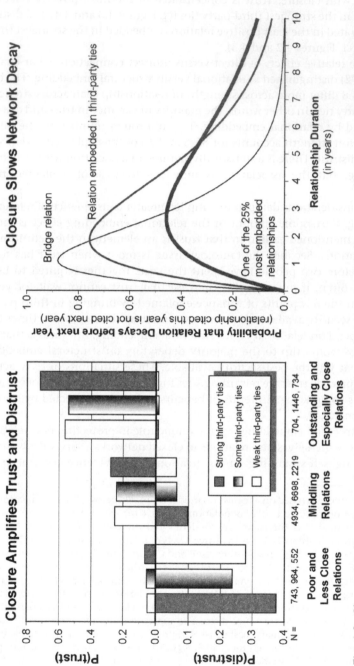

Fig. 4.8: Closure reinforces network structure, amplifying relations to extremes of trust and distrust, and slowing decay in new relations (stylized fact #4)

comes from decay rates in the banker relations. The plots of decay rates in Figure 4.6A show how structural embedding—the presence of mutual colleagues—protected new relations from decay and by the time a relationship was three years old, structural embedding had no effect on decay. The graph to the right in Figure 4.8 illustrates the point from another perspective using decay functions.[32] As a relationship ages across the horizontal axis in Figure 4.8, lines in the graph show the probability that the relationship will disappear before next year. The lines show how the risk of decay increases quickly after colleagues first meet, peaks, then declines. For bridge relations, for example, the risk peaks at 13 months. There is less risk of decay for relations within a closed network. Embedded relations have a longer honeymoon period, with decay risk peaking at 22 months—almost a year later than bridge relations. Decay is slower still for the 25% of banker relations most embedded in a network of mutual colleagues. In other words, closure has its strongest effect protecting new relations from decay. After the first three years, a bridge relation is less subject to decay than an embedded relation—but few bridges survive the three years. Relations in this population changed dramatically from year to year, so the decay functions in Figure 4.8 are probably higher than will be found elsewhere. I expect three points about the functions to generalize: decay decreases with closure, has a kinked functional form, and closure slows decay primarily by carrying relations through the initial period of a relationship, when the risk of decay is highest.

4.5.2 *Building Reputation*

The results on closure slowing change highlight a contradiction between echo and bandwidth on who owns a reputation. Under the bandwidth hypothesis, you own your reputation. You own your reputation in the sense that you define the behavior that defines your reputation. Third parties inform people about your behavior. Change in your behavior is reliably transmitted to other people in the network.

---

[32] I use a two-parameter model to describe kinked decay: $r(T) = (aT)exp(-T/b)$, where $r(T)$ is the risk of decay at time T, and a and b are parameters, b the time of the peak in decay risk (see Diekmann and Mitter, 1984; Diekmann and Englehardt, 1999: 787). If detailed data were available through the first year, I would want to separate level, shape, and time of peak decay (e.g., Brüderl and Diekmann, 1995: 162), but the two-parameter model is sufficient for illustration here. Details on creating the decay functions in Figure 4.8 from the decay data in n. 25 are given in Burt (2002: 361 n.). For bridge relations, a is 2.183, and b is 1.096 years (which, times 12, puts the peak risk of decay at 13.2 months). For embedded relations, a is 1.104 and b is 1.865 (which puts the peak decay risk at 22.4 months).

Under the echo hypothesis, you do not own your reputation. The possessive pronoun in "your reputation" refers to the subject of the reputation, not the owner. The people who own your reputation are the people in whose conversations it is built, and the goal of those conversations is not accuracy so much as bonding between the speakers. You are merely grist for the gossip-mill through which they strengthen their relationships with each other.

The ownership implications of bandwidth and echo have implications for building and managing reputation. Under bandwidth, first impressions have some disproportionate effect because of being initial data, but under echo, first impressions are critical for the gossip chain they set in motion. Reputations do not emerge from good work directly so much as from colleague stories about the work. Good work completed for people who don't talk about it is quickly forgotten. This is striking in Figure 4.6B where a banker's reputation is no more stable than random noise if the banker works with colleagues who have no connection with one another. The key to building reputation is to get people in closed networks talking to one another. Given two managers doing good work, the one whose work is more often discussed will have the more positive reputation because stories about that person's good work echo among the colleagues, amplifying individual opinions of the discussed manager. Much of what people see when you approach is not you so much as an image of you constructed in casual conversations with colleagues. This is what is meant by "building the buzz" in word-of-mouth marketing (e.g., Rosen, 2000; cf. Gladwell, 2000).

First impressions take on a new significance. You want the support of a colleague. The more closed the discussion network around the colleague, the more consequential your first impression with people in the network. A slightly positive impression will echo around the network, amplifying into trust.

A poor first impression works the same way. You can become an icon for what people in the group don't want to be. It is dangerous to leave difficult encounters to be interpreted by the locals. Not only is gossip associated with amplified negative feelings, escalating to character assassination; there are consequences beyond the immediate relationship. First, the relationship becomes less flexible because it is associated with more extreme emotions. Having reached the conclusion that you are to blame for the difficult relationship, your colleague is less likely to trust you in future (Blount, 1995; Brockner et al., 1997). Having talked to colleagues about you as the problem, things will never be the same as they were before your colleague took to assassinating your character. Second, a closed network around your colleague means that there are multiple people engaged in assassinating your character. Not only will you have difficulty working with these people in future, you will have difficulty building new relations with employees exposed to their stories. The hardening wall between you and the people around your colleague can be expected to elicit similar emotions from you (e.g., Kramer, 1994, 1999, on paranoia and distrust, Sitkin and Stickel, 1996, on distrust spawned by TQM zealots). With respect to changing your reputation, bandwidth implies that third parties transmit information on your behavior so a change in your behavior will change your reputation—allowing for the suspicion with which individuals receive data inconsistent with previous data. Under echo, your reputation is robust to changes in your behavior because the source of the reputation is stories third parties are telling one another. The mistake you once made now lives in legend within a target group where people repeat the story over and over in socializing new members of the group. Changing your reputation in the group means more than asking people in the group to accept new data. It means asking them to give up an image of you that has become part of their identity. For the mistake amplified and unforgiven in third-party gossip, you are pushed to leave the firm or fire the locals to manage your negative reputation sustained in local gossip (the right-hand graph in Figure 4.6).

4.5.3 Waiting for Orders

The people engaged in gossip do not own reputation as individuals. Theirs are the mouths through which reputation-sculpting stories pass, but reputations are owned between the people whose discussion defines a reputation. Thus ownership is removed entirely from the hands of individuals and put into the relations between individuals.

People in a closed network live with continuous echo. They offer tentative opinions to discover an acceptable position, then espouse the position, and ostentatiously reject non-believers. In the informal social networks that co-ordinate contemporary organizations, "I was just following orders" takes on new meaning. Ownership lies with the group, is discovered through discussion, but biased by echo toward predispositions. The drift toward a group standard is not a contest between peer pressure and individual will power. This is the more insidious undermining discussed in Section 4.5.2 in which ostensibly informed rationality leads to conformity: Individuals search for information by talking with colleagues, but the information they obtain is biased by etiquette, which isolates them from options not already known. This condition became popularly known in the 1970s as "groupthink" (following Janis', 1972, interpretation of group dynamics in White House actions toward Cuba in the early 1960s) and the "agentic state" (illustrated in Milgram's, 1974, experiments with people administering powerful electric shocks to a person screaming about the pain and his failing heart). People become Whyte's (1956) organization man, awaiting direction from the proper authority.

I hear senior managers bemoan the condition in terms of employees waiting for orders. The leaders are both victim and author of their misery. They are surrounded by well-intentioned subordinates trying to help. Subordinates are talking with one another about how the leader feels and what seem to be the leader's pressing concerns today. Let the leader drop a sentence about being uninterested in a particular concern, and subordinates are unlikely to bring it up again, even less likely to search for information on the wisdom of ignoring the concern. Information on the concern would not be interesting gossip. Have the leader remark that a concern is important and it will crop up in subsequent conversations. Hired consultants come in looking for ways to create value in the context of pressing concerns. They listen to what people are saying and become part of the echo. This scenario plays out in project groups, divisions, companies, regions, and countries. Think about the example with which I opened this chapter: international intelligence emerging from incomplete bits of information echoing back and forth in a closed network of allies.

What cracks the "waiting for orders" condition is having to make choices between alternatives, which takes us back to brokerage. Groupthink is thwarted by engaging contradiction, ensuring that alternatives are presented, establishing an environment of debate between alternatives, even if it means the extreme of appointing a devil's advocate (Janis, 1972). Milgram's subjects stop torturing their victim when they have to resolve contradictory commands (experiments 15 and 17 in Milgram, 1974). The central theme to the brokerage association with creativity and learning in Chapter 2 is that contacts in disparate groups provide exposure to alternative beliefs and behaviors. Engaging that diversity frees people from the adhesive beliefs and behaviors of any one group. In other words, brokerage forces people to engage contradictions, which is the cure for the hubris of uninformed certainty. People embedded in closed networks can find it difficult to make individual choices because they are so locked into beliefs and behaviors that have become routine. Recall, from Chapter 2, Weick's (1996) chilling analogy between jargon-bound academics and firefighters burned to death because they did not discard the heavy tools they were carrying. Weick (1996: 301) explains:

The reluctance to drop one's tools when threat intensifies is not just a problem for firefighters. Navy seamen sometimes refuse orders to remove their heavy steel-toed shoes when they are forced to abandon a sinking ship, and they drown or punch holes in the life rafts as a result. Fighter pilots in a disabled aircraft sometimes refuse orders to eject, preferring instead the "cocoon of oxygen" still present in the cockpit. Karl Wallenda, the world-renowned high-wire artist, fell to his death still clutching his balance pole, when his hands could have grabbed the wire below him. Dropping one's tools is a proxy for unlearning, for adaptation, for flexibility, in short, for many of the dramas that engage organization scholars.

Weick's analogy works, and generalizes to other kinds of people, because people so often identify themselves with the tools they employ in their work. Weick's (1996: 305–308) ten reasons why the firefighters did not drop their tools are a template for explaining why efforts to change organizations so often fail. Colleagues cut off and reinforcing one another in a closed network, have trouble seeing alternative ways to go. They are unlikely to give up the tools they have, and likely to insist (from a lack of alternatives) that others use the same tools. The surest way to break free of a closed network is to build attachments to another closed network, letting third parties in the new network absorb you out of the old (see Ebaugh, 1988, on people making a major transition and Rao, Davis, and Ward, 2000, on the similar network factors associated with firms switching from NASDAQ to the New York Stock Exchange; Coser, 1975, on people becoming individuals through conflicting affiliations; Starbuck, 1996, on unlearning; Sutton, 2002, on fostering creativity). Feelings of ownership and responsibility come from making a choice between alternatives. If someone else makes the choice, someone else is responsible. If group discussion obliterates alternatives from view, the group owns the choice left visible. In separating people from responsibility for their beliefs and behaviors, closed networks encourage people to be unimaginative, irresponsible drones.

4.5.4 Closure More Powerful

Echo expands the bandwidth effects in Chapter 3 to recognize closure as a more powerful, more dangerous, source of control. I described examples in Sections 3.2 and 3.3 of people working to stay aligned with colleagues. Peer pressure could be brought to bear on a person who failed to stay aligned. Recall the person on the manufacturing team who explained (Barker, 1993: 425): "If you notice that somebody's not getting anything done, then we can bring it up at a [team] meeting, you know, and ask them what the problem is, what's causing them not to be able to get their work done." The bandwidth that closure provides makes it possible for people on the team to stay informed about individual contributions to the team. The exercise of control involves peer pressure against the deviant. Echo creates a more insidious form of control. By filtering the information that reaches individuals, belief can reach higher levels of certainty and deviance can be eliminated before it is conceived. As you check with trusted contacts about a colleague, the contacts relay stories about the colleague that corroborate your existing opinion. The information you obtained in your checking around was biased by etiquette to corroborate your existing opinion, but you have done the due diligence of checking around with people. You rest assured in your opinion. Motives are a consideration. Knowing that etiquette filters what they hear, people should discount gossip. I discussed in Section 4.1.2 why people do not discount gossip, or discount it too little. My point here is that taking etiquette into account makes the reputation mechanism more powerful than it would be if it depended on peer pressure alone to maintain alignment. Where closure produces echo, people can feel that their opinion is based on a due diligence of checking opinion with others, which can take opinion to a level of self-righteous confidence that would be difficult if people were only bowing to peer pressure. Echo and bandwidth come down to the difference between belief and compliance.

More generally, echo makes closure more powerful because control no longer depends on information being consistent across a network, or accurate at any point in the network. Reputations built in conversations subject to echo can produce inconsistent reputations in adjacent groups. You do not have one reputation; you have as many as the groups in which you are discussed. People in adjacent groups can be self-righteous about inconsistent beliefs. Echo allows closure's reputation mechanism to reproduce, in fine detail, the clusters and holes in an existing social structure. Network closure does not facilitate trust so much as it amplifies predispositions to extremes of trust and distrust, creating an arthritis in which people cannot learn what they do not already know—thereby deepening the structural holes that segregate groups and allowing legacy organizations to survive in spirit long past the formal organization in which they developed. The recipe for organizational arthritis is simple: ambiguity plus network closure produces ignorant certainty.

The choice between bandwidth and echo is a minor variation within the closure argument, but has dramatic implications for understanding the link between trust and social organization. Down the bandwidth path of network closure improving information flow lies theory and practice in which people are better off when strongly connected to one another. Here lie stories about closed networks providing social capital and reputation in the spirit of Durkheim and Coleman.

Alternatively, the path presuming echo leads to understandings in which perception drifts away from empirical reality, and what closed networks produce is ignorant certainty. Closure is not associated with trust *per se*. It is associated with more certain, intense feelings. Here lie stories about groupthink, scapegoating, stereotypes, and reputations otherwise distorted by echo-amplified distrust. Here too lie positive stories amplifying trust in charismatic leaders, and transcendental visions of a better future.

We each believe that the people whose reputations we shape with our stories deserve it, but the truth is that few of us were eyewitnesses to the behavior deemed honorable or unscrupulous. Most of us were somewhere else, witnessing the behavior only vicariously through stories told by colleagues. Moreover, we have little incentive to speak directly with the person discussed. We are brought together by sharing the story with colleagues whether or not the story is true. Even if we were to speak to the story's protagonist directly, his or her version would be deemed biased by self-interest. Only gossip has the shimmer of unvarnished truth. Phantom and omnipresent, the stories we tell shape reputation and so its concrete consequences. As so nicely phrased in a sociological classic: "If men define situations as real, they are real in their consequences."[33]

---

[33] The exact quote is taken from Thomas and Thomas (1928: 572), but it also circulates as the "self-fulfilling prophecy" after Merton's (1948c) discussion of an outcome happening because people behave on the belief that the outcome is going to happen (e.g., Merton illustrates with a bank failing because people were made afraid by a rumor that the bank was going to fail, so many tried to withdraw their deposits, which caused the bank to fail). The quote in the text, which Merton (1948c: 475) also discusses as the "Thomas theorem" after its author, originates in less succinct form in Thomas and Znaniecki's (1918) report on home-country "mores and norms" affecting the "adjustment or maladjustment" of immigrants to America. I mention the original report because it contains rich source material in which one can find the reputation effects discussed in this and the preceding chapter. For example, the Borkowski letters describe the unhappy relationship between an immigrant who grew distant, and failed to support, his wife in Poland. There was no closed kinship network to enforce obligation between husband and wife, and so no effective "reputation cost" for the husband (Thomas and Znaniecki, 1918: 345): "Hence after a certain time there is nothing more left of the old affection toward his wife, and though for almost twenty years he writes from time to time and sends some money, he does it partly from pity, partly from a feeling of moral obligation. He does not make any great sacrifice; during the whole time he has sent her less than five hundred dollars, i.e., less than twenty-five dollars a year. But we must remember that he lacks any really strong motive to help her, for the feeling of obligation, not backed by the sanction of social opinion, cannot be strong."

FIVE

Images of Equilibrium

IMAGINE you could freeze a population in time. Forces at work in the population would be suspended in the frozen moment. The forces would be instantaneous in the sense of having an intensity and trajectory, but unknown outcome. Two people in an escalating argument, faces frozen in angry contortion, will probably be pulled by one another's emotions to more severe language. A person falling off the stepladder, body frozen in mid-air, will probably be pulled by gravity to the floor. A group of colleagues about to hear the punch line, faces frozen in affectionate interest, will likely move to laughter and corroborating eye contact reaffirming their camaraderie. Some trajectories are unidentified: A woman holding her cup of coffee in mid-air could be raising the cup to her lips or putting it back on the desk. Trajectory clues lie in covariates such as the woman looking at the cup to ensure lip–cup coordination, or turned back to her work confident in desk–cup coordination.

This book has been an introduction to the instantaneous effects of social capital. At any moment, the distribution of informal relations among people and groups constitute a network of dense clusters segregated by structural holes (the small world illustrated in Figure 1.1). Network models of brokerage and closure predict the distribution of social-capital advantage in the network. I anchored the discussion on four stylized facts: two facts describing the social-capital mechanism and consequence of network brokerage, and two facts describing the mechanism and consequence of network closure.

With respect to brokerage, information is more homogeneous within than between groups, so people whose networks bridge the holes between groups have a vision advantage in detecting and developing good ideas (Figure 2.3). The result is that such people are more at risk of praise and reward (Figure 1.8). Illustrated in Figure 5.1 by Robert and the material to the left of him, brokerage is about the advantages of introducing variation into group opinion and behavior.

Where third parties close the network around bridge relations, reputation pressures encourage the trust and collaboration needed to deliver the value of bridges (Figure 4.8), creating a social capital advantage defined in terms of closure across structural holes, especially at extreme levels of closure coordinating across extensive bridge relations as in a skunkworks or crisis team (Figure 3.5). Illustrated in Figure 5.1 by James and the material to the right of him, the social capital of closure is about the advantages of driving variation out of group behavior or opinion.

Looking back across the chapters, a summary conclusion is that the effects of social capital are substantial and concentrated in extreme network conditions. It is no surprise to see the substantial effects. The performance effects of brokerage and closure have been repeatedly documented in empirical research. The added refinement that effects are concentrated in extreme network conditions emerges from the diversity of research in the chapters, though the point seems obvious in retrospect. All four stylized facts, two of which are illustrated in Figure 5.1, show effects disproportionately stronger at extreme levels of brokerage and extreme levels of closure. With respect to the advantage of brokerage, illustrated in the graph to the left in Figure 5.1, connecting two contacts in an already densely connected network does not erode vision-performance as much as the first pair of contacts connected in the network. With respect to the advantage of closure, breaking the link between two contacts in a completely connected network erodes trust-performance more than breaking the link between two contacts in an already fragmented network.

A second conclusion I draw from the chapters is that brokerage and closure are twice complementary. Most obviously, they are complements because they augment one another in creating social capital. Brokerage and closure together define a network concept of social capital, structural autonomy, in which advantage is greatest when closure within a group occurs with brokerage beyond the group (Figure 3.5). Their complementarity is substantively interesting in its own right, but especially attractive for the foundation it provides to clearly compare results across studies (see Section 3.4.3). Further, brokerage and closure are complements in the sense of providing a cure for the other's failure mode. Noted at the bottom-left in Figure 5.1, unrestrained brokerage can create organization chaos, manifest in errors such as resources allocated to conflicting goals and units in the same organization competing against one another. Closure's reputation mechanism brings people back into alignment. It is no accident that reputation metrics provided by multi-point (360) evaluations were adopted in so many large organizations at about the same time that organizations were removing layers of bureaucracy, which made them more dependent on network entrepreneurs to integrate operations across groups. On the other hand, and as noted at the bottom-right in Figure 5.1, closure's reputation mechanism can create the organization arthritis discussed in Chapter 4 as groupthink, the agentic state, and ignorant certainty. Stories echoing within the closed network amplify opinion to positive and negative extremes, making the existing structure resistant to change, deepening the structural holes that segregate groups, again especially at extreme levels of closure. Brokerage has the potential to crack the closure-induced arthritis with selection and synthesis among conflicting alternatives.

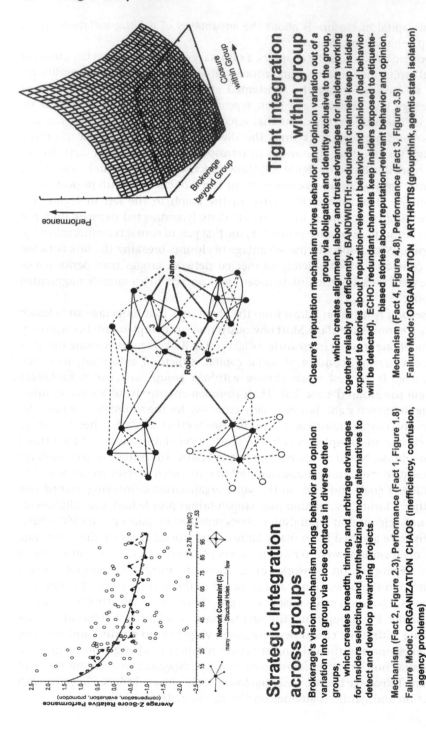

Tight Integration within group

Closure's reputation mechanism drives behavior and opinion variation out of a group via obligation and identity exclusive to the group, which creates alignment, labor, and trust advantages for insiders working together reliably and efficiently. BANDWIDTH: redundant channels keep insiders exposed to reputation-relevant behavior and opinion (bad behavior will be detected). ECHO: redundant channels keep insiders exposed to stories about reputation-relevant behavior and opinion, biased stories about reputation-relevant behavior and opinion.

Mechanism (Fact 4, Figure 4.8), Performance (Fact 3, Figure 3.5)
Failure Mode: ORGANIZATION ARTHRITIS (groupthink, agentic state, isolation)

Strategic Integration across groups

Brokerage's vision mechanism brings behavior and opinion variation into a group via close contacts in diverse other groups, which creates breadth, timing, and arbitrage advantages for insiders selecting and synthesizing among alternatives to detect and develop rewarding projects.

Mechanism (Fact 2, Figure 2.3), Performance (Fact 1, Figure 1.8)
Failure Mode: ORGANIZATION CHAOS (inefficiency, confusion, agency problems)

Fig. 5.1: Instantaneous social-capital effects

5.1 Network Model and Austrian Metaphor

The image of closure and brokerage counterbalancing one another's weaknesses raises questions about equilibrium. I focused in the preceding chapters on instantaneous forces because that is where research results are reliable and abundant. Across available panel studies of networks in heterogeneous populations, the most replicated finding is the stylized fact for Chapter 4—closure reinforces the existing structure in that strong relations are less subject to decay, and relations between friends of friends are more likely to form and survive through the initial high-decay period. In other words, closure creates inertia in social boundaries such that the existing segregation between groups is a kind of equilibrium. Clusters in a spatial display such as Figure 1.1, if left to the inertial force of closure, would tighten inward and pull away from adjacent clusters.[1] Therefore, equilibrium—defined by a lack of endogenous change disrupting the status quo—is a function of brokerage breaking free from the inertia of closure.

This is the point at which it is productive to draw an analogy between the social capital of structural holes and the market metaphor in the Austrian school of economics, here represented by Schumpeter's work on entrepreneurs and Hayek's work on markets as "telecommunication systems." The analogy is in three parts, the first two of which were the subjects of Chapters 1 and 2.[2]

---

[1] I have in mind Coleman's (1957) description of structural changes that accompany conflict escalation. More broadly, Monge and Contractor (2001, 2003) review perspectives on formation, maintenance, and decay in social networks. There are published descriptions of networks over time, several of which were cited in Chapter 4. However, the bulk of the work describes small groups, typically containing less than a few dozen people, and often with data reduced to the role of numerical illustration for a new network metric. Empirical work documenting closure effects with network panels in heterogeneous populations include Doreian et al. (1996), Gulati and Gargiulo (1999), Burt (2000a, 2002), Contractor et al. (2000), and Weesie and Raub (2000). Saying that closure reproduces itself is not to say that relations are static within groups. Figures 4.6 and 4.8 show closure slowing a high rate of decay in banker relationships. However, the factor most slowing decay is relation strength in the prior year and closure around the relationship. More generally, stability within a group tends to increase with the group's structural autonomy (Burt, 1992: 218–224), but there can be profound instability within a group as individuals jockey for secure position (as in White's, 1981, 2002a, 2002b, market model), or for status (as in Podolny's, 1993, market model, and Taylor and Coleman's, 1979, use of the model to describe network change; cf. Marsden, 1981).

[2] My remarks are not offered as an authoritative exploration of the analogy between network models of social capital and the Austrian market metaphor. I only mentioned the analogy in the first two chapters (Ch. 1, nn. 4 and 6; Ch. 2, nn. 6 and 24), and my purpose in this concluding chapter is to sketch equilibrium images implied by the instantaneous effects of social capital to set a stage for subsequent work on network dynamics. I rely on the cited primary works by Schumpeter (2002 [1911a], 1934 [1911b]) and Hayek (1937; 1945), along with expert accounts of the two scholars (respectively Swedberg, 1991, and Caldwell, 2004), and generous comments from Richard Swedberg on a draft of the chapter. I was drawn to the analogy by Birner's (1996, 1999a, 1999b) work on the network models implicit in Hayek's image of markets.

5.1.1 Context

First, the distribution of belief and behavior in the small world of organizations and markets illustrated in Figure 1.1 ensures that information is everywhere imperfect and incomplete. Knowledge about how things work in this location at this time is concentrated in a group of people with specialized experience. Knowledge unevenly distributed across groups creates local advantage. With respect to understanding the circumstances of a specific time and place, one can say (Hayek, 1945: 521–522):

> that practically every individual has some advantage over all others because he possesses unique information of which beneficial use might be made, but of which use can be made only if the decisions depending on it are left to him or are made with his active co-operation. We need to remember only how much we have to learn in any occupation after we have completed our theoretical training, how big a part of our working life we spend learning particular jobs, and how valuable an asset in all walks of life is knowledge of people, of local conditions, of special circumstances.

5.1.2 Action

Second, there is a premium (in compensation, recognition, and responsibility) given to the people who do the integrative work of creating valuable new combinations of knowledge otherwise segregated in separate groups. These bridge-builders are Schumpeter's (1934 [1911*b*]: 132) entrepreneurs: "And what have they done? They have not accumulated any kind of goods, they have created no original means of production, but have employed existing means of production differently, more appropriately, more advantageously. They have 'carried out new combinations.' They are entrepreneurs." More specifically, they are the network entrepreneurs in Chapters 1 and 2, moving into the white space between groups to add coordination where it is valuable to do so.

5.1.3 Price Incentives for Action

Third, and this is the point at which an image of equilibrium comes into focus, the benefits received for creating new combinations make visible the price for integrative work. To my understanding, this is the juncture at which the Austrian school of economics is most distinct from neoclassical economics. In neoclassical economics, there is a central mechanism, an invisible hand, by which price is determined (Rosen, 1997: 140): "the methods of neoclassical economics mainly are concerned with the establishment of economic equilibrium under fully known or (in Marshallian terminology) given conditions of resource availability, technology and preferences." In contrast, the Austrian

view is that economic systems (Rosen, 1997: 140–141): "evolve as the amal-
gamation and interactions of trials and errors among economic agents. Entrepreneurial ventures and experiments, arbitrage activities, and survival of the
fittest play crucial roles in this process.... This approach begins with the
premise that there is an enormous amount of ignorance in the system. No
one knows or can ever know what is being maximized overall. Decentralization is fundamental because specialization is extreme." Where neoclassical
economics focuses on the balance of market factors at equilibrium, the Austrian view focuses on the process by which markets move toward equilibrium
(Kirzner, 1973; Rosen, 1997).

Network entrepreneurs play a critical role in the Austrian market metaphor.
The premium they receive for their integrative work defines a price for integrative work, which affects others' decision to join in the integrative work.
People like Robert in Figure 1.1 are price makers. They are the people whose
actions reveal the price under which people like James, a price taker, subse-
quently operate. As network entrepreneurs receive disproportionate returns to
their integrative efforts, others are drawn to earn the same returns. As successive bridges are built across a structural hole, returns diminish, and the hole is
closed. The image I have in mind is people distributed across Figure 1.1,
building bridges here and there to coordinate clusters where it is practical
and valuable.[3] Their activity is the subject of entrepreneurship, an area that
has always been interesting for its substance, but has unique theoretical importance as the study of network bridge formation and decay. When incentives for brokerage are no longer visible, the existing structure has reached an
equilibrium.

---

[3] For want of authoritative evidence, I am avoiding the interesting empirical question
of how resources move between local markets around separate structural holes. One
possibility is that the bridge-builders move: Individual network entrepreneurs could
move from their work on this structural hole to build bridges across a second structural
hole. Alternatively, the incentive could move: The premium for bridging this structural
hole could move to a different set of individuals in a position to bridge the second
structural hole. If it is the bridge-builders who move, then a class of mobile network
entrepreneurs would exist as the beneficiaries of brokerage (e.g., Chinese middlemen in
the Thai economy, Siamwalla, 1978). If it is the incentive that moves, then brokerage
would be a mechanism for upward mobility and elite turnover (as in Schumpeter's
description, in n. 7 below, of the upper strata of society as a hotel always full, but of
different people). Both mechanisms probably exist in a heterogeneous population, but
balance between the two could be an informative datum on the local population in an
organization or community. For example, population response to change would be more
dependent on mobilizing the elite in the first case, and is more likely to happen because
the elite are there to be mobilized, but is less likely to provide novel solutions to
disruptive change because the people providing brokerage solutions are experienced in
solving known problems (see Section 3.3.3 on Saxenian's contrast between Route 128
and Silicon Valley).

5.1.4.   *The Path to Equilibrium*

The prices paid for integrative work should decrease in mean and variance on the path to equilibrium. Price variation decreases as buyers and sellers become more accurate in estimating price, and the average price paid for integrative work across a structural hole decreases with the number of bridges across the hole.[4] Bridge price is a function of benefit minus cost. Bridges are more costly than redundant ties for the reasons of effort and resistance discussed in Section

---

[4] Decreasing price variance around a constant equilibrium price is nicely illustrated in Smith's (1962) influential student simulations of a market. Subjects are divided into two groups, buyers and sellers, and each subject is given a card with a number on it. For the buyers, the number is the minimum price at which they can sell. Their profit is the difference from whatever higher price they can sell. For the buyers, the number on their card is the maximum price at which they can buy. Their profit is the difference from whatever lower price they can buy. The cards define supply, demand, and so an equilibrium price. A period of exchanges opens with a student announcing orally to the group a price at which the student is willing to buy or sell. Other students chime in with their offers to buy or sell. When two people agree to an exchange, their exchange price is recorded. The period stops when no further bids result in exchanges. Different numbers of periods were run under different buyer and seller distributions for a total of 49 periods (multiple periods seem to be necessary to see price variance decrease, Smith, 1962: 114 n.). Let Po be the average price at which an exchange occurred during a period. Let Pe be the equilibrium price for the period. Here are the characteristics of prices in successive periods (Smith, 1962: 117):

Period Sequence	Number	Mean (Po−Pe)/Pe	SD (Po−Pe)/Pe	Mean % variance relative to initial price variance
1	15	−.07	.18	100%
2	13	−.04	.12	55%
3	11	−.02	.07	39%
4	7	.00	.04	31%
5	2	−.00	.03	18%
6	1	−.02	—	5%

Smith ran 15 experiments in which there was a first period, 13 in which there was a second period, and so on. Across exchanges during the 15 initial periods, the average price at which exchange occurred was close to the equilibrium price (mean (Po−Pe)/Pe = −.07). Variation between prices decreases across successive periods, from .18 down to .03 in the fourth column of the table. The final column is based on Smith's measure of price variation: His "coefficient of convergence" is the standard deviation in exchange prices during a period divided by the average exchange price for the period (Po). The final column shows the rate at which price variation decreased from the variation observed in the first period (mean ratio of the coefficient of convergence for a period in an experiment divided by the first-period coefficient of convergence for the experiment). By definition, the ratio is 100% for the first period. Price variation in the second period of an experiment is on average 55% of the first-period variation. Price variation in the third period of an experiment is on average 39% of the initial. Smith (1962: 116) summarizes: "As the exchange process is repeated through successive trading periods with the same conditions of supply and demand prevailing initially in each period, the variation in exchange prices tends to decline, and to cluster more closely around the equilibrium."

4.4.2. Their higher cost is balanced against the higher benefits documented in Chapter 1. Brokerage is valuable for introducing variation, so the benefits decrease with additional redundant participants. Thus, the value created by a bridge can be expected to decrease with the number of bridges across the same structural hole. When the first entrepreneurs benefit from bridging a structural hole, others join them, decreasing the value of bridging the hole.[5] If Figure 1.1 were an academic market, for example, and Robert produced a useful idea because of a Group A technology he discovered from Contact 7, other academics in Robert's line of work would be expected to develop relationships with contacts in Group A, eventually eliminating the value to be had from the structural hole between the two groups (e.g., contacts 1 and 2 are positioned to draw on their ties to Group A).

Figure 5.2 is a notional display of benefit (white) and cost (gray) for successive bridge relations between two groups. The first pair of bars indicates high benefit and high risk for the first person to bridge the groups. The second pair indicates lower benefit with much lower risk because coordination between the groups was made more legitimate by the first bridge, and so on across additional bridges. No one knows how the bars in Figure 5.2 change across additional bridges. There is probably a typology of structural holes latent in comparative data on the issue. Even with the limited data available, the benefit of a bridge should decrease across successive bridges, and the decrease is probably steeper for the first few bridges than for the last few. Value is certainly eliminated long before everyone eligible to span the hole has done so. Holes are closed by individuals, not populations (or, in network jargon, a high density of bridges is not required to close a hole; the first few bridges suffice). To cite familiar academic work, the acclaim that Hannan and Freeman (1977) received for synthesizing organization theory from sociology and ecology, was much higher than the acclaim accorded subsequent

---

[5] Schumpeter (1934 [1911b]: 135) puts it thus: "The principle of the matter is that a new commodity is valued by purchasers much as gifts of nature or pictures by old masters, that is its price is determined without regard to cost of production. Hence the possibility that it may sell above costs, including all the expenditure connected with overcoming the innumerable difficulties of the venture. At first only a few see the new enterprise and are able to carry it out. This also is an entrepreneurial act, the carrying out of a new combination; and it yields a profit, which remains in the entrepreneur's pocket. It is true, the source dries up sooner or later." Elaborating on the dried-up source (Schumpeter, 1934 [1911b]: 147): "profit does not live eternally. Here too, necessary changes appear which put an end to it. The new combination is carried out; its results are at hand, all doubts are silenced; the advantages, and at the same time the manner of obtaining them, are henceforth evident. There is further need, at the most, of a manager or foreman, but not of the creative power of a leader. It is only necessary to repeat what has been done before to acquire the equivalent advantages. And that can and will be done without a leader. Even if resistances from friction must still be overcome, the matter has become essentially different, and easier. The advantages have become realities to all members of the community."

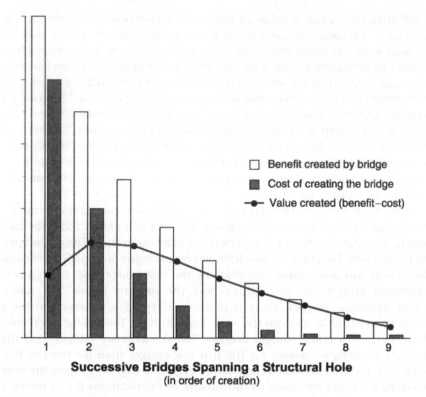

Successive Bridges Spanning a Structural Hole
(in order of creation)

Fig. 5.2: Value of successive bridges

elaboration within the population ecology of organizations. The acclaim that Granovetter (1985) received for so clearly making the case that economic transactions are affected by their sociological context was higher than the acclaim accorded subsequent elaboration within the embeddedness metaphor. In fact, the nonlinear decline in benefit is probably a nonmonotonic decline in value (benefit minus cost). Whatever the functional form of decline in benefit with additional entrants, cost must decrease more quickly because the first entrant has to create both product and market. Figure 5.2 shows cost decreasing faster than benefit, creating a second-mover advantage. Target audiences better understand the coordination benefit, and problems revealed by the first entrant can be anticipated and avoided by subsequent entrants. Whatever the benefits to the first who bridges a structural hole, benefits are probably higher for the next few entrants, then decreasing for subsequent entrants. Value declines with subsequent entrants down to some equilibrium level at which benefit is marginally higher than the cost of bridging the hole. Regardless of the rate of decline in value, there is no competitive advantage at equilibrium

to another bridge. Network entrepreneurs have moved the market to equilibrium by eliminating holes where it was valuable to do so.[6]

5.2   Enduring Advantage

The argument to this point is that brokerage provides a temporary, local advantage. Bridging structural holes, in Section 5.1.4, is a short-run advantage on the
path to equilibrium. Brokerage consumes its incentive as it speeds a system to
equilibrium. At equilibrium, there is no visible incentive for further brokerage.
As Schumpeter (1934 [1911b]: 131–132) summarized (also see n. 5): "the final
result must be a new equilibrium position, in which, with new data, the law of
cost again rules. ... the surplus of the entrepreneur in question and of his
immediate followers disappears. Not at once, it is true, but as a rule only after a
longer or shorter period of progressive diminution." The point in Section 5.1.3
is that the equilibrium is local, spanning the space within which the price paid
for a piece of integrative work is visible. A price, the incentive it creates, and
the resulting equilibrium, exist among the people for whom the price is
visible. Bridging a structural hole is a process of trial and error that can work
here, fail there, and succeed dramatically for a third person. A network entrepreneur who fails to find an attractive return here can find it over there
working with a different combination of contacts. People aware of a brokerage
opportunity can be reluctant to invest simply because they are unaware of
productive ways to develop the opportunity. If no one tries to bridge a hole, or
the rewards of successfully bridging the hole are not visible, there is no visible
incentive to bridge the hole. With no visible incentive for bridges, the hole
continues through time, awaiting the network entrepreneur who can earn a
return from bridging it. This is equilibrium of a kind, but it is distinct from the

---

[6] In the absence of empirical evidence on the relative cost and benefit of successive
bridge relations, I defined the notional bars in Figure 5.2 by the power function observed
in learning curves ($y = ax^{-b}$, see Section 3.3.5). The analogy to learning curves is obvious
in that people are learning how to coordinate across a structural hole, however, it is also
inaccurate in two ways. First, the power function predicts a much higher value and cost
for the first bridge than is indicated in Figure 5.2. If I draw a power function through the
benefits and costs given in Figure 5.2 for the second through the ninth bridges, then the
benefit of the first bridge would be about a third higher than portrayed in Figure 5.2 (a
score of 15.6 to the score of 10 in Figure 5.2). I did not see the virtue of scaling the graph
to an extreme value of the initial bridge, so I lowered the cost and benefit of the first
bridge. Second, different people are probably responsible for successive bridges across a
structural hole, so instead of learning from previous bridges (illustrated in the graph to
the right in Figure 3.7), there would be an initial learning period for each team constructing a bridge (illustrated in the graph to the left in Figure 3.7). On the other hand, if
a consulting group made a business of coordinating across a specific class of structural
holes, they would surely learn to build bridges of their specialized type more efficiently
across successive engagements.

usual understanding in neoclassical economics. As Hayek (1937: 51) described the distinction:[7] "We may therefore very well have a position of equilibrium only because some people have no chance of learning about facts which, if they knew them, would induce them to alter their plans....While such a position represents in one sense a position of equilibrium, it is clear that it is not an equilibrium in the special sense in which equilibrium is regarded as a sort of optimum position." Ignorance is an unstable foundation for equilibrium. Trial and error in the population, or exogenous shock, can make visible the value latent in unbridged structural holes. Once visible, rewards for bridging a hole elicit the efforts of network entrepreneurs, who move the population to a new equilibrium.[8]

---

[7] The distinction between global prices defined by a central market mechanism and local prices revealed by returns to entrepreneurial effort is a central point in Hayek's (1944) emphatic rejection of government bureaux directing economic markets. If a market were to clear as if it contained a central pricing mechanism, it would be because there are sufficient intermediaries to carry local prices across otherwise segregated locations (Hayek, 1945: 524–526; cf. Baker, 1984): "If we can agree that the economic problem of society is mainly one of rapid adaptation to changes in the particular circumstances of time and place, it would seem to follow that the ultimate decisions must be left to the people who are familiar with these circumstances, who know directly of the relevant changes and of the resources immediately available to meet them. We cannot expect that this problem will be solved by first communicating all this knowledge to a central board which, after integrating all knowledge, issues its orders. We must solve it by some form of decentralization. But this answers only part of our problem. We need decentralization because only thus can we insure that the knowledge of the particular circumstances of time and place will be promptly used. But the 'man on the spot' cannot decide solely on the basis of his limited but intimate knowledge of the facts of his immediate surroundings. There still remains the problem of communicating to him such further information as he needs to fit his decisions into the whole pattern of changes of the larger economic system.... This problem can be solved, and in fact is being solved, by the price system.... The whole acts as one market, not because any of its members survey the whole field, but because their limited individual fields of vision sufficiently overlap so that through intermediaries the relevant information is communicated to all."

[8] I found Hayek's market metaphor more conducive than Schumpeter's to the image in the text of local equilibria around individual structural holes. True, Hayek speaks of intermediaries carrying price information across the market so the neoclassical image of equilibrium is a possibility (see the quote in the preceding footnote). But it is a possibility, not an inevitability. Sever indirect connections through intermediaries, and price can vary across segregated locations. In contrast, Schumpeter, looking for a source of endogenous economic change, seemed more confident in competitive forces driving local prices to a central market price such that the incentive for bridges across a structural hole disappears (as expressed by the quote in the last paragraph of Section 5.1 and the quotes in n. 4, above). New entrepreneurial action will shift activity toward a new equilibrium (e.g., Schumpeter, 2002 [1911a]: 411–412), but competitive forces will again drive down the value of the new bridges pending disruption from further new entrepreneurial action (Schumpeter, 1934 [1911b]: 235): "... the action of the group of entrepreneurs has in the meanwhile altered the data of the system, upset its equilibrium, and thus started an apparently irregular movement in the economic system, which we

5.2.1   Passive and Active Structural Holes

A brokerage advantage temporary in theory could become an enduring advantage if the move to equilibrium is slowed, or repeatedly disrupted. For example, allow that information grows quickly out of date, as seems to be the case for senior managers (see Mintzberg, 1973; Stinchcombe, 1990, on the short half-life of information in organizations). As an industry of managers and organizations moves toward equilibrium, managers whose networks span structural holes have an advantage in identifying and developing the more rewarding opportunities. Technological change and events create new priorities, so the industry moves toward a new equilibrium. Again, managers whose networks span structural holes have an advantage in identifying and developing the more rewarding opportunities. With repeated change such that information grows quickly out of date, the managers whose networks span structural holes have an enduring competitive advantage, which would be visible as the association between brokerage and performance illustrated in Figure 1.8.[9]

---

conceive as a struggle towards a new equilibrium position." Even when development happens in separate sectors, Schumpeter (1911*a*: 430) believes there is something—felt more than proven—that integrates developments across the sectors: "How come, in spite of this relative independence of all individual sectors, that it is a great truth, a truth, however, which we can feel, more than prove strictly, that each element of each sector in each point in time is connected to each element of each other sector, that all situations in all sectors determine each other and belong together?" Schumpeter's felt connections between sectors could be used as a segue into a small-world story about intermediaries providing bridges that interlock the sectors, but such a story evolves into Hayek's explicit discussion of intermediaries and the segregated pricing that can occur in their absence.

[9] Enduring advantage does not mean that the same individuals benefit. Returning to the issue raised in n. 3, high returns to the brokers who bridge one structural hole can move to brokers who bridge a different structural hole. Note the triangular data distributions in some of the Figure 1.5 graphs (especially graphs D, E, and G). Managers in the high-constraint closed networks typically perform poorly, in all of the Figure 1.5 graphs. There is more performance variance between managers in the low-constraint networks. When a person performs well, the person is likely to have a low-constraint network (upper-left corner of the performance-constraint graphs). However, there are many people with low-constraint networks not performing well relative to their peers (lower-left of the performance-constraint graphs). A plausible speculation is that the variable returns to brokerage reflect the value of the structural holes spanned. High-performance brokers bridge currently valued structural holes. Low-performance brokers bridge holes less valued. Turnover in who benefits from brokerage is a central point in Schumpeter's (1934 [1911*b*]: 156) image of economic change: "The successful entrepreneur rises socially, and with him his family, who acquire from the fruits of his success a position not immediately dependent upon personal conduct. This represents the most important factor of rise in the social scale in the capitalist world. Because it proceeds by competitively destroying old businesses and hence the existences dependent upon them, there always corresponds to it a process of decline, of loss of caste, of elimination. This fate also

Or, a temporary brokerage advantage could become enduring if bridges are not absorbed into the social structure around a hole. Distinguish passive from active structural holes. A hole is passive if bridges across it are readily absorbed into the surrounding social structure. The preceding paragraph assumes passive holes. Each bridge is secure in that information flows freely across it, thereby diminishing the value of subsequent bridges across the same structural hole.

A structural hole is active if interests attached to the hole resist bridges. For example, interests can be configured such that they compete to bridge the hole so a bridge established by one group is subject to erosion by the other groups. Progress toward equilibrium with the establishment of a bridge is destabilized, resulting in a continuous disequilibrium around the structural hole. The image of social structure portrayed in this book, and illustrated in Figure 1.1, is static clusters linked here and there by productive bridges. In reality, laying a bridge between two clusters can have side-effects of more sharply segregating other clusters, or lowering the barriers to bridge relations elsewhere. There are numerous illustrations in the sociological literature, such as Simmel's (1902: 185–186) brief description of Incan rule over subject provinces and Venetian expansion onto the mainland, Pagden's (1988) description of Spanish rule in Sicily, or Barkey's (1994) description of local governors competing against bandits to be the legitimate representative of Turkish rule. Closer to the manager data used in preceding chapters, consider Finlay and Coverdill's (2002) fieldwork on the "headhunter" role in executive recruitment. They describe three interests: the manager trying to hire someone, the pool of headhunters looking for a suitable candidate, and the human resources staff (HR) responsible for the appointment process. Brokerage for the headhunter involves matching candidates with the hiring manager while buffering the manager from HR. The tension in this balance of interests is indicated by the headhunter phrase for HR staff, "weenies," and their characterization by one industry trainer, as people who "didn't have the personality to become morticians" (Finlay and Coverdill 2002: 48). Bridging structural holes in this case involves a

---

threatens the entrepreneur whose powers are declining, or his heirs who have inherited his wealth without his ability. This is not only because all individual profits dry up, the competitive mechanism tolerating no permanent surplus values, but rather annihilating them by means of just this stimulus of the striving for profit which is the mechanism's driving force; but also because in the normal case things so happen that entrepreneurial success embodies itself in the ownership of a business; and this business is usually carried on further by the heirs on what soon become traditional lines until new entrepreneurs supplant it. An American adage expresses it: three generations from overalls to overalls. And so it may be. Exceptions are rare, and are more than compensated for by cases in which the descent is still faster. Because there are always entrepreneurs and relatives and heirs of entrepreneurs, public opinion and also the phraseology of the social struggle readily overlook these facts. They constitute 'the rich' a class of inheritors who are removed from life's battle. In fact, the upper strata of society are like hotels which are indeed always full of people, but people who are forever changing."

simultaneous process of creating holes. As Finlay and Coverdill (1999: 27) conclude in an initial paper on their fieldwork: "When headhunters buffer hiring managers from HR or when they shield a client from a competitor, they open gaps in these relationships that the headhunters themselves then bridge. The success of headhunters, and their attractiveness to employers, rests on this dual function of creating and filling holes."

Then there are the holes around which interests explicitly oppose a bridge, and so ensure continuing disequilibrium as new entrants try alternative ways of bridging the hole. Tilly (1998a) provides an overview of the forms resistance can take when a group is advantaged by a structural hole (see esp. Tilly, 1998a: 8–11, 84–86). Tilly describes social mechanisms that preserve paired insider–outsider categories such as legitimate versus illegitimate, our class versus theirs, citizens versus foreigners, and other pairs of asymmetric categories defined by income, education, age, gender, ethnicity, and so on. Tilly's boundaries between social categories are examples of structural holes. His four mechanisms preserving boundaries describe interests opposing bridges across structural holes. Adapting Tilly's mechanisms to this book, a structural hole is active if (1) it provides an opportunity for insiders on one side of the hole to exploit outsiders on the other side, (2) permits insiders to hoard opportunities from outsiders, (3) makes it easier for insiders to construct new organization based on existing models in which insiders are advantaged, or (4) daily routines and valued social ties of aid, influence, and information gathering have adapted to the hole.

The fourth mechanism, "adaptation" in Tilly's analysis, is particularly important because it is a way in which passive structural holes become active. A passive hole becomes active if people adapt to the hole. For example, cotton manufacturing was brought to the United States by Francis Lowell. British producers, made prosperous by their cotton looms, closely guarded loom designs. Lowell visited Manchester in 1811, watched the looms in operation, returned to Boston, and three years later was manufacturing cotton with a system more productive than what he had observed in England (Rosegrant and Lampe, 1992: 42):

drawing on his remarkable memory, and working with an expert mechanic named Paul Moody, Lowell re-created the power loom he had studied overseas. Even more impressive is what he did with it. The looms Lowell studied in England were isolated, a discrete step in a sharply defined production process. Lowell abandoned that structure. Uniting all the main steps in textile production—from carding the raw cotton to weaving the finished cloth—under one roof. It was a deceptively simple, but profound organizational innovation. Ironically, the notion of bringing these functions together had already been conceived in Britain, but the established structure of the textile industry prohibited its implementation.

In other words, British organizations had adapted to structural holes between certain production activities such as carding and weaving. Lowell, free from the British convention, was free to create a more efficient, integrated production process.

The Clendenin case discussed in Chapter 1 involves adaptation, as it is typical in large contemporary bureaucratic organizations. The case begins with structural holes between Xerox's regional operations. Initially, the holes were passive. No one set out to create them. The holes simply reflected technological limits of production at the time that the regional operations were created. Over time, people adapted to the separate regional operations. Each region developed its own performance benchmarks, financial systems, and production control systems. Clendenin's idea of integrating production across regions required people to give up their local systems in favor of an integrated central system—and the change was rejected by the regional managers. Managing the resistance was a critical element in Clendenin's successful brokerage.

The Clendenin case illustrates resistance when people adapt daily routines and behaviors to otherwise passive structural holes. Resistance will be stronger if adaptation moves deeper. Resistance will be especially forceful against bridges between groups with conflicting beliefs, or to a group prohibiting relationships of the kind represented by a proposed bridge.[10] For example, Keller (1989: ch. 6) describes how senior-level distrust between

---

[10] These considerations define the "depth" of a structural hole (Burt, 1992: 42–44), but this is a point at which culture is a productive consideration. My comments in this section highlight the significance of Emirbayer and Goodwin's (1994) suggestion that social network analysis pay more attention to culture as a reality-structuring mechanism. As much as personal identity and beliefs emerge from the interpersonal processes discussed in Chapters 3 and 4 within closed networks, identity and belief shape understandings of interpersonal connection. Culture can discourage otherwise beneficial action (e.g., the Fur aversion discussed below in the text to working for a wage or producing beer for sale: Barth, 1967; or the initial aversion to life insurance because it involved putting a price on human life: Zelizer, 1978). It can encourage beneficial action that would otherwise be left dormant (e.g., the "Protestant ethic" that encouraged industry and trade as a godly pursuit: Weber, 1930 [1905]). The more general analytical perspective is Commons' (1924: 65–69) image of the "fifth player." The five roles to consider in analyzing a relationship are the buyer and seller in the relationship, along with the best alternative buyer, the best alternative seller, and the underlying culture (or in Commons' discussion, the legal system) that defines the may-must-can-cannot rules by which the relationship transpires. Respectively, the four verb parameters concern (1) the liberty or immunity or range of alternative behaviors you are allowed in the relationship, (2) the duty or liability or minimum you are expected to deliver in the relationship, (3) the right or power or maximum you have a right to expect from the relationship, and (4) the disability or exposure or specific behaviors prohibited to you in the relationship (see, for example, Commons, 1924: 68, 134–142, 147–148). There is a strategy argument to be made in selecting between alternative "fifth players" such as a market logic versus bureaucratic authority, or friendship (Burt, 1992: 233–236). The point in this note is merely that culture is a productive place to look for explanations of resistance to bridges making brokerage an enduring advantage.

General Motors and the United Auto Workers reversed successful labor-management collaboration in the Van Nyes plant to establish a team-based production system. Lütz (1997: 233) concludes that standard operating procedures were "one of the most important barriers" to collaboration among the manufacturers she studied in the German automobile industry.

A way to think about active structural holes is to ask why a hole observed is not already closed. If there is value to bridging the hole, why hasn't someone already done so? Consider two companies, MY-CD.com and Musicmaker.com, founded in 1998 to bridge the structural hole between music producers and customers. Instead of producers guessing demand, pressing a batch of CDs, and distributing through retail stores, the idea was that a customer could go to a website, select music, and have it pressed on a CD made just for that customer. Implementation differed between the two companies. MY-CD focused on assembling technological and financial resources needed to create and operate the site, treating as passive the hole between producers and customers. Even before Napster emerged as a challenge, MY-CD was, in the words of one observer, "a forlorn-looking site that seems to be barely alive." The problem was getting record companies to release current popular titles. Producers feared the internet as a threat to property rights. Musicmaker, in contrast, focused on assuaging record-company concerns about the internet; the founders were senior people from record companies, and the company was largely owned by record companies. Between personal ties and ownership control, Musicmaker was given access to current hits such that a senior Musicmaker officer could say at the end of 1999 that: "we've been able to do business on terms that the record companies could accept."

Even active holes can be bridged. Barth (1967) describes a structural hole in the economy of a tribe, the Fur, in central Africa. The Fur had a prohibition against exchanging labor or beer for money; it was shameful to work for a wage ("though some men have worked as migrant labor elsewhere," Barth, 1967: 153; see Zelizer, 1994, on socially enforced conceptual boundaries between kinds of money) and shameful to sell beer (Barth, 1967: 155–156): "Some women also brew beer and bring it for sale in the market-place. Though there is no dearth of buyers, especially as the afternoon wears on, the sale of beer is regarded as immoral and the women who do so are looked upon as immodest." The Fur adapted beer parties as a conversion medium (Barth, 1967: 153): "In the simplest form, two more friends may decide to work together for company, in which case they jointly cultivate each other's field in turn, he whose field is being cultivated providing a pot of beer for their joint consumption." Barth (1967: 171) tells of an entrepreneur, an Arab from the north, who put to profit the hole in the Fur economy.[11] The Arab entrepreneur

---

[11] Outsiders often play this role. For example, see Siamwalla (1978) on Chinese middlemen in the Thai economy; and Light and Karageorgis (1994) on socially excluded ethnicities for whom entrepreneurial activities are their route into society. This goes

purchased grain in an area where the price was low, brewed beer from the grain, used the beer to pay for Fur labor on his tomato crop, and sold the tomato crop for a substantial profit. "On an investment of £5 worth of millet, he obtained a return of more than £100 for his tomatoes." The success drew others over the next two years (Barth, 1967: 171–172): "more merchants, and some local people, adopted the strategy with results nearly as spectacular." There are social sanctions with which the Fur could have thwarted the entrepreneurs, but after three years of activity, at the close of Barth's fieldwork with the Fur, no reaction had emerged to block the entrepreneurs. In the words of this chapter, their bridge had been absorbed into the surrounding social structure.[12]

5.2.2   *Stability Despite Brokerage*

I close with a less exhilarating image of brokerage. It is a grand thing to speak of market-facilitating brokerage pursued by people seeking disproportionate returns to their efforts. However, many people aspire only to get paid and go home without incurring too severe a beating.[13] This includes people

---

again to the issue of incentive. Outsiders have neither established nor comfortable position creating a reputation cost inhibiting brokerage.

[12] Recalling the earlier contrast between Austrian and neoclassical images of equilibrium, it is interesting to note economist Joy's (1967: 184–185) effort to analyze Barth's work on the Fur in terms of an equilibrium model in preference to anthropologist Barth's "straight observation of disequilibrium conditions."

[13] It is productive to distinguish social capital as an effect from social capital as a goal (also see Section 1.1.6 on social capital, and Section 4.1.2 on echo-amplified opinion, as by-product rather than goal). For example, there are rules about what is healthy to eat, but I don't live by them, though I would prefer to be healthy. There are rules about how to be a more effective person, but I don't live by them, though I would like to be more effective. People whose networks span structural holes have a vision advantage associated with rewards and satisfaction—but that instantaneous effect does not mean that people optimize their relationships for the rewards of brokerage. Effect and goal are easily confused. For example, Contractor et al. (2000) describe change over the course of two years in the communication network within a public-works organization. They find that bridge relations develop less often than relations with friends of friends, from which they conclude that the brokerage argument might not apply to networks of cooperative relations. More precisely, what they found is the expected tendency for closure to reinforce the existing structure. Not knowing how performance varies across the network, it is impossible to test for social-capital effects, but the brokerage argument predicts that individuals with networks that span structural holes do better precisely because they rise above the natural evolution toward redundancy in networks. Similarly, in an early innovative paper on structural holes in organization networks, Walker, Kogut, and Shan (1997) report change over time toward redundancy in cooperation agreements between start-up firms and their partners in biotechnology. Walker et al. (1997: 109–111) test the idea that network change is motivated by individuals seeking social capital. They find that start-ups responsible for a large portion of density variance (discussed as social capital in the report, Walker et al., 1997: 115–116) are more likely to

disinterested in brokerage,[14] but also includes some number of people who enjoy brokerage benefits: It is possible for network entrepreneurs to enjoy the rewards of brokerage without having to pay the high cost of establishing bridge relations, whereupon brokerage is an enduring advantage and the existing network structure continues through time as if in equilibrium.

Return to the supply-chain managers with whom I began in Chapter 1. They worked in a large organization of social clusters in a constellation around a corporate center (Figures 1.3 and 1.4). Brokerage opportunities were abundant, visible, and rewarded—but apparently irrelevant. The supply chain continued to be plagued by structural holes. Holes continued around the supply-chain function, between the unit functional organizations, and between individuals in the function. Dramatic change could have disrupted previous integration, but that seems an unlikely explanation in this case. The supply-chain managers had been with the company for a long time (18 years on average) and connected by long-standing relationships (8 years on average).

I see evidence of structural reproduction. The point warrants attention because it describes brokerage—a mechanism for change and value creation—prevalent and rewarded in a fragmented, static organization.

There are positive and negative cycles to the reproduction. The negative cycle is clear from the results in Figures 2.1 and 2.3: managers surrounded by densely interconnected discussion partners (high network constraint) were likely to have their ideas dismissed by senior management, have their ideas seen as low-value if not dismissed, so they have learned not to express ideas. These managers can be expected to obey the maxim that a closed mouth gathers no feet, withdrawing into their local social world to wait for orders, thereby contributing to the continued segregation of groups in the supply chain (see Morrison and Milliken, 2002, on organizational silence and its correlates).

The positive cycle is less obvious. Managers whose networks spanned structural holes (low network constraint) were likely to express and discuss their ideas, likely to have their ideas engaged by senior management, and likely to have their ideas perceived as valuable. These managers can be expected to continue to have good ideas.

---

form new partnerships, and are likely to form them with partners structurally equivalent to the partners with whom other start-ups equivalent to themselves formed relations—which illustrates the reproduction of existing structure. The summary point is that the brokerage and closure effects in the preceding chapters describe the consequences of position in social structure, not the goals that led incumbents to the position.

[14] As Schumpeter (2002 [1911a]: 412) expressed it from on high (also Ch. 2, n. 6, on non-entrepreneurial people, and Section 4.5 on groupthink and the agentic state): "Most people tend to their usual daily business and have enough to do at that. Most of the time such people are on slippery ground and the effort to stand straight exhausts their energies and suppresses all appetite for further exploration. They simply do not want to perish, they want to earn their daily bread in the proven way."

But ideas alone do not disrupt the equilibrium status quo. To move to a new equilibrium, ideas have to be worked into coordination across holes in the existing structure.[15] It is not apparent that the supply-chain managers were working to implement good ideas for coordinating across structural holes in the organization. The people with whom they discussed their good ideas were colleagues with whom they were already closely connected.

Consider, as a baseline, an inertia model of social convenience. Who is most likely to be cited by a manager putting no effort into spreading or building support for an idea? The more that John speaks to the people with whom I frequently speak, the more likely that John will be present in my conversations with colleagues. If I were to have a conversation with a colleague selected at random, John has a good chance of being that colleague. In network terms, John is central in my discussion network; he speaks often to the people with whom I often discuss my work. This image of centrality is measured by the network constraint index introduced in Section 1.1.5. The more a contact is connected with others in a manager's network, the higher the constraint score for the contact.

Figure 5.3 shows contacts of the supply-chain managers sorted from most to least central. The first position contains the contact with whom the manager had the most mutual friends. This is the person most likely to be cited if social convenience determined who was selected for idea discussion. At the other extreme of the horizontal axis are the most distant contacts. Distant contacts are people with whom a manager had no mutual colleagues and people with whom the manager had the least experience.

The inertia model accounts for the distribution of good ideas, from which I infer that ideas were not discussed to change business practice so much as they were discussed to display competence and entertain familiar colleagues. The dark segments at the top of the white bars in Figure 5.3 show the colleagues who were cited for idea discussion.[16] The dark segments in Figure 5.3 are concentrated in the first few bars corresponding to colleagues at the center of a manager's network: 36% of the people cited were the most central in a manager's network, 25% were the second most central, and 13% were the third-most central. The number of citations decreases at further removes from the manager, but so does the number of contacts available to be cited. A logit

---

[15] The point is obvious and long recognized. For example, Schumpeter (1934 [1911a]: 413), after distinguishing as superior the individuals who can see entrepreneurial ideas (e.g., n. 14 above and Ch. 2, n. 6), distinguishes an elite within the superior individuals: "Then there is an even smaller minority—and this one acts. It does not matter whether they have conceived the plan of their activity themselves or have picked up one of the many plans that the just mentioned type is incessantly producing. You can always have the new combinations, but what is indispensable and decisive is the act and the force to act."

[16] Details on the construction of Figure 5.3, and estimation of effects, are given in the published report (Burt, 2004: 391–393).

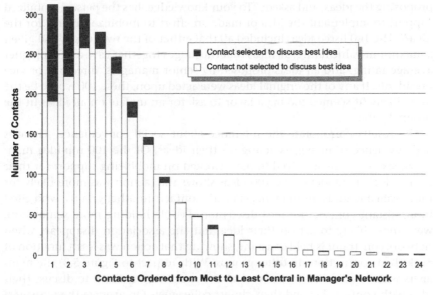

Fig. 5.3: Idea discussion and individual contacts

model predicting the probability of discussion from centrality in Figure 5.3 shows discussion likely only with the first three people, and in strongly decreasing order (z-score test statistics of 10.5, 7.8, 3.6, and 0.4 for the four closest colleagues).

The inference of social convenience guiding idea discussion strains the limits of my data. I know the names of the people with whom managers had their most detailed discussion. I do not have a census of the people with whom managers discussed their idea. Managers could have had their most detailed discussion with socially convenient colleagues, then moved on to mobilize support in subsequent discussion with people beyond their own group. I think not because there are multiple indicators of inertia: from the tendency for managers at all ranks to cite a dense circle of colleagues for work discussion (81% density on average, Figure 1.3), to the segregation of work discussion from the formal authority structure (69% of the managers excluded their immediate supervisor from their discussion network). The point remains that I do not have a census of people with whom managers discussed their best idea.

As a check on my inference, I returned to the organization (ten months after collecting the data reported in Chapter 2) to ask a favor of the long-time employee who had been promoted to run supply-chain operations for the company (not one of the original two judges who evaluated ideas). I presented a list of the top 100 ideas, with the names and business units of the people proposing the ideas, and asked: "To your knowledge, has the person mobilized support to implement the idea or made an effort to mobilize support for the idea?" The 100 listed ideas included all that either of the two judges had given a maximum-value rating, all ideas that the judges together gave a 3.5 or higher average rating, and all ideas proposed by senior managers, directors, or vice presidents. If any of the original ideas were acted upon, these 100 would be the most likely (it seemed too big a favor to ask for an update on all ideas in the original data).

The results corroborate the inference about social convenience. There is little evidence of managers acting on their ideas. Of the 100 top-idea managers, sixteen were perceived to have worked on mobilizing support for their idea. A logistic model of the 100 ideas shows that action was more likely for more valuable ideas, from managers with contacts in other groups, who cited more distant contacts for idea discussion. People holding more senior rank were more likely to act on their idea, but the association disappears when network constraint is held constant, showing that action was less a function of rank than connections to other groups. With respect to Figure 5.3, the managers who acted on their idea rose above social convenience to discuss their idea with contacts beyond their closest colleagues. On average the managers who acted on their idea cited a colleague at the fifth or sixth position in Figure 5.3. The managers not taking action cited more convenient colleagues (the second and third most central on average).

So the problem was not the lack of brokerage. It was network stability despite brokerage. There was a brokerage advantage in producing good ideas (Figure 2.1), and company systems worked correctly to reward brokers who produced good ideas (Figures 1.5A and 1.5B), but the potential value for integrating operations across the company was dissipated in the distribution of ideas. Good ideas emerged as hypothesized from the intersection of social worlds, but spread in a way that would continue segregation between the worlds.

5.3 Conclusion

The equilibrium image that emerges is one of local balance, between closure pulling groups in on themselves, and brokerage pulling them apart into new combinations. Closure is the more obvious force. People advantaged by barriers between insiders and outsiders have no incentive to bring in outsiders. People too long in their closed network have difficulty coordinating with people different than themselves. Echo within closed segments of the structure reinforce boundaries between us and them, deepening the structural holes that segregate groups. Brokerage is the source of endogenous change. Organizations and markets are viewed as illustrated in Figure 1.1, with belief and behavior, knowledge and practice, homogenous within groups relative to the heterogeneity between. People who have relations that span the structural holes between groups have a vision advantage in detecting and developing good ideas. For their integrative efforts, these people receive a premium in compensation, recognition, and responsibility. The premium signals a price for integrating the work of one group with another, and price provides a criterion for coordinating knowledge limited by time and place. However, the productive potential of brokerage as an engine of endogenous change is more clear in theory than in fact. Closure's inertial forces typically prevail, though once recognized for their role in failed brokerage, can be more effectively addressed.

Where do the holes come from? This chapter has been about the costs and benefits of bridges without etiological discussion of the holes bridged. On this point, I find myself aligned with Emirbayer and Goodwin (1994) on the significance of the cultural system through which networks are understood and acted upon. Structural holes are all around you, for the most part unseen. A hole is an empty space across which you can see the other side. Conventions in thinking, organization, and the broader environment obscure the other side, leaving us to see only empty space. This was the point in Chapter 4 on gossip serving to make opaque the boundaries around closed networks, and Section 5.2 on conditions that preserve holes such that brokerage becomes an enduring advantage. We are surrounded by holes perceived as empty space.

Optimism, wisdom, and the vicissitudes of a consolidating world make us aware of holes previously understood to be empty space. Structural holes are made apparent by the debris of legacy, as when organizations are thrown together in a merger, or technological capabilities expand such that what was previously efficient to run as separate operations is now more efficient to run as an integrated operation. Structural holes are made apparent when a person thinking more broadly than ourselves sketches the value of coordinating across what we had perceived to be empty space marking the boundary of our domain.

There is a simple moral here: when you have an opportunity to learn how someone in another group does what you do differently—go.

REFERENCES

Adams, Stephen B. (1997). *Mr. Kaiser Goes to Washington*. Chapel Hill, NC: University of North Carolina Press.

Adler, Paul S. (1990). "Shared learning." *Management Science* 36: 938–957.

—— and Kim B. Clark (1991). "Behind the learning curve: a sketch of the learning process." *Management Science* 37: 267–281.

—— and Seok-Woo Kwon (2002). "Social capital: prospects for a new concept." *Academy of Management Review* 27: 17–40.

Aldrich, Howard E. (1999). *Organizations Evolving*. Thousand Oaks, CA: Sage.

Allen, Thomas J. and Saul Cohen (1969). "Information flow in R&D labs." *Administrative Science Quarterly* 14: 12–19.

Ancona, Deborah G. and David F. Caldwell (1992*a*). "Demography and design: predictors of new product team performance." *Organization Science* 3: 321–341.

—— —— (1992*b*). "Bridging the boundary: external activity and performance in organizational teams." *Administrative Science Quarterly* 37: 634–665.

Argote, Linda (1999). *Organizational Learning*. Norwell, MA: Kluwer Academic.

Atwater, Leanne and David Waldman (1998). "Accountability in 360 degree feedback." *HR Magazine* 43: 96.

Axelrod, Robert (1984). *The Evolution of Cooperation*. New York: Basic Books.

Backbier, Esther, Johan Hoogstraten, and Katharina Meerum Terwogt-Kouwenhoven (1997). "Situational determinants of the acceptability of telling lies." *Journal of Applied Social Psychology* 27: 1048–1062.

Baker, Wayne E. (1984). "The social structure of a national securities market." *American Journal of Sociology* 89: 775–811.

—— (2000). *Achieving Success through Social Capital*. San Francisco, CA: Jossey-Bass.

—— and Robert R. Faulkner (2004). "Social networks and loss of capital." *Social Networks* 26: 91–111.

—— —— and Gene A. Fisher (1998). "Hazards of the market: the continuity and dissolution of interorganizational market relationships." *American Sociological Review* 63: 147–177.

—— and Ananth Iyer (1992). "Information networks and market behavior." *Journal of Mathematical Sociology* 16: 305–332.

Barber, Bernard (1983). *The Logic and Limits of Trust*. New Brunswick, NJ: Rutgers University Press.

Barker, James R. (1993). "Tightening the iron cage: concertive control in self-managing teams." *Administrative Science Quarterly* 38: 408–437.

Barkey, Karen (1991). "Rebellious alliances: the state and peasant unrest in early seventeenth century France and the Ottoman empire." *American Sociological Review* 56: 699–715.

—— (1994). *Bandits and Bureaucrats*. Ithaca, NY: Cornell University Press.

Barley, Stephen R. (1990). "The alignment of technology and structure through roles and networks." *Administrative Science Quarterly* 35: 61–103.

Barnes, J. A. (1969). "Networks and political processes." Pp. 51–76 in *Social Networks in Urban Situations*, ed. J. Clyde Mitchell. Manchester, England: Manchester University Press.

Baron, Robert A. and Gideon D. Markman (2003). "Beyond social capital: the role of entrepreneurs' social competence in their financial success." *Journal of Business Venturing* 18: 41–60.

Baron, Robert S., Sieg I. Hoppe, Chuan Feng Kao, Bethany Brunsman, Barbara Linneweh, and Diane Rogers (1996). "Social corroboration and opinion extremity." *Journal of Experimental Social Psychology* 32: 537–560.

Baron, Stephen, John Field, and Tom Schuller (eds.) (2001). *Social Capital*. New York: Oxford University Press.

Barth, Fredrik. (1967). "Economic spheres in Darfur." Pp. 149–174 in *Themes in Economic Anthropology*, ed. Raymond Firth. London: Tavistock.

Baum, Joel A. C., Andrew V. Shipilov, and Tim J. Rowley (2003). "Where do small worlds come from?" *Industrial and Corporate Change* 12: 697–725.

—— Tony Calabrese, and Brian S. Silverman (2000). "Don't go it alone: alliance network composition and startups' performance in Canadian biotechnology." *Strategic Management Journal* 21: 267–294.

Bavelas, Alex (1950). "Communication patterns in task oriented groups." *Journal of the Acoustical Society of America* 57: 271–282.

Becker, Gary S. and Kevin M. Murphy (1992). "The division-of-labor, coordination costs and knowledge." *Quarterly Journal of Economics* 107: 1137–1160.

Becker, Markus C. and Thorbjørn Knudsen (2002). "Schumpeter 1911: farsighted visions on economic development." *American Journal of Economics and Sociology* 61: 387–403.

Beckman, Christine M. and Pamela R. Haunschild (2002). "Network learning: the effects of partners' heterogeneity of experience on corporate acquisitions." *Administrative Science Quarterly* 47: 92–124.

Bendor, Jonathan and Dilip Mookherjee (1990). "Norms, third-party sanctions, and cooperation." *Journal of Law, Economics, and Organization* 6: 33–63.

—— Roderick Kramer, and Piotr Swistak (1996). "Cooperation under uncertainty: what is new, what is true, and what is important." *American Sociological Review* 61: 333–338.

—— Roderick Kramer, and Suzanne Stout (1991). "Cooperation in a noisy prisoner's dilemma." *Journal of Conflict Resolution* 35: 691–719.

Bielby, William T. and Denise D. Bielby (1999). "Organizational mediation of project-based labor markets: talent agencies and the careers of screenwriters." *American Sociological Review* 64: 64–85.

Bienenstock, Elisa Jayne, Phillip Bonacich, and Melvin Oliver (1990). "The effect of network density and homogeneity on attitude polarization." *Social Networks* 12: 153–172.

Biggart, Nicole Woolsey (2001). "Banking on each other: the situational logic of rotating savings and credit associations." *Advances in Qualitative Organization Research* 3: 129–153.

Birley, Sue (1985). "The role of networks in the entrepreneurial process." *Journal of Business Venturing* 1: 107–117.

Birner, Jack (1996). "Mind, market and society: network structures in the work of F. A. Hayek." Working Paper, Computable and Experimental Economics Laboratory, University of Trento.

Birner, Jack (1999a). "Making markets." Pp. 36–56 in *Economic Organization and Economic Knowledge*, ed. Sheila C. Dow and Peter E. Earl. Northhampton, MA: Edward Elgar.

—— (1999b). "Two views of social stability: an unsettled question." *American Journal of Economics and Sociology* 58: 749–780.

Black, Donald (1993). *The Social Structure of Right and Wrong*. New York: Academic Press.

—— (1995). "The epistemology of pure sociology." *Law and Social Inquiry* 20: 829–870.

—— and M. P. Baumgartner (1983). "Toward a theory of the third party." Pp. 84–114 in *Empirical Theories about Courts*, ed. Keith O. Boyum and Lynn Mather. New York: Longman.

Blau, Peter M. (1955). *The Dynamics of Bureaucratic Life*. Chicago, IL: University of Chicago Press.

—— (1964). *Exchange and Power in Social Life*. New York: John Wiley.

—— (1968). "Interaction: social exchange." Pp. 452–458 in *The International Encyclopedia of the Social Sciences*, ed. David L. Sills. New York: Free Press and Macmillan.

—— (1977). *Heterogeneity and Inequality*. New York: Free Press.

—— (1994). *Structural Contexts of Opportunities*. Chicago, IL: University of Chicago Press.

Blount, Sally (1995). "When social outcomes aren't fair: the effect of causal attribution on preferences." *Organizational Behavior and Human Decision Processes* 63: 131–144.

Boot, Arnoud W. A., Stuart I. Greenbaum and Anjan V. Thakor (1993). "Reputation and discretion in financial contracting." *American Economic Review* 83: 1165–1183.

Borgatti, Stephen P. and Pacey C. Foster (2003). "The network paradigm in organization research: a review and typology." *Journal of Management* 29: 991–1013.

—— Candace Jones, and Martin G. Everett (1998). "Network measures of social capital." *Connections* 21: 27–36.

Bothner, Matthew S. (2003). "Competition and social influence: the diffusion of the sixth generation in the global computer industry." *American Journal of Sociology* 108: 1175–1210.

Bott, Elizabeth (1957). *Family and Social Network*. New York: Free Press.

Bourdieu, Pierre (1980). "Le capital social: notes provisoires." *Actes de la Recherche en Sciences Sociales* 3: 2–3.

—— and Loïc J. D. Wacquant (1992). *An Invitation to Reflexive Sociology*. Chicago: University of Chicago Press.

Boxman, Ed A. W., Paul M. De Graaf and Hendrik D. Flap (1991). "The impact of social and human capital on the income attainment of Dutch managers." *Social Networks* 13: 51–73.

Boyer, Paul and Stephen Nissenbaum (1976). *Salem Possessed*. Cambridge, MA: Harvard University Press.

Bradach, Jeffrey L. and Robert G. Eccles (1989). "Price, authority, and trust: from ideal types to plural forms." *Annual Review of Sociology* 15: 97–118.

Brass, Daniel J., Kenneth D. Butterfield, and Bruce C. Skaggs (1998). "Relationships and unethical behavior: a social network perspective." *Academy of Management Review* 23: 14–31.

Brauer, Markus, Charles M. Judd, and Melissa D. Gliner (1995). "The effects of repeated expressions on attitude polarization during group discussions." *Journal of Personality and Social Psychology* 68: 1014–1029.

Brieger, Ronald L. (1995). "Socioeconomic achievement and the phenomenology of achievement." *Annual Review of Sociology* 21: 115–136.

Brockner, Joel, Phylllis A. Siegel, Joseph P. Daly, Tom Tyler, and Christopher Martin (1997). "When trust matters: the moderating effect of outcome favorability." *Administrative Science Quarterly* 42: 558–583.

Brouwer, Maria T. (2002). "Weber, Schumpeter and Knight on entrepreneurship and economic development." *Journal of Evolutionary Economics* 12: 83–105.

Brown, Jacqueline J. and Peter H. Reingen (1987). "Social ties and word-of-mouth referral behavior." *Journal of Consumer Research* 14: 350–362.

Brown, Penelope and Stephen C. Levinson (1987). *Politeness*. New York: Cambridge University Press.

Brüderl, Josef (2000). "The dissolution of matches: theoretical and empirical investigations." In *Management of Durable Relationships*, ed. Jeroen Weesie and Werner Raub. Amsterdam: Thela Thesis.

—— and Andreas Diekmann (1995). "The log-logistic rate model: two generalizations with an application to demographic data." *Sociological Methods and Research* 24: 158–186.

—— and Frank Kalter (2001). "The dissolution of marriages: the role of information and marital-specific capital." *Journal of Mathematical Sociology* 25: 403–421.

—— and Peter Preisendörfer (1998). "Network support and the success of newly founded businesses." *Small Business Economics* 10: 213–225.

—— and Rudolf Schüssler (1990). "Organizational mortality: the liability of newness and adolescence." *Administrative Science Quarterly* 35: 530–547.

Bulkeley, William M. and Wailen Wong (2003). "Six degrees of exploitation? New programs help companies 'mine' relationships for key business prospects." *Wall Street Journal* August 4 (2003).

Burns, Ken (1990). *The Civil War*. Burbank, CA: Public Broadcasting System.

Burt, Ronald S. (1980). "Autonomy in a Social Topology." *American Journal of Sociology* 85: 892–925.

—— (1982). *Toward a Structural Theory of Action*. New York: Academic Press.

—— (1983). *Corporate Profits and Cooptation*. New York: Academic Press.

—— (1987). "Social contagion and innovation, cohesion versus structural equivalence." *American Journal of Sociology* 92: 1287–1335.

—— (1988). "The stability of American markets." *American Journal of Sociology* 93: 356–395.

—— (1990). "Kinds of relations in American discussion networks." Pp. 411–451 in *Structures of Power and Constraint*, ed. Craig Calhoun, Marshall W. Meyer and W. Richard Scott. New York: Cambridge University Press.

—— (1991). "Measuring age as a structural concept." *Social Networks* 13: 1–34.

—— (1992). *Structural Holes*. Cambridge, MA: Harvard University Press.

—— (1997a). "The contingent value of social capital." *Administrative Science Quarterly* 42: 339–365.

—— (1997b). "A note on social capital and network content." *Social Networks* 19: 355–373.

—— (1998). "The gender of social capital." *Rationality and Society* 10: 5–46.

Burt, Ronald S. (1999*a*). "Entrepreneurs, distrust, and third parties." Pp. 213–243 in *Shared Cognition in Organizations*, ed. Leigh Thompson, John Levine and David Messick. Hillsdale, NJ: Lawrence Erlbaum.

—— (1999*b*). "The social capital of opinion leaders." *Annals* 566: 37–54.

—— (1999*c*). "Private games are too dangerous." *Computational and Mathematical Organization Theory* 5: 311–341.

—— (2000*a*). "Decay functions." *Social Networks* 22: 1–28.

—— (2000*b*). "The network structure of social capital." *Research in Organizational Behavior* 22: 345–423.

—— (2001). "Bandwidth and echo: trust, information, and gossip in social networks." Pp. 30–74 in *Networks and Markets*, ed. James E. Rauch and Alessandra Casella. New York: Russell Sage Foundation.

—— (2002). "Bridge decay." *Social Networks* 24: 333–363.

—— (2004). "Structural holes and good ideas." *American Journal of Sociology* 110: 349–399.

—— and Gregory A. Janicik. (1996). "Social contagion and social structure." Pp. 32–49 in *Networks in Marketing*, ed. Dawn Iacobucci. Thousand Oaks, CA: Sage.

—— and Marc Knez (1995). "Kinds of third-party effects on trust." *Rationality and Society* 7: 255–292.

—— and Nan Lin (1977). "Network time series from archival records." *Sociological Methodology* 8: 224–254.

—— and Don Ronchi (2004). "Teaching managers to see social capital." Unpublished paper, Graduate School of Business, University of Chicago.

—— and Thomas Schøtt (1985). "Relation contents in multiple networks." *Social Science Research* 14: 287–308.

—— and Tetsuji Uchiyama (1989). "The conditional significance of communication for interpersonal influence." Pp. 67–87 in *The Small World*, ed. Manfred Kochen. Norwood, NJ: Ablex.

—— Miguel Guilarte, Holly J. Raider, and Yuki Yasuda (2002). "Competition, contingency, and the external structure of markets." Pp. 167–217 in *Advances in Strategic Management*, vol. 19, ed. Paul Ingram and Brian Silverman. Greenwich, CT: JAI Press.

—— Robin M. Hogarth, and Claude Michaud (2000). "The social capital of French and American managers." *Organization Science* 11: 123–147.

—— Joseph E. Jannotta, and James T. Mahoney (1998). "Personality correlates of structural holes." *Social Networks* 20: 63–87.

Buskens, Vincent (1998). "The social structure of trust." *Social Networks* 20: 265–289.

—— and Jeroen Weesie (2000). "An experiment on the effects of embeddedness in trust situations: buying a used car." *Rationality and Society* 12: 227–253.

—— and Kazuo Yamaguchi (1999). "A new model for information diffusion in heterogeneous social networks." *Sociological Methodology* 29: 281–325.

Caldwell, Bruce (2004). *Hayek's Challenge*. Chicago, IL: University of Chicago Press.

Campbell, John L. (2004). *Institutional Change and Globalization*. Princeton, NJ: Princeton University Press.

Campbell, Karen E., Peter V. Marsden, and Jeanne Hurlbert (1986). "Social resources and socioeconomic status." *Social Networks* 8: 97–117.

Cappelli, Peter (2004). "Why do employers retrain at-risk workers? The role of social capital." *Industrial Relations* 43: 421–447.

Carley, Kathleen M. (1986). "An approach for relating social structure to cognitive structure." *Journal of Mathematical Sociology* 12: 137–189.

—— (1991). "A theory of group stability." *American Sociological Review* 56: 331–354.

—— Ju-Sung Lee, and David Krackhardt (2001). "Destabilizing networks," *Connections* 24: 79–92.

Caro, Robert A. (1982). *The Path to Power*. New York: Alfred A. Knopf.

Carr, James H. and Zhong Yi Tong (eds.) (2002). *Replicating Microfinance in the United States*. Baltimore, Ms: Johns Hopkins University Press.

Carrin, Guy (1987). "Drug prescribing—a discussion of its variability and (ir)rationality." *Health Policy* 7: 73–94.

Carroll, Glenn R. and Albert C. Teo (1996). "On the social networks of managers." *Academy of Management Journal* 39: 421–440.

Carter, Richard and Steven Manaster (1990). "Initial public offerings and underwriter reputation." *Journal of Finance* 45: 1045–1067.

—— Frederick H. Dark, and Ajai K. Singh (1998). "Underwriter reputation, initial returns, and the long-run performance of IPO stocks." *Journal of Finance* 53: 285–311.

Cartwright, Dorwin and Alvin Zander (eds.) (1968). *Group Dynamics*. New York: Harper & Row.

Casella, Alessandra and James E. Rauch (2002). "Anonymous market and group ties in international trade." *Journal of International Economics* 58: 19–47.

Castilla, Emilio J. (2003). "Networks of venture capital firms in Silicon Valley." *International Journal of Technology Management* 25: 113–135.

Chandrasekhar, Subrahmanyan (1987) [1975]. "Shakespeare, Newton, and Beethoven, or patterns of creativity." Pp. 29–58 in Truth and Beauty, ed. Subrahmanyan Chandrasekhar. Chicago: University of Chicago Press.

Chow, S. (1998). "Specialty group differences over tonsillectomy: pediatricians versus otolaryngologists." *Qualitative Health Research* 8: 61–75.

Cialdini, Robert B. (1989). "Indirect tactics of image management: beyond basking." Pp. 45–56 in *Impression Management in the Organization*, ed. Robert A. Giacalone and Paul Rosenfeld. Hillsdale, NJ: Lawrence Erlbaum.

—— and Noah J. Goldstein (2004). "Social influence: compliance and conformity." *Annual Review of Psychology* 55: 591–621.

Clark, Terry N. and Lorna C. Ferguson (1983). *City Money*. New York: Columbia University Press.

Cockburn, Iain M. and Rebecca M. Henderson (1998). "Absorptive capacity, coauthoring behavior, and the organization of research in drug discovery." *Journal of Industrial Economics* 64: 157–182.

Cohen, Don and Laurence Prusak (2001). *In Good Company*. Boston, MA: Harvard Business School Press.

Cohen, Wesley M. and Daniel A. Levinthal (1990). "Absorptive capacity: a new perspective on learning and innovation." *Administrative Science Quarterly* 35: 128–152.

Coleman, James S. (1957). *Community Conflict*. New York: Free Press.

—— (1988). "Social capital in the creation of human capital." *American Journal of Sociology* 94: S95–S120.

—— (1990). *Foundations of Social Theory*. Cambridge, MA: Harvard University Press.

—— Elihu Katz, and Herbert Menzel (1957). "The diffusion of an innovation among physicians." *Sociometry* 20: 253–270.

—— —— —— (1966). *Medical Innovation*. New York: Bobbs-Merrill.

Coles, Anne-marie, Lisa Harris, and Keith Dickson (2003). "Testing goodwill: conflict and cooperation in new product development networks." *International Journal of Technology Management* 25: 51–64.

Collins, Randall (1987). "A micro-macro theory of intellectual creativity: the case of German idealist philosophy." *Sociological Theory* 5: 47–69.

—— (1998). *The Sociology of Philosophies.* Cambridge, MA: Harvard University Press.

Contractor, Noshir S., Robert Whitbred, Fabio Fonti, Andrew Hyatt, Barbara O'Keefe, and Patricia Jones (2000). "Self-organizing communication networks in organizations: validation of a computational model using exogenous and endogenous theoretical mechanisms." Paper presented at Organization Science Winter Conference.

Cook, Karen S. and Richard M. Emerson (1978). "Power, equity and commitment in exchange networks." *American Sociological Review* 43: 712–739.

—— —— Mary R. Gillmore, and Toshio Yamagishi (1983). "The distribution of power in exchange networks: theory and experimental results." *American Journal of Sociology* 89: 275–305.

Corry, Bernard A. (1966). "The role of technological innovation in theories of income distribution." *American Economic Review* 56: 33–42.

Coser, Lewis (1973). "The militant collective: Jesuits and Leninists." *Social Research* 40: 110–128.

Coser, Rose Laub (1975). "The complexity of roles as a seedbed of individual autonomy." Pp. 237–263 in *The Idea of Social Structure*, ed. Lewis A. Coser. New York: Harcourt, Brace, Jovanovich.

Crane, Diana (1972). *Invisible Colleges.* Chicago: University of Chicago Press.

Cross, Rob and Andrew Parker (2004). *The Hidden Power of Social Networks.* Boston, MA: Harvard Business School Press.

—— —— Laurence Prusak, and Stephen P. Borgatti (2001). "Knowing what we know: supporting knowledge creation and sharing in social networks." *Organizational Dynamics* 30: 100–120.

Cummings, Jonathon N. and Rob Cross (2003). "Structural properties of work groups and their consequences for performance." *Social Networks* 25: 197–210.

Czernich, Christian and Chip Heath (2002). "Toward a theory of variation in idea-markets: attracting 'eyeballs' to websites during the dot-com boom and bust." Paper presented at the annual meetings of the Academy of Management.

Dahms, Harry F. (1995). "From creative action to the social rationalization of the economy: Joseph A. Schumpeter's social theory." *Sociological Theory* 13: 1–13.

Dalzell, Robert F. (1987). *Enterprising Elite.* New York: W. W. Norton.

Davis, Allison, Burleigh B. Gardner, and Mary R. Gardner (1941). *Deep South.* Chicago: University of Chicago Press.

Davis, Gerald F. and Heinrich R. Greve (1997). "Corporate elite networks and the governance changes in the 1980s." *American Journal of Sociology* 103: 1–37.

—— Mina Yoo, and Wayne E. Baker (2003). "The small world of the American corporate elite, 1991–1999." *Strategic Organization* 1:301–326.

Davis, James A. (1970). "Clustering and hierarchy in interpersonal relations: testing two graph theoretical models on 742 sociograms." *American Sociological Review* 35: 843–852.

DeCanio, Stephen J. and William E. Watkins (1998). "Information processing and organizational structure." *Journal of Economic Behavior and Organization* 36: 275–294.

Deeds, David L. and Charles W. L. Hill (1998). "An examination of opportunistic action within research alliances: evidence from the biotechnology industry." *Journal of Business Venturing* 14: 141–163.

De Long, J. Bradford (1991). "Did J. P. Morgan's men add value? An economist's perspective on financial capitalism." Pp. 205–236 in *Inside the Business Enterprise*, ed. Peter Temin. Chicago: University of Chicago Press.

DeSoto, Clinton B. (1960). "Learning a social structure." *Journal of Abnormal and Social Psychology* 60: 417–421.

Diamond, Douglas W. (1989). "Reputation acquisition in debt markets." *Journal of Political Economy* 97: 828–862.

—— (1991). "Monitoring and reputation: the choice between bank loans and directly placed debt." *Journal of Political Economy* 99: 689–721.

Diehl, Michael and Wolfgang Stroebe (1987). "Productivity loss in brainstorming groups: toward the solution of a riddle." *Journal of Personality and Social Psychology* 53: 497–509.

Diekmann, Andreas and Henriette Engelhardt (1999). "The social inheritence of divorce: effects of parent's family type in postwar Germany." *American Sociological Review* 64: 783–793.

—— and Peter Mitter (1984). "A comparison of the 'sickle function' with alternative stochastic models of divorce rates." Pp. 123–153 in *Stochastic Modelling of Social Processes*, ed. Andreas Diekmann and Peter Mitter. Orlando, FL: Academic Press.

DiMaggio, Paul (1988). "Interest and agency in institutional theory." Pp. 3–22 in *Institutional Patterns and Organizations*, ed. Lynne Zucker. Cambridge, MA: Balinger.

—— (1992). "Nadel's paradox revisited: relational and cultural aspects of organizational structure." Pp. 118–142 in *Networks and Organizations*, ed. Nitin Nohria and Robert G. Eccles. Boston, MA: Harvard Business School Press.

—— and Hugh Louch (1998). "Socially embedded consumer transactions: for what kinds of purchases do people most often use networks?" *American Sociological Review* 63: 619–637.

Doreian, Patrick and David Krackhardt (2001). "Pre-transitive balance mechanisms for signed networks." *Journal of Mathematical Sociology* 25: 43–67.

—— Roman Kapuscinski, David Krackhardt and Janusz Szczypula (1996). "A brief history of balance through time." *Journal of Mathematical Sociology* 21: 218–251.

Douthit, Mindy W. (2000). "Supervision and Social Capital." Dissertation. University of Chicago, Graduate School of Business.

Doz, Yves (1988). "Technology partnerships between larger and smaller firms: some critical issues." *International Studies of Management and Organization* 17: 31–57.

—— and Reinhard Angelmar (1991). "Ciba-Geigy/ALZA series." Fontainebleau, France: INSEAD.

—— and Gary Hamel (1998). *Alliance Advantage*. Boston, MA: Harvard University Business School Press.

Drew, Paul and John Heritage (1992). "Analyzing talk at work: an introduction." Pp. 3–65 in *Talk at Work*, ed. Paul Drew and John Heritage. New York: Cambridge University Press.

Dunbar, Robin (1996). *Grooming, Gossip, and the Evolution of Language*. Cambridge, MA: Harvard University Press.

Durkheim, Emile (1933) [1893]. *The Division of Labor in Society*, tr. George Simpson. New York: Free Press.

—— (1951) [1897]. *Suicide*, tr. John A. Spaulding and George Simpson. New York: Free Press.

Dutton, John M. and Annie Thomas (1984). "Treating progress functions as a managerial opportunity." *Academy of Management Review* 9: 235–247.

Dyer, Jeffrey H. and Kentaro Nobeoka (2000). "Creating and managing a high-performance knowledge-sharing network: the Toyota case." *Strategic Management Journal* 21: 345–367.

—— and Nile W. Hatch (2004). "Network-specific capabilities, network barriers to knowledge transfers, and competitive advantage." Paper presented at the annual meetings of the Academy of Management.

Ebaugh, Helen Rose Fuchs (1988). *Becoming an Ex*. Chicago: University of Chicago Press.

Eccles, Robert G. and Dwight B. Crane (1988). *Doing Deals*. Boston, MA: Harvard Business School Press.

Eder, Donna and Janet Lynne Enke (1991). "The structure of gossip: opportunities and constraints on collective expression among adolescents." *American Sociological Review* 56: 494–508.

Eisenstat, Russell A. (1993). "Managing Xerox's Multinational Development Center." Harvard Business School case #9-490-029. Boston, MA: Harvard Business School Press.

Ekeh, Peter P. (1974). *Social Exchange Theory*. Cambridge: Harvard University Press.

Elfenbein, Hillary Anger, Jeffrey T. Polzer, and Nalini Ambady (2004). "Emotional skills as team competencies: the case of recognizing others' emotions." Unpublished paper, Haas School of Business, University of California at Berkeley.

Elias, Norbert and John L. Scotson (1994) [1965]. *The Established and the Outsiders*. Thousand Oaks, CA: Sage.

Ellickson, Robert C. (1991). *Order without Law*. Cambridge, MA: Harvard University Press.

Ellis, Paul D. (1998). "Hong Kong's emerging tertius role in the global economy." *Business Horizons* 41: 37–43.

—— (2000). "Social ties and foreign market entry." *Journal of International Business Studies* 31: 443–469.

—— (2002). "Social ties and partner identification in Sino-Hong Kong international joint ventures." *Journal of International Business Studies* 33: 267–289.

—— (2003). "Social structure and intermediaries: market-making strategies in international exchange." *Journal of Management Studies* 40: 1683–1708.

Elster, Jon (1983). *Sour Grapes*. New York: Cambridge University Press.

Emirbayer, Mustafa and Jeff Goodwin (1994). "Network analysis, culture, and the problem of agency." *American Journal of Sociology* 99: 1411–1454.

Erickson, Bonnie H. (1996). "Culture, class, and connections." *American Journal of Sociology* 102: 217–251.

Erikson, Kai T. (1966). *Wayward Puritans*. New York: John Wiley.

Farber, Henry S. (1994). "The analysis of interfirm worker mobility." *Journal of Labor Economics* 40: 554–593.

Faust, Katherine and John Skvoretz (2002). "Comparing networks across space and time, size and species." *Sociological Methodology* 32: 267–299.

Feld, Scott L. (1981). "The focused organization of social ties." *American Journal of Sociology* 86: 1015–1035.

—— (1982). "Social structural determinants of similarity among associates." *American Sociological Review* 47: 797–801.

—— (1997). "Structural embeddedness and stability of interpersonal relations." *Social Networks* 19: 91–95.

Fenster, Thelma and Daniel Lord Smail (eds.) (2003). *Fama*. Ithaca, NY: Cornell University Press.

Fernandez, Roberto M. and Roger V. Gould (1994). "A dilemma of state power: brokerage and influence in the national health policy domain." *American Journal of Sociology* 99: 1455–1491.

Ferrary, Michel (2003). "Managing the disruptive technologies lifecycle by externalising the research: social network and corporate venturing in the Silicon Valley." *International Journal of Technology Management* 25: 165–180.

Festinger, Leon, Stanley Schachter, and Kurt W. Back (1950). *Social Pressures in Informal Groups*. Stanford, CA: Stanford University Press.

Fichman, Mark and Daniel A. Levinthal (1991). "Honeymoons and the liability of adolescence: a new perspective on duration dependence in social and organizational relationships." *Academy of Management Review* 16: 442–460.

Fine, Gary Alan (1986). "The social organization of adolescent gossip: the rhetoric of moral education." Pp. 405–423 in *Children's Worlds and Children's Language*, ed. Jenny Cook-Gumperz, William A. Corsaro and Jürgen Streeck. New York: Mouton de Gruyter.

—— (1996). "Reputational entrepreneurs and the memory of incompetence: melting supporters, partisan warriors, and images of President Harding." *American Journal of Sociology* 101: 1159–1191.

—— (2001). *Difficult Reputations*. Chicago: University of Chicago Press.

Finifter, Bernard M. (1972). "The generation of confidence: evaluating research findings by random subsample replication." *Sociological Methodology* 4: 112–175.

Finlay, William and James E. Coverdill (1999). "The search game: organizational conflicts and the use of headhunters." *Sociological Quarterly* 40: 11–30.

—— —— (2000). "Risk, opportunism, and structural holes: how headhunters manage clients and earn fees." *Work and Occupations* 27: 377–405.

—— —— (2002). *Headhunters*. Ithaca, NY: Cornell University Press.

Fischer, David Hackett (1994). *Paul Revere's Ride*. Oxford: Oxford University Press.

Flap, Hendrik D. and Ed Boxman (2001). "Getting started: the influence of social capital on the start of the occupational career." Pp. 159–181 in *Social Capital*, ed. Nan Lin, Karen S. Cook and Ronald S. Burt. New York: Aldine de Gruyter.

—— Beate Völker, and Bert Bulder (2000). "Social capital at the workplace and job satisfaction." Pp. 102–105 in *Management of Durable Relationships*, ed. Jeroen Weesie and Werner Raub. Amsterdam: Thesis.

Flap, Henk and Beate Volker (eds.) (2004). *Creation and Returns of Social Capital*. New York: Routledge.

Fleck, Ludwik (1979) [1935]. *Genesis and Development of a Scientific Fact*, tr. Fred Bradley and Thaddeus J. Trenn. Chicago: University of Chicago Press.

Fleming, Lee (2002). "Finding the organizational sources of technological breakthroughs: the story of Hewlett-Packard's thermal ink-jet." *Industrial and Corporate Change* 11: 1059–1084.

—— Lyra J. Colfer, Alexandra Marin, and Jonathan McPhie (2004). "Why the Valley went first: agglomeration and emergence in regional inventor networks." Paper presented at the annual meetings of the Academy of Management.

Fligstein, Neil (1997). "Social skill and institutional theory." *American Behavioral Scientist* 40: 397–405.

Foley, Michael W. and Bob Edwards (1999). "Is it time to disinvest in social capital?" *Journal of Public Policy* 19: 141–173.

Frank, Kenneth A. and Jeffrey Y. Yasumoto (1998). "Linking action to social structure within a system: social capital within and between subgroups." *American Journal of Sociology* 104: 642–686.

Freeman, Linton C. (1977). "A set of measures of centrality based on betweenness." *Sociometry* 40: 35–40.

—— "Filling in the blanks: a theory of cognitive categories and the structure of social affiliation." *Social Psychology Quarterly* 55: 118–127.

Friedkin, Noah E. (1983). "Horizons of observability and limits of informal control in organizations." *Social Forces* 62: 54–77.

—— (1998). *A Structural Theory of Social Influence*. New York: Cambridge University Press.

—— (1999). "Choice shift and group polarization." *American Sociological Review* 64: 856–875.

—— (2004). "Social cohesion." *Annual Review of Sociology* 30: 409–425.

Gabbay, Shaul M. (1997). *Social Capital in the Creation of Financial Capital*. Champaign, IL: Stipes.

—— and Ezra W. Zuckerman (1998). "Social capital and opportunity in corporate R & D: the contingent effect of contact density on mobility expectations." *Social Science Research* 27: 189–217.

Galaskiewicz, Joseph (1985). *Social Organization of an Urban Grants Economy*. New York: Academic Press.

—— (1997). "An urban grants economy revisited: corporate charitable contributions in the twin cities, 1979–81, 1987–89." *Administrative Science Quarterly* 42: 445–471.

—— and Ronald S. Burt (1991). "Interorganization contagion in corporate philanthropy." *Administrative Science Quarterly* 36: 88–105.

Gambetta, Diego (1988a). "Mafia: the price of distrust." Pp. 158–175 in *Trust*, ed. Diego Gambetta. New York: Blackwell.

—— (ed.) (1988b). *Trust*. New York: Blackwell.

—— (1993). *The Sicilian Mafia*. Cambridge, MA: Harvard University Press.

—— (1994). "Godfather's gossip." *Archives Europeennes de Sociologie* 35: 199–223.

Gargiulo, Martin and Mario Benassi (2000). "Trapped in your own net: network cohesion, structural holes, and the adaptation of social capital." *Organization Science* 11: 183–196.

Garmaise, Mark J. and Tobias J. Moskowitz (2003). "Informal financial networks: theory and evidence." *Review of Financial Studies* 16: 1007–1040.

Gatignon, Hubert and Thomas S. Robertson (1985). "A propositional inventory for new diffusion research." *Journal of Consumer Research* 11: 849–867.

Geertz, Clifford (1978). "The bazaar economy: information and search in peasant marketing." *American Economic Review* 68: 28–32.

Geletkanycz, Marta A. and Donald C. Hambrick (1997). "The external ties of top executives: implications for strategic choice and performance." *Administrative Science Quarterly* 42: 654–681.

Gennep, Arnold Van (1960) [1908]. *The Rites of Passage*. Chicago: University of Chicago Press.

Geroski, Paul and Mariana Mazzucato (2002). "Learning and the sources of corporate growth." *Industrial and Corporate Change* 11: 623–644.

Ghosh, Amitav (1992). *In an Antique Land*. New Delhi: Ravi Dayal.

Gibbons, Robert (1992). *Game Theory for Applied Economists*. Princeton: Princeton University Press.

Gibson, David R. (2003). "Participation shifts: order and differentiation in group conversation." *Social Forces* 81: 1335–1381.

—— (2004). "Taking turns and talking ties: networks and conversation interactions." *American Journal of Sociology* 110: In Press.

Gilovich, Thomas (1987). "Secondhand information and social judgment." *Journal of Experimental Social Psychology* 23: 59–74.

Giuffe, Katherine A. (1999). "Sandpiles of Opportunity: Success in the Art World." *Social Forces* 77: 815–832.

Gladwell, Malcolm (2000). *The Tipping Point*. New York: Little, Brown and Company.

—— (2004). "Something borrowed." *New Yorker*, November 22, 40.

Gluckman, Max (1963). "Gossip and scandal." *Current Anthropology* 4: 307–316.

Godechot, Olivier and Nicolas Mariot (2004). "Les deux formes due capital social: structure relationnelle des jurys de thèses et recrutement en science politique." *Revue Française de Sociologie* 45: 243–282.

Goitein, S. D. (1967). *A Mediterranean Society, Vol. 1: Economic Foundations*. Berkeley, CA: University of California Press.

Goleman, Daniel (1995). *Emotional Intelligence*. New York: Bantam Books.

Goodwin, Charles and John Heritage (1990). "Conversation analysis." *Annual Review of Anthropology* 19: 283–307.

Goodwin, Marjorie Harness (1982). "'Instigating': storytelling as social process." *American Ethnologist* 9: 799–819

Goody, Esther N. (ed.) (1978). *Questions and Politeness*. New York: Cambridge University Press.

Gordon, Yefim and Vladimir Rigmant (2002). *Tupolev Tu-4*, tr. Sergey Komissarov and Dmitriy Komissarov. Hinckley, England: Midland Publishing.

Gorton, Gary (1996). "Reputation formation in early bank note markets." *Journal of Political Economy* 104: 346–397.

Grabowski, Richard (1999). "Market evolution and economic development: the evolution of interpersonal markets." *American Journal of Economics and Sociology* 58: 699–712.

Granovetter, Mark S. (1973). "The strength of weak ties." *American Journal of Sociology* 78: 1360–1380.

—— (1985). "Economic action, social structure, and embeddedness." *American Journal of Sociology* 91: 481–510.

—— (1992). "Problems of explanation in economic sociology." Pp. 29–56 in *Networks and Organization*, ed. Nitin Nohria and Robert G. Eccles. Boston, MA: Harvard Business School Press.

—— (1995) [1974]. *Getting a Job*. Chicago: University of Chicago Press.

—— (2002). "A theoretical agenda for economic sociology." Pp. 46–80 in *The New Economic Sociology*, ed. Mauro F. Guillén, Randall Collins, Paula England and Marshall Meyer. New York: Russell Sage Foundation.

Greif, Avner (1989). "Reputation and coalitions in medieval trade: evidence on the Maghribi traders." *Journal of Economic History* 49: 857–882.

Greif, Avner (1993). "Contract enforceability and economic institutions in early trade: the Maghribi traders' coalition." *American Economic Review* 83: 524–548.

—— (1994). "On the political foundations of the late medieval commercial revolution: Genoa during the twelfth and thirteenth centuries." *Journal of Economic History* 54: 271–287.

—— Paul Milgrom, and Barry R. Weingast (1994). "Coordination, commitment, and enforcement: the case of the merchant guild." *Journal of Political Economy* 102: 745–776.

Grice, H. Paul (1975). "Logic and conversation." Pp. 41–58 in *Syntax and Semantics*, ed. Peter Cole and Jerry L. Morgan. New York: Academic Press.

Gulati, Ranjay (1995). "Social Structure and Alliance Formation Patterns: A Longitudinal Analysis." *Administrative Science Quarterly* 40: 619–652.

—— and Martin Gargiulo (1999). "Where do interorganizational networks come from?" *American Journal of Sociology* 104: 1439–1493.

—— and James D. Westphal (1999). "Cooperative or controlling? The effects of CEO-board relations and the content of interlocks on the formation of joint ventures." *Administrative Science Quarterly* 44: 473–506.

Hackman, J. Richard (1976). "Group influences on individuals." Pp. 1455–1525 in *Handbook of Industrial and Organizational Psychology*, ed. Marvin D. Dunette. Chicago: Rand McNally.

Han, Shin-Kap (1993). "Churning firms in stable markets." *Social Science Research* 21: 406–418.

—— (1994). "Mimetic isomorphism and its effect on the audit services market." *Social Forces* 73: 637–664.

—— (2004). "The other ride of Paul Revere: reassessing historical evidence and recalibrating conceptual scope." Paper presented at the annual meetings of the American Sociological Association.

Hannan, Michael T. (1998). "Rethinking age dependence in organizational mortality: logical formalizations." *American Journal of Sociology* 104: 126–164.

—— and John H. Freeman (1977). "The population ecology of organizations." *America Journal of Sociology* 82: 929–964.

—— —— (1989). *Organizational Ecology*. Cambridge, MA: Harvard University Press.

Hansen, Morten T. (1999). "The search-transfer problem: the role of weak ties in sharing knowledge across organization subunits." *Administrative Science Quarterly* 44: 82–111.

—— Joel M. Podolny, and Jeffrey Pfeffer (2001). "So many ties, so little time: a task contingency perspective on the value of social capital in organizations." *Research in the Sociology of Organizations* 18: 21–57.

Hardy, G. H. (1940). *A Mathematician's Apology*. New York: Cambridge University Press.

Hargadon, Andrew B. (2003). *How Breakthroughs Happen*. Boston, MA: Harvard Business School Press.

—— and Robert I. Sutton (1997). "Technology brokering and innovation in a product development firm." *Administrative Science Quarterly* 42: 716–749.

Hatch, Mary Jo (1999). "Exploring the empty spaces of organizing: how improvisational jazz helps redescribe organizational structure." *Organization Studies* 20: 75–100.

Hatch, Nile W. and David C. Mowery (1998). "Process innovation and learning by doing in semiconductor manufacturing." *Management Science* 44: 1461–1477.

Haveman, Heather A. and Lisa E. Cohen (1994). "The ecological dynamics of careers: the impact of organizational founding, dissolution, and merger on job mobility." *American Journal of Sociology* 100: 104–152.

Hayek, Friedrich A. (1937). "Economics and Knowledge." *Economica* 5: 33–54.

—— (1944). *The Road to Serfdom.* London: G. Routledge.

—— (1945). "The use of knowledge in society." *American Economic Review* 35: 519–530.

Heaton, Tim B. (1990). "Marital stability throughout the child-rearing years." *Demography* 27: 55–63.

Hechter, Michael (1987). *Principles of Group Solidarity.* Berkeley, CA: University of California Press.

—— (1990). "On the inadequacy of game theory for the solution of real-world collective action problems." Pp. 240–249 in *The Limits of Rationality*, ed. Karen S. Cook and Margaret Levi. Chicago: University of Chicago Press.

Hedström, Peter and Richard Swedberg (1998). "Social mechanisms: an introductory essay." Pp. 1–31 in *Social Mechanisms*, ed. Peter Hedström and Richard Swedberg. New York: Cambridge University Press.

Heider, Fritz (1958). *The Psychology of Interpersonal Relations.* New York: John Wiley.

Heinz, John P., Edward O. Laumann, Robert L. Nelson, and Robert H. Salisbury (1993). *The Hollow Core.* Cambridge, MA: Harvard University Press.

Heise, David R. (1979). *Understanding Events.* New York: Cambridge University Press.

Hennart, Jean-François, Dong-Jeo Kim, and Ming Zeng (1998). "The impact of joint venture status on the longevity of Japanese stakes in U.S. manufacturing affiliates." *Organization Science* 9: 382–395.

Higgins, E. Tory (1992). "Achieving 'shared reality' in the communication game: a social action that creates meaning." *Journal of Language and Social Psychology* 11: 107–131.

—— (1999). "'Saying is believing' effects: when sharing reality about something biases knowledge and evaluations." Pp. 33–48 in *Shared Cognition in Organizations*, ed. Leigh L. Thompson, John M. Levine and David M. Messick. Mawah, NJ: Lawrence Erlbaum.

Higgins, Monica C. and Ranjay Gulati (2003). "Getting off to a good start: the effects of upper echelon affiliations on underwriter prestige." *Organization Science* 14: 244–263.

Hite, Julie M. and William S. Hesterly (2001). "The evolution of firm networks: from emergence to early growth of the firm." *Strategic Management Journal* 22: 275–286.

Hoffer, Eric (1951). *The True Believer.* New York: Harper & Row.

Hogarth, Robin M. (2001). *Educating Intuition.* Chicago: University of Chicago Press.

Homans, George C. (1950). *The Human Group.* New York: Harcourt, Brace & World.

—— (1961). *Social Behavior.* New York: Harcourt, Brace & World.

Hudson, R. A. (1980). *Sociolinguistics.* New York: Cambridge University Press.

Isenberg, Daniel J. (1986). "Group polarization: a critical review and meta-analysis." *Journal of Personality and Social Psychology* 50: 1141–1151.

Jacob, John, Thomas Z. Lys, and Margaret A. Neale (1999). "Expertise in Forecasting Performance of Security Analysts." *Journal of Accounting and Economics* 28: 51–82.

Jang, Ho (1997). "Market Structure, Performance, and Putting-Out in the Korean Economy." Dissertation. University of Chicago, Department of Sociology.

Janicik, Gregory A. (1998). "Social Expertise in Social Networks: Examining the Learning of Relations." Dissertation. University of Chicago, Graduate School of Business.

—— and Richard P. Larrick (2005). "Social network schemas and the learning of incomplete networks" *Journal of Personality abd Social Psychology* 88: 348–364.

Janis, Irving L. (1972). *Victims of Groupthink*. New York: Houghton Mifflin.

Jensen, Michael (2003). "The role of network resources in market entry: commercial banks' entry into investment banking 1991–1997." *Administrative Science Quarterly* 48: 466–497.

Johansen, Bruce E. (1982). *Forgotten Founders*. Boston, MA: Harvard Common Press.

Johnson, J. David (2004). "The emergence, maintenance, and dissolution of structural hole brokerage within consortia." *Communication Theory* 14: 212–236.

Johnson, Jeffrey C. and Marc L. Miller (1983). "Deviant social positions in small groups: the relation between role and individual." *Social Networks* 5: 51–69.

Joy, Leonard (1967). "An economic homologue of Barth's presentation of economic spheres in Darfur." Pp. 175–189 in *Themes in Economic Anthropology*, ed. Raymond Firth. London: Tavistock.

Just, Marcel Adam, Vladimir L. Cherkassky, Timothy A. Keller and Nancy J. Minshew (2004). "Cortical activation and synchronization during sentence comprehension in high-functioning autism: evidence of underconnectivity." *Brain* 127: 1811–1821.

Kadushin, Charles (1995). "Friendship among the French financial elite." *American Sociological Review* 60: 201–221.

Kaldor, Nicholas (1985). *Economics Without Equilibrium*. Armonk, NY: M. E. Sharpe.

Kalleberg, Arne L., David Knoke, Peter V. Marsden and Joe L. Spaeth (eds.) (1996). *Organizations in America*. Thousand Oaks, CA: Sage.

Katz, Elihu and Paul F. Lazarsfeld (1955). *Personal Influence*. New York: Free Press.

Kavolis, Vytautas (1966). "Community dynamics and artistic creativity." *American Sociological Review* 31: 208–217.

Keller, Maryann (1989). *Rude Awakening*. New York: William Morrow.

Kenny, David A. and Linda Albright (1987). "Accuracy in interpersonal perception: a social relations analysis." *Psychological Bulletin* 102: 390–402.

Khurana, Rakesh (2002). *Searching for a Corporate Savior*. Princeton, NJ: Princeton University Press.

Kidder, Tracy (1981). *The Soul of a New Machine*. New York: Atlantic-Little Brown.

Kilduff, Martin and David Krackhardt (1994). "Bringing the Individual back in: A Structural Analysis of the Internal Market for Reputation in Organizations." *Academy of Management Journal* 37: 87–108.

—— and Wenpin Tsai (2003). Social Networks and Organizations. Thousand Oaks, CA: Sage.

King, Charles W. and John O. Summers (1970). "Overlap of opinion leadership across consumer product categories." *Journal of Marketing Research* 7: 43–50.

Kirkpatrick, David (2003). "I get by with a little help from my friends of friends of friends: ties created by social-networking sites have people excited." *Fortune* Tuesday September 30.

Kirzner, Israel M. (1973). *Competition and Entrepreneurship*. Chicago, IL: University of Chicago Press.

Kish, Leslie and Martin R. Frankel (1974). "Inference from complex samples." *Journal of the Royal Statistical Society* A 36: 1–37.

Klapp, Orin E. (1978). *Opening and Closing*. New York: Cambridge University Press.

Klayman, Joshua (1995). "Varieties of confirmation bias." *The Psychology of Learning and Motivation* 32: 385–418.

Klerks, Peter (2001). "The network paradigm applied to criminal organizations: theoretical nitpicking or a relevant doctrine for investigators? Recent developments in the Netherlands." *Connections* 24: 53–65.

Knez, Marc and Colin Camerer (1994). "Creating expectational assets in the laboratory: coordination in weakest-link games." *Strategic Management Journal* 15: 101–119.

Knoke, David (2001). *Changing Organizations*. Boulder, CO: Westview Press.

Kock, Carl J. and Mauro F. Guillén (2001). "Strategy and structure in developing countries: business groups as an evolutionary response to opportunities for unrelated diversification." *Industrial and Corporate Change* 10: 77–113.

Kogut, Bruce (1989). "The stability of joint ventures: reciprocity and competitive rivalry." *Journal of Industrial Economics* 38: 183–198.

—— (2000). The network as knowledge: generative rules and the emergence of structure. *Strategic Management Journal* 21: 405–425.

—— and Gordon Walker (2001). "The small world of Germany and the durability of national networks." *American Sociological Review* 66: 317–335.

—— and Udo Zander (2000). "Did socialism fail to innovate? A natural experiment of the two Zeiss companies." *American Sociological Review* 65: 169–190.

Kohn, Melvin L. and Carmi Schooler (1983). *Work and Personality*. Norwood, NJ: Ablex.

Kollock, Peter (1994). "The emergence of exchange structures: an experimental study of uncertainty, commitment, and trust." *American Journal of Sociology* 100: 313–345.

Koput, Kenneth and Walter W. Powell (2003). "Organizational growth and alliance capability: science and strategy in a knowledge-intensive industry." Unpublished paper, College of Business and Public Administration, University of Arizona.

Koza, Mitchell P. and Arie Y. Lewin (1999). "The coevolution of network alliances: a longitudinal analysis of an international professional service network." *Organization Science* 10: 638–653.

Krackhardt, David (1990). "Assessing the political landscape: structure, cognition, and power in organizations." *Administrative Science Quarterly* 35: 342–369.

—— (1992). "The strength of strong ties: the importance of philos in organizations." Pp. 216–239 in *Networks and Organizations*, ed. Nitin Nohria and Robert G. Eccles. Boston, MA: Harvard Business School Press.

—— (1996). "Comment on Burt and Knez's third-party efects on trust." *Rationality and Society* 8: 113–118.

—— (1998). "Simmelian ties: super strong and sticky." Pp. 21–38 in *Power and Influence in Organizations*, ed. Roderick M. Kramer and Margaret A. Neale. Thousand Oaks, CA: Sage.

—— (1999). "The ties that torture: Simmelian ties in organizations." *Research in the Sociology of Organizations* 16: 183–210.

—— and Martin Kilduff (2002). "Structure, culture and Simmelian ties in entrepreneurial firms." *Social Networks* 24: 279–290.

—— and Robert N. Stern (1988). "Informal networks and organizational crisis: an experimental simulation." *Social Psychology Quarterly* 51: 123–140.

Kramer, Roderick M. (1994). "The sinister attribution error." *Motivation and Emotion* 18: 199–231.

—— (1999). "Trust and distrust in organizations: emerging perspectives, enduring questions." *Annual Review of Psychology* 50: 569–598.

Kreps, David M. (1990). "Corporate culture and economic theory." Pp. 90–143 in *Perspectives on Positive Political Economy*, ed. James E. Alt and Kenneth A. Shepsle. New York: Cambridge University Press.

Kruskal, Joseph B. (1964). "Multidimensional scaling by optimizing goodness of fit to a nonmetric hypothesis." *Psychometrika* 29: 1–27.

Kuhn, Thomas S. (1970) [1962]. *The Structure of Scientific Revolutions*. Chicago: University of Chicago Press.

—— (2000). *The Road Since Structure*, ed. James Conant and John Haugeland. Chicago: University of Chicago Press.

Kuran, Timur (1997). *Private Truths, Public Lies*. Cambridge, MA: Harvard University Press.

Labianca, Giuseppe and Daniel J. Brass (2004). "Exploring the social ledger: negative relationships and negative asymmetry in social networks in organizations." *Academy of Management Review* 29: In Press.

—— Daniel J. Brass and Barbara Gray (1998). "Social networks and perceptions of intergroup conflict: the role of negative relationships and third parties." *Academy of Management Journal* 41: 55–67.

Lamm, Helmut (1988). "A review of our research on group polarization: eleven experiments on the effects of group discussion on risk acceptance, probability estimation, and negotiation positions." *Psychological Reports* 62: 807–813.

Lamont, Michèle (1987). "How to become a dominant French philosopher: the case of Jacques Derrida." *American Journal of Sociology* 93: 584–622.

Lane, Frederic Chapin (2001) [1951]. *Ships for Victory*. Baltimore, MD: Johns Hopkins University Press.

Laumann, Edward O. (1966). *Prestige and Association in an Urban Community*. New York: Bobbs-Merrill.

—— (1973). *Bonds of Pluralism*. New York: Wiley-Interscience.

Lawler, Edward J. and Jeongkoo Yoon (1993). "Power and the emergence of commitment behavior in negotiated exchange." *American Sociological Review* 58: 465–481.

—— —— (1998). "Network structure and emotion in exchange relations." *American Sociological Review* 63: 871–894.

Lazarsfeld, Paul F., Bernard R. Berelson and Hazel Gaudet (1944). *The People's Choice*. New York: Duell, Sloan and Pierce.

Lazega, Emmanuel (2001). *The Collegial Phenomenon*. Oxford: Oxford University Press.

—— and Philippa E. Pattison (1999). "Mutliplexity, generalized exchange and cooperation in organizations: a case study." *Social Networks* 21: 67–90.

Le Guin, Ursula K. (1997). *Lao Tzu, Tao Te Ching*. Boston, MA: Shambhala.

Leana, Carrie R. and Harry J. Van Buren III (1999). "Organizational social capital and employment practices." *Academy of Management Review* 24: 538–555.

Lebowitz, Fran (1981). *Social Studies*. New York: Random House.

Lee, Nancy Howell (1969). *The Search for an Abortionist*. Chicago: University of Chicago Press.

Lee, Steve S. (2004). "Predicting cultural output diversity in the radio industry, 1989–2002." *Poetics* 32: 325–342.

Leenders, Roger T. A. J. and Shaul M. Gabbay (eds.) (1999). *Corporate Social Capital and Liability*. Amsterdam: Kluwer Academic.

Lesser, Eric L. (ed.) (2000). *Knowledge and Social Capital*. Boston, MA: Butterworth-Heinemann.

Levi, Margaret (2001). "Sociology of trust." Pp. 15922–15926 in *International Encyclopedia of the Social and Behavioral Sciences*, ed. Neil J. Smelser and Paul B. Baltes. New York: Elsevier.

Levin, Daniel Z. and Rob Cross (2004). "The strength of weak ties you can trust: the mediating role of trust in effective knowledge transfer." *Management Science* 50: In Press.

Levinthal, Daniel A. and Mark Fichman (1988). "Dynamics of inter organizational attachments: auditor-client relationships." *Administrative Science Quarterly* 33: 345–368.

Lewis, Michael (1989). *Liar's Poker.* New York: W. W. Norton.

Light, Ivan and Stavros Karageorgis (1994). "The ethnic economy." Pp. 647–671 in *The Handbook of Economic Sociology*, ed. Neil J. Smelser and Richard Swedberg. Princeton, NJ: Princeton University Press.

Lin, Nan (1999). "Social networks and status attainment." *Annual Review of Sociology* 25: 467–487.

—— (2002). *Social Capital.* New York: Cambridge University Press.

—— Karen S. Cook and Ronald S. Burt (eds.) (2001). *Social Capital.* New York: Aldine de Gruyter.

—— Alfred Dean and Walter M. Ensel (1986). *Social Support, Life Events, and Depression.* New York: Academic Press.

—— Walter Ensel and John Vaughn (1981). "Social resources and strength of ties: structural factors in occupational status attainment." *American Sociological Review* 46: 393–405.

—— Yang-chih Fu and Ray-May Hsung (2001). "The position generator: measurement techniques for investigations of social capital." Pp. 57–81 in *Social Capital*, ed. Nan Lin, Karen S. Cook and Ronald S. Burt. New York: Aldine de Gruyter.

Lincoln, James R. and Michael L. Gerlach (2004). *Japan's Network Economy.* New York: Cambridge University Press.

Llobrera, Joseph T., David R. Meyer, and Gregory Nammacher (2000). "Trajectories of industrial districts: impact of strategic intervention in medical districts." *Economic Geography* 76: 68–98.

Locke, Richard M. (1995). *Remaking the Italian Economy.* Ithaca, NY: Cornell University Press.

Lofstrom, Shawn M. (2000). "Absorptive capacity in strategic alliances: investigating the effects of individuals' social and human capital on inter-firm learning." Paper presented at the Organization Science Winter Conference.

Lustgarten, S. H. (1975). "The impact of buyer concentration in manufacturing industries." *Review of Economics and Statistics* 57: 125–132.

Lütz, Susanne (1997). "Learning through intermediaries: the case of inter-firm research collaborations." Pp. 220–237 in *The Formation of Inter-Organizational Networks*, ed. Mark Ebers. Oxford: Oxford University Press.

Macaulay, Stewart (1963). "Non-contractual relations in business: a preliminary study." *American Sociological Review* 28: 55–67.

Macy, Michael W. (1991). "Learning to cooperate: stochastic and tacit collusion in social exchange." *American Journal of Sociology* 97: 808–843.

—— and John Skvoretz (1998). "Trust and cooperation between strangers." *American Sociological Review* 63: 638–660.

March, James G. (1991). "Exploration and exploitation in organization learning." *Organization Science* 2: 71–87.

Markovsky, Barry, David Willer, and Travis Patton (1988). "Power relations in exchange networks." *American Sociological Review* 53: 220–236.

Marks, Stephen R. (1977). "Multiple roles and role strain: some notes on human energy, time, and commitment." *American Sociological Review* 42: 921–936.

Markusen, Ann (1996). "Sticky places in slippery space: a typology of industrial districts." *Economic Geography* 72: 293–313.

Marsden, Peter V. (1981). "Introducing influence processes into a system of collective decisions." *American Journal of Sociology* 86: 1203–1235.

—— (1990). "Network data and measurement." *Annual Review of Sociology* 16: 435–463.

—— (2001). "Interpersonal ties and social capital in employer staffing practices." Pp. 105–121 in *Social Capital*, ed. Nan Lin, Karen S. Cook, and Ronald S. Burt. New York: Aldine de Gruyter.

—— (2004). "Recent developments in network measurement." In *Models and Methods in Social Network Analysis*, ed. Peter J. Carrington, John Scott and Stanley Wasserman. New York: Cambridge University Press.

—— and Karen E. Campbell (1985). "Measuring tie strength." *Social Forces* 63: 482–501.

—— and Elizabeth H. Gorman (1999). "Social capital in internal staffing practices." Pp. 180–196 in *Corporate Social Capital and Liability*, ed. Roger T. A. J. Leenders and Shaul M. Gabbay. Amsterdam: Kluwer Academic.

—— and Jeanne Hurlbert (1988). "Social resources and mobility outcomes: a replication and extension." *Social Forces* 66: 1038–1059.

—— and Joel M. Podolny (1990). "Dynamic analysis of network diffusion processes." Pp. 197–214 in *Social Networks through Time*, ed. Jeroen Weesie and Henk Flap. Utrecht, Netherlands: ISOR.

Marshall, S. L. A. (1978) [1947]. *Men Against Fire*. Gloucester, MA: Peter Smith.

McClelland, David C. (1961). *The Achieving Society*. Princeton: Van Nostrand.

McEvily, Bill and Akbar Zaheer (1999). "Bridging ties: a source of firm heterogeneity in competitive capabilities." *Strategic Management Journal* 20: 1133–1156.

—— and Alfred Marcus (2002). "Embeddedness and the acquisition of competitive capabilities." Unpublished Paper, Graduate School of Industrial Administration, Carnegie Mellon University.

McGuckin, Maryanne, Richard Waterman, Lois Porten, Sandra Bello, Mary Caruso, Barbara Juzaitis, Elyse Krug, Sherry Mazer, and Stanley Ostrawski (1999). "Patient education model for increasing handwashing compliance." *American Journal of Infection Control* 27: 309–314.

McGuire, Patrick and Mark Granovetter (2003). "The social construction of the electric utility industry, 1878–1919." In *Constructing Industries and Markets*, ed. Joe Porac and Marc Ventresca. New York: Pergamon Press.

McPherson, J. Miller, and Lynn Smith-Lovin (1987). "Homophily in voluntary organizations: status distance and the composition of face-to-face groups." *American Sociological Review* 52: 370–379.

—— —— and J. M. Cook (2001). "Birds of a feather: homophily in social networks." *Annual Review of Sociology* 27: 415–444.

Mehra, Ajay, Martin Kilduff, and Daniel J. Brass (2001). "The social networks of high and low self-monitors: implications for workplace performance." *Administrative Science Quarterly* 46: 121–146.

Melbin, Murray (1987). *Night as Frontier*. New York: Free Press.

Menon, Tanya and Jeffrey Pfeffer (2003). "Valuing internal vs. external knowledge: explaining the preference for outsiders." *Management Science* 49: 497–513.

Merry, Sally Engle (1984). "Rethinking gossip and scandal." Pp. 271–302 in *Toward a General Theory of Social Control*, Vol. 1, ed. Donald Black. New York: Academic Press.

Merton, Robert K. (1936). "The unanticipated consequences of purposive social action." *American Sociological Review* 1: 894–904.

—— (1948a). "Discussion." *American Sociological Review* 13:164–168.

—— (1948b). "The bearing of empirical research upon the development of social theory." Pp. 156–171 in Merton (1968).

—— (1948c). "The self-fulfilling prophecy." Pp. 475–490 in Merton (1968).

—— (1949). "Patterns of influence: local and cosmopolitan influentials." Pp. 441–474 in Merton (1968).

—— (1957). "Continuities in the theory of reference group behavior." Pp. 335–440 in Merton (1968).

—— (1968). *Social Theory and Social Structure*. New York: Free Press.

—— (1984). "Socially expected durations: a case study of concept formation in sociology." Pp. 262–283 in *Conflict and Consensus*, ed. Walter W. Powell and Richard Robbins. New York: Free Press.

Meurling, John and Richard Jeans (1997). *The Ugly Duckling*. Stockholm: Ericsson Mobile Communications.

Meyerson, Eva M. (1994). "Human capital, social capital and compensation: the relative contribution of social contacts to managers' incomes." *Acta Sociologica* 37: 383–399.

Milgram, Stanley (1967). "The small world problem." *Psychology Today* 1: 61–67.

—— (1974). *Obedience to Authority*. New York: Harper & Row.

Milgrom, Paul and John Roberts (1992). *Economics, Organization, and Management*. New York: Prentice-Hall.

Mill, John Stuart (1987) [1848]. *Principles of Political Economy*. Fairchild, NJ: Augustus M. Kelley.

Mintzberg, Henry (1973). *The Nature of Managerial Work*. New York: Harper and Row.

Mitchell, Lawrence E. (2003). "Structural holes, CEOs, and informational monopolies: the missing link in corporate governance." Unpublished Paper, Law School, George Washington University.

Mizruchi, Mark S. (1992). *The Structure of Corporate Political Action*. Cambridge: Harvard University Press.

—— and Linda Brewster Sterns (2001). "Getting deals done: the use of social networks in bank decision making." *American Sociological Review* 66: 647–671.

Monge, Peter R. and Noshir S. Contractor (2001). "Emergence of communication networks." Pp. 440–502 in *The New Handbook of Organizational Communication*, ed. Fredric M. Jablin and Linda L. Putnam. Thousand Oaks, CA: Sage.

—— —— (2003). *Theories of Communication Networks*. New York: Oxford University Press.

Montgomery, James D. (1998). "Toward a role-theoretic conception of embeddedness." *American Journal of Sociology* 104: 92–125.

Moreno, Jacob L. (1940). "Mental catharsis and the psychodrama." *Sociometry* 3: 209–243.

—— (1955). "Theory of spontaneity-creativity." *Sociometry* 18: 105–118.

Morgan, Stephen L. and Aage B. Sørensen (1999). "A test of Coleman's social-capital explanation of school effects." *American Sociological Review* 64: 661–681.

Morrill, Calvin (1995). *The Executive Way*. Chicago: University of Chicago Press.

Morris, Desmond and Peter Marsh (1988). *Tribes*. Salt Lake City, UT: Gibbs-Smith.

Morrison, Elizabeth Wolfe and Frances J. Milliken (2002). "Organizational silence: a barrier to change and development in a pluralistic world." *Academy of Management Review* 25: 706–725.

Morselli, Carlo (2001). "Structuring Mr. Nice: entrepreneurial opportunities and brokerage positioning in the cannabis trade." *Crime, Law, and Social Change* 35: 203–244.

—— (2003). "Career opportunities and network-based privileges in the Cosa Nostra." *Crime, Law, and Social Change* 37: 383–418.

—— and Pierre Tremblay (2004). "Criminal achievement, offender networks and the benefits of low self-control." *Criminology* 42: 773–804.

Mouw, Ted (2003). "Social capital and finding a job: do contacts matter?" *American Sociological Review* 68: 868–898.

Mullen, Brian, Craig Johnson, and Eduardo Salas (1991). "Productivity loss in brainstorming groups: a meta-analytic integration." *Basic and Applied Social Psychology* 12: 3–24.

Murphy, Kate (2003). "To cut—or not to cut?" *BusinessWeek*, July 7, 98–99.

Murray, Stephen O., Joseph H. Rankin, and Dennis W. Magill (1981). "Strong ties and job information." *Sociology of Work and Occupations* 8: 119–136.

Myers, David G. and Helmut Lamm (1976). "The group polarization phenomenon." *Psychological Bulletin* 83: 602–627.

Nahapiet, Janine and Sumantra Ghoshal (1998). "Social capital, intellectual capital, and the organization advantage." *Academy of Management Review* 23: 242–266.

Nicolaou, Nicos and Sue Birley (2003*a*). "Academic networks in a trichotomous categorisation of university spinouts." *Journal of Business Venturing* 18: 333–359.

—— —— (2003*b*). "Social networks in organizational emergence: the university spinout phenomenon." *Management Science* 49: 1702–1725.

Nohria, Nitin and Robert G. Eccles (eds.) (1992). *Networks and Organizations*. Boston: Harvard Business School Press.

Northway, Mary L. and Margaret McCallum Rooks (1955). "Creativity and sociometric status in children." *Sociometry* 18: 194–201.

Nyberg, David (1993). *The Varnished Truth*. Chicago: University of Chicago Press.

O'Malley, John W. (1993). *The First Jesuits*. Cambridge, MA: Harvard University Press.

O'Reilly, Charles (1989). "Corporations, culture, and commitment: motivation and social control in organizations." *California Management Review* 31: 9–25.

—— and Jennifer A. Chatman (1996). "Culture as social control: corporations, cults, and commitment." *Research in Organizational Behavior* 18: 157–200.

O'Reilly, Francis A. (2003). *The Fredericksburg Campaign*. Baton Rouge, LA: Louisiana State University Press.

Osgood, Charles E., George J. Suci, and Percy H. Tannenbaum (1957). *The Measurement of Meaning*. Chicago: University of Illinois Press.

Padgett, John F. and Christopher K. Ansell (1993). "Robust action and the rise of the Medici, 1400–1434." *American Journal of Sociology* 98: 1259–1319.

Pagden, Anthony (1988). "The destruction of trust and its economic consequences in the case of eighteenth-century Naples." Pp. 127–141 in *Trust*, ed. Diego Gambetta. New York: Blackwell.

Park, Seung Ho and Yadong Luo (2001). "Guanxi and organizational dynamics: organizational networking in Chinese firms." *Strategic Management Journal* 22: 455–477.

Paulus, Paul B., Timothy S. Larey, and Anita H. Ortega (1995). "Performance and perceptions of brainstormers in an organizational setting." *Basic and Applied Social Psychology* 17: 249–265.

Pennings, Johannes M., Kyungmook Lee, and Arjen van Witteloostuijn (1998). "Human capital, social capital, and firm dissolution." *Academy of Management Journal* 41: 425–440.

Peters, Lawrence H. (2002). "Introduction: Tracy Kidder's *The Soul of a New Machine*." *Academy of Management Executive* 16: 43–44.

Peters, Tomas J. and Robert H. Waterman, Jr. (1982). *In Search of Excellence*. New York: Harper & Row.

Peterson, Richard A. and David G. Berger (1975). "Cycles in symbol production: the case of popular music." *American Sociological Review* 40: 158–173.

Peterson, Trond, Ishak Saporta, and Marc-David Seidel (2000). "Offering a job: meritocracy and social networks." *American Journal of Sociology* 106: 763–816.

Pfeffer, Jeffrey (1983). "Organizational demography." *Research in Organizational Behavior* 5: 299–357.

—— and Robert I. Sutton (2000). *The Knowing-Doing Gap*. Boston, MA: Harvard Business School Press.

Phillips, Damon J. (2001). "The promotion paradox: organizational mortality and employee promotion chances in Silicon Valley law firms, 1946–1996." *American Journal of Sociology* 106: 1058–1098.

—— and Ezra W. Zuckerman (2001). "Middle-status conformity: theoretical restatement and empirical demonstration in two markets." *American Journal of Sociology* 107: 379–429.

—— and Jesper B. Sørensen (2003). "Competitive position and promotion rates: commercial television station top management, 1953–1988." *Social Forces* 81: 812–841.

Piore, Michael J. and Charles F. Sabel (1992). *The Second Industrial Divide*. New York: Basic Books.

Piskorski, Mikola Jan (2001). "Structural closure and exposure: managerial autonomy in the market for corporate control." Dissertation. Harvard University, School of Business Administration.

Planck, Max (1968) [1949]. *Scientific Autobiography and Other Papers*. Westport, CT: Greenwood Publishing Group.

Platteau, Jean-Philippe (1994). "Behind the market stage where real societies exist—part I: the role of public and private order institutions." *Journal of Development Studies* 30: 533–577.

Podolny, Joel M. (1993). "A status-based model of market competition." *American Journal of Sociology* 98: 829–872

—— (2001). "Networks as the pipes and prisms of the market." *American Journal of Sociology* 107: 33–60.

—— and James N. Baron (1997). "Relationships and resources: social networks and mobility in the workplace." *American Sociological Review* 62: 673–693.

Polanyi, Michael (1983) [1966]. *The Tacit Dimension*. Gloucester, MA: Peter Smith.

Pollock, Timothy G., Joseph F. Porac, and James B. Wade (2004). "Constructing deal networks: brokers as network architects in the U.S. IPO market and other examples." *Academy of Management Review* 29: 50–72.

Portes, Alejandro (1998). "Social capital: its origins and applications in modern sociology." *Annual Review of Sociology* 24: 1–24.

—— and Margarita Mooney (2002). "Social capital and community development." Pp. 303–329 in *The New Economic Sociology*, ed. Mauro F. Guillén, Randall Collins, Paula England and Marshall Meyer. New York: Russell Sage Foundation.

Powell, Walter W. and Laurel Smith-Doerr (1994). "Networks and economic life." Pp. 368–402 in *The Handbook of Economic Sociology*, ed. Neil J. Smelser and Richard Swedberg. Princeton: Princeton University Press.

—— and Kaisa Snellman (2004) "The knowledge economy." *Annual Review of Sociology* 30: 199–220.

Provan, Keith G. and H. Brinton Milward (1995). "A preliminary theory of inter-organizational network effectiveness: a comparative study of four community mental health systems." *Administrative Science Quarterly* 40: 1–33.

Putnam, Robert D. (1993). *Making Democracy Work*. Princeton, NJ: Princeton University Press.

—— (2000). *Bowling Alone*. New York: Simon and Schuster.

—— and Lewis Feldstein (2003). *Better Together*. New York: Simon & Schuster.

—— Robert Leonardi, Raffaella Y. Nanetti, and Franco Pavoncello (1983). "Explaining institutional success: the case of Italian regional government." *American Political Science Review* 77: 55–74.

Raider, Holly J. (2003). "The Governance of Economic Exchange: Technology, Relationships, and the Structure of Contracts." Dissertation. Columbia University, Department of Sociology.

Rao, Hayagreeva, Gerald F. Davis, and Andrew Ward (2000). "Embeddedness, social identity and mobility: why firms leave the NASDAQ and join the New York Stock Exchange." *Administrative Science Quarterly* 45: 268–292.

Rapping, Leonard (1965). "Learning and World War II production functions." *Review of Economics and Statistics* 47: 81–86.

Ratliff, Evan (2000). "O, engineers." *Wired* 8.12: 357–367.

Raub, Werner and Jeroen Weesie (1990). "Reputation and efficiency in social interactions: an example of network effects." *American Journal of Sociology* 96: 626–654.

Reagans, Ray and Bill McEvily (2003). "Network structure and knowledge transfer: the effects of cohesion and range." *Administrative Science Quarterly* 48: 240–267.

—— and Ezra W. Zuckerman (2001). "Networks, diversity, and performance: the social capital of corporate R&D units." *Organization Science* 12: 502–517.

—— —— and Bill McEvily (2005). "How to make the team: social networks versus demography as criteria for designing effective teams." *Administrative Science Quarterly* 49: 101–133.

Rees, Albert (1966). "Information networks in labor markets." *American Economic Review* 56: 559–566.

Renzulli, Linda A., Howard E. Aldrich, and James Moody (2000). "Family matters: gender, networks, and entrepreneurial outcomes." *Social Forces* 79: 523–546.

Rich, Ben R. and Leo Janos (1994). *Skunk Works*. Boston, MA: Back Bay Books.

Roberts, Gilbert and Thomas N. Sherratt (1998). "Development of cooperative relationships through increasing investment." *Nature* 394: 175–179.

Robertson, Paul J. (1995). Review of *Regional advantage*, by Annalee Saxenian. *Journal of Economic History* 55: 198–199.

Robinson, Dawn T. and Lynn Smith-Lovin (2001). "Getting a laugh: gender, status, and humor in task discussion." *Social Forces* 80: 123–158.

Rochlin, Gene I., Todd R. LaPore, and Karlene H. Roberts (1987). "The self-designing high-reliability organization: aircraft carrier flight operations at sea." *Naval War College Review* 40: 76–90.

Rodin, Judith (1985). "The application of social psychology." Pp. 805–881 in *The Handbook of Social Psychology*, Vol. 2, ed. Gardner Lindsey and Elliot Aronson. New York: Random House.

Rogers, Everett M. (1995). *Diffusion of Innovations*. New York: Free Press.

—— (1997). *A History of Communication Study*. New York: Free Press.

Romney, A. Kimball and Roy G. D'Andrade (1964). "Cognitive aspects of English kin terms." *American Anthropologist* 566: 146–170.

Rosegrant, Susan and David R. Lampe (1992). *Route 128*. New York: Basic Books.

Rosen, Emanuel (2000). *The Anatomy of Buzz*. New York: Doubleday.

Rosen, Sherwin (1997). "Austrian and neoclassical economics: any gains from trades?" *Journal of Economic Perspectives* 11: 139–152.

Rosen, Sidney and Abraham Tesser (1970). "On reluctance to communicate undesirable information: the MUM effect." *Sociometry* 33: 253–263.

Rosenthal, Elizabeth A. (1996). "Social networks and team performance." Dissertation. University of Chicago, Graduate School of Business.

Rosnow, Ralph L. and Gary Alan Fine (1976). *Rumor and Gossip*. New York: Elsevier.

Ross, Lee and Craig A. Anderson (1982). "Shortcomings in the attribution process: on the origins and maintenance of erroneous social assessments." Pp. 129–152 in *Judgment Under Uncertainty*, ed. Daniel Kahneman, Paul Slovic and Amos Tversky. New York: Cambridge University Press.

Ross, Michael and Garth J. O. Fletcher (1985). "Attribution and social perception." Pp. 73–122 in *The Handbook of Social Psychology*, Vol. 2, ed. Gardner Lindsey and Elliot Aronson. New York: Random House.

Rowley, Timothy J. and Joel A. C. Baum (2004). "Sophistication of interfirm network strategies in the Canadian investment banking industry." *Scandinavian Journal of Management* 20: 103–124.

Ruef, Martin (2002). "Strong ties, weak ties and islands: structural and cultural predictors of organizational innovation." *Industrial and Corporate Change* 11: 427–449.

Runco, Mark A. (2004). "Creativity." *Annual Review of Psychology* 55: 657–687.

Sandefur, Rebecca L. and Edward O. Laumann (1998). "A paradigm for social capital." *Rationality and Society* 10: 481–501.

Sawai, K. (1994). "A study on how Coleman's book on diffusion of new drugs has been cited in subsequent published articles." *Library and Information Science* 32: 105–122.

Saxenian, Annalee (1994). *Regional Advantage*. Cambridge, MA: Harvard University Press.

Schumpeter, Joseph A. (2002) [1911a]. "Theorie der wirtschaftlichen Entwicklung," tr. Markus C. Becker and Thorbjørn Knudsen. *American Journal of Economics and Sociology* 61: 405–437.

—— (1934) [1911b]. *The Theory of Economic Development*, tr. Redvers Opie. Cambridge, MA: Harvard University Press.

—— (1947). "The creative response in economic history." *Journal of Economic History* 7: 149–159.

Scott, John P. (2000). *Social Network Analysis*. Thousand Oaks, CA: Sage.

Seabright, Mark A., Daniel A. Levinthal, and Mark Fichman (1992). "Role of individual attachments in the dissolution of interorganizational relationships." *Academy of Management Journal* 35: 122–160.

Searle, Allen D. (1945). "Productivity changes in selected wartime shipbuilding programs." *Monthly Labor Review* 61: 1132–1147.

Sediatis, Judith (1998). "The alliances of spin-offs versus start-ups: social ties in the genesis of post-Soviet alliances." *Organization Science* 9: 368–381.

Seibert, Scott E., Maria L. Kraimer, and Robert C. Liden (2001). "A social capital theory of career success." *Academy of Management Journal* 44: 219–237.

Seidel, Marc-David L., Jeffrey T. Polzer, and Katherine J. Stewart (2000). "Friends in high places: the effects of social networks on discrimination in salary negotiations." *Administrative Science Quarterly* 45: 1–24.

Sellers, Patricia (1996). "Can Home Depot fix its sagging stock?" *Fortune* 133: 139–146.

Shane, Scott and Daniel Cable (2002). "Network ties, reputation, and the financing of new ventures." *Management Science* 48: 364–381.

Shapiro, Susan P. (1984). *Wayward Capitalists*. New Haven, CT: Yale University Press.

—— (1987). "The social control of impersonal trust." *American Journal of Sociology* 93: 623–658.

Sherif, Muzafer (1935). "A study of some factors in perception," *Archives of Psychology*, No. 187.

Shils, Edward A. and Morris Janowitz (1948). "Cohesion and disintegration in the Wehrmacht in World War II." *Public Opinion Quarterly* 12: 280–315.

Siamwalla, Ammar (1978). "Farmers and middlemen: aspects of agriculture marketing in Thailand." *Economic Bulletin for Asia and the Pacific* 29: 38–50.

Sieber, Sam D. (1974). "Toward a theory of role accumulation." *American Sociological Review* 39: 567–578.

Simmel, Georg (1902). "The number of members as determining the sociological form of the group, II," tr. A. Small. *American Journal of Sociology* 8: 158–196.

—— (1955) [1922]. *Conflict and the Web of Group Affiliations*. New York: Free Press.

Simonton, Dean Keith (1984). *Genius, Creativity, and Leadership*. Cambridge, MA: Harvard University Press.

Sitkin, Sim B. and Darryl Stickel (1996). "The road to hell: the dynamics of distrust in an era of quality." Pp. 196–215 in *Trust in Organizations*, ed. Roderick M. Kramer and Tom R. Tyler. Thousand Oaks, CA: Sage.

Simons, Daniel J. and Christopher F. Chabris (1999). "Gorillas in our midst: sustained inattentional blindness for dynamic events." *Perception* 28: 1059–1074.

Smelser, Neil J. and Robin Content (1980). *The Changing Academic Market*. Berkeley, CA: University of California Press.

—— and Richard Swedberg (eds.) (1994). *Handbook of Economic Sociology*. Princeton: Princeton University Press.

Smith, Adam (1982) [1766]. *Lectures on Jurisprudence*. Indianapolis, IN: Liberty Fund.

Smith, Vernon L. (1962). "An experimental study of competitive market behavior." *Journal of Political Economy* 70: 111–137.

Smith-Lovin, Lynn (1987). "Impressions from events." *Journal of Mathematical Sociology* 13: 35–70.

Smock, Pamela J. (2000). "Cohabitation in the United States: an appraisal of research themes, findings, and implications." *Annual Review of Sociology* 26: 1–20.

Snijders, Chris and Werner Raub (1998). "Revolution and risk: paradoxical consequences of risk aversion in interdependent situations." *Rationality and Society* 10:
405–425.
Sørensen, Jesper B. (1999). "Executive Migration and Interorganizational Competition." *Social Science Research* 28: 289–315.
—— (2000). "The longitudinal effects of group tenure composition on turnover."
American Sociological Review 65: 298–310.
Sorenson, Olav and Toby E. Stuart (2001). "Syndication networks and the spatial
distribution of venture capital investments." *American Journal of Sociology* 106:
1546–1588.
Sparrowe, Raymond T. and Pamela A. Popielarz (1995). "Weak ties and structural
holes: the effects of network structure on careers." Paper presented at the annual
meetings of the Academy of Management.
—— Robert C. Liden, Sandy J. Wayne, and Maria L. Kraimer (2001). "Social networks and the performance of individuals and groups." *Academy of Management
Journal* 44: 316–325.
Spratling, Gary R. (2001). "Detection and deterrence: rewarding informants for
reporting violations." *George Washington Law Review* 69: 798–823.
Starbuck, William (1996). "Unlearning ineffective or obsolete technologies." *Inter-
national Journal of Technology Management* 11: 725–737.
Staw, Barry M. and Jerry Ross (1987). "Behavior in escalation situations: antece-
dents, prototypes, and solutions." *Research in Organizational Behavior* 9: 39–78.
Steier, Lloyd and Royston Greenwood (2000). "Entrepreneurship and the Evolution
of Angel Financial Networks." *Organization Studies* 21: 163–192.
Stephan, Paula E. and Sharon G. Levin (1992). *Striking the Mother Lode in Science*.
New York: Oxford University Press.
Sterns, Carl W. and George Stalk (eds.) (1998). *Perspectives on Strategy*. New York:
Wiley.
Stevens, R. Blake and Edward C. Ezell (1992). *The Black Rifle*. Cobourg, Canada:
Collector Grade Publications.
Stewart, Alex (1990). "The bigman metaphor for entrepreneurship: a 'library
tale' with morals on alternatives for further research." *Organization Science* 1:
143–159.
Stewart, Thomas A. (1996). "The great conundrum: you vs. the team." *Fortune* 134
(November): 165–166.
Stigler, George J. (1986) [1982]. "The process and progress of economics."
Pp. 134–149 in *The Essence of Stigler*, ed. Kurt R. Leube and Thomas Gale Moore.
Stanford, CA: Hoover Institution Press.
Stinchcombe, Arthur L. (1990). *Information and Organizations*. Berkeley, CA: Uni-
versity of California Press.
Stirling, Rebecca B. (1956). "Some psychological mechanisms operative in gossip."
Social Forces 34: 262–267.
Stokes, Donald E. (1997). *Pasteur's Quadrant*. Washington, DC: Brookings Institu-
tion.
Strang, David and Sarah A. Soule (1998). "Diffusion in organizations and social
movements." *Annual Review of Sociology* 24: 265–290.
—— and Nancy Brandon Tuma (1993). "Spatial and temporal heterogeneity in
diffusion." *American Journal of Sociology* 99: 614–639.
Stroebe, Wolfgang and Michael Diehl (1994). "Why groups are less effective than
their members: on productivity losses in idea-generating groups." Pp. 271–303 in

European Review of Social Psychology, ed. Wolfgang Stroebe and Miles Hewstone. London: Wiley.

Stuart, Toby E. (1998). "Producer network positions and propensities to collaborate: an investigation of strategic alliance formations in a high-technology industry." *Administrative Science Quarterly* 43: 668–698.

—— and Joel M. Podolny (1999). "Positional causes and correlates of strategic alliances in the semiconductor industry." *Research in the Sociology of Organizations* 16: 161–182.

—— Ha Hoang, and Ralph C. Hybels (1999). "Interorganizational endorsements and the performance of entrepreneurial ventures." *Administrative Science Quarterly* 44: 315–349.

Susskind, Alex M., Vernon D. Miller, and J. David Johnson (1998). "Downsizing and structural holes—their impact on layoff survivors' perceptions of organizational chaos and openness to change." *Communication Research* 25: 30–65.

Sutton, Robert I. (2002). *Weird Ideas that Work*. New York: Free Press.

—— and Andrew B. Hargadon (1996). "Brainstorming groups in context: effectiveness in a product design firm." *Administrative Science Quarterly* 41: 685–718.

Swedberg, Richard (ed.) (1990). *Economics and Sociology*. Princeton, NJ: Princeton University Press.

—— (ed.) (1991). *Joseph A. Schumpeter*. Princeton, NJ: Princeton University Press.

—— (ed.) (1993). *Explorations in Economic Sociology*. New York: Russell Sage Foundation.

—— (2003). *Principles of Economic Sociology*. Princeton, NJ: Princeton University Press.

Talmud, Ilan (1994). "Relations and profits: the social organizations of Israeli industrial competition." *Social Science Research* 23: 109–135.

—— and Gustavo S. Mesch (1997). "Market embeddedness and corporate instability: the ecology of inter-industrial networks." *Social Science Research* 26: 419–441.

Tarrow, Sidney (1996). "Making social science work across space and time: a critical reflection on Robert Putnam's *Making Democracy Work*." *American Political Science Review* 90: 389–397.

Täube, Volker G. (2004). "Measuring the social capital of brokerage roles." *Connections* 26: 29–52.

Taylor, D. Garth and James S. Coleman (1979). "Equilibrating processes in social networks: a model for conceptualization and analysis." Pp. 257–300 in *Perspectives on Social Network Research*, ed. Paul W. Holland and Samuel Leinhardt. New York: Academic Press.

Taylor, Maureen and Marya L. Doerfel (2003). "Building international relationships that build nations." *Human Communication Research* 29: 153–181.

Thomas, William I. and Dorothy S. Thomas (1928). *The Child in America*. New York: Alfred A. Knopf.

—— and Florian Znaniecki (1918). *The Polish Peasant in Europe and America*, Vol. 2. Boston, MA: Gorham.

Thompson, Peter (2001). "How much did the Liberty shipbuilders learn? New Evidence for an old case study." *Journal of Political Economy* 109: 103–137.

Thoreau, Henry D. (2004) [1854]. *Walden*, ed. Jeffrey S. Cramer. New Haven, CT: Yale University Press.

Thornton, Patricia H. (1999). "The sociology of entrepreneurship." *Annual Review of Sociology* 25: 19–46.

Thurstone, L. L. (1919). "The learning curve equation." *Psychological Monographs* 26: No. 3.

Tillman, Robert and Michael Indergaard (1999). "Field of schemes: health insurance fraud in the small business sector." *Social Problems* 46: 572–590.

Tilly, Charles (1998a). *Durable Inequality*. Berkeley, CA: University of California Press.

—— (1998b). "Contentious conversation." *Social Research* 65: 491–510.

Topper, Curtis M. and Kathleen M. Carley (1999). "A structural perspective on the emergence of network organizations." *Journal of Mathematical Sociology* 24: 67–96.

Travers, Jeffrey and Stanley Milgram (1969). "An experimental study of the small world problem." *Sociometry* 32: 425–443.

Trolander, Paul and Zeynep Tenger (2004). "Katherine Philips and coterie critical practices." *Eighteenth-Century Studies* 37: 367–387.

Tullock, Gordon (1985). "Adam Smith and the prisoner's dilemma." *Quarterly Journal of Economics* 100: 1073–1081.

Tushman, Michael L. and Thomas J. Scanlan (1981a). "Characteristics and external orientations of boundary spanning individuals." *Academy of Management Journal* 24: 83–98.

—— —— (1981b). "Boundary spanning individuals: their role in information transfer and their antecedents." *Academy of Management Journal* 24: 289–305.

Ulrich, Dave, Jack Zenger, and Norman Smallwood (1999). *Results-Based Leadership*. Boston, MA: Harvard Business School Press.

Uzzi, Brian (1996). "The sources and consequences of embeddedness for the economic performance of organizations: the network effect." *American Sociological Review* 61: 674–698.

—— (1999). "Embeddedness in the making of financial capital: how social relations and networks benefit firms seeking finance." *American Sociological Review* 64: 481–505.

—— and J. J. Gillespie (2002). "Knowledge spillover in corporate financing networks: embeddedness and the firm's debt performance." *Strategic Management Journal* 23: 595–618.

—— and Ryon Lancaster (2004). "Embeddedness and the price of legal services in the large law firm market." *American Sociological Review* 69: 319–344.

Valente, Thomas W. (1995). *Network Models of the Diffusion of Innovation*. Cresskill, NJ: Hampton Press.

Van de Ven, Andrew H., Raghu Garud, Douglas E. Polley, and Sankaran Venkataraman (1999). *The Innovation Journey*. New York: Oxford University Press.

Van den Bulte, Christophe and Gary L. Lilien (2001). "*Medical Innovation* revisited: social contagion versus marketing effort." *American Journal of Sociology* 106: 1409–1435.

Van Maanen, John (1978). "The asshole." Pp. 121–138 in *Policing*, ed. Peter K. Manning and John Van Maanen. New York: Random House.

Van Meter, Karl M. (2001). "Terrorists/liberators: researching and dealing with adversary networks." *Connections* 54: 66–78.

Von Hippel, Eric (1988). *The Sources of Innovation*. New York: Oxford University Press.

Walker, Gordon, Bruce Kogut, and Weijian Shan (1997). "Social capital, structural holes and the formation of an industry network." *Organization Science* 8:109–125.

Wasserman, Stanley and Katherine Faust (1994). *Social Network Analysis*. New York: Cambridge University Press.

Watts, Duncan J. (1998). *Small Worlds*. Princeton, NJ: Princeton University Press.

—— (1999). "Networks, dynamics, and the small-world phenomenon." *American Journal of Sociology* 105: 493–527.

—— and Steven H. Strogatz (1998). "Collective Dynamics of 'Small-World' Networks." *Nature* 393: 440–442.

Weber, Max (1930) [1905]. *The Protestant Ethic and the Spirit of Capitalism* (tr. Talcott Parsons). New York: Charles Scribner's Sons.

Weesie, Jeroen, and Werner Raub (eds.) (2000). *The Management of Durable Relations*. Amsterdam: Thela Thesis.

Weick, Karl E. (1996). "Drop your tools: an allegory for organizational studies." *Administrative Science Quarterly* 41: 301–313.

—— and Karlene H. Roberts (1993). "Collective mind in organizations: heedful interrelating on flight decks." *Administrative Science Quarterly* 38: 357–381.

Westphal, James D., Ranjay Gulati, and Steve M. Shortell (1997). "Customization or conformity? An institutional and network perspective on the content and consequences of TQM adoption." *Administrative Science Quaterly* 42: 366–394.

White, Harrison C. (1981). "Where do markets come from?" *American Journal of Sociology* 87: 517–547.

—— (1993). *Careers and Creativity*. Boulder, CO: Westview Press.

—— (2002a). *Markets from Networks*. Princeton, NJ: Princeton University Press.

—— (2002b). "Markets and firms: notes on the future of economic sociology." Pp. 129–147 in *The New Economic Sociology*, ed. Mauro F. Guillén, Randall Collins, Paula England and Marshall Meyer. New York: Russell Sage Foundation.

White, Lynn K. (1990). "Determinants of divorce: a review of research in the eighties." *Journal of Marriage and the Family* 52: 904–912.

Whyte, William H. (1956). *The Organization Man*. New York: Simon & Schuster.

Willer, David (1999). *Network Exchange Theory*. New York: Praeger.

Williams, Katherine Y. and Charles A. O'Reilly III (1998). "Demography and diversity in organizations: a review of 40 years of research." *Research in Organizational Behavior* 20: 77–140.

Williams, Phil (1998). "The nature of drug-trafficking networks." *Current History* 97: 154–159.

Williams, Steve and Robert J. Taormina (1992). "Group polarization in business decisions in Singapore." *Journal of Social Psychology* 132: 265–267.

Windolf, Paul and Sebastian Schief (1999). "Corporate networks in East Germany." *Kolner Zeitschrift fur Soziologie und SozialPsychologie* 51: 260–282.

Wittek, Rafael and Rudi Wielers (1998). "Gossip in organizations." *Computational and Mathematical Organization Theory* 4: 189–204.

Wong, Peter Leung-Kwong and Paul Ellis (2002). "Social ties and partner identification in Sino-Hong Kong international joint ventures." *Journal of International Business Studies* 33: 267–289.

Woolcock, Michael (1998). "Social capital and economic development: toward a theoretical synthesis and policy framework." *Theory and Society* 27: 151–208.

—— and Deepa Narayan (2001). "Social capital: implications for development theory, research, and policy." *World Bank Research Observer* 15: 225–249.

Wright, T. P. (1936). "Factors affecting the cost of airplanes." *Journal of the Aeronautical Sciences* 3: 122–128.

Yair, Gad and Daniel Maman (1996). "The persistent structure of hegemony in the Eurovision song contest." *Acta Sociologica* 39: 309–325.

Yamaguchi, Kazuo (1994). "The flow of information through social networks: diagonal-free measures of inefficiency and the structural determinants of inefficiency." *Social Networks* 16: 57–86.

Yasuda, Yuki (1996). *Network Analysis of Japanese and American Markets*. Tokyo: Bokutaku-sha.

Yelle, Louis E. (1979). "The learning curve: historical review and comprehensive survey." *Decision Sciences* 10: 302–328

Zelizer, Viviana (1978). "Human values and the market: the case of life insurance and death in 19th century America." *American Journal of Sociology* 84: 591–610.

Ziegler, Rolf (1982). "Market structure and cooptation." Unpublished paper, Department of Sociology, Universität München.

Zucker, Lynne G. (1977). "The role of institutionalization in cultural persistence." *American Sociological Review* 42: 726–743.

—— (1986). "Production of trust: institutional sources of economic structure, 1840–1920." *Research in Organizational Behavior* 8: 53–111.

Zuckerman, Ezra W. (1999). "The categorical imperative: securities analysts and the legitimacy discount." *American Journal of Sociology* 104: 1398–1438.

INDEX